Policy Responses to the Interwar Economic Crisis

Adnan Türegün

Policy Responses to the Interwar Economic Crisis

Contending Ideas of the Economy

palgrave
macmillan

Adnan Türegün
Department of Sociology and Anthropology
Carleton University
Ottawa, ON, Canada

ISBN 978-3-030-96952-3   ISBN 978-3-030-96953-0 (eBook)
https://doi.org/10.1007/978-3-030-96953-0

© The Editor(s) (if applicable) and The Author(s), under exclusive licence to Springer Nature Switzerland AG 2022

This work is subject to copyright. All rights are solely and exclusively licensed by the Publisher, whether the whole or part of the material is concerned, specifically the rights of translation, reprinting, reuse of illustrations, recitation, broadcasting, reproduction on microfilms or in any other physical way, and transmission or information storage and retrieval, electronic adaptation, computer software, or by similar or dissimilar methodology now known or hereafter developed.

The use of general descriptive names, registered names, trademarks, service marks, etc. in this publication does not imply, even in the absence of a specific statement, that such names are exempt from the relevant protective laws and regulations and therefore free for general use.

The publisher, the authors and the editors are safe to assume that the advice and information in this book are believed to be true and accurate at the date of publication. Neither the publisher nor the authors or the editors give a warranty, expressed or implied, with respect to the material contained herein or for any errors or omissions that may have been made. The publisher remains neutral with regard to jurisdictional claims in published maps and institutional affiliations.

This Palgrave Macmillan imprint is published by the registered company Springer Nature Switzerland AG.

The registered company address is: Gewerbestrasse 11, 6330 Cham, Switzerland

Preface

Historically minded students of economic policy can be divided into two groups: those who are interested in stable, normal times and those in chaotic, extraordinary times. I would like to think that I belong to the second group. I find times of crisis with all their negative connotations more interesting as a research topic since they mark both the end of good times and the beginning of experimentation that often paves the way for new good—sometimes better—times. What better way to make this point than studying the interwar economic crisis? Even in its near centennial, the Great Depression continues to capture scholarly interest and popular imagination. It has in fact become the standard reference point for subsequent international crises, including the stagflation of the 1970s and 1980s, the global financial crisis of 2008–2009, and the recent COVID-19 pandemic. What made the interwar crisis an enduring image was not just its severity or the spectacular failure of economic and political arrangements, both globally and for most countries. Equally important was the breadth of economic policy responses to the crisis that ranged from the most ardent defence of the status quo to various experiments heralding the future.

I wrote this book with three specific objectives in mind: (a) to bring the full range of responses into focus based on a holistic, but nuanced, conception of economic policy; (b) to compare a sample of national responses representing that range among both large states and small states; and (c) to highlight the role in policy variation of ideas and strategies, particularly those of ruling parties, concerning three major groups of interest—business, labour, and agrarians—without losing sight of the context in the most general sense. I developed these objectives in a critical dialogue with the comparative public policy literature, which has been building in Western Europe and North America since the late 1970s.

States diverged greatly in responding to the Great Depression just as they had converged on a relatively liberal course when reconstructing their war-torn economies in the 1920s. All departed from orthodox liberalism but to a different degree and in a variety of ways. Some were more innovative than others but still kept some aspect of liberalism. Conversely, those states which were generally more conservative broke with certain liberal principles decisively. Existing, otherwise rich, comparative literature mainly informed by political science and historical sociology has failed to capture this messy reality because it has a fragmented view of economic policy. This book aims to achieve just that by conceptualizing broad policy patterns or paradigms. In this effort, I use the comprehensive, yet analytical, perspective of economic historians and identify three dimensions of economic policy: international (finance and trade), microeconomic (industry and agriculture), and macroeconomic (money and budget). I thus distinguish three emerging policy alternatives—namely, protectionism, proto-Fordism, and neomercantilism with its developmental variant—to classical liberalism reigning in the pre-crisis period.

The book is equally motivated by the lack of comparative rigour in existing public policy literature on the interwar economic crisis. Whereas the literature tends to draw mainly on large states and democratic polities for comparison, I bring in a wide array of cases to represent the variation in economic policy across large states and small states, as well as across democracies and dictatorships. My sample includes six large states of the period and 12 small states, namely, those of the Balkans, Scandinavia, three self-governing British Dominions, as well as Austria. However, I do not treat all cases evenly as I highlight those exemplifying the three emerging policy patterns for more detailed analysis and use borderline or mixed cases for checking the validity of my argument. As the most common type of response, protectionism had some of its exemplary manifestations in the British Empire. Particularly, the United Kingdom, Australia, and Canada stood out in their resolution to stay the course. New Zealand did experiment with a mixture of protectionism, proto-Fordism, and even developmental neomercantilism. It thus provides an interesting contrast to those three cases; so does France which had a proto-Fordist interlude. The United States and Sweden went deeper than any other state in experimenting with proto-Fordism while Denmark and Norway produced much weaker versions. Among the large states, Germany was the exemplar of neomercantilism, with the semi-industrial Italian case having a developmental streak. Austria was the only small and industrialized state which delivered something resembling neomercantilism in its response. The Soviet Union and Turkey developed a variant geared to industrialization whereas the other Balkan responses were barely distinguishable from protectionism.

When one casts the net wide in both policy conception and case selection as I do in this book, no factor can plausibly be singled out as an explanation of cross-national variation in responses to the crisis. In fact, the comparative literature abounds with explanations centring on three broad clusters of factors, either individually or in some combination. These are the so-called 3Is (ideas, interests, and institutions). This book, too, takes account of them but not in a random, eclectic, or "even-handed" manner. First, I give primacy to rulers' ideas of, and strategies for, the economy with its three major groups of interest (in the interwar context): business, labour, and, not to be overlooked, agrarians. Unlike some ideationally oriented scholars who see interests as a derivative of ideas, I recognize interests as real and do not consider their articulation or representation terribly problematic. What is problematic is not so much the transition from interests to ideas informing collective action as it is the transition from interests to ideas informing public policy. Many things happen in that second transition, including, most notably, rulers' own ideas and strategies, which do not necessarily overlap with those of business, labour, or agrarians. Second, I incorporate economic and political institutions into my explanation as factors intermediating (constraining or facilitating) collective action and policy decision. For example, financial/banking systems or electoral arrangements under democracy filtered purposeful action and decision making in the interwar period. Third, I underline a limiting context for 3Is at both the world-historical and national-structural levels. World-historical (secular and cyclical) trends of the period and national-structural (not to be confused with institutional) features, such as level of economic development and type of political regime, all put limits to what rulers and other actors could do.

Under the given limiting and mediating conditions, crisis-time governments approached sectional interests in different ways, each one of which helped shape a distinct policy pattern. The most common approach came from those governments (e.g., UK, Australian, and Canadian governments) which privileged business and accommodated agrarian interests out of necessity but excluded organized labour altogether. The policy outcome of this approach was protectionism, a conservative departure from classical liberalism. Some governments (e.g., Nazi, Fascist, and Austrofascist governments) went beyond accommodating the agrarian sector to promote it ideologically and politically as the bedrock of national purity and rejuvenation while still observing the general reign of business and suppressing organized labour. This approach resulted in a more aggressive policy response in the form of neomercantilism. A small number of governments (e.g., US and Swedish governments) steered the three groups of interest into cross-sectoral and cross-class compromises, thus clearing the way for an innovative, proto-Fordist policy mix containing something from each group. Even a smaller number of governments (e.g., Soviet and Turkish governments) regimented or suppressed business, put agriculture into the use of industrialization by applying financial coercion and, in the extreme case, socializing it, and allowed no autonomous organization of labour. This approach yielded a developmental variant of neomercantilism.

Chapter 1 lays out the theoretical and methodological framework of the book. After briefly reviewing the comparative literature, it presents a typology of economic policy responses in their international, microeconomic, and macroeconomic aspects. It then offers an explanation of the cross-national variation and substantiates the selection of country cases representing that variation across the democracy–dictatorship and small state–large state divides. Chapter 2 elaborates on the world-historical and national-structural limits of the possible for economic policy choice. Taking the interwar period as a critical juncture, it first identifies secular and cyclical trends in both the liberal convergence of the 1920s and the interventionist expansion of policy space in the 1930s. It then shifts to the national level to portray actually existing policies and refer to their structurally possible alternatives in the 18 country cases. Chapters 3, 4, 5, and 6 form the substantive core of the book. Each one deploys the argument of the book in the primary and secondary cases of a particular policy paradigm. Chapter 3 takes up the UK, Australian, and Canadian responses as the primary cases of protectionism, using the French and New Zealand responses as secondary cases. Chapter 4 follows suit for the US and Swedish responses as the primary cases of proto-Fordism, and the Danish and Norwegian responses as secondary cases. In Chap. 5, I analyse the German, Italian, and Austrian responses in their protectionist and neomercantilist phases. Similarly, Chap. 6 reviews the Soviet and Turkish developmentalist responses, along with their weaker counterparts in the

Balkans, against the broadly liberal background of the 1920s. In the concluding chapter, I revisit the core theoretical themes to reflect on them in light of the material presented in substantive chapters.

This book has been a long time coming. In the process, I accumulated a lot of intellectual and personal debt. John Myles was single-handedly responsible for changing my research outlook from abstract class analysis to comparative historical analysis. My work tremendously benefitted in both style and content from Rianne Mahon's detailed and critical reading. Wally Clement was always there to support me in my hours of need as a foreign graduate student in Canada. I can never fully appreciate the intellectual lifeline that the late Gertrud Neuwirth extended to me when I became a sort of scholar at risk. Over the years, many anonymous reviewers of my work helped me better organize my thoughts and sharpen my argument. I must confess that I came to appreciate the role of ideas in human life more and more, and hold no one responsible for that.

A small fellowship from the American Research Institute in Turkey went a long way to start my Canadian journey. Staff at Carleton University's MacOdrum Library have been extremely efficient and patient with my constant requests for interlibrary loans.

My greatest debt, however, is to my wife, Nezahat, who took on more than her fair share of responsibilities for raising our son, Bengi, and kept me going throughout my difficulties on and off the academic field. I dedicate this book to her.

Ottawa, ON, Canada
January 2022

Adnan Türegün

Contents

1 The Interwar Economic Crisis in Comparative Research Perspective — 1

2 Limits of the Possible for Economic Policy Choice — 43

3 Protectionism: A Safe Haven or Missed Opportunity? — 99

4 Proto-Fordism: Seizing the Moment Under Democracy — 139

5 Neomercantilism, Mark I, Under Dictatorship with an Agro-Industrial Base — 173

6 Neomercantilism, Mark II, Under Dictatorship of the Bureaucracy — 201

7 Conclusion — 235

References — 241

Index — 283

Abbreviations

3Is	ideas, institutions, and interests
AAA	Agricultural Adjustment Administration
ADGB	Allgemeiner Deutscher Gewerkschaftsbund (General Trade Union Federation)
AFL	American Federation of Labor
AK	Arbetslöshetskommissionen (Unemployment Commission)
ALP	Australian Labor Party
AMS	Arbetsmarknadsstyrelsen (Labour Market Board)
BZNS	Bŭlgarski Zemedelski Naroden Sŭyuz (Bulgarian Agrarian National Union)
CCF	Co-operative Commonwealth Federation
CGT	Confédération générale du travail
CHF	Cumhuriyet Halk Fırkası (Republican People's Party)
CIO	Committee for Industrial Organization / Congress of Industrial Organizations
GNP	gross national product
IMI	Istituto Mobiliare Italiano (Italian Industrial Finance Institute)
IRI	Istituto per la Ricostruzione Industriale (Institute for Industrial Reconstruction)
İTF	İttihad ve Terakki Fırkası (Union and Progress Party)
LO	Landsorganisationen (Trade Union Confederation)
LSR	League for Social Reconstruction
Metall	Metallindustriarbetareförbundet (Metalworkers' Union)
MFN	most favoured nation
NAM	National Association of Manufacturers
NEC	National Employment Commission
NEP	*Novaya Ekonomicheskaya Politika* (New Economic Policy)

NRA	National Recovery Administration
RBNZ	Reserve Bank of New Zealand
RCBCC	Royal Commission on Banking and Currency in Canada
RCDPR	Royal Commission on Dominion–Provincial Relations
RIIA	Royal Institute of International Affairs
SAF	Svenska Arbetsgivareföreningen (Swedish Employers' Federation)
SAP	Socialdemokratiska Arbetarepartiet (Social Democratic Workers' Party)
SCF	Serbest Cumhuriyet Fırkası (Free Republican Party)
SDAP	Sozialdemokratische Arbeiterpartei (Social Democratic Workers' Party)
Socred	Social Credit Party
SPD	Sozialdemokratische Partei Deutschlands (Social Democratic Party)
TCF	Terakkiperver Cumhuriyet Fırkası (Progressive Republican Party)
TLC	Trades and Labour Congress
TUC	Trades Union Congress
UFA	United Farmers of Alberta
USBC	US Bureau of the Census
VF	Verkstadsföreningen (Engineering Employers' Association)

List of Figures

Fig. 1.1	Three emergent economic policy paradigms in the 1930s	15
Fig. 1.2	Modes of economic policy determination	19
Fig. 2.1	World-historical and political regime limits of economic policy choice	44

List of Tables

Table 1.1	Selected socioeconomic indices for the 18 country cases	33
Table 3.1	Points of convergence and divergence in the protectionist camp	102
Table 4.1	Points of convergence and divergence in the proto-Fordist camp	142
Table 5.1	Neomercantilism, mark I: (semi-)industrial varieties	176
Table 6.1	Neomercantilism, mark II: developmental varieties	203

CHAPTER 1

The Interwar Economic Crisis in Comparative Research Perspective

Some 60 years ago, Thomas Kuhn ([1962] 1970) observed that periods of normalcy are regularly punctuated by those of crisis. To follow his observation a little further, normalcy is provided by the hegemony of a paradigm that defines both problems and solutions. When the hegemonic paradigm can no longer ignore or cope with anomalies (new puzzles), however, it gives way to a crisis situation whereby alternative paradigms compete for hegemony with their sets of problems and solutions. The crisis culminates in a paradigm shift (a "revolution") which seals the hegemony of one of the alternative paradigms to start a new round of normalcy.

Kuhn was, of course, a philosopher of science reflecting on the history of disciplines such as physics, chemistry, and biology. Yet his theory of how "normal science" operates and how it is periodically interrupted by "scientific revolutions" has caught the imagination of many social scientists about the workings of not just their disciplines but also, more critically, their real-world areas of interest, including public policy. As will be seen later in the chapter, the Kuhnian concept of paradigm-centred scientific practice has been a useful analogy in the policy context, that is, in identifying and describing formal mechanisms that govern the relations within and across meaningful policy sets as dependent variables. Otherwise, the concept does not offer much help in substantive terms to account for what goes into the preference (or rejection) of one policy set over (or in favour of) its alternatives.

© The Author(s), under exclusive license to Springer Nature Switzerland AG 2022
A. Türegün, *Policy Responses to the Interwar Economic Crisis*, https://doi.org/10.1007/978-3-030-96953-0_1

In this book, I use the concept of paradigm to portray the international policy scene before and during the interwar economic crisis. Looking at three main areas of state intervention in the economy—foreign, microeconomic, and macroeconomic—I develop a typology of economic policy paradigms to group national responses to the crisis. The reigning classical liberal paradigm defended the international gold standard, free trade, sound money, balanced budget, and self-regulating market. Three alternative paradigms emerged as the crisis deepened: protectionism, proto-Fordism, and neomercantilism. Protectionism included tariff and nontariff protection, a generally procyclical macroeconomic framework, and a weak, selective intervention in the "real" economy. Proto-Fordism differed from protectionism in its preference for freer trade in industry but stronger protection of agriculture (both externally and internally), generally countercyclical macroeconomic framework, and institutionalization of employer–union relations and regulation of the industrial labour market. Contrasting sharply with proto-Fordism, neomercantilism was built on autarky, a staunchly conservative macroeconomic framework, and a physical, *dirigiste* mode of intervention in the domestic economy, including a repressive industrial relations system. A developmental variant of neomercantilism added to this list the exploitation of agriculture for industrialization purposes.

In explaining these divergent departures from classical liberalism, I give primacy to ideas among the so-called 3Is (ideas, institutions, and interests) while, at the same time, recognizing the world-historical and national-structural limitations on purposeful action guided by 3Is. More specifically, I argue that rulers' ideas and strategies concerning three major groups of interest—business, labour, and, most critically, agrarians—were the single most important determinant of economic policy variation across nations. Crisis-time governments approached these groups in four different ways, each one of which helped shape a distinct policy pattern. The most common approach came from those governments which privileged business and accommodated agrarian interests out of necessity but excluded organized labour altogether. The policy outcome of this approach was protectionism, a conservative departure from classical liberalism as the hegemonic paradigm of the pre-crisis period. Some governments went beyond accommodating the agrarian sector to promote it ideologically and politically as the bedrock of national existence while still observing the general reign of business. At the same time, they suppressed organized labour. This approach resulted in a more aggressive policy response in the form of neomercantilism. A small number of governments steered the three groups into cross-sectoral and cross-class compromises, thus clearing the way for an innovative, proto-Fordist policy mix containing something from each group. Even a smaller number regimented or suppressed business, put agriculture into the use of industrialization by applying financial coercion and, in the extreme case, socializing it, and allowed no autonomous organization of labour. This approach yielded a developmental variant of neomercantilism.

I apply this explanatory framework to six large states and 12 small states. I do not, however, deal with each case in the same depth and length as I highlight the exemplary cases of each policy paradigm for more detailed analysis and use borderline or mixed cases for secondary analysis in both the large state and small state contexts. The primary cases are the United Kingdom, Australia, and Canada for protectionism, the United States and Sweden for proto-Fordism, Germany and (by default) Austria for neomercantilism, and the Soviet Union and Turkey for developmental neomercantilism. French protectionism briefly interrupted by the proto-Fordist Blum experiment and Italian neomercantilism with a developmental streak are secondary cases in the large state context. For secondary analysis in the small state context, I bring in New Zealand (whose response mixed elements from all three paradigms), the two other Scandinavian countries (Denmark and Norway, which delivered a weaker version of proto-Fordism), and the rest of the Balkans (Bulgaria, Greece, Romania, and Yugoslavia, whose responses fell somewhere between protectionism and neomercantilism).

This chapter lays out the theoretical and methodological framework of the book. The first section briefly reviews the comparative public policy literature in terms of policy conception, case selection, and mode of explanation. This is followed by a typology of economic policy paradigms in their international, microeconomic, and macroeconomic aspects, which all emerged as alternatives to the classical liberal orthodoxy. In the third section, I offer an explanation of the cross-national variation in responses by highlighting the role of ruling ideas and strategies about business, labour, and agrarian interests while, at the same time, recognizing the world-historical and national-structural limitations on policy choice. The last section substantiates the selection of country cases representing the cross-national policy variation.

Taking 3Is Seriously and Putting Them in Their Place

The comparative public policy literature has produced plenty of material on the role of ideas, institutions, and interests—individually or in some combination—in responses to the interwar economic crisis. My intervention in the literature will be at two levels. First, I will emphasize the world-historical and national-structural limitations on the way 3Is shape economic policy. Second, and with that recognition, I will zero in on the ideational and strategic orientation of rulers (individuals, factions, and parties that are in power) towards three major groups of interest: business, labour, and agrarians. But let me first briefly review how the 3Is framework has been applied comparatively to the interwar crisis.

New institutionalism, particularly its historical variant, emerged in the 1980s as a reaction to the ahistorical behaviouralism and social determinism that had dominated American political science for most of the twentieth century, and to reclaim the earlier historical-institutional tradition and bring institutions back in (Robertson 1993; also Immergut 1998, 2006). With its emphasis on path dependency and rules of the game whereby change occurs in predictable ways, historical institutionalism is favourably disposed to explain institutional continuity or stability (Hall and Taylor 1996; Harty 2005; Lecours 2005a; Pierson 2000; Pierson and Skocpol 2002; Steinmo 2008). This historical-institutional return has given a big spurt to the comparative economic and social policy literature, especially in North America and Western Europe (for a review, see Evans et al. 1985; Lecours 2005b; Steinmo et al. 1992; Thelen 1999).

In their analysis of fiscal policies in the United Kingdom, Sweden, and the United States, Margaret Weir and Theda Skocpol (1985) deliver a major comparative application of historical institutionalism to the interwar crisis. They attribute UK orthodoxy, and Swedish and US proto-Keynesianism to the organizational and policy-historical features of the three national bureaucracies. According to this, functioning as both the ministry of finance and a department overseeing the entire civil service, the UK Treasury successfully guarded the orthodox policy legacy of the 1920s thanks to its institutional impermeability to political intervention. In contrast, the US federal civil service had no orthodox legacy to defend and was fragmented and permeable, thus leaving sufficient room for an innovative administration to experiment with demand management in the late 1930s. In the Swedish case, an open but centralized bureaucracy was part of peculiar and "long-established mechanisms for bringing experts, bureaucrats, and political representatives together for sustained planning of public policies" (Weir and Skocpol 1985, 129).

The policy legacy argument was also used in analysing responses to industrial decline and unemployment. For instance, Hugh Heclo (1974, 65–154) accounts for the contrasting UK and Swedish approaches to unemployment during the crisis—insurance versus work, respectively—by their antecedents earlier in the century. The Swedish work approach was a continuation and expansion of the relief work programmes that were first initiated with the outbreak of World War I. Likewise, the UK insurance approach grew out of a national unemployment insurance system that was introduced even before the war and had its coverage extended subsequently. In a similar vein, Frank Dobbin (1993) highlights cultural legacy to explain the industrial policy responses of the United Kingdom, France, and the United States. He maintains that, when failed to counter the depression, the three countries abandoned their traditional, culturally defined industrial policies (UK firm-centred *laissez-faire*, French *étatisme*, and US market regulation) in favour of rationalization (monopolization), liberalism, and state-led cartelization, respectively. Yet these shifts proved to be brief aberrations in the face of revivified traditional industrial cultures and, hence, policies.

These three studies speak to both the strengths and weaknesses of historical institutionalism. First, the (im)permeability and (de)centralization of national bureaucracies strongly reinforce that institutions serve as filters for the efficacy of ideas and interests. Second, policy and cultural legacies point to the "stickiness" of institutional arrangements and memories, and the path dependency of change whenever and wherever it occurs. Third, these studies also attest to the limits of historical institutionalism in explaining change. Attributing the fiscal stance of a country to its civil service organization ignores both the world-historical and national-structural limitations on policy, and the role in it of purposeful action guided by ideas and interests. Without considering these factors, it is impossible to explain, for example, Sweden's opposite fiscal responses to two similar economic downturns (namely, the depressions of 1921–1922 and the early 1930s) under the same type of bureaucracy. Similarly, institutional legacies and memories seem to fit the bill nicely when things are stable over time as in UK and Swedish approaches to unemployment, recurrent industrial policies in the United Kingdom, France, and the United States, or Weimar Germany's monetary and fiscal orthodoxy given the memory of hyperinflation in the early 1920s (Eichengreen 1992, 394). Yet, when things change and do so fundamentally, historical institutionalism does not offer much help. A case in point was Nazi Germany's demand stimulus experiment, which constituted a clean break with the past in fiscal policy.

Failing to incorporate institutional changes into its theoretical core, historical institutionalism treated them as the results of exogenous shocks or disturbances (Blyth 1997; Harty 2005, 52, 59; Lecours 2005a, 12). The renewed emphasis on the role of ideas in public policy has been a response to this failure. Many historically minded institutionalists have turned to ideas to explain path-shaping (as opposed to path-dependent) change in which seemingly insurmountable, institutional obstacles are overcome. These scholars of ideational or discursive persuasion still call their work (new) institutionalist because they see institutions as both contexts constraining actors and constructs shaped by the same actors (see, e.g., Béland 2005, 2009; Béland and Cox 2011; Campbell and Pedersen 2001, 2015; Schmidt 2008, 2010, 2011).

Even before the "ideational turn" in new institutionalism, the comparative public policy literature began to feature studies using ideas in their theoretical, calculative, and programmatic forms to account for some of the cross-national variation in economic policy during the interwar crisis. There are two ways in which economic theory is used as an explanation of policy. One is the unmediated, simplistic understanding of causation. According to this, choosing one policy over another is just a matter of following a more "scientific" theory. For instance, Donald Winch (1969, 178) asserts that the "underlying cause of the log-jam" to fiscal innovation before Keynes published *The General Theory of Employment, Interest and Money* was the theoretical failure of neoclassical economics to discover the connections between government budgets and the general economy. Thus, 1936 was a watershed between the fiscal orthodoxy of the UK Labour government in 1929–1931 and the "fiscal revolution" of the US Democratic administration in 1938. The other understanding of economics as a cause of policy concerns not just the kind of theory but also the kind of advice that is available from economists. For instance, in accounting for the earlier occurrence of Sweden's experiment with demand management than that of the United States (1933 versus 1938), Lars Jonung (1981) maintains that Swedish economists had a deeper understanding of the crisis and hence came up with more appropriate policy recommendations than those of their US counterparts. Similarly, Mark Blyth gives economic theory and theorists an elevated status to explain the same problematic: "By developing a demand-side model of the economy within a dynamic open-economy framework, the Stockholm School was far ahead of American economists ... Consequently, the theory of underconsumption and the theoretical case for compensatory institutions were developed faster and more readily in Sweden than they were in the United States" (2002, 106).[1]

Whether guided by theory, ideology, or some other conviction, the calculus of policymakers is another way in which ideas can affect policy. Two studies will be cited to make this point. Bradford Lee (1989) claims that despite situational necessity and intellectual innovation, the United Kingdom, France, and the United States did not experience a proto-Keynesian policy "revolution" in the 1930s because policymakers in these countries were concerned that a possible deficit-financed recovery strategy would decrease state autonomy *vis-à-vis* society, particularly the financial community as the largest potential source of any government borrowing. They thus strove to balance the budget in order to maintain the state–society equilibrium. Tobias Straumann (2010) resorts to a similar explanation in studying the fixed exchange rate regimes of seven European small states for most of the twentieth century, including the interwar period: "My main finding is that for most of the twentieth century, small European states preferred having their exchange rates fixed or pegged and that the reason for this preference was not institutional or economic in nature but rather the result of a deeply rooted fear that a floating exchange rate would hamper trade and complicate monetary policy" (xvii).

When they are adopted in a programmatic form by political parties, ideas become more powerful and also easier to measure in terms of their efficacy. How these ideas affected national policy responses has been argued most forcefully by Sheri Berman (1998a, 1998b, 2006). In her account of the contrasting responses of the German and Swedish Social Democrats, Berman assigns the deciding role to the two parties' "long-held ideas and the distinct policy legacies these ideas helped create" (1998b, 7). With programmatic beliefs such as an undogmatic view of Marxism, a commitment to reform work, and a mild view of the class conflict, the Swedish Social Democrats were prepared to respond to the crisis in innovative ways. In contrast, subscribing to a dogmatic view of Marxism, the futility of reform work, and a strident view of the class conflict, the German Social Democrats saw no choice but to wait for the downward business cycle to run its course (Berman 1998a, 380–95).[2]

The ideational reorientation of new institutionalism was meant to endogenize change and free the historical variant of its pro-continuity bias. Ideational institutionalism tries to achieve these goals by bringing in ideas both as another filter for the definition of interests alongside institutions and as a driver of purposeful action wherever it emanates from—individuals, groups, or broader collectivities. As it was applied to the interwar economic crisis, this variant has broadened our understanding of the policy process and problematized institutions such as state bureaucracies as arenas and agents of contestation. Yet, like their historical counterparts, existing ideational studies work with a narrow concept of economic policy, are confined to Western democracies, and pay insufficient, if any, attention to factors limiting policy choices. Moreover, while emphasizing the mutual causation of ideas and institutions, these studies often project a one-way transition from ideas to interests, whereby one cannot distinguish interests from ideas, all interests are ideas, and ideas constitute interests (Schmidt 2008, 317; see also Hay 2011, 79).

Two levels of transition between interests and ideas need to be distinguished for a full assessment of ideationalism. At the level of policy decision, it provides a nuanced view of the transition by highlighting the ideas, preferences, and choices of policymakers as distinct from those of collective actors representing particular interests. At the level of collection action, however, ideationalism misses the mark. It is true that interests are not "out there" regardless of individual or collective actors who can relate to them. Actors construct their own interests but, to paraphrase Marx, they do not do so under the circumstances of their own choosing. In other words, their material conditions will most likely come into play when they define their interests: High-income earners probably have interests in flat-rate taxes as opposed to progressive taxes and exporters in a lower, rather than higher, exchange value for their national currencies.

Informed by interest group and neo-Marxist perspectives, interest-based explanations had a head start in the comparative public policy literature. Yet some of the best examples of these explanations have been produced in response to new institutionalism in the 1980s and 1990s. A few studies pertaining to the interwar crisis will confirm this point. While not dealing with economic policy per se, Gøsta Esping-Andersen (1985, 71–113) delivers a fine rendition of the class coalition thesis when he studies the rise of Scandinavian social democracy in the 1930s. His argument is that labour's alignment with independent farmers in the context of a split bourgeoisie was critical to the social democratic breakthrough in all three countries. Likewise, with a focus on industrial policy in the small open economies of northwestern Europe, including Scandinavia, Peter Katzenstein (1985, 136–90) traces the origins of "democratic corporatism" in its liberal and social variants to labour's historical compromise with employers and farmers in the 1930s.

Peter Gourevitch (1984, 1986, 124–66) provides arguably the most eloquent comparative account of economic policy responses to the Great Depression from an interest-based perspective. He examines five national responses within the protectionist to demand stimulus policy range. His argument is that where labour and farmers found a common ground with some segments of business, the outcome was demand stimulus. Where there was no such ground, protectionist neo-orthodoxy got the upper hand. In the United States and Sweden, demand stimulus was made possible by a coalition of organized labour, independent farmers, and segments of business—initially domestic-market industries, subsequently export industries. The Nazi demand stimulus coalition, in contrast, included both domestic and weakened export industries, the agricultural sector, the unemployed, and urban middle strata. On the conservative side of the divide, the United Kingdom followed neo-orthodoxy mainly because of its highly internationalized financial sector identified with the City, which led a fiscally orthodox coalition involving all but labour. In France, a similar coalition, involving Catholic unions as well, got the upper hand in the 1930s except for the Popular Front interlude. The Front government's abortive experiment with demand stimulus had the support of major unions, parts of the agricultural sector, and the "Republican" bourgeoisie.

In following the contrasting trajectories of Swedish and US industrial relations and social policies in the twentieth century, Peter Swenson (2002) comes up with an employer-centred view of cross-class alliances, whereby politically adept capitalist classes subtly manipulate their labour counterparts and policymakers, thus determining the pace and extent of social reform. He maintains that the New Deal gave the United States a progressive head start on Sweden because of the "progressive social policy inclinations of a small if articulate minority of politically significant large employers during the 1930s in the United States, when New Deal legislation was passed, and the absence of the same in Sweden at the same time" (2002, 42). Bill Winders (2005) provides a corrective to this view when he traces the class coalitions behind the divergent policy trajectories of three New Deal initiatives. While the New Deal coalition in general consisted of "southern planters, labor, some segments of capital, and farmers in the corn and wheat belts," Winders notes, coalitions supporting different policies varied in membership and changed over time (2005, 392). Thus, the Wagner Act initially had the support of all but capital, received only a weak support from all but industrial labour in wartime, and was left with the support of only industrial and (partly) craft labour in the immediate postwar period. As a result, pro-labour policy had setbacks during and after the war. In contrast, New Deal agricultural policy had steady support from southern planters and farmers in the corn and wheat belts and, therefore, became increasingly generous over those years. Social security policy remained largely unchanged behind an all-inclusive coalition in which capital's role grew stronger and that of southern planters weaker.

In his study of the divergent responses to labour and farmer unrest in Canada and the United States, Barry Eidlin (2018, 159–90) brings in an element of political contingency that receives little or no attention from other interest-based explanations.[3] His explanation hinges on ruling parties' strategies. In the United States, the Democratic Party under Franklin D. Roosevelt adopted a co-optive strategy, using the unrest to build a coalition that was able to deliver benefits to workers and farmers in the form of industrial relations reform, agricultural support programmes, and social security. In contrast, Canada's Conservative and Liberal ruling parties adopted an exclusionary strategy that included policies of repression and neglect in responding to labour and farmer demands. This divergence resulted in the incorporation of labour and agrarian protest movements into a ruling party coalition in the United States, on one hand, and the search for an independent left third party that would draw on similar movements in Canada, on the other.

These studies show us that there is an alignment of interests behind every policy piece or package although, as Colin Hay (2004, 215) mentions, exhibited behaviour may not (always) reflect material interests. While ideational and historical studies point out the ways in which ideas define interests and institutions filter the latter, interest-based studies remind us of the irreducibility of material interests to their ideationally and institutionally mediated expressions. As Eidlin's study demonstrates, both Canadian and US workers strove to better their lot in the 1930s but did so differently because they encountered different political strategies developed by their federal governments. All this goes to show that there is no straight path from interests to ideas and institutions.

As reviewed above, the comparative public policy literature on economic policy responses to the interwar crisis can be critiqued from three angles: policy conception, case selection, and explanation. All of the studies in question work with a narrow conception of economic policy and thus fail to capture the full scope of national responses. It is usually fiscal or industrial policies—occasionally monetary or labour market policies—that are compared and any variation in these particular areas is presented as the one in national responses. This truncated view allows Gourevitch, for instance, to elevate fiscal policy to a general policy posture and thus lump Nazi Germany's economic response together with those of New Deal United States, Social Democratic Sweden, and Popular Front France. That all four countries tried fiscal stimulus should be placed in a context that included sharp differences in all other economic policy areas between the Nazi and three other responses. Any comparative project claiming to capture the full range of economic responses has to work with a broad policy conception covering international, microeconomic, and macroeconomic dimensions.

The comparative literature also suffers from a case selection skewed towards the industrial economies and democratic polities of Europe and North America. None of the studies reviewed has a sufficient number of cases to represent the diversity of responses among the large states or small states. Gourevitch's four cases—the United Kingdom, France, the United States, and Germany—come close to representing large state responses. His exclusion of the Soviet Union, however, leaves the picture incomplete. All comparisons in the small state context are region-specific with Scandinavia, or northwestern Europe in general, being the favourite universe for sampling. There is yet to be a comparison of sufficient number of cases representing the diversity of national responses across both the small state–large state and democratic–dictatorial divides. This book aims to do just that.

Policy conception and case selection problems are, of course, related to those of explanation. Emerging in the aftermath of the post-World War II economic order and growth, new institutionalisms and their interest-based rebuttals focused on the origins of Keynesianism and industrial policy (along with the welfare state) in Western Europe and North America to the extent that they dealt with the interwar crisis. Therefore, the interwar origins of the developmentalist state in its Soviet and Third World iterations hardly registered within the 3Is framework. Because of this narrow focus, the comparative public policy literature has overlooked two limiting factors in economic policy, world-historical and national-structural. As a world-historical event, the interwar crisis not only excluded classical liberalism as a policy option but also paved the way for neomercantilism, including its developmental variant, as well as protectionism and proto-Fordism. The literature's failure to pay attention to the national-structural limits of economic policy is equally noteworthy. As I will elaborate later in this chapter, two such limits stand out: political regime and sectoral profile. *Pace* Gourevitch, who produced one of the finest pieces of work on comparative responses to international crises, political regimes put limits on what actors can push for and choose as policy.[4] In this context, speaking of a Nazi demand stimulus coalition of employers, agrarians, urban middle strata, and the unemployed is simply not possible since none of these actors had either the medium or the means to negotiate and form alliances in Nazi Germany. Similarly, the sectoral profile of an economy can be a limiting factor. For example, the small size of the UK agricultural sector was a barrier to forming an agrarian–labour alliance in the 1930s.

As reviewed above, the comparative literature is about the triaging of 3Is guiding purposeful action. No work of substance singles out one "I" to the exclusion of the other "I"s. My approach is not different. In explaining the economic policy variation—within world-historical and national-structural limits—across the 18 cases, I give the "tipping point" priority to rulers' ideas and strategies while, at the same time, taking account of sectoral and class interests as well as of the institutional settings in which all actors operate. The rest of the chapter elaborates on the three aspects of the research programme: policy conception, case selection, and explanation.

PATHS OF DEPARTURE FROM CLASSICAL LIBERALISM

Writing in the midst of the crisis, British economist Lionel Robbins lamented that "[a]ll over the world, Governments to-day are actively engaged, on a scale unprecedented in history, in restricting trade and enterprise and undermining the basis of capitalism" (1934, 197).[5] While an orthodox contemporary like Robbins genuinely believed that there was a concerted assault on capitalism, economic historian Peter Temin (1989, 89–137) referred to the 1930s as "socialism in many countries" in analogy to Stalin's Soviet Union. Perhaps Karl Polanyi put it best when he noted that the "emerging regimes of fascism, socialism, and the New Deal were similar only in discarding *laissez-faire* principles" (1944, 244). The general interventionist tenor of the time was unmistakable.

However, this interventionism came in many forms and shapes. To capture and contextualize them, I will use the Kuhnian concepts of paradigm and paradigm shift. The allure of these concepts for policy scholarship has been twofold. First, social scientists found them useful for understanding the operation of their disciplines in an epistemic sense. For instance, Donald Winch (1969, 167–97) saw a Kuhnian paradigm shift in the rise of Keynesianism as an alternative to neoclassical economics in the 1930s. Second, it did not take long for policy scholars to adapt the Kuhnian framework to the policy field itself in the sense of political practice. In his study of the United Kingdom's transition from Keynesianism to monetarism in the 1970s and 1980s, Peter Hall (1993) broke new ground for this enterprise. The resurgence of monetarism was a paradigm shift in UK economic policy, he concluded, because it amounted to a third order change involving the overarching goals that guide policy, not just first order change (precise setting or levels of policy instruments) and second order change (techniques or policy instruments used to attain policy goals) (1993, 277–81).[6] Later scholarship was very prolific in applying the Kuhnian framework to both the disciplinary and policy dimensions of the economy (for a comprehensive review, see Béland and Cox 2013; Skogstad 2011).

I use the concepts of paradigm and paradigm shift to construct my dependent variable, which is economic policy. My idea of economic policy paradigm pertains to three main domains: international (finance and trade), microeconomic (sectoral), and macroeconomic (monetary and fiscal). It thus differs from the narrow conceptions reviewed above, including Hall's macroeconomic (Keynesian and monetarist) paradigms and Gourevitch's asymmetrical options—classical liberalism, (trade) protectionism, (fiscal) demand stimulus, and (industrial) mercantilism (1986, 35–54). Unlike Hall's restriction of policy change to either first, second, or third order change, this broad and nuanced view allows for different degrees of change across different components of the same paradigm, which is closer to what happens on the ground. My idea of policy paradigms as generic forms also differs from that of national policy traditions such as UK liberalism, French *étatisme*, German institutionalism, and US market regulation (Allen 1989; Dobbin 1993; Shonfield [1965] 1969). It is, however, historically more specific and elastic than the traditional Marxist conception of modes of state intervention in the economy, which is based on the changing requirements of capital accumulation or capitalist development over the *longue durée*. Mercantilism in the seventeenth and eighteenth centuries, liberalism in the nineteenth and early twentieth centuries, and developmentalism and/or Keynesianism after World War II were such modes (Wallerstein 1974, 2011; Wolfe 1981).

The classical liberal paradigm was the economic policy orthodoxy of the immediate pre-Great Depression period. Even a Soviet Union bent on destroying capitalism had used market incentives and liberal trade route to revive its economy under the New Economic Policy (NEP) of 1921–1928. By the mid-1920s, states came to a consensus on economic policy or how they should connect to the economy. The policy consensus involved all three main aspects of economic activity: foreign finance and trade, money and budget, and the "real" economy (particularly agriculture and industry as the most important productive sectors of the time). In foreign finance and trade, states subscribed to a liberal regime based on the international gold standard, which they were all tied to directly or indirectly, and free trade in the second half of the 1920s. The macroeconomic component of the consensus was a procyclical stance (going with the cycle) on credit and spending, that is, the "sound money and balanced budget" orthodoxy. This meant tightening credit and cutting spending in a contractionary cycle. As UK Chancellor of the Exchequer Winston Churchill put it, "whatever might be the political or social advantages, very little additional employment and no permanent additional employment can in fact and as a general rule be created by State borrowing and State expenditure" (UK House of Commons 1929, c54). Things were not as straightforward at the microeconomic level but, on balance, states acted to facilitate, not thwart, the self-regulation of the market. In short, classical liberalism was normal economic policy before the crisis.

Although no government gave a full rendition of classical liberalism as an "ideal type," it was a hegemonic idea, a policy standard that governments would aspire to. It did not thus go away quickly and entirely when the crisis hit in 1929. While multilateral free trade collapsed, the idea of free trade was rejuvenated bilaterally and within trade blocs. Similarly, government after government abandoned the gold standard but many stuck to it until the late 1930s or never lost the hope of returning to it at an opportune time. At the microeconomic level, the idea of self-regulating market was always the weakest link of classical liberalism and would lose whatever credibility it had during the crisis. At the macroeconomic level, however, the "sound finance and balanced budget" orthodoxy lingered in many quarters until the late 1930s, when the armaments buildup accelerated.

As a result, all three emergent policy paradigms—protectionism, proto-Fordism, and neomercantilism—carried an element of the classical liberal orthodoxy. Figure 1.1 presents the unique and intersecting aspects of the emergent policy paradigms.

The hallmark of the protectionist departure from the orthodoxy was its trade centrism. In the absence of the international gold standard as the linchpin of a liberal finance and trade regime, the protectionist response incorporated what the rest of the world was doing to protect the domestic market and export the ills of the depression: tariff and nontariff protection, currency devaluation, and other incentives for exports. Export promotion was, in fact, the main countercyclical aspect of the protectionist response. In macroeconomic terms, protectionism generally upheld the procyclical orthodoxy but not without practical deviations such as lowering the interest rate for credit ease and "unintended" deficit spending in the face of declining tax revenues. State physical intervention in the

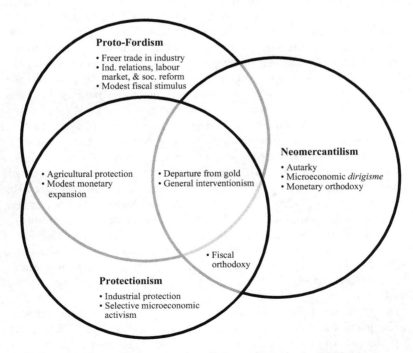

Fig. 1.1 Three emergent economic policy paradigms in the 1930s

domestic economy mainly aimed to facilitate the production and marketing of export-oriented primary products but also to encourage or enforce cartelization schemes in selected industries. This type of response is also called "neo-orthodoxy" because all of its components were tried universally at some point in the crisis (Gourevitch 1986, 43–8).

Assessed against Hall's three orders of change, protectionism represented a third order change only in international finance and trade. It replaced free movement of capital and goods with domestic market protection ("beggar-thy-neighbour") as the overarching policy goal by making first and second order changes such as currency devaluation, tariff increases, exchange controls, and nontariff measures. In the microeconomic field, however, changes were limited to those of first and second order. The state continued to facilitate the operation of the market but, in so doing, increased or introduced production, price, and marketing controls for primary producers and industries. Protectionism was most conservative in the macroeconomic field. Whatever changes occurred in monetary and fiscal policy were limited to those of first order, including cuts in interest rate and out-of-necessity increases in spending.

In contrast to protectionism, the proto-Fordist response came from a small number of states. This pattern was an innovative mix of classical liberalism, incipient Keynesianism, and "macrosocial" activism, a mix that would bear fruit fully as the postwar hegemonic policy paradigm in most of the Western world.[7] What was liberal about it was, first, its relatively open stance on foreign finance and trade in a world of economic closure. Freer trade concerned mainly manufactured goods with primary products remaining subject to external and internal protection. Second, proto-Fordism remained true to the spirit of classical liberalism by generally eschewing physical intervention in the domestic economy. However, this required two unorthodox forms of intervention. One was the fiscal experimentation with countercyclical demand management based on proto-Keynesian ideas and backed up by a low interest rate. The other intervention, which complemented macroeconomic activism, took on a "macrosocial" form aimed at institutionalizing employer–union relations, regulating the industrial labour market, and supporting the non-market population.

The paradigm shift proto-Fordism brought about was in the macroeconomic (particularly fiscal policy) and "macrosocial" fields. Deficit spending, not out of necessity as in protectionism (declining tax revenues coupled with a floor on expenditures) but for countercyclical purposes (demand stimulus), became the guiding principle of fiscal policy in a contractionary cycle. One area where classical liberalism was absent and where proto-Fordism created a niche for itself was industrial relations, labour market, and welfare state regulation, which aimed to improve the conditions of wage labour and people out of the labour force. In contrast, only first and second order changes were made in foreign finance and trade, as well as in the microeconomic field, under proto-Fordism. The liberal ideal remained largely intact in both areas with the notable exception of agriculture and with new instruments such as trade bilateralism.

The neomercantilist response was equally innovative but sharply contrasted with the proto-Fordist response.[8] Neomercantilism aimed to maximize production and exports and to minimize consumption and imports within a generally restrictive macroeconomic framework. Its defining feature in foreign finance and trade was autarky, which meant not so much economic independence as trade closure and the eclipse of monetary transactions in favour of state-organized or state-mediated quasi bartering. Microeconomic policy, however, was the cutting edge of this response pattern. State ownership and entrepreneurship ranging from ad hoc nationalization to full-scale collectivization, industrial or comprehensive planning, compulsory cartelization and marketing schemes, and, as a result of all this, circumscription of private economic activity and industrial organization were the components of a physical, *dirigiste* mode of intervention in the domestic economy. In contrast, neomercantilist monetary and fiscal policies drew closer to classical liberalism, producing the most successful applications of the "sound finance and balanced budget" orthodoxy. Reflecting a desire to catch up with the industrialized world, the developmental variant of neomercantilism was more *dirigiste* and statist in all three areas of economic policy.

Neomercantilism effected a paradigm shift both internationally and domestically. Autarky became the overarching policy goal in foreign finance and trade, going beyond first and second order changes, including clearing trade. Similarly, microeconomic *dirigisme* was not confined to what was included in protectionism and additional policy instruments such as sectoral or national planning. It also redefined the role of the state. Policy no longer targeted facilitation or even regulation of the market; instead, it regimented or, in the extreme case of the Soviet Union, suppressed the market. In macroeconomic terms, however, neomercantilism stuck to the "sound finance and balanced budget" orthodoxy of the classical liberal paradigm while making first and second order changes (e.g., price suppression, higher levels and new forms of taxation, and off-budget spending).

Before proceeding any further, a caveat is in order. Just as no state replicated "ideal-typical" classical liberalism in normal times, no response to the crisis fully matched any of the protectionist, proto-Fordist, and neomercantilist patterns. Individual state responses exemplified, approximated, or, as in many cases, mixed these alternative paradigms. Some responses came closer to them than others but always fell short of the ideal types. Many responses combined elements of two or even all three patterns. And, to the extent they drew closer to a response pattern, it was fairly common for individual states to shift from one pattern (usually protectionism) to another (usually proto-Fordism and neomercantilism) in the course of the crisis. Nevertheless, we need these constructs to isolate tendencies within the fluidity of reality and make a meaningful attempt at explanation, which the next section will take up.

Limits and Drivers of Economic Policy Choice

This section establishes the framework of an explanation of the paradigm shift as outlined above. In the first step, I specify the world-historical and national-structural limits of economic policy choice. Policymakers were not free to choose just any policy. The international conjuncture, along with domestic economic and political structures, defined what is possible and what is not. In the second step, I offer an ideational explanation of the variation within what is possible. Rulers' ideas about business, labour, and agrarian interests and the strategies they developed in response to demands by these sectoral and class interests largely shaped their economic policy choices. Figure 1.2 sketches these modes of policy determination.

The Interwar Critical Juncture and National Structures

The breakdown of the classical liberal paradigm in the interwar crisis was not a foregone conclusion. That it broke down and gave way to alternative policy paradigms was a result of the conjunction of several world-historical (secular and cyclical) trends cutting across national and broader regional boundaries, trends that made the interwar period a truly critical juncture. Once these trends took hold, they constituted a limiting context for economic policy options in a dual sense, closing off classical liberalism and opening up space for alternative paradigms. At the national level,

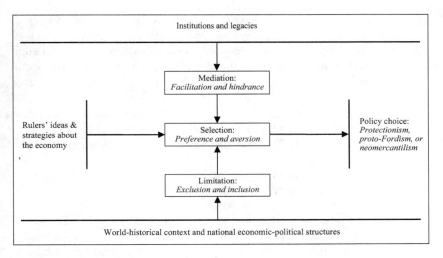

Fig. 1.2 Modes of economic policy determination

economic and political structures, particularly economies' sectoral profile and political regime types, further limited policy options. I argue that a full-fledged neomercantilism including autarky and *dirigisme* was not an option for democracies, just as proto-Fordism with its liberal approach to trade and partnership model of industrial relations was not an option for dictatorships. As for economies' sectoral profile, it limited political alignments and thus, indirectly, policy choices. For example, a small agricultural sector was an obstacle to agrarian–labour coalitions or a small industrial sector (lack of industrialization) left the bureaucracy as a main political player in society.

Systems theory can help us better appreciate the world-historical context, particularly critical junctures as expanded opportunities for change. Based on the idea of an irreducible whole, the theory makes a distinction between closed systems (mainly of the inanimate world), where no material enters to and leaves from, and open systems, where "there is import and export and, therefore, change of the components" (von Bertalanffy 1950, 23). In open systems, which are also called ecosystems, parts (subsystems) not only are interrelated but also interact with the whole (system) that, in turn, transacts with other systems. An open system and its environment composed of other, neighbouring systems form a supra-system. With its holistic and relational understanding of open systems, this theory can also help us move past the sterile debate between historical and newer institutionalisms as to the exogeneity versus endogeneity of sources of change, a debate premised on the assumption of closed systems. Change may originate from the inside, outside, or intersection of systems. Social sciences have yet to fully utilize systems theory as originated in "exact" sciences such as physics and biology. The few social science applications of it that are available come mostly from the fields of educational psychology and family therapy, where the unit of analysis is individual or family (see, e.g., Cooper and Upton 1990; Tyler 1996; Whitchurch and Constantine 1993).

As defined by historical institutionalists, critical junctures (alternatively called "defining moments," "points of critical choice" or "moments of flux," and "turning points") bear a strong resemblance to periods of scientific revolutions in the Kuhnian terminology. The former refer to the presence of a (usually exogenous) triggering event, rupture of the routine, realignment of actors, widening of options, and the eventual triumph of one possible option among many. More specifically, critical junctures are "shorter phases of fluidity and change alternating with longer periods of stability and adaptation" and concern those moments of path-dependent institutions in which "uncertainty as to the future of an institutional arrangement allows for political agency and choice to play a decisive role in setting an institution on a certain path of development, a path that then persists over a long period of time" (Capoccia 2015, 147–8; see also Capoccia and Kelemen 2007; Soifer 2012).

One does not need to accept the concept of critical junctures in toto as defined by historical institutionalists to use it as a theoretical tool. First, when countries are thought of as units (subsystems) of a whole (suprasystem), it really does not matter where the change-triggering event begins within the whole. Second, critical junctures are not necessarily shorter in duration than the periods preceding or succeeding them. For example, the interwar crisis combined with the two world wars lasted as long as, perhaps even longer than, the subsequent period of stability in Western Europe and North America. Third, why critical junctures should only concern "path-dependent institutions" is a problematic proposition. If critical junctures are associated with a high probability of change, they encompass the whole system, not just particular units such as path-dependent institutions.

The interwar period was doubly a critical juncture in world history. On one hand, the first part of the period from the end of World War I to the late 1920s witnessed efforts to restore the nineteenth-century order that had been disrupted by the war. That liberal order was based on a balance of power system, the international gold standard, the self-regulating market, and the "liberal state" in Polanyi's words (1944, 3–19). In their economic, political, and ideological facets, these four pillars of the nineteenth-century order also supported, or became part and parcel of, the classical liberal policy paradigm. Indeed, with the end of World War I, a concerted effort was underway to restore the status quo ante. The establishment of the League of Nations, a wave of returns to the gold standard, liberalization of international trade, withdrawal of the states from wartime spheres of intervention, and political opening were all indications—albeit in altered forms—of that effort. On the other hand, the second part of the period marked a spectacular failure of the restoration project and, with it, the breakdown of the classical liberal paradigm. The League of Nations never lived up to its lofty goals, the gold standard collapsed, the self-regulating market was discredited, and a series of democratic breakdowns ensued.

The League of Nations, a Wilsonian idea for international cooperation, was doomed ironically by the nonparticipation of the United States because of an isolationist Congress. A League without the membership of the strongest nation emerging from the war, as Eric Hobsbawm put it with a dose of exaggeration, "proved an almost total failure, except as an institution for collecting statistics" (1994, 34). International cooperation was also hampered by issues of war reparations and debts. Given the lack of international cooperation (Eichengreen 1992) or the absence of a hegemonic power (Kindleberger [1973] 2013), the restoration of the gold standard that had supported a liberal finance and trade regime from the 1870s to the outbreak of World War I rested on shaky ground. The United Kingdom left the gold standard at the first stress test in 1931 and many states followed suit. On the trade front, the United States signalled a protectionist turn even before the Great Crash by introducing what would eventually become the Smoot–Hawley Tariff Act of 1930 (Irwin 2011).

The liberal restoration project did not fare any better domestically. The golden age of classical liberalism had been sustained by a law-and-order state which, unconstrained from below within an exclusionary political framework, would spend only residually on the "social question." Although states began to withdraw from wartime spheres of intervention, government at arm's length was no longer possible. Two related developments necessitated state economic activism in industrial and semi-industrial nations. One was the increasing pace of proletarianization in the labour force that made unemployment and distributional conflicts permanent features of economic life. The other development was an unintended consequence of the war, namely, the politicization of society, including the activation of agrarian and labour movements, mass mobilization for universal suffrage, and the emergence of radical movements such as fascism and Third International communism. In both cases, the result was the end of elite politics and the beginning of mass politics with its distributional and systemic conflicts (Feinstein et al. 2008, 23).

The classical liberal policy paradigm could not stand against these world-historical trends and it crumbled. Yet, as seen above, its bits and pieces were picked up by the three emergent paradigms. As noted by critical junctures analysts, policy space was significantly expanded in the 1930s. However, not all policy options were available to individual nations. What policies governments could choose were constrained directly by where they stood on the democratic–dictatorial divide and indirectly by their economies' sectoral features.

Issues of affinity between economic policies and political arrangements were novel for the interwar period both because of a wave of democratization along with new forms of dictatorship (Luebbert 1987, 1991, part 2) and because of the expanding scope of economic policy. With a minimalist approach to state economic intervention, classical liberalism had been neutral to different *nondemocratic* political arrangements, liberal and authoritarian alike. Similarly, protectionism—the emerging orthodoxy of the late 1920s and early 1930s—was largely polity-neutral as everybody tried it in one way or another. In contrast, proto-Fordism and neomercantilism required a certain political arrangement; the former emerged in a limited number of democracies and the latter in modern dictatorships. Why they did so had to do with their defining features. Neomercantilism's autarky and *dirigisme* could only be possible under dictatorship (of a modern type), just as proto-Fordist industrial relations and trade policies could only find a hospitable environment under democracy.[9] So the choice in the 1930s was between protectionism and proto-Fordism under democracy, and between protectionism and neomercantilism under dictatorship.

I also recognize the limiting, if indirect, role of national economies' sectoral profile on policy choice. As the next section will argue in more detail, how governments approached and helped shape cross-sectoral and cross-class alignments was critical to their policy choices, and the sectoral structure determined whether these alignments were possible in the first place. A few examples will suffice to make this point. A small agricultural sector as in the UK case or the structural weakness of an independent farming class as in the Australian case hindered agrarian–labour alliances in the 1930s. Conversely, in countries where industrial and financial sectors were both small and weak (lack of industrialization and commercialization), capitalist and working classes remained on the margins, if anywhere, of politics, leaving a vast but partially commodified agricultural sector at the mercy of state bureaucracy as the main player. The Soviet Union and Turkey were the prime examples of this configuration.

Within the world-historical and national-structural limits sketched above, governments and other actors had room to manoeuvre. This is where ideas and strategies come to play a deciding role in the particular course of action to be followed. Especially the ideas and strategies of those in power about three major groups of interest—business, labour, and agrarians—tipped the balance in favour of one policy option against the other. What follows is an outline of this mechanism.

Ideas That Matter

In May 1930, 1028 economists from across the United States petitioned against the protectionist Smoot–Hawley tariff bill, addressing Congress and the President (Irwin 2011, 222–6). They first pointed out that the bill was unnecessary for the home market which faced no significant competition either in primary products or in manufactured goods. If it were to be enacted, they then warned, it would increase domestic prices for consumers and invite retaliatory measures abroad to hurt primary and manufactured exports. Nevertheless, Congress carried on and President Herbert Hoover signed the bill into law in June. After it was introduced to a Republican-dominated Congress in early 1929, the bill had snowballed in coverage and level of protection during the legislative process, reflecting the typical "logrolling" and "pork barrel" mechanisms of US politics.

This legislative case illustrates the interaction of 3Is. Despite the warnings of the 1028 economists and a minority of Congressmen, the President and the Republican Party acted in the belief that they were serving the interests of farmers and manufacturers by pushing the protective tariff bill. Once the legislative process got underway, familiar Congressional instruments (logrolling and pork barrel) were at work to deliver a more comprehensive and protective tariff than originally intended (Lake 1988, 193–201). The ruling Republicans' ideology of farming and manufacturing interests got the upper hand over the calculative logic of the economists. And the US polity helped strengthen the Republican protectionist agenda in ways that were not anticipated.

I will argue that how rulers (in this case, Republicans) articulated interests and pursued them via available (legislative and executive) channels in a specific area of concern (foreign trade) can be scoped to general economic policy across nations irrespective of where they stood on the democratic–dictatorial divide and the sectoral limitations on their policy choice. Interest articulation is necessarily an ideational—if structurally limited and institutionally mediated—process whereby actors, ruling or otherwise, contest for supremacy with their alternative definitions of reality and what to do about it. In this context, Vivien Schmidt's distinctions between and within ideas and discourse come in handy (2008, 2011). Ideas refer to substantive content or "text" and can be differentiated in terms of both scope (philosophical, programmatic, and policy ideas) and type (cognitive and normative ideas). Discourse encompasses not only ideas (what) but also the context (who, where, when, how, and why). Two forms of discourse are differentiated: (a) the coordinative discourse taking place in the policy sphere and among policy actors and (b) the communicative discourse taking place in the political sphere and between political actors and the general public.

While Schmidt's distinctions are useful, they do not tell us much about the translation of ideas in their variety into policy. This is where Jal Mehta's conception of transitions between different levels of ideas—corresponding largely to philosophical, programmatic, and policy ideas in Schmidt's work—complements the latter's work. Mehta (2011) identifies three levels of ideas. At the highest level, ideas are public philosophies or *zeitgeist*. More critical for our discussion here are mid-level ideas as problem definitions. By emphasizing some elements of a complex reality to the neglect of others, a problem definition frames that reality and thus circumscribes the scope of potential solutions. How does a particular problem definition prevail over its alternatives, then? Mehta lists six factors for an answer: (a) power and resources of the claimants; (b) how claimants portray the issues (framing); (c) venue or context in which the problem is heard; (d) who takes ownership of the problem; (e) whether there is a solution for a given problem definition; and (f) fit between the problem definition and the broader environment (2011, 35–8). Once a problem definition becomes prevalent, a corresponding solution emerges from considerations of policy, administrative, and political viability (see also Hall 1989, 370–5). Policy solutions are thus the third level in Mehta's hierarchy of ideas.

Some of Schmidt's and Mehta's "discursive" categories are more relevant than others to this study whose subject matter is general economic policy and whose unit of comparative analysis is nation-state. First, programmatic and policy ideas or mid- and low-level ideas (problem definitions and solutions), rather than philosophical ones, are of concern to me. Second, I am more interested in normative than in cognitive ideas (for example, the Republican versus academic views of the Smoot–Hawley tariff bill, respectively). Third, the discursive or contextualized expression of these ideas in their communicative form brings the policy process into sharper focus. Fourth, the elevation of one idea or set of ideas as qualified above over its alternatives as policy solution is mediated by interest-based and institutional factors listed by Mehta.

Governments that privileged business interests and accommodated those of the agrarians to the exclusion of labour gave a protectionist response to the crisis. This was the case initially with all governments that had dropped classical liberalism or parts thereof and still with quite a large number of governments throughout the 1930s. The United Kingdom, Australia, and Canada were among the latter group and produced exemplary cases of the protectionist neo-orthodoxy. France took a detour to proto-Fordism in 1936 before quickly returning to the protectionist fold, whereas New Zealand made a determined effort to break with the latter by mid-decade.

The United Kingdom neared the orthodox perfection under a Labour government from 1929 to 1931. Believing in the futility of countercyclical action in the absence of socialism, the Labour leadership embraced the orthodox Treasury doctrine, the gold standard, and free trade as the main planks of a heavily internationalized financial sector. However, the succeeding Conservative-dominated governments caught up with the times and effected a protectionist shift. While fiscal policy remained conservative, leaving the gold standard allowed monetary relaxation. In addition to credit ease, industry also received higher tariffs as part of an intra-Empire trade closure, cartelization, and sectoral/regional help. The small and domestic market-oriented agriculture, too, received tariff protection as well as marketing help. It is true that the UK agricultural sector was too small to support an agrarian–labour alliance. Yet what was also missing was the initiative on the part of the political arm of the labour movement. Political party orientation and strategies were critical to UK economic policy in its both classical liberal and protectionist phases. Labour Party leadership succumbed to the orthodoxy of the Treasury, the Bank of England, and the City representing the financial sector, whereas the Conservatives were able to activate their pro-Empire agenda and, in so doing, to devise policies favourable to industry, finance, and agriculture. The one party that proposed a proto-Fordist alternative to protectionism were the Liberals, but the first-past-the-post system reduced them to a small minority in parliament.

Like its UK counterpart, the Australian Labor Party (ALP) ruled in the initial years of the crisis with a fatalistic view of socialism. Operating in an export-dependent economy, however, the ALP government was compelled to leave the gold standard, devalue the currency, and support primary producers, as well as raising the industrial tariffs. And it did so by sticking to monetary and fiscal orthodoxy. The "bourgeois" parties, which ruled for most of the 1930s, largely remained within these parameters. With its capitalist relations of production generating sharp class divisions, the Australian agrarian/pastoral sector did not feature a strong independent farming class. This structural limitation, coupled with the ALP's orthodox thinking, reduced the possibility for a political rapprochement between labour and independent farmers. What took place instead was a polarization between the ALP representing urban and rural workers, on one hand, and the non-Labor parties which, when ruling, catered to (industrial and pastoral) capitalist and farming interests, on the other. On the macroeconomic front, countercyclical proposals did emerge from within the broader labour movement, but they were stifled by either the ALP leadership or federal constitutional arrangements.

Under both the Liberals and the Conservatives, the Canadian response conformed to the protectionist policy paradigm, including industrial tariff protection, limited marketing support to agriculture, ad hoc industrial policy measures, and a largely procyclical use of fiscal and monetary policy until the late 1930s. Both parties privileged business interests (with the Liberals leaning towards extractive industries and the Conservatives towards manufacturing industries) and provided only residual support to agriculture, while totally ignoring economic demands from organized labour. The resurgent agrarian and labour movements were the seat of innovative policy ideas, but they were hampered not only by internal divisions along multiple lines but also by the first-past-the-post system and federal–provincial disputes. Under these circumstances, only the mainstream parties could give voice to agrarian and labour demands at the national level. The Liberals were not prepared ideationally or politically to do that, whereas the Conservatives at least made a half-hearted attempt at mid-decade.

The case of New Zealand presents an interesting contrast to those mentioned above. With an export-dependent pastoral economy, New Zealand initially responded to the crisis in a typical protectionist fashion under a non-Labour coalition. However, the Labour Party's electoral victory in 1935 changed all that. The Labour government took daring initiatives in trade and banking regulation, industrialization, job creation, protection of wage earners and primary producers, and social security—initiatives that would infuse a measure of proto-Fordism and even neomercantilism into protectionism. It was able to do so for two related reasons. First, unlike its UK and Australian counterparts, the New Zealand Labour Party was not encumbered by the kind of socialism that counselled the classical liberal orthodoxy for as long as capitalism prevailed. Its economic ideology was informed by popular socialism. Second, unlike traditional labour or socialist parties appealing mainly to workers, it came to represent smallholders as well, thus effectively embodying an agrarian–labour alliance.

Among the large states, France attempted a proto-Fordist shift in 1936–1937 but quickly reverted to protectionism. Despite the astounding parade of right-wing and centrist governments before then, the French response was resolutely conservative. They all clung to the "national" policy consensus built around the gold standard, deflation, and budget balancing while, at the same time, providing cartelization schemes to industry, subsidies to agriculture, and trade protection to both. The Popular Front government of the Socialist, Communist, and left Radical parties punctured this consensus with the "Blum experiment." The short-lived experiment included an underconsumptionist purchasing power policy, enhanced marketing support for primary producers, labour peace negotiated between union and employers' federations, and improvements in employment conditions, as well as long-due departure from the gold standard. By early 1937, the Front government would be brought into the conservative fold under stress from within and without, most notably, fracturing support from employers, unions, and farming interests.

Where France failed, the United States succeeded in the transition from protectionism to proto-Fordism. Under the Republican administration of 1929–1932, the US response was protectionist only in the narrow (foreign trade) sense of the term, with its domestic component being largely reliant on market forces. The succeeding Democratic administration first strengthened domestic protectionism with various regulatory schemes for banking, industry, and agriculture under the First New Deal. It then transitioned to the proto-Fordist Second New Deal (freer trade, demand stimulus, industrial relations reform, and social security) that would redefine US economic policy for a long time to come. The key to this innovation were the willingness and ability of a Democratic Party not burdened by economic orthodoxy to serve as a common medium and interlocutor for employers, industrial workers, and farmers in the context of a national crisis. From the mid-1920s on, the Democrats had begun a self-renewal process to win over urban and industrial constituencies while maintaining a strong rural representation. They thus seized on the opportunity accorded by the crisis to add industrial labour as a constituency, as well as giving prominence in policy platforms to those businessmen who had spearheaded corporate liberalism.

Sweden went further than any other small state in fashioning a proto-Fordist response. Until the Social Democrats came to power in 1932, the Swedish response remained mildly protectionist as manifested in such measures as departure from the gold standard, currency devaluation, special protection of agriculture, and monetary reflation. The Social Democratic government maintained a freer trade approach in industry but enhanced agricultural protection in return for deficit-financed public works and other relief works as part of a deal with the Agrarian Party. It introduced a modest unemployment insurance scheme in another deal—this time with the Liberals. The Social Democratic–Agrarian rapprochement, formalized in a coalition government in 1936, prompted the employers' and labour federations to strike a compromise of their own later in the decade. The cross-sectoral and cross-class compromises, and whatever policy innovation they led to, owed their existence in large part to an ideational and strategic renewal process that transformed the Social Democrats from a working-class ghetto party into one of "people's home."

Denmark and Norway reached similar cross-sectoral and cross-class compromises to those of Sweden. In Denmark, the Social Democratic–Radical Liberal coalition negotiated a crisis agreement with the agrarian Liberals in early 1933 and the employers' and union federations had been working within a collective bargaining framework since the turn of the century. The Norwegian Labour and Agrarian parties, on one hand, and employers' and union federations, on the other, struck their respective agreements in 1935. Yet Denmark's and Norway's economic policies were not nearly as proto-Fordist as Sweden's. The Danish response distinguished itself by exchange controls and trade restrictions, and the Norwegian response by attempts at import-substituting industrialization. The two social democratic parties' ideational and strategic orientation, along with the two economies' sectoral profile, was what made the difference in policy. Developed against the background of a trade-dependent pastoral economy, the Danish party had a liberal streak and was thus weak in its domestic policy thrust. In contrast, the Norwegian party went as radical as joining the Third International in the early 1920s and somewhat retained its ideological rigidity in a resource economy sharply divided along the rural–urban line.

The one constant in all the cases above that experienced some degree of proto-Fordism was a rapprochement between organized labour and farmers with express or tacit support from business quarters. That only the United States and Sweden went the distance in proto-Fordist experimentation shows that cross-sectoral and cross-class alignments were not sufficient for determining actual policy content. The ideas held, and strategies used, by the ruling Democrats and Social Democrats proved decisive in US and Swedish policy outcomes. As will be seen in the next three cases, governments' ideational orientation and political strategies played a similar role in the rise of neomercantilism. The Nazis, Fascists, and Austrofascists promoted the agrarian sector ideologically and politically as the bedrock of national existence but, at the same time, observed the general rule of big business and suppressed organized labour.

Weimar Germany met the crisis with a Social Democratic-led coalition government. The economic orthodoxy of the Social Democrats was more rigid than that of the UK and Australian labour parties, and they would pay a much heavier price for it. When its neoclassical remedies did not work, the coalition government collapsed and made way for a procession of unstable minority governments which would increasingly rule by decree. Nevertheless, these governments put Germany on a protectionist course by imposing exchange and import controls, introducing clearing trade, and undertaking financial/industrial rescue measures within a restrictive macroeconomic framework. What the Nazis did was mobilize Weimar-era trade instruments (including a nominal allegiance to the gold standard and thus an overvalued mark) for autarkic goals, introduce national—if not comprehensive or detailed—planning, and spend boldly first for public works and then for armaments. The Nazis' willingness and ability to innovate by building on the "marriage of iron and rye" contrasted sharply with the Social Democrats' failure to break with dogmatic

Marxism and try new ways despite countercyclical proposals coming from the union wing.

Until the Nazi takeover in 1933, Germany's and Austria's responses were remarkably similar in part because they faced similar international constraints as losers of World War I. By the time Austria installed its own (Austro)fascism in early 1933, its economic policy had already undergone a Weimar-style switch from classical liberalism to protectionism under the Christian Socials. The "corporatist" Dollfuss/Schuschnigg regime of 1933–1938 privileged agrarian interests and promoted cartelization in industry, but its domestic *dirigiste* thrust remained much weaker than its Nazi counterpart. Thus, the Austrian response was a conservative iteration of neomercantilism in the context of an industrialized economy. A German–Austrian comparison would make it clear that Austrofascism was rather a top-down affair falling well short of the ideological and political reach of Nazism, and that the small Austrian economy was doubly vulnerable to international pressures with its large foreign sector and ongoing financial obligations to external creditors.

On the southern flank of Europe, Fascist Italy rendered a statist edition of neomercantilism in a semi-industrialized economy. Reflecting the world-historical trends, the Fascists showed an extraordinary flexibility in economic policy during the interwar period. From 1922 to 1925 (the so-called *Liberista* period), they wholeheartedly embraced the rhetoric and practice of "Manchester liberalism" by privatizing state enterprises, encouraging foreign investment, reducing taxes for business, downsizing state bureaucracy, and curtailing labour rights. They then gradually shifted to protectionism, particularly seeking self-sufficiency in agriculture and exalting the virtues of rural life. The world economic crisis sharpened their resolve to solidify the new course and expanded their room for manoeuvring. Fascist economic policy came to include, most notably, an all-out autarkic campaign, growing state entrepreneurship in finance and industry but not in agriculture, and monetary (if not fiscal) conservatism that preached a strong lira at any cost both at home and abroad at least until the collapse of the gold bloc in 1936.

The developmental variant of neomercantilism as exemplified by the Soviet and Turkish responses was informed by a different government approach that regimented or suppressed business, put agriculture into the use of industrialization by applying financial coercion and, in the Soviet case, socializing it, and allowed no autonomous organization of labour. Soviet economic policy followed a strikingly similar trajectory to the Italian one during the period. After securing their rule in 1920, the Bolsheviks put into effect NEP that would reintroduce market incentives and reopen the economy for international finance and trade. In the late 1920s, however, they reversed NEP in the direction of "socialist industrialization." The key question among the Bolshevik leadership in the lead-up to the first five-year plan (to be launched in 1928) was what to do with agriculture as the obvious fiscal source of industrialization. One group advocated a gradualist strategy to win over the landed, middle peasantry. The other group, which would get the upper hand, pushed for a crash collectivization programme to be incorporated into the plan. As in the Italian case, the Great Depression gave a big jolt to the new orientation. Unlike its Western counterparts, however, Soviet neomercantilism was built on comprehensive and detailed planning and made possible by the suppression and expropriation (rather than exaltation and protection) of the landed peasantry. While preaching monetary and fiscal conservatism like all neomercantilist responses, Soviet policy used non-monetary and non-budgetary instruments for its expansionary ways.

Among small states, Turkey's interwar economic policy trajectory was arguably closest to those of the Soviet Union and Italy. In the 1920s, the incipient Kemalist rule favoured an export-oriented, agriculturally driven development strategy encouraging foreign and domestic private investment. It then adopted a typical protectionist stance in 1929–1931 before resolving to launch a statist industrialization strategy in a heavily agricultural economy. While autarkic closure and macroeconomic conservatism were the common features of all small state responses in southeastern Europe, Turkish neomercantilism added a unique level of microeconomic *dirigisme* involving state ownership and entrepreneurship, industrial planning, and circumscription of private enterprise. Like its Stalinist counterpart, the Kemalist bureaucracy implemented its industrialization project on the back of the agricultural sector. However, it did so without any attempt to change the agrarian class structure via land reform, let alone collectivization; rather, it heavily taxed the peasantry and manipulated the internal terms of trade against agriculture to finance industrialization. Thus, the Kemalist approach to agriculture also differed from its Nazi and Fascist counterparts in that its homage to the peasantry was limited to pure rhetoric.

The rest of the small Balkan states (Greece, Bulgaria, Romania, and Yugoslavia) straddled between protectionism and neomercantilism. Like their industrialized Austrian counterpart, these largely agricultural states lacked domestic, particularly industrial, *dirigisme* but were highly protective of their agrarians. The main reason for this divergence between the Turkish and other Balkan responses lay in the pre-existing sectoral structures towards which the rulers developed strategies. Unlike Turkey, where the vast agricultural sector was left untouched in terms of property relations and where there was no industry of considerable size, the other Balkan states implemented radical land redistribution schemes in the aftermath of World War I, thus creating egalitarian sectors of small producers and strong agrarian movements. As well, they experienced some measure of industrial growth via tariffs and other incentives in the 1920s. The upshot for the 1930s was a limited room for the rulers of the "European" Balkans in both the economy and polity, compared with the Turkish bureaucracy which found itself unchallenged by any societal force, if not internally, once it underwent an ideational reorientation.

Methodological Considerations on Case Selection

Six large states and 12 small ones. Some fully industrialized, some predominantly agricultural, and many somewhere in between. Many remained democratic and some dictatorial, but the rest experienced a democratic breakdown. Among the large states, the United Kingdom, France, and the United States remained democratic, Italy and the Soviet Union became increasingly dictatorial, and Germany switched from democracy to dictatorship in the interwar period. Among small states, Austria's democratic breakdown was as sharp as Germany's while the Balkan states, starting from a weaker democratic base, turned increasingly, though varyingly, dictatorial. The rest retained democracy. As can be seen in Table 1.1, both groups of states were also well represented on either side of the agricultural–industrial divide as measured by labour force distribution. The United Kingdom, France, the United States, and Germany were industrialized economies with large agricultural sectors except for the UK case, whereas Italy and especially the Soviet Union were still agriculture-heavy economies. The 12 small states diverged even more: Austria and Sweden were industrially mature, the rest of Scandinavia and the three Dominions depended on primary exports but had a significant industrial base, and the Balkans were heavily agricultural.

So, if sectoral profile or political regime does not define the small state–large state distinction, what does? Population and economic size does matter but not always. For example, China and India had the two largest

Table 1.1 Selected socioeconomic indices for the 18 country cases

Country group	Population, 1938 (in millions)	National income, 1938 (in millions of US dollars)	Per capita income, 1938 (in US dollars)	Year	Agriculture, fishing	Manufacturing, handicraft
Large states						
United Kingdom	47.5	22,100	465	1930	7	32
France	41.1	10,800	260	1931	36	32
United States	129.8	67,375	519	1930	22	30
Germany	68.6	23,000	335	1933	29	36
Italy	43.7	5830	133	1936	48	28
Soviet Union	170.0	17,850	105	1930	67	n/a
Small states						
Australia	6.9	3825	556	1933	20	30
Canada	11.2	3986	357	1931	31	25
New Zealand	1.6	907	567	1936	28	24
Sweden	6.3	2830	449	1930	36	31
Denmark	3.8	1170	308	1930	36	28
Norway	2.9	1000	345	1930	35	26
Austria	6.8	1051	154	1934	32	33
Turkey	17.8	1060	60	1935	82	8
Bulgaria	6.2	682	110	1934	80	8
Greece	7.1	550	77	1928	54	16
Romania	n/a	n/a	n/a	1930	78	7
Yugoslavia	15.4	2640	171	1931	79	11

Sources: Woytinsky and Woytinsky (1953, 389–90), for population and income; League of Nations (1945, 26–7), for labour force distribution

populations in the world and their economies were larger than Italy's (Woytinsky and Woytinsky 1953, 389–90). Yet, by interwar standards, either of the former cannot plausibly be considered as a large state while Italy can. China and India may be extreme cases. What about Australia and Canada whose economies were not much smaller than Italy's? The former were still small states despite their vast territories and sizable economies.

This is because they lacked influence in the interstate system. The political, relational nature of the distinction was equally on display in two marginal cases of large states, namely, Italy and the Soviet Union. Italy was an international player on account of its sphere of influence in the northeastern Mediterranean and the widespread inspiration of Fascism as a social movement. Even the young Soviet Union grew in international stature in the interwar period by exerting indirect influence via the Third International in the domestic politics of many nations with significant Communist presence.[10]

Concerning the identification of small states in particular, a political, relational approach using position in the interstate system as the main yardstick is superior to existing alternatives ranging from "we know a small state when we see it" (Streeten 1993, 197) to identifying one based on empirical cut-off points demarking it from both large and "very small" or "micro" ones. Measures used for this purpose include population, geography, economy, military, and other indicators (Veenendaal and Corbett 2015, 529). As seen above, however, size (economic or otherwise) does not always matter. Vulnerability, real or perceived, is a more insightful indicator used in the comparative public policy literature to distinguish small states from the large ones (Bishop 2012; Cameron 1978; Castles 1988; Katzenstein 1985, 2003). In my previous writing, I followed this literature and generalized the impact of external coercion, trade dependency (economic openness in general), and partner dependency on small state identity and behaviour (Türegün 1994, 2016, 2017). I now see that these mechanisms do not have that reach and that their impact is limited mainly to foreign finance and trade.

In addition to clarifying the small state–large state distinction, I would also like to highlight what my sample leaves out as alternative cases. Japan pursued an aggressive neomercantilism in the 1930s. I could have rounded out large state cases to seven by including it in the study. Yet, with Germany and Italy covering that policy option, I thought the Japanese experience would not add further analytical value to the study. Among small states, South Africa, Argentina, and Uruguay were alternative and interesting cases of protectionism from the perspectives of Canada and the Antipodes. As "consociational" democracies, Belgium, Switzerland, and the Netherlands approached Scandinavia in political arrangements but not so much in policy experiments. While the Austrian case was unique in bringing together a small state, an industrialized economy, a fascist dictatorship, and a conservative neomercantilism, the Balkan experiences had their counterparts in Latin America, particularly Mexico and Brazil, and perhaps in Iberia, namely, Portugal. However, including these cases in the comparison by doing justice to them and the actual cases would have been a daunting task and I did not take it on.

Before closing, a few words about the unit of analysis are in order. I use the words "country" and "nation" interchangeably and in a generic sense. In more specific terms, the study's comparative unit of analysis is (nation-)state, an entity which controls an internationally recognized territory, thus organizing a polity and an economy on it. The only exception to this is when I deal with the world-historical context of the interwar period in the next chapter. In that case, my international unit of analysis is the interstate system with its economic and political arrangements.

Notes

1. Blyth (2002) makes this point as part of a larger problematic, that is, the emergence of US liberal democratic "embedded liberalism" (49–95) and of its Swedish social democratic counterpart (96–125).
2. See also Martin (1973, 44–5, 1975, 22–4), and Stephens (1979, 145), for a similar contrasting of the ideological orientations of the Swedish Social Democrats and their German counterparts (and the UK Labour Party).
3. This comparison is part of Eidlin's attempt to explain the higher union density in Canada than in the United States during the post-World War II period: What made the difference was the existence of a Canadian independent left third party (Co-operative Commonwealth Federation and its successor New Democratic Party) that spurred the "class idea," as opposed to the incorporation of US labour into the Democratic Party as an interest group among many.
4. Gourevitch sees no linkages between political regime and economic policy: "[S]ince different political systems pursued the same policies, and similar political systems pursued different ones, there is no connection between the two and economic policies are polymorphous—anyone can take up any policy through any political system, so no linkages can be established" (1984, 103, also 1986, 129–31). For similar views, see also Garraty 1973; Zimmerman and Saalfeld 1988.
5. Robbins would come to regret this observation as the "greatest mistake" of his professional career and as a "fundamental misconception" (1971, 154–5).
6. Neil Bradford (1999) uses the concept of paradigm shift similarly in the Canadian context, in which neoliberalism replaced "Technocratic Keynesianism" in the 1980s and 1990s. Unlike Hall, however, he points

out that neoliberalism got the upper hand over an alternative paradigm, "Progressive Competitiveness" (just as "Technocratic Keynesianism" had risen by defeating "Social Keynesianism" in the 1930s and 1940s).
7. I would have called this policy mix "neoliberalism" if it had not been for the entirely different meaning stuck to the term since the market-oriented experiments of Ronald Reagan and Margaret Thatcher in the 1980s. In adopting the term "proto-Fordism," I was inspired by the French regulation school which conceptualized Fordism in the 1980s and 1990s as the postwar "regime of accumulation" with a corresponding "social mode of regulation" under advanced capitalism (see, e.g., Boyer [1986] 1990; Lipietz [1985] 1987). In line with my policy conception, however, I view (proto-)Fordism as a more plastic arrangement susceptible to politics.
8. As used here, the concept of neomercantilism refers to a general economic policy pattern, not particularly to an assertive industrial policy that France and Japan are often associated with in the post-World War II period (see, e.g., Brown 1980; Johnson 1982).
9. At this point, one might rightly warn that democracies themselves were in peril as a series of democratic breakdowns occurred in Europe and elsewhere in the interwar period (Stephens 1989). However, why democracies did not fare well would constitute another problematic within the world-historical context of the time.
10. Thus, unlike the core–periphery–semi-periphery distinction of the world-systems analysis (Wallerstein 1974), this political conception of the small state–large state distinction does not conflate a state's position in the interstate system with its position in the international economy. The two positions reinforce each other but one does not necessarily beget the other.

References

Allen, Christopher S. 1989. "The Underdevelopment of Keynesianism in the Federal Republic of Germany." In *The Political Power of Economic Ideas: Keynesianism across Nations*, edited by Peter A. Hall, 263–89. Princeton: Princeton University Press.

Béland, Daniel. 2005. "Ideas, Interests, and Institutions: Historical Institutionalism Revisited." In *New Institutionalism: Theory and Analysis*, edited by André Lecours, 29–50. Toronto: University of Toronto Press.

Béland, Daniel. 2009. "Ideas, Institutions, and Policy Change." *Journal of European Public Policy* 16, no. 5: 701–18. https://doi.org/10.1080/13501760902983382.

Béland, Daniel, and Robert H. Cox, eds. 2011. *Ideas and Politics in Social Science Research*. New York: Oxford University Press.

Béland, Daniel, and Robert H. Cox, eds. 2013. "Special Issue: The Politics of Policy Paradigms." *Governance* 26, no. 2: 189–328.
Berman, Sheri. 1998a. "Path Dependency and Political Action: Reexamining Responses to the Depression." *Comparative Politics* 30, no. 4: 379–400. https://doi.org/10.2307/422330.
Berman, Sheri. 1998b. *The Social Democratic Moment: Ideas and Politics in the Making of Interwar Europe*. Cambridge, MA: Harvard University Press.
Berman, Sheri. 2006. *The Primacy of Politics: Social Democracy and the Making of Europe's Twentieth Century*. New York: Cambridge University Press.
Bishop, Matthew L. 2012. "The Political Economy of Small States: Enduring Vulnerability?" *Review of International Political Economy* 19, no. 5: 942–60. https://doi.org/10.1080/09692290.2011.635118.
Blyth, Mark M. 1997. "'Any More Bright Ideas?' The Ideational Turn of Comparative Political Economy." *Comparative Politics* 29, no. 2: 229–50. https://doi.org/10.2307/422082.
Blyth, Mark M. 2002. *Great Transformations: Economic Ideas and Institutional Change in the Twentieth Century*. New York: Cambridge University Press.
Boyer, Robert. [1986] 1990. *The Regulation School: A Critical Introduction*. Translated from the French by Craig Charney. New York: Columbia University Press.
Bradford, Neil. 1999. "The Policy Influence of Economic Ideas: Interests, Institutions and Innovation in Canada." *Studies in Political Economy*, no. 59: 17–60. https://doi.org/10.1080/19187033.1999.11675266.
Brown, C. J. F. 1980. "Industrial Policy and Economic Planning in Japan and France." *National Institute Economic Review*, no. 93: 59–75. https://doi.org/10.1177/002795018009300107.
Campbell, John L., and Ove K. Pedersen, eds. 2001. *The Rise of Neoliberalism and Institutional Analysis*. Princeton: Princeton University Press.
Campbell, John L., and Ove K. Pedersen. 2015. "Policy Ideas, Knowledge Regimes and Comparative Political Economy." *Socio-Economic Review* 13, no. 4: 679–701. https://doi.org/10.1093/ser/mwv004.
Cameron, David R. 1978. "The Expansion of the Public Economy: A Comparative Analysis." *American Political Science Review* 72, no. 4: 1243–61. https://doi.org/10.2307/1954537.
Capoccia, Giovanni. 2015. "Critical Junctures and Institutional Change." In *Advances in Comparative-Historical Analysis*, edited by James Mahoney and Kathleen Thelen, 147–79. Cambridge: Cambridge University Press.
Capoccia, Giovanni, and R. Daniel Kelemen. 2007. "The Study of Critical Junctures: Theory, Narrative, and Counterfactuals in Historical Institutionalism." *World Politics* 59, no. 3: 341–69. https://doi.org/10.1017/S0043887100020852.

Castles, Francis G. 1988. *Australian Public Policy and Economic Vulnerability: A Comparative and Historical Perspective.* Sydney: Allen and Unwin.

Cooper, Paul, and Graham Upton. 1990. "An Ecosystemic Approach to Emotional and Behavioural Difficulties in Schools." *Educational Psychology* 10, no. 4: 301–21. https://doi.org/10.1080/0144341900100402.

Dobbin, Frank R. 1993. "The Social Construction of the Great Depression: Industrial Policy during the 1930s in the United States, Britain, and France." *Theory and Society* 22, no. 1: 1–56. https://doi.org/10.1007/BF00993447.

Eichengreen, Barry J. 1992. *Golden Fetters: The Gold Standard and the Great Depression, 1919–1939.* New York: Oxford University Press.

Eidlin, Barry. 2018. *Labor and the Class Idea in the United States and Canada.* New York: Cambridge University Press.

Esping-Andersen, Gøsta. 1985. *Politics against Markets: The Social Democratic Road to Power.* Princeton: Princeton University Press.

Evans, Peter B., Dietrich Rueschemeyer, and Theda Skocpol, eds. 1985. *Bringing the State Back In.* Cambridge: Cambridge University Press.

Feinstein, Charles H., Peter Temin, and Gianni Toniolo. 2008. *The World Economy between the World Wars.* Oxford: Oxford University Press.

Garraty, John A. 1973. "The New Deal, National Socialism, and the Great Depression." *American Historical Review* 78, no. 4: 907–44. https://doi.org/10.2307/1858346.

Gourevitch, Peter A. 1984. "Breaking with Orthodoxy: The Politics of Economic Policy Responses to the Depression of the 1930s." *International Organization* 38, no. 1: 95–129. https://doi.org/10.1017/S0020818300004288.

Gourevitch, Peter A. 1986. *Politics in Hard Times: Comparative Responses to International Economic Crises.* Ithaca: Cornell University Press.

Hall, Peter A. 1989. "Conclusion: The Politics of Keynesian Ideas." In *The Political Power of Economic Ideas: Keynesianism across Nations,* edited by Peter A. Hall, 361–91. Princeton: Princeton University Press.

Hall, Peter A. 1993. "Policy Paradigms, Social Learning, and the State: The Case of Economic Policymaking in Britain." *Comparative Politics* 25, no. 3: 275–96. https://doi.org/10.2307/422246.

Hall, Peter A., and Rosemary C. R. Taylor. 1996. "Political Science and the Three New Institutionalisms." *Political Studies* 44, no. 5: 936–57. https://doi.org/10.1111/j.1467-9248.1996.tb00343.x.

Harty, Siobhán. 2005. "Theorizing Institutional Change." In *New Institutionalism: Theory and Analysis,* edited by André Lecours, 51–79. Toronto: University of Toronto Press.

Hay, Colin. 2004. "Ideas, Interests and Institutions in the Comparative Political Economy of Great Transformations." *Review of International Political Economy* 11, no. 1: 204–26. https://doi.org/10.1080/0969229042000179811.

Hay, Colin. 2011. "Ideas and the Construction of Interests." In *Ideas and Politics in Social Science Research*, edited by Daniel Béland and Robert H. Cox, 65–82. New York: Oxford University Press.

Heclo, Hugh. 1974. *Modern Social Politics in Britain and Sweden: From Relief to Income Maintenance*. New Haven: Yale University Press.

Hobsbawm, Eric. 1994. *Age of Extremes: The Short Twentieth Century, 1914–1991*. London: Michael Joseph.

Immergut, Ellen M. 1998. "The Theoretical Core of the New Institutionalism." *Politics and Society* 26, no. 1: 5–34. https://doi.org/10.1177/0032329298026001002.

Immergut, Ellen M. 2006. "Historical-Institutionalism in Political Science and the Problem of Change." In *Understanding Change: Models, Methodologies and Metaphors*, edited by Andreas Wimmer and Reinhart Kössler, 237–59. London: Palgrave Macmillan.

Irwin, Douglas A. 2011. *Peddling Protectionism: Smoot–Hawley and the Great Depression*. Princeton: Princeton University Press.

Johnson, Chalmers A. 1982. *MITI and the Japanese Miracle: The Growth of Industrial Policy, 1925–1975*. Stanford: Stanford University Press.

Jonung, Lars. 1981. "The Depression in Sweden and the United States: A Comparison of Causes and Policies." In *The Great Depression Revisited*, edited by Karl Brunner, 286–315. Boston: Martinus Nijhoff.

Katzenstein, Peter J. 1985. *Small States in World Markets: Industrial Policy in Europe*. Ithaca: Cornell University Press.

Katzenstein, Peter J. 2003. "*Small States* and Small States Revisited." *New Political Economy* 8, no. 1: 9–30. https://doi.org/10.1080/1356346032000078705.

Kindleberger, Charles P. [1973] 2013. *The World in Depression, 1929–1939*. 40th anniversary ed. Berkeley: University of California Press.

Kuhn, Thomas S. [1962] 1970. *The Structure of Scientific Revolutions*. 2nd ed. Chicago: University of Chicago Press.

Lake, David A. 1988. *Power, Protection, and Free Trade: International Sources of U.S. Commercial Strategy, 1887–1939*. Ithaca: Cornell University Press.

League of Nations. 1945. *Industrialization and Foreign Trade*. Geneva: League of Nations.

Lecours, André. 2005a. "New Institutionalism: Issues and Questions." In *New Institutionalism: Theory and Analysis*, edited by André Lecours, 3–25. Toronto: University of Toronto Press.

Lecours, André, ed. 2005b. *New Institutionalism: Theory and Analysis*. Toronto: University of Toronto Press.

Lee, Bradford A. 1989. "The Miscarriage of Necessity and Invention: Proto-Keynesianism and Democratic States in the 1930s." In *The Political Power of Economic Ideas: Keynesianism across Nations*, edited by Peter A. Hall, 129–70. Princeton: Princeton University Press.

Lipietz, Alain. [1985] 1987. *Mirages and Miracles: The Crises of Global Fordism*. Translated from the French by David Macey. London: Verso.
Luebbert, Gregory M. 1987. "Social Foundations of Political Order in Interwar Europe." *World Politics* 39, no. 4: 449–78. https://doi.org/10.2307/2010288.
Luebbert, Gregory M. 1991. *Liberalism, Fascism, or Social Democracy: Social Classes and the Political Origins of Regimes in Interwar Europe*. New York: Oxford University Press.
Martin, Andrew. 1973. *The Politics of Economic Policy in the United States: A Tentative View from a Comparative Perspective*. Beverly Hills: Sage.
Martin, Andrew. 1975. "Is Democratic Control of Capitalist Economies Possible?" In *Stress and Contradiction in Modern Capitalism: Public Policy and the Theory of the State*, edited by Leon N. Lindberg, Robert Alford, Colin Crouch, and Claus Offe, 13–56. Lexington: D. C. Heath.
Mehta, Jal. 2011. "The Varied Roles of Ideas in Politics: From 'Whether' to 'How'." In *Ideas and Politics in Social Science Research*, edited by Daniel Béland and Robert H. Cox, 23–46. New York: Oxford University Press.
Pierson, Paul. 2000. "Increasing Returns, Path Dependence, and the Study of Politics." *American Political Science Review* 94, no. 2: 251–67. https://doi.org/10.2307/2586011.
Pierson, Paul, and Theda Skocpol. 2002. "Historical Institutionalism in Contemporary Political Science." In *Political Science: The State of the Discipline*, edited by Ira Katznelson and Helen V. Milner, 693–721. New York: W. W. Norton.
Polanyi, Karl. 1944. *The Great Transformation: The Political and Economic Origins of Our Time*. Boston: Beacon.
Robbins, Lionel. 1934. *The Great Depression*. London: Macmillan.
Robbins, Lionel. 1971. *Autobiography of an Economist*. London: Macmillan.
Robertson, David. B. 1993. "The Return to History and the New Institutionalism in American Political Science." *Social Science History* 17, no. 1: 1–36. https://doi.org/10.1017/S0145553200016734.
Schmidt, Vivien A. 2008. "Discursive Institutionalism: The Explanatory Power of Ideas and Discourse." *Annual Review of Political Science* 11: 303–26. https://doi.org/10.1146/annurev.polisci.11.060606.135342.
Schmidt, Vivien A. 2010. "Taking Ideas and Discourse Seriously: Explaining Change through Discursive Institutionalism as the Fourth 'New Institutionalism'." *European Political Science Review* 2, no. 1: 1–25. https://doi.org/10.1017/S175577390999021X.
Schmidt, Vivien A. 2011. "Reconciling Ideas and Institutions through Discursive Institutionalism." In *Ideas and Politics in Social Science Research*, edited by Daniel Béland and Robert H. Cox, 47–64. New York: Oxford University Press.

Shonfield, Andrew. [1965] 1969. *Modern Capitalism: The Changing Balance of Public and Private Power*. 2nd ed. London: Oxford University Press.

Skogstad, Grace, ed. 2011. *Policy Paradigms, Transnationalism, and Domestic Politics*. Toronto: University of Toronto Press.

Soifer, Hillel D. 2012. "The Causal Logic of Critical Junctures." *Comparative Political Studies* 45, no. 12: 1572–97. https://doi.org/10.1177/0010414012463902.

Steinmo, Sven. 2008. "Historical Institutionalism." In *Approaches and Methodologies in the Social Sciences: A Pluralist Perspective*, edited by Donatella della Porta and Michael Keating, 118–38. New York: Cambridge University Press.

Steinmo, Sven, Kathleen Thelen, and Frank Longstreth, eds. 1992. *Structuring Politics: Historical Institutionalism in Comparative Perspective*. Cambridge: Cambridge University Press.

Stephens, John D. 1979. *The Transition from Capitalism to Socialism*. London: Macmillan.

Stephens, John D. 1989. "Democratic Transition and Breakdown in Western Europe, 1870–1939: A Test of the Moore Thesis." *American Journal of Sociology* 94, no. 5: 1019–77. https://doi.org/10.1086/229111.

Straumann, Tobias. 2010. *Fixed Ideas of Money: Small States and Exchange Rate Regimes in Twentieth-Century Europe*. New York: Cambridge University Press.

Streeten, Paul. 1993. "The Special Problems of Small Countries." *World Development* 21, no. 2: 197–202.

Swenson, Peter A. 2002. *Capitalists against Markets: The Making of Labor Markets and Welfare States in the United States and Sweden*. New York: Oxford University Press.

Temin, Peter. 1989. *Lessons from the Great Depression: The Lionel Robbins Lectures for 1989*. Cambridge: MIT Press.

Thelen, Kathleen A. 1999. "Historical Institutionalism in Comparative Politics." *Annual Review of Political Science* 2: 369–404. https://doi.org/10.1146/annurev.polisci.2.1.369.

Türegün, Adnan. 1994. "Small-State Responses to the Great Depression, 1929–39: The White Dominions, Scandinavia, and the Balkans." Unpublished PhD Thesis, Carleton University. https://curve.carleton.ca/389cf024-c165-4063-8b5a-4ff838e97529 (accessed 17 December 2021).

Türegün, Adnan. 2016. "Policy Response to the Great Depression of the 1930s: Turkish Neomercantilism in the Balkan Context." *Turkish Studies* 17, no. 4: 666–90. https://doi.org/10.1080/14683849.2016.1227684.

Türegün, Adnan. 2017. "Revisiting Sweden's Response to the Great Depression of the 1930s." *Scandinavian Economic History Review* 65, no. 2: 127–48. https://doi.org/10.1080/03585522.2017.1286258.

Tyler, Ken. 1996. "Systems Thinking and Ecosystemic Psychology." *Educational Psychology* 16, no. 1: 21–34. https://doi.org/10.1080/0144341960160102.
UK House of Commons. 1929. "Debates, 15 April 1929." *Hansard*, Series 5, Volume 227: cc53–6. http://hansard.millbanksystems.com/commons/1929/apr/15/disposal-of-surplus (accessed 25 April 2021).
Veenendaal, Wouter P., and Jack Corbett. 2015. "Why Small States Offer Important Answers to Large Questions." *Comparative Political Studies* 48, no. 4: 527–49. https://doi.org/10.1177/0010414014554687.
von Bertalanffy, Ludwig. 1950. "The Theory of Open Systems in Physics and Biology." *Science*, new series 111, no. 2872: 23–9. https://doi.org/10.1126/science.111.2872.23.
Wallerstein, Immanuel M. 1974. "The Rise and Future Demise of the World Capitalist System: Concepts for Comparative Analysis." *Comparative Studies in Society and History* 16, no. 4: 387–415. https://doi.org/10.1017/S0010417500007520.
Wallerstein, Immanuel M. 2011. *The Modern World-System*, vol. 4, *Centrist Liberalism Triumphant, 1789–1914*. Berkeley: University of California Press.
Weir, Margaret, and Theda Skocpol. 1985. "State Structures and the Possibilities for 'Keynesian' Responses to the Great Depression in Sweden, Britain, and the United States." In *Bringing the State Back In*, edited by Peter B. Evans, Dietrich Rueschemeyer, and Theda Skocpol, 107–63. Cambridge: Cambridge University Press.
Whitchurch, Gail G., and Larry L. Constantine. 1993. "Systems Theory." In *Sourcebook of Family Theories and Methods: A Contextual Approach*, edited by Pauline G. Boss, William J. Doherty, Ralph LaRossa, Walter R. Schumm, and Suzanne K. Steinmetz, 325–52. New York and London: Plenum Press.
Winch, Donald. 1969. *Economics and Policy: A Historical Study*. London: Hodder and Stoughton.
Winders, Bill. 2005. "Maintaining the Coalition: Class Coalitions and Policy Trajectories." *Politics and Society* 33, no. 3: 387–423. https://doi.org/10.1177/0032329205278461.
Wolfe, David A. 1981. "Mercantilism, Liberalism and Keynesianism: Changing Forms of State Intervention in Capitalist Economies." *Canadian Journal of Political and Social Theory* 5, nos. 1–2: 69–96.
Woytinsky, Wladimir S., and E. S. Woytinsky. 1953. *World Population and Production: Trends and Outlook*. New York: Twentieth Century Fund.
Zimmerman, Ekkart, and Thomas Saalfeld. 1988. "Economic and Political Reactions to the World Economic Crisis of the 1930s in Six European Countries." *International Studies Quarterly* 32, no. 3: 305–34. https://doi.org/10.2307/2600445.

CHAPTER 2

Limits of the Possible for Economic Policy Choice

Writing in the midst of World War II, Karl Polanyi (1944) reflected on the passing of the "hundred years' peace" that had been secured by the nineteenth-century order or "civilization" with its four institutions mentioned earlier (balance of power system, international gold standard, self-regulating market, and liberal state). The interesting point in this reflection was that the peace did not end with World War I or II, or in the 1920s. Rather, it ended with the "great transformation" of the nineteenth-century order in the 1930s (Polanyi 1944, 20–30).[1] This sharp contrasting of the 1920s as part of an earlier order and the 1930s transforming that order should not, however, lead us to ignore that they were two sides of the interwar critical juncture. As I will show in this chapter, international and domestic efforts in the 1920s to restore the prewar order proved futile despite initial successes on all four institutional fronts.

The overarching goal of the chapter is to define the limits of the possible for economic policy choice during the Great Depression. In the first section, I review world-historical developments in the interwar period both across the 1920s–1930s divide and along the international–domestic, secular–cyclical, and economic–political lines. The upshot of these developments for policy choice was their exclusion of classical liberalism and inclusion of protectionism, proto-Fordism, and neomercantilism. The second section brings down the policy options to two at the country level by factoring in the political regime limits of policy choice. The choice was between protectionism and proto-Fordism under democracy, and between

© The Author(s), under exclusive license to Springer Nature Switzerland AG 2022
A. Türegün, *Policy Responses to the Interwar Economic Crisis*, https://doi.org/10.1007/978-3-030-96953-0_2

protectionism and neomercantilism under dictatorship. These relations of limitation are presented in Fig. 2.1.

The World-Historical Context

The world-historical context is not a *deus ex machina*. It is not entirely independent of the actions of individual states. Yet it takes on a life of its own once states, interstate institutions, and other international entities begin to think and act in the general direction of a certain prescription. The so-called Washington consensus was one such prescription, which both stamped the "neoliberal" practices of the 1980s and constituted a policy template for the remainder of the century. This example also shows that there is a cyclical, as well as secular, aspect to the world-historical context. Classical liberalism, discredited in the interwar period as much as any policy or philosophy has ever been, made a triumphant comeback in the 1980s just as its successors in the post-World War II period were spectacularly thrown aside in that decade. The interwar period was Janus-faced and each face (1920s and 1930s) deserves their own treatment.

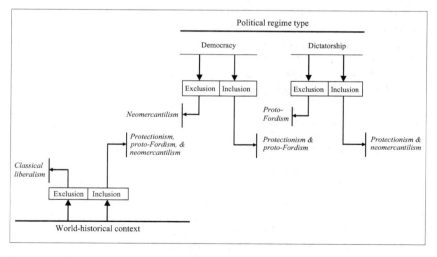

Fig. 2.1 World-historical and political regime limits of economic policy choice

The 1920s: Striving to Restore the Nineteenth-Century Order

Any story of the nineteenth-century order should probably start with the international gold standard. The internationalization of the gold standard dated back to the 1870s when major European powers such as Germany and France, as well as the United States, at last followed the UK lead in adopting it (Eichengreen and Flandreau [1985] 1997, 3–5; Gallarotti 1995, 18–26). As an international exchange standard and as coinage in circulation, gold ensured a fixed parity between national currencies from 1871, when Germany adopted the standard, to 1914, when all major powers suspended it with the outbreak of World War I. The gold standard also underlay a regime of free trade although newly industrializing nations in Europe, North America, and elsewhere had room to use protection selectively. Neither the gold standard nor the free trade regime it spawned, however, was on some kind of automatic pilot. Whether the United Kingdom had a hegemonic status in the pre-World War I period is still a matter of contention as will be seen in discussions concerning the interwar period. Yet the United Kingdom was indisputably the most powerful nation at the time with its massive domestic (commodity) market, world financial centre (London), and internationally predominant currency (pound sterling) among other things. And it was willing to use its position to elicit cooperation in the world economy and the interstate system. Embedded in a liberal but not necessarily democratic polity, the UK state intervened in the domestic economy largely to facilitate the operation of the market, thus giving rise to notions of self-regulation and *laissez-faire*.

The long stagnation of 1873–1896, also known in economic historiography as the first Great Depression, was instrumental in the emergence of new powers alongside the United Kingdom and France. While Germany, Italy, Japan, Russia, and the United States had dealt with the political problems of nation building previously (German unification in 1871, Italian *Risorgimento* in 1870, Japanese Meiji restoration in 1868, abolition of Russian serfdom in 1861, and end of the US Civil War in 1865), they all entered this period of crisis without a matching economic base to their political accomplishments. The crisis afforded them the opportunity to build that base, in the form of industrialization, with protective tariff and other measures of intervention. These national projects did not, however, mean the end of the liberal order. On the contrary, the discipline of the gold standard extremely narrowed the range of international dissent. The period came to be defined with the first wave of globalization in terms of financial mobility, commodity trade, foreign direct investment, and migration (see, e.g., Berger 2013).

World War I, by and large an intra-European affair, brought an abrupt end to the 44 years of unprecedented openness and growth in the world economy as well as tranquillity and cooperation in the interstate system. States, belligerent and neutral alike, suspended the gold standard, imposed exchange and import/export controls, regimented the market, and resorted to expansionary financing. Moreover, for the first time in the history of modern warfare, belligerent states had to mobilize the full economic resources of their nations. The resultant war economies featured, though on an ad hoc basis, many of the most *dirigiste* characteristics of the 1930s economies, including autarky and planning.

As victors of the war, the Allied powers led by the United Kingdom and France, along with the United States as an Associated power, set out to restore the prewar liberal order with its international and intranational components. As in the 1870s, the gold standard was at the centre of efforts to establish a global financial regime. Between 1919 and 1928, most nations returned to a revised international gold standard whereby gold was removed from circulation as coinage but remained as an exchange standard.[2] The United Kingdom and most small states in northwestern Europe returned to gold at the prewar parity; another group, including France and Italy, significantly depreciated their currencies against their prewar gold parities; and a third group made up of losers of the war as the Central powers, notably Germany, returned to gold with new currencies after experiencing hyperinflation in the early 1920s (Aldcroft 1977, 125–55; Crafts and Fearon 2013, 19; Eichengreen 1992, 188–91; Feinstein et al. 2008, 46; Moggridge 1989, 250–95). Even the Soviet Communists decided, in 1922, to make a transition to a gold-based currency (Kuruç 2011, 79–80; Nove [1969] 1992, 86).

The restoration of the gold standard was complemented with the removal of war-induced trade restrictions around the globe. Again, trade liberalization found its most enthusiastic practitioners in the least expected quarters. Putting an end to "War Communism," the Soviet Union opened its economy to Western trade and investment for most of the 1920s under the New Economic Policy (NEP). The Italian Fascists expressed even more enthusiasm towards economic openness. Their first years in power, which came to be known as the *Liberista* period (1922–1925), were a testament to liberal internationalism. Combined with adherence to the gold standard, liberal trade policies across nations paved the way for a relatively open and prosperous world economy in the second half of the decade.

Politically, liberal internationalism also had a promising start. The Treaty of Versailles that the Allied and Associated powers concluded with Germany in June 1919 included a League of Nations covenant (Paris Peace Conference 1919, part 1). Beginning its operations in January 1920 and increasing its membership for the rest of the decade, the League of Nations embodied a new, institutional form of cooperation in the interstate system. In it, small states found an international standing forum for the first time. Moreover, it was very much an agent of liberal economic orthodoxy as exemplified by its financial control of Austrian reconstruction from 1922 to 1926 (Marcus 2018).

A parallel liberal campaign was underway in the domestic sphere. Following the unprecedented growth of their economic role during the war, states were now willing or forced to withdraw from many areas of intervention. The prewar orthodoxy of sound money and balanced budget resonated not just with its traditional backers in the West but also with the politically most *dirigiste* regimes such as Soviet Communism and Italian Fascism. The Italian case was particularly telling because the wholehearted rhetoric and practice of "Manchester liberalism" during the *Liberista* period far exceeded any of their contemporaries. Italian economic policy in the early 1920s embodied a massive liberalization programme, including privatization, encouragement of foreign investment, tax reductions for business, downsizing in state bureaucracy, and curtailment of labour rights (Clough 1964, 222–30; de Cecco 1989, 202–7; Welk 1938, 163).

Yet the liberal restoration project was resting on shaky ground. National differences in timing and mode of return to the gold standard, a sign of lack of concerted action, resulted in wild swings in international capital flows as exemplified by "gold hoarding" by the United States and France from 1928 on (Crafts and Fearon 2013, 15; Feinstein et al. 2008, 18). Concerning the instability of the interwar gold standard and economic order in general, many refer as the main causes to the decline of UK hegemony and the absence of any power emerging to replace it notwithstanding the rise of the United States (Aldcroft 1977, 1997; Block 1977; Boyce 2009; Brown 1949; Carr [1939] 1946; Feinstein et al. 2008; Temin and Vines 2013). Charles Kindleberger came to exemplify this group with his apt statement: "The world economic system was unstable unless some country stabilized it, as Britain had done in the nineteenth century and up to 1913. In 1929, the British couldn't and the United States wouldn't" ([1973] 2013, 292). However, considering that the most successful period of the classical gold standard coincided with the rise of the United States, Germany, and other competitors to the United Kingdom, others put a Polanyian emphasis on the lack of international cooperation (balance of power system), along with the lack of public confidence, to account for the troubles of the interwar gold standard (see, e.g., Eichengreen 1992; Wolf 2013).

In any case, there was neither international hegemony nor, as it turned out, international cooperation in the interwar period. The postwar settlement enshrined in the Treaty of Versailles (and adjacent treaties with other losers of the war) left unresolved or created three sticky issues: war debts, reparations, and the League of Nations. To finance their war efforts and those of other Allies, the United Kingdom and France had heavily borrowed mainly from the United States, which would thus transform itself into a net creditor country (Eichengreen 1992, 81–8). For the Allies, France in particular, the payment of war debts was contingent on the reparations to be exacted from Germany, which also had to grant them the "most favoured nation" (MFN) status for a period of five years under the treaty. When Germany failed to meet its reparations commitments, France and Belgium occupied the Ruhr region in January 1923. This prompted a US-led effort (Dawes Plan) in 1924 to reschedule German reparations payment (Boyce 2009, 126; Feinstein et al. 2008, 37–8; Kindleberger [1973] 2013, 31–57). While massive US lending that ensued financed Germany's reconstruction and, in part, reparations payments, Weimar governments of all political colours built foreign policy on the theme of reparations—their presumably debilitating consequences for the German economy and society.[3]

The reparations issue dragged on well into the 1930s. With US lending to Germany and elsewhere coming to a halt in the summer of 1928 after the United States raised the interest rate to a more attractive level for domestic investors, the German government began to push for a renegotiation of the reparations. The result was another US-brokered deal (Young Plan of 1930), which considerably reduced the amount and eased the terms of payment. However, Weimar governments were not satisfied even with this deal and kept using the reparations both as the linchpin of foreign policy and as an excuse for monetary contraction and fiscal retrenchment in the face of Europe's severest depression. Germany would finally have its way with the issue in the Lausanne Conference of 1932, which put a practical end to its reparations payments (Pollard and Holmes 1973, 300–1; Ritschl 2013, 117; Schacht 1956, 197).

At a more general level, the reparations issue was instrumental in prompting some level of central bank cooperation in negotiations leading up to the Young Plan. In May 1930, the Bank for International Settlements was established to receive and disburse reparations (Boyce 2009, 222–30; Clavin 2000, 93). However, the bank failed to serve either as a "reparations bank" or as a significant venue for international monetary cooperation. In the end, it "transformed itself into an institution for economic analysis ... and for the collection of statistics about the world economy" (James 2001, 95). It failed as a debt collection agency because France and the United Kingdom remained far apart over the terms of reparations payments with the former opposing any dilution of the Young Plan. What sealed the fate of the bank, however, was the absence of US membership. The United States which helped create the bank did not permit the Federal Reserve System (central bank) to join it for fear of entanglement in European affairs.

This fear of entanglement defined US foreign policy for the greater part of the interwar period. The League of Nations, very much a Wilsonian idea, was beset by the refusal of an isolationist US Congress to ratify the League covenant and join the organization (Boyce 2009, 23–76; Lake 1999, 78–127). The absence of US membership rendered the League particularly ineffective in responding to international crises such as the Japanese invasion of Manchuria in 1931 and the Italian invasion of Ethiopia in 1935, not to mention the catastrophic developments later in the decade. It might not have "proved an almost total failure" (Hobsbawm 1994, 34) but did certainly lay bare the fundamental cracks in liberal internationalism.

Domestically, the liberal restoration project did not fare any better. The ideal state in the golden age of classical liberalism was a law-and-order state which would have intervened in the economy and spent on the "social question" only residually. To the extent that actually existing states approached this ideal, an exclusionary political framework helped insulate them from popular pressure. However, this would change fundamentally with the increasing pace of industrialization and consequent proletarianization from the 1870s on, coupled with mass (military and civilian) mobilization during World War I. These processes let the political genie out of the bottle.

The Russian Revolution of 1917, regardless of its future trajectory, played a pivotal role in the politicization of society across the world. First, it not only revolutionized a significant section of organized labour under the Third International but also galvanized the entire labour movement to push for political and economic rights such as universal suffrage and social legislation. The postwar wave of democratization and social democratic (or socialist/labour) participation in government in the West owed much of its impetus to this mobilization (Rueschemeyer et al. 1992, 79–154; Stephens 1989; Therborn 1977). Although initial labour radicalism died down by the mid-1920s, there was no turning back to nineteenth-century elite politics. Second, the Russian Revolution was also instrumental in the radicalization of peasantry for land redistribution and political participation as in southeastern Europe (Mitrany 1951), and, more generally and indirectly, in the rise of agrarian protest movements in Europe, North America, and elsewhere. Third, it eventually received a fascist response in the generic sense of the term. As a reactionary social movement, fascism found adherents among the urban middle class, peasantry, and even the working class, thus providing further proof of the arrival of mass politics with its distributional conflicts (Feinstein et al. 2008, 23).

The new political reality would be on a collision course not only with the defence of the gold standard at any cost (Eichengreen 1992, 31) but also with the continuation of government at arm's length. With the political–economic and national–international supports crumbling around it by the late 1920s, the classical liberal paradigm was no longer tenable. Policy space would expand in the interventionist direction but what particular forms it would come to include was not predetermined. That would be shaped by the reactions of states to the ensuing crisis.

The 1930s: The Making of a Transitional (Dis)order

Viewed against the foregoing background, it is hard to pinpoint whether the Great Depression was the result of one particular event such as the crash of the New York Stock Exchange in October 1929, US Smoot–Hawley Tariff Act of June 1930, or European financial crisis in the summer of 1931. The crisis was dotted by many such events and defined by unprecedented levels of decline in world prices, production, trade, and employment (Eichengreen and Hatton 1988, 6–7; Feinstein et al. 2008, 94, 96; Hill 1988, 31–2; Lewis 1949, 58, 61; Safarian [1959] 2009, 98; Tracy 1972, 108). Yet the crisis was not just about an economic downturn. It also occasioned new forms of economic organization that informed alternative policy paradigms.

Most states clung to the international gold exchange standard well into the crisis. Ironically, the very state that presided over the gold standard in its classical period and returned to it at the prewar parity was the first large state to have a clean break with it. The UK decision to go off gold and devalue the pound sterling on 21 September 1931 was a world-historical one. This decision came on the heels of several momentous developments in that year. Reeling from the cessation in late 1928 and subsequent reversal of US foreign lending but also from self-imposed orthodox monetary and fiscal policies, Germany and states succeeding the Austro-Hungarian Empire began to search for ways to sidestep currency exchange in foreign trade. One way was clearing trade as will be seen shortly, another way being a proposed customs union between Germany and Austria in March 1931 (Pollard and Holmes 1973, 382–4). Yet the French-led opposition to the proposal caused further capital flight from the region, thus triggering a regional financial crisis. The first country to be in the spotlight was Austria where the leading bank (Credit-Anstalt) declared insolvency in May, threatening to take down with it numerous industrial ventures that it financed across central Europe (Eichengreen 2015, 134–47). Waking up to the severity of the region's and Europe's problems, the US administration issued a one-year moratorium the following month on all war debts and reparations payments. However, this move was too little, too late to stem the flow of gold to the United States (and France) from the rest of the world. Immersed in its own banking crisis, Germany imposed foreign exchange controls in July and thus effectively severed its ties with the gold standard.

Following the US departure from gold and currency devaluation in March–April 1933, the gold standard had one final chance to maintain its international stature. Convening in June, the London Monetary and Economic Conference issued a declaration at the end of the month to affirm the gold standard as the international measure of exchange value (Pollard and Holmes 1973, 387–8; see also Clavin 1996, 117–41; Eichengreen 1992, 317–47). However, this statement of principle did not even survive the conference. Having just taken the dollar off gold and devalued it, US President Franklin D. Roosevelt sent a "bombshell message" to the conference on 3 July, opposing any proposal for exchange rate stabilization: "The sound internal economic system of a nation is a greater factor in its well-being than the price of its currency in changing terms of the currencies of other nations" (in Pollard and Holmes 1973, 388). This was the end of the international gold exchange standard.

After the London conference, international monetary relations came to be defined by five main exchange rate regimes (Brown 1949, 45; Chandler 1970, 105; Irwin 2012, 45; Kindleberger [1973] 2013, 247–61; Moggridge 1989, 298–300). The United Kingdom and numerous small states (in the British Empire, Europe, South America, and the Near East) that had followed its lead in going off the gold standard formed the sterling area as a bloc of managed currencies.[4] A similar area would be formed around the US dollar following the London conference. The gold standard still had its adherents, especially among those European states which had returned to it with devalued currencies. Thus, France, Italy, and five small states (Belgium, Luxemburg, the Netherlands, Poland, and Switzerland) came together under the gold bloc. Yet it would survive only until September 1936, when the United States and the United Kingdom convinced France to leave the gold standard and devalue the franc under the Tripartite Monetary Agreement (Pollard and Holmes 1973, 424–5; see also Eichengreen 1992, 348–89; Straumann 2010, 126–69). A fourth grouping was the so-called blocked currency bloc bringing together states, notably Germany, which had abandoned gold in spirit, if not in letter, by controlling the cross-border movement of gold and currency. The Japanese-led yen bloc had a similar function in the Far East.

Regionalization was also at work in international trade relations (Kindleberger 1989, 190–6). The Soviet Union had already been on a course of autarkic closure when the crisis began, but that was singularly a national experiment as part of "socialism in one country." The first significant dent in the relatively free trade environment of the 1920s came from the US Smoot–Hawley Tariff Act of June 1930, which had been in the making since 1928 (Irwin 2011, 2012). Although this protective act did not discriminate for or against particular nations, it did elicit international responses favouring bilateralism and regionalism as well as protectionism.[5] Weimar Germany became the first large state to take a bilateral and regional route to trade. Lacking foreign funds to import from countries to its west, it devised clearing trade bypassing currency exchange in 1931 to import raw materials and primary products from, and export finished products to, countries in east-central and southeastern Europe and elsewhere. France read this clearing trade offensive—correctly as it turned out—as part of Germany's aspirations to create an area of dependency in the region and of German revisionism in general. The French response was in the form of leading a conference (Stresa Conference) of the Danube countries in September 1932 to find ways of liquidating their agricultural surpluses without German involvement (Boyce 2009, 366–72, 382–4). However, that was to no avail and, under the Nazis, clearing trade would become an explicit tool to establish and solidify the region as Germany's "living space" (*Lebensraum*). Japan sought to create a similar space in its vicinity, the so-called East Asia Co-Prosperity Sphere, whereas Italy had to be content with a smaller space in the northeast of the Mediterranean basin until its invasion of Ethiopia.

The UK turn to regionalism and protectionism in late 1931 was particularly dramatic after 85 years of internationalism and free trade since the repeal of the Corn Laws in 1846. The United Kingdom faced pressure from two groups of small states after 1930. The Scandinavian and Low countries that came together for a low tariff cause under the Oslo Convention in December 1930 invited the United Kingdom to join the group in an effort to stem the tide of protectionism but also to safeguard them against the brewing tension between France and Germany (Boyce 2009, 283, 372–5; van Roon 1989). By then, however, the mood in the United Kingdom had turned inward in no small part because of the push from the Dominions facing difficulties exporting their primary products. The Ottawa Agreements of 1932 with the Dominions formally instituted a British preferential trading system.

The trade blocs of the 1930s served a dual, seemingly contradictory purpose. On one hand, they embodied a generalized, discriminatory protectionism against non-members, employing tariff and nontariff measures such as import and export quotas.[6] On the other hand, they amounted to mini free trade systems within themselves, thus having the best of both worlds.[7] An indication of this was the significant increase in intra-bloc trade from 1929 to 1938 (Irwin 2011, 137). For example, clearing trade taking place largely in the German zone of influence came to account for about 12% of world trade in 1937 (League of Nations 1942, 70).

Even after the United States took a more open trade stance with the Reciprocal Trade Agreements Act of 1934, bilateralism—if not so much regionalism—was still the rule of the day. Moving away from the non-discriminatory protectionism of the Smoot–Hawley tariff, the 1934 Act (Cordell Hull trade programme) paved the way for a series of bilateral, reciprocal trade agreements, beginning with Canada in 1935, that would lower the tariff barriers for the parties involved (Lake 1988, 202–12). The most important one of these agreements in the decade was the US–UK

Reciprocal Trade Agreement of 1938, which went beyond a bilateral agreement in influence by sealing the fate of the British preferential trading system.

States also spawned new forms of economic organization on the domestic front, ranging from joint industrial organization by employers and unions to central and comprehensive state planning. The retreat of the market as both reality and myth was uneven across nations but, at the very least, included various schemes of cartelization in industry and marketing arrangements in agriculture. The United Kingdom and, except for the Blum experiment of the Popular Front interlude, France went only this far. The Blum experiment brought employers and unions together in a hasty arrangement (Matignon Accord) for a new industrial relations system but could not hold them together for long and ended in dismal failure. In comparison, the US New Deal laying the legal and institutional groundwork for such a system, not to mention the exemplary cases of Scandinavia, proved successful and durable in its consequences. Planning was perhaps the hallmark of the period in microeconomic terms. While planning was an enduring theme in the French tradition, the United Kingdom began to debate it and even ventured into regional planning later in the 1930s. Industrial planning of sorts found its way into US economic policy under the National Recovery Administration (NRA) early in the New Deal. Yet the limits of planning were tested by the Soviet Union in its all-out drive for industrialization and agricultural collectivization. Italy and Turkey came close to the Soviet experiment in state industrial ownership whereas Germany's New Plans and Japan's industrial policy were based nominally on private ownership but no less *dirigiste* than the Italian and Turkish cases.

At the macroeconomic level, states produced two innovations to counter the economic downturn: monetary reflation and fiscal expansion. Many states tried some measure of monetary reflation. The rest, including France, stuck to the monetary orthodoxy to the end. Fiscally, the cards were dealt differently. Only a handful of states, including the United States and Sweden on the democratic front, explicitly used budget as a countercyclical tool. Nazi Germany, along with Japan (Broadbridge 1989; Hadley 1989; Nanto and Takagi 1985; Yamamura 1972; Yasuba 1988), resorted to expansionary financing mainly for armaments buildup and actually contributed to economic recovery in the process.

In this diversity of economic experimentation sketched above at both international and domestic levels, one can discern three meaningful, relatively consistent patterns that were conceptualized as policy paradigms in Chap. 1. Protectionism, proto-Fordism, and neomercantilism (including a developmental variant) capture the range of variation in states' particular economic behaviour. Could states act differently from how they actually did? They could plausibly do so. Then, would a combination of such counterfactuals add up to a fourth paradigm? Extremely unlikely—because the classical liberal option had been exhausted previously. A more accountable and interesting question is what options states had other than the ones they tried among the three world-historically possible paradigms. As I will elaborate in the next section, my answer is that, in a given political regime context, they could choose only one other option as an alternative to their actual choice.

Political Regime Limits

Of the 18 cases in this study, nine were by and large democracies in the sense that their governments were formed and changed hands according to the popular will as expressed via (near) universal suffrage. These democracies shaped their policy responses along the protectionist–proto-Fordist continuum. The United Kingdom, Australia, and Canada stuck with protectionism until the end; France had a brief proto-Fordist experiment before returning to the protectionist fold; New Zealand, Denmark, and Norway stood somewhere in-between; and the United States and Sweden came closest to the proto-Fordist pole. The other nine cases were dictatorships of varying degree and type, and similarly shaped their responses along a continuum, that of protectionism–neomercantilism. Germany and Italy, along with the Soviet Union and Turkey with a developmental bent, were on the neomercantilist end whereas Austria, Bulgaria, Greece, Romania, and Yugoslavia drew closer to the middle of the continuum.

The following four substantive chapters will discuss why possible options (proto-Fordism under democracy and neomercantilism under dictatorship) were realized in some cases and partly or never realized in other cases. The rest of this chapter will focus on the limiting role of political regimes in policy choice. I argue that, at the basic level of differentiation (democratic versus dictatorial), political regimes were policy-selective not in the sense of preferring one piece of policy to another but in that of including and excluding whole policy sets. Protectionism and proto-Fordism but not neomercantilism were possible sets under democracy; so were protectionism and neomercantilism but not proto-Fordism under dictatorship. This can best be substantiated in view of the actual policy performance of the democracies and dictatorships in our sample.

Democracies: Protectionism and Proto-Fordism Versus Neomercantilism

Among the nine democracies, the United Kingdom, Australia, and Canada resolutely stayed on the protectionist course, never giving proto-Fordism a chance. France was similarly protectionist except for the aborted Blum experiment. The New Zealand, Danish, and Norwegian cases were interesting in that their combined responses included extremely protectionist policies such as exchange controls, nontariff measures, and import-substituting industrialization, as well as industrial relations and social reform. They had a middle-of-the-road policy stance between protectionism and proto-Fordism. The United States and Sweden fully realized the proto-Fordist potential. Neomercantilism was out of the question for these democratic cases. Even New Zealand, Denmark, and Norway, which resorted to exchange and nontariff import controls, never sought autarky or regimented the domestic market.

United Kingdom. A Labour government had been in charge when the crisis arrived. Until its downfall in August 1931, the government drew closer to classical liberal perfection, including external stability (gold standard and free trade), sound money, and balanced budget. Yet this policy mix was not world-historically sustainable and Labour gave way to a Conservative-dominated "National" government, which would put UK economic policy on a protectionist course (Arndt 1944, 94–134; Checkland 1989, 628–38; Lewis 1949, 74–89; Winch 1969, 114–44). After going off the gold standard in September 1931, the new government devalued the pound sterling. This was coupled with the Import Duties Act of 1932 representing a protectionist turn in UK trade policy since the repeal of the Corn Laws in 1846. The Ottawa Agreements concluded with the Dominions later in 1932 projected an imperial trading bloc and the sterling exchange standard actually created a regional currency bloc, thus signalling a reversal of age-old UK internationalism (Booth 1993, 41–2; Drummond 1974, 184).

Domestically, the UK response combined a measure of microeconomic activism with monetary expansion and fiscal conservatism (Aldcroft 1970, 295–349; Booth 1993, 51; Middleton 1985, 174–5, 1998, 195, 2013, 250). In addition to ad hoc subsidy programmes and various marketing boards created for controlling output and setting prices in agriculture (Dewey 2003, 279; Williams 1960, 11–21), the government introduced cartelization schemes for selected industries (such as coal mining, cotton textiles, and ship building) and induced others to "rationalize" and reorganize their operations (Garside 2000, 14; Greaves 2000, 115; Smith 1998, 25, 33–4). When initiatives to relocate industries regionally are also considered, one can conclude that a sort of patchwork planning made its way into UK economic policy. It also helped that the government had unemployment insurance (as well as residual relief mechanisms) at its disposal to protect the unemployed. At the macroeconomic level, a cheap money policy was pursued from 1932 to 1935 but fiscal conservatism was a constant of the entire period (Middleton 1998, 194; Solomou 1996, 112–31). Both the Labour and National governments aimed for balanced budgets by cutting back expenditures and by raising taxes and national insurance premiums. And they were largely successful at that until the beginning of armaments buildup in 1938.[8]

The United Kingdom, whose past policies had informed the classical liberal paradigm, made a remarkable break with it except for fiscal orthodoxy. The favourite policy instruments of the time, including clearing trade, cartelization, and planning, made their way into the UK response under Conservative-dominated governments. By using these and similar policy instruments for protectionism, the Conservatives went as far as they could in a democratic polity. The United Kingdom could also plausibly try proto-Fordism, but it did not. That story has to wait for the next chapter.

Australia. Like the United Kingdom, Australia met the crisis with a "Labor" government. Although the Australian Labor Party (ALP) government proved monetarily and fiscally conservative like its UK counterpart, the former left the gold standard (effectively in November 1929, officially in January 1931), devalued the currency (which would then be pegged to the pound sterling and eventually be part of the sterling bloc of currencies), beefed up industrial tariff protection (Scullin tariff of November 1929), and extended production and marketing support to the primary sector in 1931 (Eichengreen 1988; Knox 1939, 49, 58; Louis and Turner 1968, 124–9). The ALP's "bourgeois" successors made no significant changes to the protectionist course in the rest of the 1930s (Castles 1988, 94). The Australian Commonwealth (federal) government relied primarily on tariff protection to deal with the problems of industry, leaving direct relief as the only option for the unemployed in the absence of unemployment insurance until 1944 (Birch 1955, 236; Millmow 2010, 38–42; Schedvin 1970, 87–95).

Australian monetary policy remained consistently procyclical except for a modest cut in interest rate as part of the Premiers' Plan of June 1931. Institutionally, efforts to create a central bank out of the Commonwealth Bank of Australia came to fruition only in 1939 (Plumptre 1940, 86–96). In fiscal policy, both Labor and non-Labor governments toed the neoclassical line. As the exclusive agency of industrial dispute resolution and wage fixing, the Commonwealth Court of Conciliation and Arbitration used its powers in the service of fiscal orthodoxy first by adjusting wages to the "reduced cost of living" and then by ordering a wage cut by 10% in January 1931. In so doing, it departed from the "living wage" convention (Castles 1988, 133–62; Millmow 2010, 235–38). The three-year Premiers' Plan involving federal and state governments paralleled the court decisions, requiring a 20% cut in all government expenditures and tax increases to restore balanced budgets (Alhadeff 1985; Fisher 1934, 766–73; Green and Sparks 1988; Millmow 2010, 87–94; Schedvin 1970, 213–82).

The Australian response was more conservative than its UK counterpart in a dual sense. Whereas the United Kingdom made a paradigm shift from classical liberalism to protectionism, Australia did not actually add anything new to its pre-existing economic and social protection package (Murphy 2010). Moreover, the Australian response represented a reversal of some of the gains achieved in labour protection, or what Francis Castles (1988, 91–104) calls "domestic defence" generally, earlier in the twentieth century. As in the United Kingdom, a proto-Fordist response was conceivable but did not materialize. In the Canadian case, which will be taken up next, that possibility became a public policy topic at least for a fleeting moment in mid-decade.

Canada. Canada officially clung to the gold standard until the US departure in April 1933 (Brecher 1957, 177–91; Curtis 1931, 109–10; Drummond 1981, 63–4; Knox 1939; Marcus 1954, 22–7; Noble 1938, 270). Unlike other governments abandoning gold, the Canadian government did not devalue its currency; it simply let the dollar fluctuate. By 1934, the dollar regained its pre-crisis parity with the US dollar and the pound sterling (Brecher 1957, 178; Knox 1939, 3). Instead of exchange rate policy, the Canadian government used tariff policy to promote exports as well as protecting the domestic market and jobs. The first tariff increase (Dunning tariff) came in May 1930 under the Liberals (Hart 2002, 105–8; McDonald et al. 1997; O'Brien and McDonald 2009, 335; Perry

1955, 279). The succeeding Conservatives elevated tariff protection to new heights while, at the same time, promoting intra-Empire trade with the Ottawa Agreements in 1932 (Drummond 1972, 205–18; Mackintosh [1939] 1964, 164; Perry 1955, 278–84; RCDPR 1940a, 157–60; Stacey 1972, 204–6, 209–11). By mid-decade, however, the same Conservatives began to negotiate a trade agreement with the United States, which the incoming Liberals would conclude in November 1935 to signal a continental turn in Canadian trade policy (Drummond and Hillmer 1989; Hart 2002, 123–4; McDiarmid 1946, 290–4; O'Brien and McDonald 2009, 333–4; Perry 1955, 282–4).

The Canadian government was much less active on the home front. Cartelization was rarely used in industry (Stacey 1972, 240–1). With no unemployment insurance in place until 1940, the federal government extended direct relief to the unemployed between 1930 and 1939 (MacKinnon 1990). Relief works were tried only on an ad hoc basis (Struthers 1983, 81).[9] Similarly, the federal government and its provincial counterparts in the Prairies responded to the hardships of that region's wheat farmers initially with direct relief efforts and, only later, with more active measures such as debt relief and resettlement programmes. The centrepiece of federal intervention in agriculture, however, was the establishment in 1935 of the Canadian Wheat Board with the mandate of price fixing, purchasing, and marketing (Fowke 1957, 256–78; Pomfret 1981, 147–64; Stacey 1972, 219–21). At the macroeconomic level, the Canadian response was strictly procyclical until the end of the decade. Monetary policy was contractionary both before and after the establishment of the central bank (Bank of Canada) in March 1935 (Knox 1939, 28–44; Plumptre 1940, 145–9; Stacey 1972, 257–60). Fiscally, the federal government played catch-up in the face of declining tax revenues and increasing relief spending, thus ending up with budget deficits (Bryce 1985, 12, 1986, 108–9). Only against the background of a new recession in 1937–1938 did the Liberals cautiously move to try a public works programme to be financed by deficit budget (Bryce 1986, 115–21; Struthers 1983, 190).

No account of the Canadian response will be complete without reference to the so-called Bennett New Deal, which constituted a proto-Fordist counterfactual to actually existing protectionism. Towards the end of his mandate, Conservative Prime Minister Richard B. Bennett launched a public campaign for economic and social reform in a series of radio speeches in January 1935, declaring that the "old order is gone" (1935,

9). These speeches formed the basis of a legislative package that would never pass the Constitutional test. Regardless of what motivated Bennett to take the initiative as will be discussed in Chap. 3, it represented an alternative policy paradigm.

France. Unlike the "Bennett New Deal," the Blum experiment in France embodied a policy break with protectionism. Except for that interlude, however, the French response proved more conservative than most of its democratic counterparts (Arndt 1944, 135–51; Jackson 1985, 27–34, 53–111; Kemp 1972, 99–114, 129–61, 1989, 738–51; Lewis 1949, 98–103; Villa 2003). Various right-wing and centrist governments staunchly supported the gold standard and France led the gold bloc from its inception in 1933 until its dissolution in 1936. Adherence to the gold standard did not, however, go hand in hand with free trade; on the contrary, French trade policy not only was generally protectionist but also gave more prominence to nontariff measures than to tariff measures. Domestically, agricultural prices were supported by price fixing, restriction of crop areas, and government purchasing of staple products whereas industry was the subject of both compulsory and voluntary cartelization schemes involving production quotas, market sharing by existing firms, entry restrictions for new firms, and investment controls (Kemp 1972, 166). On the macroeconomic front, French conservatism was unparalleled. Governments defended the exchange and domestic value of the franc as a fixed policy objective. Although leaving the gold standard in 1936 put an end to the external component of this policy, the "anti-inflation" mindset, along with that of fiscal retrenchment, survived the Blum experiment (Jackson 1985, 167–211).

Following its electoral victory in May 1936, the Popular Front of Socialist, Communist, and left Radical parties formed a majority government, a rare phenomenon in the Third Republic. From June 1936 to March 1937, the Front government headed by Socialist Léon Blum attempted to redefine industrial relations and reflate the economy by increasing the purchasing power of the masses (Jackson 1988, 159–88; Kalecki 1938; Kemp 1972, 115–28; Marjolin 1938). The government first brought the main union and employers' federations together to negotiate a comprehensive agreement (Matignon Accord), which would recognize workers' right to join unions and strike, institute collective bargaining and shop stewardship, and increase wages substantially (see Jackson 1988, 305–6; or Pollard and Holmes 1973, 404–5). It followed this up with pro-labour legislation introducing, among other things, a two-week annual paid leave and a 40-hour workweek. Farmers, too, benefitted from the purchasing power policy in the form of higher floor prices and strengthened marketing arrangements.[10] Standing for "neither devaluation nor deflation" (Schwarz 1993), the Front government also launched off-budget public works programmes for job creation. The Tripartite Monetary Agreement, signed with the United States and the United Kingdom in September 1936, created a leeway for more macroeconomic activism by helping France abandon the gold standard and devalue the franc (Eichengreen 1992, 348–89; Kindleberger [1973] 2013, 247–61). Instead, the government reverted to the fiscal orthodoxy of its predecessors and scrapped the entire experiment in early 1937.

The French response uniquely reverted to protectionism after taking a proto-Fordist turn. What accounted for that turn and its reversal makes an interesting research question. In this sense, the French case provides an instructive contrast to more consistent responses in either direction. What follows is one such response.

New Zealand. The New Zealand response defined the limits of protectionism under a democracy, particularly after the formation of a Labour government in 1935. With only an indirect connection to gold via the pound sterling, the New Zealand pound remained pegged to the former after the UK departure, thus conforming to the sterling exchange standard and becoming part of the sterling bloc (Belshaw 1933; Hawke 1971, 1988; Quigley 1992, 8–18; Singleton 2003). The Liberal/United and Reform party coalition followed that up with a major (30%) devaluation of the pound in early 1933, also taking protective tariff and nontariff measures (Endres and Jackson 1993, 153–5). Domestically, the coalition introduced a voluntary unemployment insurance scheme in 1930 but would make the scheme completely self-financing after ending subsidies to the insurance fund in 1932 (Endres and Jackson 1993, 150; Hawke 1985, 14–9). At the same time, the coalition took an expansionary step by cutting the interest rate by 20%, in addition to establishing the Reserve Bank of New Zealand (RBNZ) as a central bank. Yet it remained resolutely conservative in fiscal policy with measures such as a 10% wage cut by the Court of Arbitration, a 20% cut in public service salaries by legislation, and tax increases to curb budget deficits (Brown 1962, 146–7; Hawke 1985, 148–55; Simpson 1990, 58–60).

The innovative edge of the Labour government was in microeconomic policy. Its "insulationism" in foreign finance and trade (for example, targeted use of tariffs, re-imposition of exchange controls, and introduction of import licensing in 1938) was geared towards import-substituting industrialization (Hawke 1985, 163–6; RBNZ 2007, 13). In agriculture, the government controlled the entire space between the production and marketing of primary products. Part of this effort were the strengthening of the cooperative movement and the creation of two marketing agencies for export products and domestically consumed primary products. Domestic activism did not end there; it also took over industrial relations and social protection (Brady 1941, 225–32, 1958, 277–83; Simpson 1990, 86–92). Reorganized in 1936, the Court of Arbitration restored minimum wage requirement and became a labour-organizing agency by tying industrial awards to union membership. The omnibus Social Security Act of 1938 introduced a comprehensive social protection scheme, also improving and expanding unemployment insurance. These measures, coupled with increased spending on public works, were destined to have an expansionary effect at the macroeconomic level.[11]

Labour went as far as it could to deliver a statist rendition of proto-Fordism. In so doing, it was both limited and driven by a pastoral economy. It put its creative energy into the microeconomic domain because it had few options monetarily or fiscally in a heavily primary-producing economy. That economy also gave Labour the incentive to encourage import-substituting industrialization by imposing financial and trade restrictions. The United States and Sweden had no such limitation and, hence, drew closer to the proto-Fordist template.

United States. Likewise, the US response developed in two stages. Yet they were not clear-cut along partisan lines; while the Republican administration of 1929–1932 was protectionist only in the narrow (foreign trade) sense of the term, its Democratic successor added a domestic component to protectionism before moving on to the proto-Fordist stage. The Hoover administration stayed on the gold standard but introduced the Smoot–Hawley tariff in June 1930, the signature act of the administration's entire term that substantially and universally increased the rate of protection for raw materials and agricultural goods in particular (Lake 1988, 195; see also Irwin 2011). Domestically, the market was supposed to take care of the crisis with the aid of conservative monetary and fiscal policies.

The Roosevelt administration left the gold standard and devalued the dollar in April 1933. The following year, Congress passed the Reciprocal Trade Agreements Act (Cordell Hull trade programme) that authorized the executive to negotiate bilateral agreements based on the MFN principle (Haggard 1988). Compared with the general, non-discriminatory protectionism of the Smoot–Hawley tariff, the new trade programme adopted bilateral, discriminatory liberalization while continuing to protect agriculture by various nontariff measures (Lake 1988, 194; Oye 1992, 71–104). Yet it was first and foremost on the domestic front that the Roosevelt administration broke new ground with the New Deal (Arndt 1944, 34–70; Fishback and Wallis 2013; Lewis 1949, 104–14; Stein 1990; Winch 1969, 219–51). For industry, the NRA introduced cartelization schemes freeing employers from antitrust laws. Each branch of industry had price fixing privileges and codes of entry and production whereas workers received minimum wage guarantee, 40-hour workweek, and the right to unionize and bargain collectively. The agricultural counterpart of the NRA was the Agricultural Adjustment Administration (AAA), which aided farmers with subsidies, cheap credit, and crop and acreage controls.

When the Supreme Court ruled the NRA and AAA legislations unconstitutional in 1935–1936, the New Deal had already headed to a second, proto-Fordist phase. The Wagner Act of 1935 established the National Labor Relations Board by incorporating and strengthening the pro-labour provisions of the NRA legislation. The Roosevelt administration shed its microeconomic *dirigisme* in industry but continued to support agriculture by resuscitating the AAA legislation in 1938. It also undertook distributional and institutional reforms such as an omnibus social security legislation (including unemployment insurance), a labour standards legislation (including minimum wages and maximum hours of work), reinforced antitrust regulations, and progressive taxation. In macroeconomic terms as well, the New Deal was transformative of US economic policy. The administration tackled the massive failures in the banking sector with an institutional reform legislation, Glass–Steagall Act of 1933, requiring banks to choose between commercial and investment banking (Born [1977] 1983, 276–8; Sobel 1994, 26). Substantively, Democratic monetary policy was an expansionary one making use of the low interest rate. Although the administration did not give up on the discourse of balanced budgets until after the onset of a new recession in 1937, the federal government budget ran consecutive deficits in the decade, except for 1930, due to increased spending on public works and other relief efforts (USBC 1965, 711).[12] An explicit Keynesian turn in US fiscal policy came with the deficit-financed budget of 1938 to fight the new recession.

Although the New Deal would move away from micro-regulation by mid-decade, the "codification" of industry under the NRA in particular led to comparisons with the authoritarian regimes of regulation. Before the Third International switched to a "Popular Front" strategy in 1935, Soviet economists viewed the New Deal as "disguised fascism" (Day 1981, 248–84). Alternatively, many in the West branded it as a democratic variant of either "socialism" or, more fashionably, "corporatism" (Garraty 1973, 912–915, 1986, 182–211; Letwin 1989, 649–53; Temin 1989, 107–112; Winch 1969, 231). Yet these comparisons are misplaced for three reasons. First, general interventionism as a world-historical tendency does not make a policy regime. Second, fascism, socialism, and corporatism are political categories, not policy categories. Third, policy instruments per se do not make a policy regime; they may cut across policy regimes.

Sweden. No small state went as far as Sweden in experimenting with policy innovation. Leaving the gold standard immediately after the UK departure, the Liberal government devalued the krona and established a floating exchange standard (Lundberg [1953] 1957, 12–3; Möller 1938, 64–5). The succeeding Social Democrats adopted the sterling exchange standard by pegging the krona to the pound sterling in 1933. In international trade, Sweden had a dual policy. Agriculture was protected mainly by nontariff measures such as export subsidies, import monopolies, and domestic milling quotas (Braatoy 1939, 68–71; Cole 1938; Lundberg, [1953] 1957, 14–5, 107; Ovesen 1958). For manufacturing and extractive industries needing no such measures, in contrast, Swedish trade policy targeted market expansion and diversification. Initiatives in this direction included the Oslo Convention of 1930 for a freer trade area of Scandinavia and the Low countries (Cole 1938, 236–7; Olsson 2010; van Roon 1989) and bilateral agreements with the United Kingdom in 1933 (Rooth 1986), Germany in 1934 (Hedberg 2010), and the United States in 1935 (Sallius 1961).

Domestically, the Swedish response also differentiated along the agricultural–industrial line. Early in the crisis, the Liberals brought agriculture under an elaborate support programme ranging from price formation to product distribution (Braatoy 1939, 71–8; Dahmén [1950] 1970, 38–43; Lundberg [1953] 1957, 51–2; Ovesen 1958, 43–9). Agriculture made further gains under the Social Democrats. In the Crisis Agreement ("cow deal" or *kohandel*) they struck with the Agrarians in May 1933, the Social Democrats gave up free trade and cheap foodstuffs for protectionism to get the Agrarian support for their public works initiatives (Morell 2010, 147–8; Olsson 1968, 91–7; Söderpalm [1973] 1975). In contrast, industry avoided physical intervention. The state not only refrained from enforcing or even encouraging cartelization but also strove to check private moves in that direction (Lundberg [1953] 1957, 16). In the aftermath of the Kreuger industrial crash of 1932, the Social Democratic government passed a new banking legislation in 1933 to curtail banks' direct industrial involvement. Yet the banks circumvented the legislation by setting up nonbanking subsidiaries and thus transferring their industrial shareholdings to them (Larsson 1991, 91–5; Olsen 1992, 61; Olsson 1991, 33).

The innovative edge of the Swedish response was in labour market, industrial relations, and macroeconomic regulation. In 1933, the Social Democrats launched a new public works (*beredskapsarbeten*) programme to fight unemployment as part of the Crisis Agreement, in addition to preexisting suite of relief works (*reservarbeten*) and direct relief (Clark 1941, 71–111; Lindström 1985, 157; Möller 1938).[13] The following year, they introduced with the Liberal support a voluntary unemployment insurance scheme to be funded and administered by unions but subsidized by the state with no contribution from employers (Clark 1941, 125–30; Heclo 1974, 211–26; Jörberg and Krantz 1989, 1095–100; Rothstein 1990, 333–5). Labour market reform was crowned with the establishment in 1939 of the Labour Market Board as a common forum of unions, employers, and government to administer labour exchanges and unemployment relief. Unlike the labour market, industrial relations were regulated largely and autonomously by union and employers' federations. In 1938, they took a historic step by reaching a Basic Agreement, better known as the Saltsjöbaden compromise, which drew the general framework of collective bargaining between their affiliates and specified the conditions of strikes, lockouts, and other industrial actions (Hansson 1939, 85–105).

Undergirding the domestic activism of the Swedish response was an unorthodox macroeconomic policy mix. Fearing inflation after the departure from gold and devaluation in September 1931, the Riksbank (central bank) took an unusual step by raising the interest rate and launching a price stabilization programme to maintain the domestic purchasing power of the krona (Berg and Jonung 1999; Jonung 1979, 1981; Kjellstrom 1934, 42–79; Montgomery 1938, 34–44; Thomas 1936, 187–205). Beginning in 1932, however, the bank responded favourably to the emerging fiscal activism by gradual reductions in interest rate. The Social Democratic innovation in fiscal policy, which built on the Liberal experience of 1930–1932 and which came after the Crisis Agreement, was putting more emphasis on the demand stimulus effects of both the loan-financed and ordinary budget expenditures. First, social policy expenditures, traditionally conceived of as a burden on the economy, became part and parcel of the economic recovery programme (Jörberg and Krantz 1989, 1096). Second, and as a corollary of the first, the government increased spending on, and made improvements in, existing programmes such as unemployment relief and social services. Third, it introduced loan-financed and open market-based public works to confront the crisis head on (Braatoy 1939, 21–4; Clark 1941, 131–65; Möller 1938, 68–9).[14]

Denmark and Norway struck remarkably similar political compromises to those of Sweden (Lindström 1985, 156–9; Lindvall 2012, 250–2; Söderpalm [1973] 1975, 274–5). Yet the Danish and Norwegian economic responses were not as similar to the Swedish one.

Denmark. Denmark's intriguing turn to restrictive and protective policies began shortly after it abandoned the gold standard and devalued its currency in September 1931 (Johansen 1987, 53–9; Kristensen 1958; RIIA 1951, 54–60; Salmon 2003, 234–45). Later the same year, it brought in an exchange control and import licensing system to be administered by the Exchange Control Office (Larsen 2010, 94–6). This paved the way for an era of physical restrictions while tariff levels remained relatively stable. Significantly, the trade-diverting measures by that office concerned not just industry but also agriculture that had long been Denmark's niche in international competition. Following the Crisis Agreement (*Kanslergadeforliget*) with the agrarian Liberals in January 1933, the Social Democratic–Radical Liberal coalition government pegged the krone to the pound sterling and joined the sterling bloc.

Agriculture came under increasing state protection on the domestic front as well. Between 1931 and 1933, the Social Democratic-led government set up an extensive support programme involving debt relief, subsidies, production controls, and price fixing (Johansen 1987, 47–53). At the same time, the government encouraged domestic manufacturing industries via both nontariff protection and monopoly pricing. Although the Crisis Agreement gave an impetus to public works programmes, direct relief remained the main form of unemployment relief (Topp 2008, 84–89). The Danish response was also conservative in the areas of unemployment insurance and industrial relations; however, that was for a different reason. In both areas, Denmark was a trendsetter for Scandinavia. Already in place had been a union-administered scheme of unemployment insurance and a collective bargaining framework that was drawn by the

September compromise of 1899 between labour and employers' federations (Kuhnle 1978, 25). At the macroeconomic level, Denmark followed a mixed policy. Monetary policy served a countercyclical purpose (Johansen 1987, 63–69). After raising the interest rate upon departure from the gold standard and currency devaluation, the central bank pursued a low interest rate policy from 1932 to 1935. Fiscally, however, Denmark was a successful follower of orthodoxy (Garside and Topp 2001; Topp 1988). In fact, the central government ran uninterrupted budget surpluses throughout the crisis (Johansen 1987, 66–9).

Norway. Like Sweden and Denmark, Norway pegged its currency to the pound sterling and joined the sterling bloc in 1933 after leaving the gold standard and devaluing its currency in 1931. Regardless of their political party composition, all Norwegian governments were protective of industry and especially agriculture (Grytten 2008a, 284; Hodne 1983, 70–82; Værholm 2010, 38–43). The two common trade practices concerning agricultural staples were quantitative import restrictions and price dumping to export the domestic surplus. For industry, in contrast, the state relied primarily on tariff protection.

These protective trade measures were echoed domestically. Intent on preserving the traditional family farm, the state central marketing board gave product-specific cooperatives a monopoly position in pricing and marketing. In industry as well, the state introduced or encouraged cartelization schemes and, more importantly, supported import substitution via tariff protection and other incentives (Grytten 2008a, 284–8). Like the Danes, the Norwegians emphasized direct relief in dealing with unemployment. Although the Liberals in 1933, and the Labour government after the Crisis Agreement (*Kriseforliket*) with the Agrarians in March 1935, initiated public works programmes, the "dole" remained the main source of relief for the unemployed until 1938. The unemployment insurance legislation of 1938 introduced a compulsory scheme for the industrial labour force to replace existing union-administered scheme, which had been very limited in its coverage (Kuhnle 1978, 25). In industrial relations, however, Norway drew closer to Sweden. The five-year Main Agreement between national union and employers' federations in 1935, to be enforced by the signatories themselves, established an industrial code of conduct (Hodne 1983, 96–7).

Norwegian monetary and fiscal policies fully converged with Danish ones. The Norwegian central bank raised the interest rate immediately after departure from the gold standard and currency devaluation but took an expansionary course thereafter by gradually lowering the interest rate until 1933 (Grytten 1998, 98, 2008a, 289–93; Øksendal 2010, 70–6). While increasing funding to crisis-specific programmes at the expense of ordinary programmes in the 1935–1936 fiscal year, the Labour government did not make a clear break with the orthodox course of its predecessors (Grytten 2008a, 288–9; Hanisch 1978; Hodne 1983, 94). As in Denmark, central government budgets resulted in surpluses throughout the decade (Hodne 1983, 95).

The Danish and Norwegian cases clearly show that agrarian–labour and employer–union compromises per se do not ensure economic policy innovation. While all three Scandinavian states converged in monetary management and agricultural protection, Denmark and Norway lagged behind Sweden in labour market, industrial relations, and demand management, as well as generally being far more restrictive than the latter in foreign finance and trade. In this sense, they—together with New Zealand—are useful contrasts to Sweden and the United States whose responses came closest to proto-Fordism.

Dictatorships: Protectionism and Neomercantilism Versus Proto-Fordism

Political democracy came in the aftermath of World War I with few exceptions. Before then, authoritarian rule was the rule rather than the exception. However, the interwar period spawned a new type of authoritarian rule which came to be known as modern dictatorship or totalitarianism. Unlike top-down, elitist traditional dictatorships, modern dictatorships, including Soviet Communism, Italian Fascism, and German Nazism, involved a militant mass following and penetrated all aspects of society (hence, the appellation totalitarian) with a collectivist ideal. For the Soviet Communists, that ideal was a classless society; for the Italian Fascists, German Nazis, and their counterparts elsewhere in the world, it was a corporatist society (Goldfrank 1978; Landes 1969, 398–419; Maier 1987, 70–120; Milward 1976). As will be discussed in Chaps. 5 and 6, the traditional–modern authoritarian regime differentiation was relevant to economic policy choice between protectionism and neomercantilism. All authoritarian polities, however, were exclusive of proto-Fordism. This section portrays nine authoritarian regime responses along the protectionist–neomercantilist continuum.

Germany. Three full years of economic crisis had elapsed under several Weimar governments before the Nazis took power in January 1933. These years formed an exceptional period of monetary and fiscal orthodoxy in the history of German economic policy (Borchardt 1990, Hentschel 1989, 801–6; Holtfrerich 1990a, 1990b). Regardless of their political stripes, the governments stuck to the procyclical course of deflation and retrenchment. They raised the interest rate, cut taxes, and reduced spending, particularly, on wages and salaries as well as social insurance benefits (Overy 1982, 23). Agriculture, however, was exempted from this restrictive macroeconomic framework; it received cheap credit, debt relief, and tariff and extra-tariff protection. Moreover, the banking crisis of July 1931 prompted a general protectionist turn in the German response. In addition to rescuing three major banks by "nationalizing" them, the Brüning government imposed exchange controls and introduced clearing trade, which, together with maintaining a nominal allegiance to the gold standard, were designed to help Germany's foreign balances (James 1986, 283–323, 2013). These measures, coupled with the cessation of all foreign debt payments in 1931 and the end of the reparations issue in 1932 (Schacht 1956, 197), would help the Nazis pursue their economic agenda.

Nazi economic policy had three building blocks: (a) autarky in foreign finance and trade; (b) microeconomic *dirigisme*; and (c) a mix of monetary conservatism and fiscal stimulus (Arndt 1944, 152–206; Dobb [1947] 1963, 374–8; Guillebaud 1939, 1941; Hentschel 1989, 806–13; Hirschman 1945, 34–40; James 1986, 343–418, 1993; Kindleberger [1973] 2013, 238–41; Lewis 1949, 90–7; Overy 1975, 1982; Rimlinger 1989, 592–5; Silverman 1988; Ziegler 2013). Like its predecessors, the Nazi government nominally stayed on the gold standard while maintaining exchange controls and thus avoided currency devaluation. An overvalued mark formed part of the autarkic trade drive that was launched under the New Plan of 1934. The plan, a brainchild of Reichsbank President and Economy Minister Hjalmar Schacht, refashioned the late Weimar trade initiatives to make up the loss of Western export markets and funding sources by creating areas of dependency such as the self-declared *Lebensraum* (east-central and southeastern Europe) and South America. By quasi barter clearing and payments trade with these areas, Germany was able to dispose of its manufactures in exchange for the raw materials and agricultural products that it badly needed (Overy 1982, 29; Schacht 1956, 301–5). A necessary corollary of the New Plan was complete state control over the foreign finance and trade sector. Moreover, the growth of quasi barter trade resulted in the eclipse of monetary exchanges in the country's foreign economic relations.[15]

Domestically, the Nazi government intervened in the economy by enforcing its political priorities and also using market incentives (Ziegler 2013). The two four-year plans it launched in 1933 and 1936 were the closest experiments to economic planning (James 1993, 88; Temin 1991). These, however, were specific schemes of intervention in selected sectors and industries, lacking comprehensiveness and coherence. Significantly, the Nazis did not resort to any formal nationalization. They even reprivatized the three large banks that had been taken under state control during the financial crisis of 1931 (Born [1977] 1983, 267–8; James 1993, 89; Ziegler 2013, 141). This said, private business was subject to a command type of regulation which not only circumscribed the general investment environment by price, exchange, and trade controls but also was involved in direct resource allocation by more physical measures. The Nazi government was even more interventionist in agriculture. It protected agricultural prices from domestic and international fluctuations, as in the late Weimar period, but also brought new arrangements to the sector such as the "estate" organization under which independent peasant farmsteads were made legally inalienable (Temin 1991, 577–8).

At the macroeconomic level, the Nazis had a mixed record. They clung to a conservative monetary course on the whole (Overy 1982, 51). Fiscally, however, they were more innovative. Until they subjected fiscal policy to an overt rearmament campaign by mid-decade, they carried out large public works projects, including housing and road construction in particular, for the explicit purpose of fighting unemployment (Overy 1975, 472–7). Yet, even before then, they camouflaged some of military spending as spending on work creation (James 1989, 240–3, 1993, 78; see also Arndt 1944, 156; Lewis 1949, 95–6; Temin 1989, 117). They also complemented direct (military or otherwise) public investment with incentives (such as cheap credit, subsidies, and tax rebates) to private investment, particularly, in the capital goods sector and armaments industries.

Translated into practice, the Nazi corporatist ideal became a tool of social control and labour repression in particular. In industry, for example, the "estate" organization and numerous complementary schemes (such as "social honour courts," "labour trustees," and the "labour front") served to restrict labour mobility, enforce compulsory service, and push women out of paid employment. The corporatist ideal turned into a similar tool in Austria and Italy, too.

Austria. Germany and Austria followed remarkably similar economic policies in the interwar period until they both fell for fascism in 1933. Losing World War I, they experienced postwar hyperinflation, heavily borrowed for reconstruction, occupied themselves with the reparations issue, and had a severe financial crisis in 1931. Austria's financial crisis, which preceded Germany's, broke out when the country's leading commercial bank, Credit-Anstalt, announced insolvency in May. The Christian Social government responded to the crisis by bailing out and practically taking over the Credit-Anstalt and, indirectly, an extensive network of industrial enterprises that the bank had a stake in across the territory of the former Austro-Hungarian Empire (James 2013, 126; Marcus 2018, 298–334; Senft 2003, 40–2; Wessels 2007, 244–7). This was followed by exchange controls, currency devaluation (but no departure from the gold standard), and a League of Nations-negotiated loan in return for Austria's renouncing of a proposed customs union with Germany and its pledge to continue with monetary and fiscal orthodoxy (Klausinger 2002, 8–9, 2003, 66–7; Wessels 2007, 250, 261–2, 291). With the constriction of international finance, Austrian trade relations turned protectionist. Tariff levels were raised regularly but the real story was the shift towards bilateral clearing trade bolstered by physical controls (Senft 2003, 39–40; Wessels 2007, 256–7, 262–3).

On the domestic front, the Austrian response under both democracy and dictatorship was a textbook example of neoclassical economics in monetary and fiscal terms but proved pragmatic in microeconomic terms. The single most important act of intervention in industry was the bailout of the Credit-Anstalt group. Aside from that, the state, especially the self-advertised Corporate State (*Ständestaat*), helped industries lower wages with a labour-repressive regime and industries themselves were involved in cartelization (Klausinger 2002, 19; Senft 2003, 34–5, 45). Agriculture, however, was a totally different story. Both the Christian Social governments and the Corporate State privileged, and sought autarky in, the sector with an intricate system of physical controls and subsidies (Berger 2003, 89; Kirk 2003, 22; Miller 2003). Austrian macroeconomic policy was remarkably consistent over the entire decade. The Christian Social governments and their Corporate State successors firmly stuck to the sound money and balanced budget orthodoxy and were largely successful on both counts with policies of deflation, lower spending, and higher taxation (Klausinger 2002, 11; Senft 2003, 36; Wessels 2007, 247–51, 291).

Austrofascism delivered only a faint version of neomercantilism for reasons to be discussed in Chap. 5. In contrast, Italian fascism, whose corporatist ideal provided a model for the Austrian Corporate State, tested the limits of *dirigisme* in a capitalist economy.

Italy. Unfolding against the background of a semi-industrial economy, the Italian response had a developmental drive. Like most other neomercantilist responses, it combined microeconomic *dirigisme* with monetary and fiscal conservatism (Clough 1964, 241–59; Kindleberger [1973] 2013, 241–2; Ricossa 1976, 282–90; Toniolo and Piva 1988; Welk 1938, 159–242; Zamagni 1993, 243–71). The Fascist government did everything, including exchange controls, to keep the exchange value of the lira at *Quota Novanta* or *Quota 90* (approximately 90 lire per pound sterling) that was established at the time of Italy's return to the gold standard in 1927. However, an overvalued lira could not last beyond the dissolution of the gold bloc in 1936, when it was indeed devalued. Already visible in the late 1920s as in the self-sufficiency "Battle for Grain" (Pollard 1998, 79), autarkic tendencies in foreign trade gained momentum in the early 1930s. As in Germany and Austria, physical restrictions (including quotas, prohibitions, as well as exchange controls), rather than tariff increases, discouraged imports (Zamagni 1993, 269). Conversely, various subsidies and clearing agreements were used to promote exports.

No national response was more statist than Italy's response except for the Soviet Union's (Cohen 1988). The Italian state physically intervened in the economy not just by subjecting private enterprise to a fiat mode of regulation, as in Germany, but also by engaging in direct financial and industrial entrepreneurship. In 1931, the Istituto Mobiliare Italiano (IMI) was established as a state institution to meet the long-term financing needs of crisis-stricken private industry. Later on, the IMI took control of many of the enterprises which it helped rescue, thus growing into a holding company. In 1933, the Fascist government raised the level of state ownership to a new high by establishing a second holding company, Istituto per la Ricostruzione Industriale (IRI). The IRI acquired the financial and industrial assets of the country's three largest universal banks that had been in crisis. State ownership was complemented with planning in industry, including investment licensing, and production and price controls (Zamagni 1993, 254). Statism did not penetrate agriculture, but the state was no less active in the sector. The Fascists backed up their pro-agrarian discourse with actual policies such as land reclamation, marketing facilities, price supports, and various incentives for independent family farming.

In contrast to its microeconomic boldness, the Italian response was highly defensive on the macroeconomic front. When high interest rate, credit restrictions, and wage and salary cuts simply made things worse early in the crisis, the government stepped up microeconomic *dirigisme* and relaxed fiscal policy rather than reversing the course of deflation.[16] Although the Fascists initiated numerous public works programmes, they gave fiscal stimulus only a subordinate role in fighting unemployment. This job was left primarily to supply-side measures including, among other things, the removal of women from paid employment and the reduction of the workweek.

As in Germany and Austria, the corporatist ideal served as a legitimation tool, rather than informing economic policy (Maier 1987, 81; Pollard 1998, 87; Welk 1938, 171). Instead of representing and regulating all sectors of society as presented, the so-called Fascist corporations primarily served the latent function of labour control on a coercive, and often persuasive, basis. These organs, combined with the Labour Charter of 1927 and a nationwide network of "labour education and recreation" (Clough 1964, 234–5; Clough et al. 1968, 280–4), were responsible for crushing autonomous labour organizations, prohibiting strikes, and limiting labour mobility with an internal passport system.[17] The classless society ideal served a similar, perhaps more effective, function in the Soviet Union.

Soviet Union. Soviet neomercantilism was unique in its systematic and total subjection of economic processes to the political will of rulers. The Nazis in Germany, or the Fascists in Italy, too, aimed to steer the economy in the direction of their political image but turned out to be rather piecemeal and ad hoc in doing so (Temin 1991). After experimenting with a relatively open, mixed economy (state industry, private agriculture) under NEP in the mid-1920s, the Bolsheviks turned to all-out industrialization based on central and comprehensive planning that made use of autarky in foreign finance and trade, collectivization in agriculture, and a semblance of macroeconomic constriction (Davies 1989; Kuruç 2011, 67–85, 174–211; Nove [1969] 1992, 78–114, 133–58). In the late 1920s and early 1930s, the industrializing economy needed capital and intermediate goods imports for which it only had primary goods to offer in a largely barter-based exchange framework (Gregory and Sailors 2003). Still, with a gold-backed currency, the Soviet Union was conservative in its foreign economic relations and never defaulted on its obligations.

Unlike its German and Italian counterparts, Soviet neomercantilism put agricultural policy in the service of industrial policy. In the context of autarky, the planners targeted agriculture as the primary source of funding for industrialization. This is known as the "primitive accumulation" of capital in Soviet economic historiography, which meant the expropriation of the rich peasantry (*kulak*s) and voluntary or, mostly, forced participation of independent peasantry in collective farming (Hunter and Szyrmer 1992, 90–104; Nove [1969] 1992, 159–225). That the Bolsheviks were able to trade with Weimar Germany for the initial requirements of industrialization for capital and intermediate goods was an outcome made possible by the rise of an anti-Versailles sentiment in both countries as well as by the institution of clearing trade subsequent to the withdrawal of Western financial capital from central and eastern Europe (Hunter and Szyrmer 1992, 124–35). To the extent that money remained as a medium of exchange, Soviet monetary policy followed a conservative course by repressing prices (Kuruç 2011, 79–80; Nenovsky 2015; Nove [1969] 1992, 86).

Developmental neomercantilism was the economic building block of "socialism in one country" within a totalitarian political framework. Turkey used the crisis to take a similar policy route.

Turkey. Turkish neomercantilism was similarly driven by a developmental goal but in the context of a far more backward economy and a less totalitarian polity. In the course of the crisis, the Kemalist government shifted from relative openness to autarky in foreign economic policy and from an industrialization policy privileging the private sector to statism. In macroeconomic terms, however, the Kemalists stuck to the orthodox goals of sound money and balanced budget. Turkey established an exchange controls regime in 1930 and progressively expanded its scope by issuing periodic decrees (Kuyucak 1939, 17–33). It also established an indirect parity with gold for the lira and thus avoided currency devaluation.[18] Complementing strong currency policy was one that sought trade surpluses. The tariff schedule was made more protective with the introduction of new schedules in 1933 (Tekeli and İlkin 1982, 221–45; Tezel [1982] 1986, 138–43). Tariff protection, however, was only a subordinate element of Turkish trade policy which would rely primarily on physical controls. The government introduced a detailed scheme of import controls in 1931, imposing quotas and other restrictions for both specific goods and countries (Boratav [1974] 1982, 92; Kuyucak 1939, 34–43). With such measures, bilateral clearing trade became Turkey's primary trading mechanism.[19]

Domestically, the Kemalist government largely maintained its pro-business stance in the initial years of the crisis. In July 1932, however, it turned to statism (*étatisme* as preferred locally) by bringing in a comprehensive policy package that would redefine the state's role in the economy. The statist approach to industrialization eventually opted for a holding company (Sümerbank) model in industrial organization and planning (Boratav [1974] 1982, 197–9; Tekeli and İlkin 1982, 175–9; Thornburg et al. 1949, 28–9). Launched in 1934, the first five-year industrial plan was a project of state investments in a limited number of industries whose raw materials were domestically available (Boratav [1974] 1982, 111–3; Göymen 1976, 134–8; Günçe 1967, 13–7; Hershlag [1958] 1968, 80–4; Tekeli and İlkin 1982, 184–201; Tezel [1982] 1986, 251–60). The government contemplated a second industrial plan by establishing another holding company (Etibank) in 1938 but scrapped it in the worsening international climate. The state also became an active agent in other ways ranging from the nationalization of public utilities and mining companies to the participation in joint ventures with the private sector, which had to operate under a system of regimentation consisting of price controls, financial inspections, and regional relocation. In agriculture, however, statism made little headway. The government intervened in agriculture in ways that supported industrialization, leaving the traditional organization of the sector largely intact. Nevertheless, two pieces of legislation in the July 1932 package marked the beginning of a more interventionist agricultural policy. One initiated monopoly marketing of the opium crop and the other support purchase of wheat by the Agricultural Bank, which also organized producers' cooperatives in regions producing cash crops (Silier 1981, 77–91). Later in the decade, the government contemplated an agricultural plan and passed a Constitutional amendment allowing land reform (Avcıoğlu 1968, 485–7). However, other than a new Office for Soil Products, nothing would come out of these initiatives.

At the macroeconomic level, the Kemalist government successfully followed the orthodox course while innovating institutionally (Owen and Pamuk 1999, 20; Pamuk 2000, 333, 2014, 191–2). The institution of central banking in 1930 (İlkin 1975, 572–82; Tekeli and İlkin 1977, 115–9, 1981, appendix 20), combined with industrial and commercial banking under the aegis of the new holding companies and specialized banks, would make the state the principal agent in finance as well. In substantive terms, Turkish monetary policy was strictly deflationary (Hale 1981, 69; Tezel [1982] 1986, 111). Fiscally, the government lived up to its balanced budget creed while, at the same time, implementing an aggressive industrialization programme.[20] Given the financing requirement of the nationalization and industrialization programmes, this is an intriguing performance which can be explained in part by the fiscal organization of the Turkish state. Excluded from the central government budget were the accounts of profit-oriented state enterprises (e.g., Sümerbank and Etibank) and most public utility companies (Tezel [1982] 1986, 182; Thornburg et al. 1949, 146–51).

Turkey realized its neomercantilist potential after initially responding to the crisis in a typically protectionist fashion. For the rest of the small Balkan states, which I will turn to next, the line between protectionism and neomercantilism was blurred.

Rest of the Balkans. Bulgaria, Greece, Romania, and Yugoslavia converged with Turkey in autarkic trade and orthodox macroeconomic policies but diverged from it by trailing in industrial *dirigisme* and by providing more protection to their primary producers. With a direct or indirect link to the gold standard, all four states introduced exchange controls and, with the exception of Greece, avoided currency devaluation. Greece was uniquely exposed to the crisis with a heavy debt burden administered by international creditors and had to formally abandon the gold standard and devalue its currency in 1932 (Brégianni 2012, 7; Christodoulakis 2012, 15; Freris 1986, 77–82; Mazower 1991, 143–78). Nevertheless, like Turkey, the rest of the Balkan states turned autarkic in foreign trade, replacing currency exchange with bartering through bilateral clearing agreements—with, first and foremost, Germany (Basch 1944, 165–93; Berend and Ránki 1974, 265–84; Ellis 1941, 257–70; Lampe and Jackson 1982, 456–69; Ránki 1983, 123–60).

Unlike Turkish *étatisme* targeting industry rather than agriculture, the other Balkan responses showed their interventionist edge in agriculture and limited their industrial policies largely to protectionist measures such as cartelization schemes, protection of the domestic market, and various financial incentives (Lampe and Jackson 1982, 448–56, 482–519; Ránki 1985, 64–72; Ránki and Tomaszewski 1986, 21–40; Teichova 1989, 939–61). In Bulgaria, the state monopolized the marketing of agricultural products while, at the same time, providing effective debt relief to producers (Asenova 2012; Lampe 1986, 78–104; Ránki and Tomaszewski 1986, 23). Tariff protection, the highest in the northern Balkans (Lampe and Jackson 1982, 413), was the main form of support given to Bulgarian industry within a conservative macroeconomic framework (Kolev 2009,

25). Despite defaulting on its international debt, Greece continued to give marketing, price, and debt relief support to agricultural producers. In industry, however, a more concerted policy would have to wait until after the installation of the Metaxas regime in 1936 (Freris 1986, 89–97; Mazower 1991, 278–302). Romania and Yugoslavia were similarly protective of their agricultural sectors with monopolistic marketing, price, and debt relief policies (Ránki and Tomaszewski 1986, 23). In industry, Romania encouraged cartelization that made its sector the most cartelized in the northern Balkans (Lampe and Jackson 1982, 498–9), but Yugoslavia was not as successful with a similar scheme for its sector defined by high levels of foreign investment (Singleton and Carter 1982, 68–9).

Summing Up the Problematic

While international crises expand the policy space, they do not do so randomly. The background against which a crisis unfolds is one factor that limits the range of policy options. That background includes a pre-existing hegemonic policy paradigm as well as its underlying processes and institutions at both international and domestic levels. Moreover, the crisis itself opens up new possibilities and leads to new institutions relatively independently of any single state or non-state actor. I call this conjunction of background and foreground factors the world-historical context, which puts limits on policy choice by excluding the pre-existing hegemonic option and including previously untenable or unimaginable options in the realm of the possible.

In the interwar crisis, the classical liberal policy paradigm, along with its supporting institutions—UK hegemony or balance of power system depending on one's outlook, international gold standard, self-regulating or minimally regulated market, and a liberal but not necessarily democratic polity—constituted the background factors. The crisis, first and foremost a crisis of these institutions and of the policy paradigm they underlaid, discredited classical liberalism as a policy option. It also unleashed new dynamics such as international discordance (especially between large states), regionalization (currency and trade blocs), bilateral and barter-based trade mechanisms, and various strands of innovation in domestic economic organization ranging from cartelization through planning to demand management. In their international and domestic aspects, these dynamics occasioned and supported three alternative policy paradigms in the world: protectionism, proto-Fordism, and neomercantilism.

A second limitation on policy choice is political regime. The position of the public policy literature on the role of democracies, dictatorships, and their subtypes in economic policy is varied. Some see no connection, but others claim a necessary and full correspondence between political regime and economic policy. This controversy largely hinges on differing definitions of economic policy; if one's focus is on a particular policy area, s/he can easily point to either the relevance or irrelevance of political regime to economic policy. For example, fiscal policy with its taxing, spending, and, in almost all cases, borrowing components can take any direction under any political arrangement. In contrast, microeconomic policy concerning particularly industry and industrial relations has a low tolerance for political regime variation. Industrial *dirigisme* requires a certain degree of authoritarian fiat whereas a negotiated industrial relations system presupposes a democratic environment, first and foremost, autonomously organized employers' and labour federations. If one takes up economic policy as a package as I do here, the picture gets complicated. Some policy packages may still be entirely politically neutral, but others are distinguished by their politically defined features.

States displayed both facets of economic policy in their responses to the interwar crisis. As the most conservative package outside of the discredited classical liberalism, protectionism had no political regime mark and was thus tried by all states at some point during the crisis. In contrast, proto-Fordism and neomercantilism carried the hallmarks of democracy and dictatorship, respectively. Tried only by a handful of democracies, the proto-Fordist package had democracy-specific elements making autonomous interest articulation and representation possible just as the neomercantilist package featured policies that required the monopolization of decision making at the hands of an unaccountable, authoritarian bureaucratic elite. Thus, individual states had only two options available to them: protectionism and proto-Fordism under democracy, and protectionism and neomercantilism under dictatorship.

The next four chapters account for why some states stuck with protectionism while others made a transition to either proto-Fordism or neomercantilism and still others stopped short of full transition. In each country case, I will use a counterfactual to the actual policy choice: Proto-Fordism was the counterfactual for democracies that stuck with protectionism and neomercantilism for their dictatorial counterparts. For states that made the transition to either proto-Fordism or neomercantilism, protectionism was the counterfactual, which they tried but did not stick with.

NOTES

1. In Polanyian perspective, the 1930s experience can actually be seen as the second "great transformation" with the first one being the rise of market liberalism itself in the nineteenth century. I would like to thank an anonymous reviewer for drawing my attention to this point.
2. For this reason, the interwar gold standard is often called the gold exchange standard to differentiate it from the original, prewar version (Aldcroft 1977, 156–86; Brown 1949; Eichengreen 1992, 193).
3. On paper, reparations were astronomical, amounting to 260% of Germany's 1913 gross domestic product (Ritschl 2013, 113). "In reality, however," according to Feinstein et al. (2008, 87), "reparations amounted at most to one-third of gross receipts from abroad. In the period 1924–30, the total amount paid in reparations amounted approximately $2.4 billion (about 2.3 percent of Germany's aggregate national income over these years), whereas the gross inflow of capital during the same period amounted to approximately $7000 million, or 6.6 percent of national income." Hjalmar Schacht (1956, 196), President of the German central bank (Reichsbank) from 1923 to 1930 and again from 1933 to 1939 (as well as Minister of Economic Affairs from 1934 to 1937), claims that, between 1924 and 1932, Germany actually paid about 10% of the 120 billion gold marks originally assessed as reparations.
4. Economic historians generally agree that the gold standard applied a pro-cyclical, deflationary pressure on national economies by limiting domestic monetary and fiscal choices during the depression (see, e.g., Bernanke 2000; Eichengreen 1992). The evidence provided is that nations that severed their "golden fetters" recovered more quickly than nations bound with them.
5. Kenneth Oye (1992, 71–104) argues that the non-discriminatory Smoot–Hawley tariff had a general trade-limiting effect whereas the subsequent discriminatory (bilateral and regional) protectionism of other nations in the 1930s, as well as the discriminatory liberalization of the US Reciprocal Trade Agreements Act of 1934, liberated trade between nations and within regions.
6. According to Douglas Irwin (2012, 159–66), trade restrictions of the 1930s were closer to mercantilism in the sense of pervasive practices of import minimization aiming to improve the balance of payments, than to protectionism in the sense of selective practices sheltering import-competing industries from foreign competition.
7. In this sense, trade blocs often overlapping with currency blocs had the potential to solve the "impossible trinity" or "trilemma" that states face: Of the three policies of a stable exchange rate, capital mobility, and auton-

omous monetary policy, only two can be mutually consistent (Straumann 2010, 4). Within a trade bloc, however, policymakers "can continue to benefit from unrestricted international capital mobility, pursue autonomous monetary policy … and maintain stable exchange rates" (Wolf 2013, 77; but see also Irwin 2012). Nations in the sterling area that were also part of the British preferential trading system might have come closest to this solution in the Depression era.

8. Although the central government budget ran continuous deficits throughout the 1930s, they were minor except for those of 1938 and 1939 (Feinstein 1972, T31–2).
9. At any point between 1932 and 1939, the proportion of people on relief works to those on direct relief remained below 10% (calculated from Bryce 1985, 10–2).
10. Under the Blum experiment, nationalization was limited to parts of the armaments industry. Nevertheless, the government reorganized the Bank of France as a semi-public institution and established a National Ministry of Economy.
11. Institutionally, the RBNZ was reorganized with increased powers in 1936 (Plumptre 1940, 15–21).
12. Economists argue that these deficits were too small to have a Keynesian effect on the economy (see, e.g., Fishback 2010, 403).
13. The public works component of the unemployment relief system would progressively grow so that the ratio of the workers employed in public works to those in other relief works increased from 1:10 in 1933 to 3:1 in 1938 (calculated from Jörberg and Krantz 1989, 1082).
14. Viewed over the entire decade, Swedish fiscal policy effected a different type of budget balancing. The aggregate deficits of the 1931–1932 to 1934–1935 fiscal years were compensated for by the aggregate surpluses of 1935–1936 to 1938–1939 (Wigforss 1938, 34).
15. By 1938, over 50% of German foreign trade came to be done with bilateral clearing and payments agreements (Overy 1982, 30).
16. For this reason, Marcello de Cecco (1989, 207–14) calls Fascist economic policy "bastard Keynesianism," meaning the organization of supply rather than demand.
17. To do justice to Fascist labour policy, however, one must also mention the foundation of a paternalistic social security system introducing health insurance and family allowance, and covering sickness, old age, invalidity, maternity, and unemployment.
18. Against the US dollar, for example, the lira rose from 47 cents in 1930 to 78 cents in 1939 (Thornburg et al. 1949, 260).

19. Clearing trade accounted for no less than 80% of Turkish foreign trade in the second half of the 1930s (Kuyucak 1939, table 17 [no paging]; Tezel [1982] 1986, 152).
20. Between the 1929–1930 and 1937–1938 fiscal years, the government ran only three deficit budgets, whose aggregate deficits amounted to no more than 20% of the aggregate surpluses of the remaining six budgets (Kuyucak 1939, table 6 [no paging]).

References

Aldcroft, Derek H. 1970. *The Inter-War Economy: Britain, 1919–1939*. New York: Columbia University Press.
Aldcroft, Derek H. 1977. *From Versailles to Wall Street, 1919–1929*. Berkeley: University of California Press.
Aldcroft, Derek H. 1997. *Studies in the Interwar European Economy*. Aldershot: Ashgate.
Alhadeff, Peter. 1985. "Public Finance and the Economy in Argentina, Australia and Canada during the Depression of the 1930s." In *Argentina, Australia and Canada: Studies in Comparative Development, 1876–1965*, edited by D. C. M. Platt and Guido di Tella, 161–78. London: Macmillan.
Arndt, Heinz W. 1944. *The Economic Lessons of the Nineteen-Thirties*. London: Oxford University Press.
Asenova, Vera. 2012. "Small States' Responses to the Great Depression: A Case Study of Bulgaria." Paper presented at the general conference of the European Consortium for Political Research, 25–27 August, Reykjavik.
Avcıoğlu, Doğan. 1968. *Türkiye'nin Düzeni (Dün-Bugün-Yarın)*, book 1. Ankara: Bilgi Yayınevi.
Basch, Antonín. 1944. *The Danube Basin and the German Economic Sphere*. London: Kegan Paul.
Belshaw, H. 1933. "Crisis and Readjustment in New Zealand." *Journal of Political Economy* 41, no. 6: 750–76.
Bennett, Richard B. 1935. *The Premier Speaks to the People – The First Address*. Ottawa: Dominion Conservative Headquarters.
Berend, Iván T., and György Ránki. 1974. *Economic Development in East-Central Europe in the 19th and 20th Centuries*. New York: Columbia University Press.
Berg, Claes, and Lars Jonung. 1999. "Pioneering Price Level Targeting: The Swedish Experience 1931–1937." *Journal of Monetary Economics* 43, no. 3: 525–51.
Berger, Peter. 2003. "The League of Nations and Interwar Austria: Critical Assessment of a Partnership in Economic Reconstruction." In *The Dollfuss/Schuschnigg Era in Austria: A Reassessment*, edited by Günter Bischof, Anton Pelinka, and Alexander Lassner, 73–92. London and New York: Routledge.

Berger, Suzanne. 2013. "Puzzles from the First Globalization." In *Politics in the New Hard Times: The Great Recession in Comparative Perspective*, edited by Miles Kahler and David A. Lake, 150–68. Ithaca: Cornell University Press.

Bernanke, Ben S. 2000. *Essays on the Great Depression*. Princeton: Princeton University Press.

Birch, Anthony H. 1955. *Federalism, Finance and Social Legislation in Canada, Australia, and the United States*. Oxford: Oxford University Press.

Block, Fred L. 1977. *The Origins of International Economic Disorder: A Study of United States International Monetary Policy from World War II to the Present*. Berkeley: University of California Press.

Booth, Alan. 1993. "The British Reaction to the Economic Crisis." In *Capitalism in Crisis: International Responses to the Great Depression*, edited by W. Redvers Garside, 30–55. London: Pinter.

Boratav, Korkut. [1974] 1982. *Türkiye'de Devletçilik*. 2nd ed. Ankara: Savaş Yayınları.

Born, Karl E. [1977] 1983. *International Banking in the 19th and 20th Centuries*. Translated from the German by Volker R. Berghahn. New York: St. Martin's.

Borchardt, Knut. 1990. "A Decade of Debate About Brüning's Economic Policy." In *Economic Crisis and Political Collapse: The Weimar Republic, 1924–1933*, edited by Jürgen B. von Kruedener, 99–151. Oxford: Berg.

Boyce, Robert. 2009. *The Great Interwar Crisis and the Collapse of Globalization*. Basingstoke: Palgrave Macmillan.

Braatoy, Bjarne. 1939. *The New Sweden: A Vindication of Democracy*. London: Thomas Nelson.

Brady, Alexander. 1941. "Democracy in the Overseas Dominions." In *Canada in Peace and War: Eight Studies in National Trends since 1914*, edited by C. Martin, 212–44. London: Oxford University Press.

Brady, Alexander. 1958. *Democracy in the Dominions: A Comparative Study in Institutions*. 3rd ed. Toronto: University of Toronto Press.

Brecher, Irving. 1957. *Monetary and Fiscal Thought and Policy in Canada, 1919–1939*. Toronto: University of Toronto Press.

Brégianni, Catherine. 2012. "The Gold-Exchange Standard, the Great Depression and Greece; Lessons (?) from the Interwar Greek Default." Paper presented at the symposium on "The Euro: (Greek) Tragedy or Europe's Destiny? Economic, Historical and Legal Perspectives on the Common Currency," 11–12 January, Bayreuth.

Broadbridge, Seymour A. 1989. "Aspects of Economic and Social Policy in Japan, 1868–1945." In *The Cambridge Economic History of Europe*, vol. 8, *The Industrial Economies: The Development of Economic and Social Policies*, edited by Peter Mathias and Sidney Pollard, 1106–45. Cambridge: Cambridge University Press.

Brown, Bruce. 1962. *The Rise of New Zealand Labour: A History of the New Zealand Labour Party from 1916 to 1940.* Wellington: Price Milburn.

Brown, William A., Jr. 1949. "Gold as a Monetary Standard, 1914–1919." *Journal of Economic History* 9, supplement S1: 39–49. https://doi.org/10.1017/S0022050700064032.

Bryce, Robert B. 1985. "The Canadian Economy in the 1930s: Unemployment Relief under Bennett and Mackenzie King." In *Explorations in Canadian Economic History: Essays in Honour of Irene M. Spry*, edited by Duncan Cameron, 7–26. Ottawa: University of Ottawa Press.

Bryce, Robert B. 1986. *Maturing in Hard Times: Canada's Department of Finance through the Great Depression.* Kingston and Montreal: McGill-Queen's University Press.

Carr, Edward H. [1939] 1946. *The Twenty Years' Crisis, 1919–1939: An Introduction to the Study of International Relations.* 2nd ed. London: Macmillan.

Castles, Francis G. 1988. *Australian Public Policy and Economic Vulnerability: A Comparative and Historical Perspective.* Sydney: Allen and Unwin.

Chandler, Lester V. 1970. *America's Greatest Depression, 1929–1941.* New York: Harper and Row.

Checkland, S. G. 1989. "British Public Policy, 1776–1939." In *The Cambridge Economic History of Europe*, vol. 8, *The Industrial Economies: The Development of Economic and Social Policies*, edited by Peter Mathias and Sidney Pollard, 607–40. Cambridge: Cambridge University Press.

Christodoulakis, Nicos. 2012. "Currency Crisis and Collapse in Interwar Greece: Predicament or Policy Failure?" GreeSE Paper No. 60, Hellenic Observatory Papers on Greece and Southeast Europe. http://eprints.lse.ac.uk/44881/1/GreeSE%20No60.pdf (accessed 25 June 2021).

Clark, Harrison. 1941. *Swedish Unemployment Policy – 1914 to 1940.* Washington, D.C.: American Council on Public Affairs.

Clavin, Patricia. 1996. *The Failure of Economic Diplomacy: Britain, Germany, France and the United States, 1931–36.* Basingstoke: Macmillan.

Clavin, Patricia. 2000. *The Great Depression in Europe, 1929–1939.* New York: St. Martin's.

Clough, Shepard B. 1964. *The Economic History of Modern Italy.* New York: Columbia University Press.

Clough, Shepard B., Thomas Moodie, and Carol G. Moodie, eds. 1968. *Economic History of Europe: Twentieth Century.* New York: Walker.

Cohen, Jon S. 1988. "Was Italian Fascism a Developmental Dictatorship? Some Evidence to the Contrary." *Economic History Review*, 2nd series 41, no. 1: 95–113. https://doi.org/10.2307/2597334.

Cole, G. D. H. 1938. "Sweden in World Trade." In *Democratic Sweden*, edited by Margaret Cole and Charles Smith, 226–43. New York: Greystone.

Crafts, Nicholas, and Peter Fearon. 2013. "Depression and Recovery in the 1930s: An Overview." In *The Great Depression of the 1930s: Lessons for Today*, edited by Nicholas Crafts and Peter Fearon, 1–44. Oxford: Oxford University Press.

Curtis, C. A. 1931. "Canada and the Gold Standard." *Queen's Quarterly* 38, no. 1: 104–20.

Dahmén, Erik. [1950] 1970. *Entrepreneurial Activity and the Development of Swedish Industry, 1919–1939*. Translated from the Swedish by Axel Leijonhufvud. Homewood: Richard D. Irwin.

Davies, Robert W. 1989. "Economic and Social Policy in the USSR, 1917–41." In *The Cambridge Economic History of Europe*, vol. 8, *The Industrial Economies: The Development of Economic and Social Policies*, edited by Peter Mathias and Sidney Pollard, 984–1047. Cambridge: Cambridge University Press.

Day, Richard B. 1981. *The "Crisis" and the "Crash": Soviet Studies of the West (1917–1939)*. London: New Left Books.

de Cecco, Marcello. 1989. "Keynes and Italian Economics." In *The Political Power of Economic Ideas: Keynesianism across Nations*, edited by Peter A. Hall, 195–229. Princeton: Princeton University Press.

Dewey, Peter. 2003. "Agriculture, Agrarian Society and the Countryside." In *A Companion to Early Twentieth-Century Britain*, edited by Chris Wrigley, 270–85. Oxford: Blackwell Publishing.

Dobb, Maurice. [1947] 1963. *Studies in the Development of Capitalism*. Revised ed. New York: International.

Drummond, Ian M. 1972. *British Economic Policy and the Empire, 1919–1939*. London: George Allen and Unwin.

Drummond, Ian M. 1974. *Imperial Economic Policy, 1917–1939: Studies in Expansion and Protection*. London: George Allen and Unwin.

Drummond, Ian M. 1981. *The Floating Pound and the Sterling Area, 1931–1939*. Cambridge: Cambridge University Press.

Drummond, Ian M., and Norman Hillmer. 1989. *Negotiating Freer Trade: The United Kingdom, the United States, Canada, and the Trade Agreements of 1938*. Waterloo: Wilfrid Laurier University Press.

Eichengreen, Barry J. 1988. "The Australian Recovery of the 1930s in International Comparative Perspective." In *Recovery from the Depression: Australia and the World Economy in the 1930s*, edited by Robert G. Gregory and Noel G. Butlin, 33–60. Cambridge: Cambridge University Press.

Eichengreen, Barry J. 1992. *Golden Fetters: The Gold Standard and the Great Depression, 1919–1939*. New York: Oxford University Press.

Eichengreen, Barry J. 2015. *Hall of Mirrors: The Great Depression, the Great Recession, and the Uses – and Misuses – of History*. New York: Oxford University Press.

Eichengreen, Barry J., and Marc Flandreau. [1985] 1997. "Editors' Introduction." In *The Gold Standard in Theory and History*, 2nd ed., edited by Barry J. Eichengreen and Marc Flandreau, 1–21. London and New York: Routledge.

Eichengreen, Barry J., and Tim J. Hatton. 1988. "Interwar Unemployment in International Perspective: An Overview." In *Interwar Unemployment in International Perspective*, edited by Barry J. Eichengreen and Tim J. Hatton, 1–59. Dordrecht: Kluwer.

Ellis, Howard S. 1941. *Exchange Control in Central Europe*. Cambridge, MA: Harvard University Press.

Endres, A. M., and Kenneth E. Jackson. 1993. "Policy Responses to the Crisis: Australasia in the 1930s." In *Capitalism in Crisis: International Responses to the Great Depression*, edited by W. Redvers Garside, 148–65. London: Pinter.

Feinstein, Charles H. 1972. *National Income, Expenditure and Output of the United Kingdom, 1855–1965*. Cambridge: At the University Press.

Feinstein, Charles H., Peter Temin, and Gianni Toniolo. 2008. *The World Economy between the World Wars*. Oxford: Oxford University Press.

Fishback, Price. 2010. "US Monetary and Fiscal Policy in the 1930s." *Oxford Review of Economic Policy* 26, no. 3: 385–413. https://doi.org/10.1093/oxrep/grq029.

Fishback, Price, and John J. Wallis. 2013. "What Was New about the New Deal?" In *The Great Depression of the 1930s: Lessons for Today*, edited by Nicholas Crafts and Peter Fearon, 290–327. Oxford: Oxford University Press.

Fisher, Allan G. B. 1934. "Crisis and Readjustment in Australia." *Journal of Political Economy* 42, no. 6: 753–82.

Fowke, Vernon C. 1957. *The National Policy and the Wheat Economy*. Toronto: University of Toronto Press.

Freris, Andrew F. 1986. *The Greek Economy in the Twentieth Century*. New York: St. Martin's.

Gallarotti, Giulio M. 1995. *The Anatomy of an International Monetary Regime: The Classical Gold Standard, 1880–1914*. New York and Oxford: Oxford University Press.

Garside, W. Redvers. 2000. "The Political Economy of Structural Change: Britain in the 1930s." In *After the Slump: Industry and Politics in 1930s Britain and Germany*, edited by C. Buchheim and W. Redvers Garside, 9–31. Frankfurt am Main: Peter Lang.

Garside, W. Redvers, and Niels-Henrik Topp. 2001. "Nascent Keynesianism? Denmark in the 1930s." *History of Political Economy* 33, no. 4: 717–41.

Garraty, John A. 1973. "The New Deal, National Socialism, and the Great Depression." *American Historical Review* 78, no. 4: 907–44. https://doi.org/10.2307/1858346.

Garraty, John A. 1986. *The Great Depression: An Inquiry into the Causes, Course, and Consequences of the Worldwide Depression of the Nineteen-Thirties, as Seen by*

Contemporaries and in the Light of History. San Diego: Harcourt Brace Jovanovich.

Goldfrank, Walter L. 1978. "Fascism and World Economy." In *Social Change in the Capitalist World Economy*, edited by Barbara H. Kaplan, 75–117. Beverly Hills: Sage.

Göymen, Korel. 1976. "Stages of Etatist Development in Turkey: The Interaction of Single-Party Politics and Economic Policy in the 'Etatist Decade,' 1930–1939." *METU Studies in Development*, no. 10: 89–114.

Greaves, Julian. 2000. "British Steel in the 1930s: Adaptation under Duress?" In *After the Slump: Industry and Politics in 1930s Britain and Germany*, edited by C. Buchheim and W. Redvers Garside, 111–30. Frankfurt am Main: Peter Lang.

Green, Alan G., and Gordon R. Sparks. 1988. "A Macro Interpretation of Recovery: Australia and Canada." In *Recovery from the Depression: Australia and the World Economy in the 1930s*, edited by Robert G. Gregory and Noel G. Butlin, 89–112. Cambridge: Cambridge University Press.

Gregory, Paul R., and Joel Sailors. 2003. "The Soviet Union during the Great Depression: The Autarky Model." In *The World Economy and National Economies in the Interwar Slump*, edited by Theo Balderston, 191–210. Basingstoke: Palgrave Macmillan.

Grytten, Ola H. 1998. "Monetary Policy and Restructuring of the Norwegian Economy during the Years of Crises, 1920–1939." In *Economic Crises and Restructuring in History: Experiences of Small Countries*, edited by Timo Myllyntaus, 93–124. St. Katharinen: Scripta Mercaturae Verlag.

Grytten, Ola H. 2008a. "A Small Country's Policy Response to Global Economic Disintegration during the Interwar Years of Crisis." In *Pathbreakers: Small European Countries Responding to Globalisation and Deglobalisation*, edited by Margrit Müller and Timo Myllyntaus, 271–96. Bern: Peter Lang.

Guillebaud, Claude W. 1939. *The Economic Recovery of Germany: From 1933 to the Incorporation of Austria in March 1938*. London: Macmillan.

Guillebaud, Claude W. 1941. *The Social Policy of Nazi Germany*. Cambridge: At the University Press.

Günçe, Ergin. 1967. "Early Planning Experiences in Turkey." In *Planning in Turkey (Selected Papers)*, edited by Selim İlkin and E. İnanç, 1–27. Ankara: METU Publications.

Hadley, Eleanor M. 1989. "The Diffusion of Keynesian Ideas in Japan." In *The Political Power of Economic Ideas: Keynesianism across Nations*, edited by Peter A. Hall, 291–309. Princeton: Princeton University Press.

Haggard, Stephan. 1988 "The Institutional Foundations of Hegemony: Explaining the Reciprocal Trade Agreements Act of 1934." *International Organization* 42, no. 1: 91–119. https://doi.org/10.1017/S0020818300007141.

Hale, William M. 1981. *The Political and Economic Development of Modern Turkey*. London: Croom Helm.

Hanisch, Tore. 1978. "The Economic Crisis in Norway in the 1930s: A Tentative Analysis of Its Causes." *Scandinavian Economic History Review* 26, no. 2: 145–55. https://doi.org/10.1080/03585522.1978.10415624.

Hansson, Sigfrid. 1939. "Employers and Workers in Sweden." In *Sweden's Economic Progress*, edited by the Royal Swedish Commission, 1–113 (separately paged). New York: Royal Swedish Commission.

Hart, Michael. 2002. *A Trading Nation: Canadian Trade Policy from Colonialism to Globalization*. Vancouver: University of British Columbia Press.

Hawke, G. R. 1971. "New Zealand and the Return to Gold in 1925." *Australian Economic History Review* 11, no. 1: 48–58.

Hawke, G. R. 1985. *The Making of New Zealand: An Economic History*. Cambridge: Cambridge University Press.

Hawke, G. R. 1988. "Depression and Recovery in New Zealand." In *Recovery from the Depression: Australia and the World Economy in the 1930s*, ed. Robert G. Gregory and Noel G. Butlin, 113–34. Cambridge: Cambridge University Press.

Heclo, Hugh. 1974. *Modern Social Politics in Britain and Sweden: From Relief to Income Maintenance*. New Haven: Yale University Press.

Hedberg, Peter. 2010. "Bilateral Exchange Clearing with Germany during the 1930s: The Experiences of the Scandinavian Countries." In *Managing Crises and De-globalisation: Nordic Foreign Trade and Exchange, 1919–39*, edited by Sven-Olof Olsson, 101–20. London: Routledge.

Hentschel, Volker. 1989. "German Economic and Social Policy, 1815–1939." In *The Cambridge Economic History of Europe*, vol. 8, *The Industrial Economies: The Development of Economic and Social Policies*, edited by Peter Mathias and Sidney Pollard, 752–813. Cambridge: Cambridge University Press.

Hershlag, Zvi Y. [1958] 1968. *Turkey: The Challenge of Growth*. 2nd ed. Leiden: E. J. Brill.

Hill, Kim Q. 1988. *Democracies in Crisis: Public Policy Responses to the Great Depression*. Boulder: Westview.

Hirschman, Albert O. 1945. *National Power and the Structure of Foreign Trade*. Berkeley: University of California Press.

Hobsbawm, Eric. 1994. *Age of Extremes: The Short Twentieth Century, 1914–1991*. London: Michael Joseph.

Hodne, Fritz. 1983. *The Norwegian Economy, 1920–1980*. London: Croom Helm.

Holtfrerich, Carl-Ludwig. 1990a. "Was the Policy of Deflation in Germany Unavoidable?" In *Economic Crisis and Political Collapse: The Weimar Republic, 1924–1933*, edited by Jürgen B. von Kruedener, 63–80. Oxford: Berg.

Holtfrerich, Carl-Ludwig. 1990b. "Economic Policy Options and the End of the Weimar Republic." In *Weimar: Why Did German Democracy Fail?*, edited by Ian Kershaw, 58–91. London: Weidenfeld and Nicholson.

Hunter, Holland, and Janusz M. Szyrmer. 1992. *Faulty Foundations: Soviet Economic Policies, 1928–1940*. Princeton: Princeton University Press.
Irwin, Douglas A. 2011. *Peddling Protectionism: Smoot–Hawley and the Great Depression*. Princeton: Princeton University Press.
Irwin, Douglas A. 2012. *Trade Policy Disaster: Lessons from the 1930s*. Cambridge, MA: MIT Press.
İlkin, Selim. 1975. "Türkiye'de Merkez Bankası Fikrinin Gelişimi." In *Türkiye İktisat Tarihi Semineri: Metinler/Tartışmalar (8–10 Haziran 1973)*, edited by Osman Okyar and H. Ünal Nalbantoğlu, 537–82. Ankara: Hacettepe Ünverstesi Yayınları.
Jackson, Julian. 1985. *The Politics of Depression in France, 1932–1936*. Cambridge: Cambridge University Press.
Jackson, Julian. 1988. *The Popular Front in France: Defending Democracy, 1934–38*. Cambridge: Cambridge University Press.
James, Harold. 1986. *The German Slump: Politics and Economics, 1924–1936*. Oxford: Clarendon Press.
James, Harold. 1989. "What Is Keynesian about Deficit Financing? The Case of Interwar Germany." In *The Political Power of Economic Ideas: Keynesianism across Nations*, edited by Peter A. Hall, 231–62. Princeton: Princeton University Press.
James, Harold. 1993. "Innovation and Conservatism in Economic Recovery: The Alleged 'Nazi Recovery' of the 1930s." In *Capitalism in Crisis: International Responses to the Great Depression*, edited by W. Redvers Garside, 70–95. London: Pinter.
James, Harold. 2001. *The End of Globalization: Lessons from the Great Depression*. Cambridge, MA: Harvard University Press.
James, Harold. 2013. "The 1931 Central European Banking Crisis Revisited." In *Business in the Age of Extremes: Essays in Modern German and Austrian Economic History*, edited by Hartmut Berghoff, Jürgen Kocka, and Dieter Ziegler, 119–30. Cambridge: Cambridge University Press.
Johansen, Hans C. 1987. *The Danish Economy in the Twentieth Century*. London: Croom Helm.
Jonung, Lars. 1979. "Knut Wicksell's Norm of Price Stabilization and Swedish Monetary Policy in the 1930's." *Journal of Monetary Economics* 5, no. 4: 459–96.
Jonung, Lars. 1981. "The Depression in Sweden and the United States: A Comparison of Causes and Policies." In *The Great Depression Revisited*, edited by Karl Brunner, 286–315. Boston: Martinus Nijhoff.
Jörberg, Lennart, and Olle Krantz. 1989. "Economic and Social Policy in Sweden, 1850–1939." In *The Cambridge Economic History of Europe*, vol. 8, *The Industrial Economies: The Development of Economic and Social Policies*, edited

by Peter Mathias and Sidney Pollard, 1048–105. Cambridge: Cambridge University Press.

Kalecki, M. 1938. "The Lesson of the Blum Experiment." *Economic Journal* 48, no. 189: 26–41. https://doi.org/10.2307/2225475.

Kemp, Tom. 1972. *The French Economy, 1913–39: The History of a Decline.* London: Longman.

Kemp, Tom. 1989. "Economic and Social Policy in France." In *The Cambridge Economic History of Europe*, vol. 8, *The Industrial Economies: The Development of Economic and Social Policies*, edited by Peter Mathias and Sidney Pollard, 691–751. Cambridge: Cambridge University Press.

Kindleberger, Charles P. [1973] 2013. *The World in Depression, 1929–1939.* 40th anniversary ed. Berkeley: University of California Press.

Kindleberger, Charles P. 1989. "Commercial Policy between the Wars." In *The Cambridge Economic History of Europe*, vol. 8, *The Industrial Economies: The Development of Economic and Social Policies*, edited by Peter Mathias and Sidney Pollard, 161–96. Cambridge: Cambridge University Press.

Kirk, Tim. 2003. "Fascism and Austrofascism." In *The Dollfuss/Schuschnigg Era in Austria: A Reassessment*, edited by Günter Bischof, Anton Pelinka, and Alexander Lassner, 10–31. London and New York: Routledge.

Kjellstrom, Erik T. H. 1934. *Managed Money: The Experience of Sweden.* New York: Columbia University Press.

Klausinger, Hansjörg. 2002. "The Austrian School of Economics and the Gold Standard Mentality in Austrian Economic Policy in the 1930s." Center for Austrian Studies Working Paper 02-2, University of Minnesota, Minneapolis. https://econwpa.ub.uni-muenchen.de/econ-wp/mhet/papers/0501/0501001.pdf (accessed 8 May 2021).

Klausinger, Hansjörg. 2003. "How Far Was Vienna from Chicago in the 1930s? The Economists and the Depression." In *The Dollfuss/Schuschnigg Era in Austria: A Reassessment*, edited by Günter Bischof, Anton Pelinka, and Alexander Lassner, 56–72. London and New York: Routledge.

Knox, Frank A. 1939. "Dominion Monetary Policy, 1929–1934: A Study Prepared for the Royal Commission on Dominion–Provincial Relations." Unpublished report, Ottawa.

Kolev, Stefan. 2009. "The Great Depression in the Eyes of Bulgaria's Inter-War Economists." Discussion Paper No. DP/79/2009, Bulgarian National Bank, Sophia.

Kristensen, Thorkil. 1958. "State Intervention and Economic Freedom." In *Scandinavian Democracy: Development of Democratic Thought and Institutions in Denmark, Norway and Sweden*, edited by Joseph A. Lauwerys, 192–219. Copenhagen: Danish Institute.

Kuhnle, Stein. 1978. "The Beginnings of the Nordic Welfare States: Similarities and Differences." *Acta Sociologica* 21, supplement: 9–35.

Kuruç, Bilsay. 2011. *Mustafa Kemal Döneminde Ekonomi: Büyük Devletler ve Türkiye*. İstanbul: İstanbul Bilgi Üniversitesi Yayınları.
Kuyucak, Hazım A. 1939. "Memorandum on Exchange Control in Turkey." Paper submitted to the 12th Session of the International Studies Conference, Bergen, April.
Lake, David A. 1988. *Power, Protection, and Free Trade: International Sources of U.S. Commercial Strategy, 1887–1939*. Ithaca: Cornell University Press.
Lake, David A. 1999. *Entangling Relations: American Foreign Policy in Its Century*. Princeton: Princeton University Press.
Lampe, John R. 1986. *The Bulgarian Economy in the Twentieth Century*. New York: St. Martin's.
Lampe, John R., and Marvin R. Jackson. 1982. *Balkan Economic History, 1550–1950: From Imperial Borderlands to Developing Nations*. Bloomington: Indiana University Press.
Landes, David S. 1969. *The Unbound Prometheus: Technological Change and Industrial Development in Western Europe from 1750 to the Present*. Cambridge: At the University Press.
Larsen, Hans K. 2010. "Danish Exchange Rate Policy and the Trades: The Interwar Experience." In *Managing Crises and De-globalisation: Nordic Foreign Trade and Exchange, 1919–39*, edited by Sven-Olof Olsson, 82–100. London: Routledge.
Larsson, Mats. 1991. "State, Banks and Industry in Sweden, with Some Reference to the Scandinavian Countries." In *The Role of Banks in the Interwar Economy*, edited by Harold James, Håkan Lindgren, and Alice Teichova, 80–103. Cambridge: Cambridge University Press.
League of Nations. 1942. *Commercial Policy in the Interwar Period*. Geneva: League of Nations.
Letwin, William. 1989. "American Economic Policy, 1865–1939." In *The Cambridge Economic History of Europe*, vol. 8, *The Industrial Economies: The Development of Economic and Social Policies*, edited by Peter Mathias and Sidney Pollard, 641–90. Cambridge: Cambridge University Press.
Lewis, W. Arthur. 1949. *Economic Survey, 1919–1939*. London: George Allen and Unwin.
Lindström, Ulf. 1985. *Fascism in Scandinavia, 1920–1940*. Stockholm: Almqvist and Wiksell International.
Lindvall, Johannes. 2012. "Politics and Policies in Two Economic Crises: The Nordic Countries." In *Coping with Crisis: Government Reactions to the Great Recession*, edited by Nancy Bermeo and Jonas Pontusson, 233–60. New York: Russell Sage Foundation.
Louis, L. J., and Ian Turner, eds. 1968. *The Depression of the 1930s*. Melbourne: Cassell Australia.

Lundberg, Erik. [1953] 1957. *Business Cycles and Economic Policy.* Translated from the Swedish by J. Potter. London: George Allen and Unwin.

MacKinnon, Mary. 1990. "Relief Not Insurance: Canadian Unemployment Relief in the 1930s." *Explorations in Economic History* 27, no. 1: 46–83. https://doi.org/10.1016/0014-4983(90)90004-I.

Mackintosh, William A. [1939] 1964. *The Economic Background of Dominion–Provincial Relations.* Reprint. Toronto: McClelland and Stewart.

Maier, Charles S. 1987. *In Search of Stability: Explorations in Historical Political Economy.* Cambridge: Cambridge University Press.

Marcus, Edward. 1954. *Canada and the International Business Cycle, 1927–1939.* New York: Bookman.

Marcus, Nathan. 2018. *Austrian Reconstruction and the Collapse of Global Finance, 1921–1931.* Cambridge, MA: Harvard University Press.

Marjolin, Robert. 1938. "Reflections on the Blum Experiment." *Economica,* new series 5, no. 18: 177–91. https://doi.org/10.2307/2549020.

Mazower, Mark. 1991. *Greece and the Inter-War Economic Crisis.* Oxford: Clarendon Press.

McDiarmid, Orville J. 1946. *Commercial Policy in the Canadian Economy.* Cambridge, MA: Harvard University Press.

McDonald, Judith A., Anthony Patrick O'Brien, and Colleen M. Callahan. 1997. "Trade Wars: Canada's Reaction to the Smoot–Hawley Tariff." *Journal of Economic History* 57, no. 4: 802–26. https://doi.org/10.1017/S0022050700019549.

Middleton, Roger. 1985. *Towards the Managed Economy: Keynes, the Treasury and the Fiscal Policy Debate of the 1930s.* London: Methuen.

Middleton, Roger. 1998. *Charlatans or Saviours? Economists and the British Economy from Marshall to Meade.* Cheltenham: Edward Elgar.

Middleton, Roger. 2013. "Can Contractionary Fiscal Policy Be Expansionary? Consolidation, Sustainability, and Fiscal Policy Impact in Britain in the 1930s." In *The Great Depression of the 1930s: Lessons for Today,* edited by Nicholas Crafts and Peter Fearon, 212–57. Oxford: Oxford University Press.

Miller, James W. 2003. "Engelbert Dollfuss and Austrian Agriculture." In *The Dollfuss/Schuschnigg Era in Austria: A Reassessment,* edited by Günter Bischof, Anton Pelinka, and Alexander Lassner, 122–42. London and New York: Routledge.

Millmow, Alex. 2010. *The Power of Economic Ideas: The Origins of Keynesian Macroeconomic Management in Interwar Australia, 1929–39.* Canberra: ANU E Press.

Milward, Alan S. 1976. "Fascism and the Economy." In *Fascism, a Reader's Guide: Analyses, Interpretations, Bibliography,* edited by Walter Z. Laqueur, 379–412. Berkeley: University of California Press.

Mitrany, David. 1951. *Marx against the Peasant: A Study in Social Dogmatism.* Chapel Hill: University of North Carolina Press.
Moggridge, Donald E. 1989. "The Gold Standard and National Financial Policies, 1919–39." In *The Cambridge Economic History of Europe,* vol. 8, *The Industrial Economies: The Development of Economic and Social Policies,* edited by Peter Mathias and Sidney Pollard, 250–314. Cambridge: Cambridge University Press.
Montgomery, G. Arthur. 1938. *How Sweden Overcame the Depression, 1930–1933.* Translated from the Swedish by Leonard B. Eyre. Stockholm: Alb. Bonniers Boktryckeri.
Morell, Mats. 2010. "Trade Crisis and Regulation of the Farm Sector: Sweden in the Interwar Years." In *Managing Crises and De-globalisation: Nordic Foreign Trade and Exchange, 1919–39,* edited by Sven-Olof Olsson, 137–57. London: Routledge.
Murphy, John. 2010. "Path Dependence and the Stagnation of Australian Social Policy Between the Wars." *Journal of Policy History* 22, no. 4: 450–73. https://doi.org/10.1017/S0898030610000229.
Möller, Gustav. 1938. "The Unemployment Policy." *Annals of the American Academy of Political and Social Science* 197, no. 1: 47–71. https://doi.org/10.1177/000271623819700107.
Nanto, Dick K., and Shinji Takagi. 1985. "Korekiyo Takahashi and Japan's Recovery from the Great Depression." *American Economic Review* 75, no. 2: 369–74.
Nenovsky, Nikolay. 2015. "The Soviets Monetary Experience (1917–1924) through the Perspective of the Discussion on Unity and Diversity of Money." MPRA Paper No. 79864. https://mpra.ub.uni-muenchen.de/79864/3/MPRA_paper_79864.pdf (accessed 30 June 2021).
Noble, S. R. 1938. "The Monetary Experience of Canada during the Depression." *Canadian Banker* 45, no. 3: 269–77.
Nove, Alec. [1969] 1992. *An Economic History of the USSR 1917–1991.* 3rd ed. London: Penguin.
O'Brien, Anthony P., and Judith A. McDonald. 2009. "Retreat from Protectionism: R. B. Bennett and the Movement to Freer Trade in Canada, 1930–1935." *Journal of Policy History* 21, no. 4: 331–65. https://doi.org/10.1017/S0898030609990121.
Olsen, Gregg M. 1992. *The Struggle for Economic Democracy in Sweden.* Aldershot: Avebury.
Olsson, Carl-Axel. 1968. "Swedish Agriculture during the Interwar Years." *Economy and History* 11, no. 1: 67–107. https://doi.org/10.1080/00708852.1968.10418874.
Olsson, Sven-Olof. 2010. "Nordic Trade Cooperation in the 1930s." In *Managing Crises and De-globalisation: Nordic Foreign Trade and Exchange, 1919–39,* edited by Sven-Olof Olsson, 17–33. London: Routledge.

Olsson, Ulf. 1991. "Comparing the Interwar Banking History of Five Small Countries in North-West Europe." In *The Role of Banks in the Interwar Economy*, edited by Harold James, Håkan Lindgren, and Alice Teichova, 26–34. Cambridge: Cambridge University Press.
Overy, R. J. 1975. "Cars, Roads, and Economic Recovery in Germany, 1932–8." *Economic History Review*, 2nd series 28, no. 3: 466–83. https://doi.org/10.2307/2593594.
Overy, R. J. 1982. *The Nazi Economic Recovery, 1932–1938*. London: Macmillan.
Ovesen, Thorkild. 1958. "Swedish Agricultural Policy and Agricultural Production from 1930 to 1940." *Economy and History* 1, no. 1: 43–64. https://doi.org/10.1080/00708852.1958.10418864.
Owen, Roger, and Şevket Pamuk. 1999. *A History of Middle East Economies in the Twentieth Century*. Cambridge, MA: Harvard University Press.
Oye, Kenneth A. 1992. *Economic Discrimination and Political Exchange: World Political Economy in the 1930s and 1980s*. Princeton: Princeton University Press.
Pamuk, Şevket. 2000. "Intervention during the Great Depression: Another Look at Turkish Experience." In *The Mediterranean Response to Globalization before 1950*, edited by Şevket Pamuk and Jeffrey G. Williamson, 321–39. London: Routledge.
Pamuk, Şevket. 2014. *Türkiye'nin 200 Yıllık İktisadi Tarihi: Büyüme, Kurumlar ve Bölüşüm*. İstanbul: Türkiye İş Bankası Kültür Yayınları.
Paris Peace Conference. 1919. "Treaty of Peace with Germany (Treaty of Versailles)." June 28, 1919. https://www.census.gov/history/pdf/treaty_of_versailles-112018.pdf (accessed 6 March 2022).
Perry, Harvey J. 1955. *Taxes, Tariffs, and Subsidies: A History of Canadian Fiscal Development*, vol. 1. Toronto: University of Toronto Press.
Plumptre, A. F. W. 1940. *Central Banking in the British Dominions*. Toronto: University of Toronto Press.
Polanyi, Karl. 1944. *The Great Transformation: The Political and Economic Origins of Our Time*. Boston: Beacon.
Pollard, John. 1998. *The Fascist Experience in Italy*. London and New York: Routledge.
Pollard, Sidney, and Colin Holmes, eds. 1973. *Documents of European Economic History*, vol. 3, *The End of the Old Europe, 1914–1939*. London: Edward Arnold.
Pomfret, Richard. 1981. *The Economic Development of Canada*. Toronto: Methuen.
Quigley, Neil C. 1992. "Monetary Policy and the New Zealand System: An Historical Perspective." Reserve Bank of New Zealand Discussion Paper No. G92/1, Wellington. https://silo.tips/download/monetary-policy-and-the-an-historical-perspective (accessed 14 June 2021).
Ránki, György. 1983. *Economy and Foreign Policy: The Struggle of the Great Powers for Hegemony in the Danube Valley, 1919–1939*. New York: Columbia University Press.

Ránki, György. 1985. "Problems of Southern European Economic Development (1918–38)." In *Semiperipheral Development: The Politics of Southern Europe in the Twentieth Century*, edited by Giovanni Arrighi, 55–85. Beverly Hills: Sage.

Ránki, György, and Jerzy Tomaszewski. 1986. "The Role of the State in Industry, Banking and Trade." In *The Economic History of Eastern Europe, 1919–1975*, vol. 2, *Interwar Policy, the War and Reconstruction*, edited by Michael C. Kaser and E. A. Radice, 3–48. Oxford: Clarendon.

RBNZ (Reserve Bank of New Zealand). 2007. *The Reserve Bank and New Zealand's Economic History*. https://www.rbnz.govt.nz/research-and-publications/fact-sheets-and-guides/factsheet-the-reserve-bank-and-nzs-economic-history (accessed 14 June 2021).

RCDPR (Royal Commission on Dominion–Provincial Relations). 1940a. *Report*, book 1, *Canada: 1867–1939*. Ottawa: Queen's Printer.

Ricossa, Sergio. 1976. "Italy, 1920–1970." In *The Fontana Economic History of Europe*, vol. 6, *Contemporary Economies*, part 2, edited by Carlo M. Cipolla, 266–322. Glasgow: Fontana.

RIIA (Royal Institute of International Affairs). 1951. *The Scandinavian States and Finland: A Political and Economic Survey*. London: RIIA.

Rimlinger, G. V. 1989. "Labour and the State on the Continent, 1800–1939." *The Cambridge Economic History of Europe*, vol. 8, *The Industrial Economies: The Development of Economic and Social Policies*, edited by Peter Mathias and Sidney Pollard, 549–606. Cambridge: Cambridge University Press.

Ritschl, Albrecht O. 2013. "Reparations, Deficits, and Debt Default: The Great Depression in Germany." In *The Great Depression of the 1930s: Lessons for Today*, edited by Nicholas Crafts and Peter Fearon, 110–39. Oxford: Oxford University Press.

Rooth, T. J. T. 1986. "Tariffs and Trade Bargaining: Anglo–Scandinavian Economic Relations in the 1930s." *Scandinavian Economic History Review and Economy and History* 34, no. 1: 54–71. https://doi.org/10.1080/03585522.1986.10408059.

Rothstein, Bo. 1990. "Marxism, Institutional Analysis, and Working-Class Power: The Swedish Case." *Politics and Society* 18, no. 3: 317–45. https://doi.org/10.1177/003232929001800302.

Rueschemeyer, Dietrich, Evelyne H. Stephens, and John D. Stephens, 1992. *Capitalist Development and Democracy*. Chicago: University of Chicago Press.

Safarian, A. E. [1959] 2009. *The Canadian Economy in the Great Depression*. 3rd ed. Montreal and Kingston: McGill-Queen's University Press.

Sallius, Per-Ove. 1961. "Swedish–American Treaty Policy, 1920–1935." *Economy and History* 4, no. 1: 65–89. https://doi.org/10.1080/00708852.1961.10418983.

Salmon, Patrick. 2003. "Paternalism or Partnership? Finance and Trade in Anglo-Danish Relations in the 1930s." In *Britain and Denmark: Political, Economic and Cultural Relations in the 19th and 20th Centuries*, edited by Jørgen Sevaldsen, Bo Bjørke, and Claus Bjørn, 231–49. Copenhagen: Museum Tusculanum Press.

Schacht, Hjalmar H. G. 1956. *Confessions of "The Old Wizard": The Autobiography of Hjalmar Horace Greeley Schacht*. Translated from the German by Diana Pyke. Boston: Houghton Mifflin.

Schedvin, C. B. 1970. *Australia and the Great Depression: A Study of Economic Development and Policy in the 1920s and 1930s*. Sydney: Sydney University Press.

Schwarz, L. D. 1993. "Searching for Recovery: Unbalanced Budgets, Deflation and Rearmament in France during the 1930s." In *Capitalism in Crisis: International Responses to the Great Depression*, edited by W. Redvers Garside, 96–113. London: Pinter.

Senft, Gerhard. 2003. "Economic Development and Economic Policies in the *Ständestaat* Era." In *The Dollfuss/Schuschnigg Era in Austria: A Reassessment*, edited by Günter Bischof, Anton Pelinka, and Alexander Lassner, 32–55. London and New York: Routledge.

Silier, Oya. 1981. *Türkiye'de Tarımsal Yapının Gelişimi (1923–1938)*. İstanbul: Boğaziçi Üniversitesi Yayınları.

Silverman, Dan P. 1988. "National Socialist Economics: The *Wirtschaftswunder* Reconsidered." In *Interwar Unemployment in International Perspective*, edited by Barry J. Eichengreen and Tim J. Hatton, 185–220. Dordrecht: Kluwer.

Simpson, Tony. 1990. *The Slump; The 1930s Depression: Its Origins and Aftermath*. Auckland: Penguin Books.

Singleton, Fred, and Bernard Carter. 1982. *The Economy of Yugoslavia*. London: Croom Helm.

Singleton, John. 2003. "New Zealand in the Depression: Devaluation without a Balance of Payments Crisis." In *The World Economy and National Economies in the Interwar Slump*, edited by Theo Balderston, 172–90. Basingstoke: Palgrave Macmillan.

Smith, Malcolm. 1998. *Democracy in a Depression: Britain in the 1920s and 1930s*. Cardiff: University of Wales Press.

Sobel, Andrew C. 1994. *Domestic Choices, International Markets: Dismantling National Barriers and Liberalizing Securities Markets*. Ann Arbour: University of Michigan Press.

Solomou, Solomos. 1996. *Themes in Macroeconomic History: The UK Economy, 1919–1939*. Cambridge: Cambridge University Press.

Stacey, C. P., ed. 1972. *Historical Documents of Canada*, vol. 5, *The Arts of War and Peace, 1914–1945*. Toronto: Macmillan.

Stein, Herbert. [1969] 1990. *The Fiscal Revolution in America*. 2nd ed. Washington, D.C.: American Enterprise Institute.

Stephens, John D. 1989. "Democratic Transition and Breakdown in Western Europe, 1870–1939: A Test of the Moore Thesis." *American Journal of Sociology* 94, no. 5: 1019–77. https://doi.org/10.1086/229111.
Straumann, Tobias. 2010. *Fixed Ideas of Money: Small States and Exchange Rate Regimes in Twentieth-Century Europe*. New York: Cambridge University Press.
Struthers, James. 1983. *No Fault of Their Own: Unemployment and the Canadian Welfare State, 1914–1941*. Toronto: University of Toronto Press.
Söderpalm, Sven A. [1973] 1975. "The Crisis Agreement and the Social Democratic Road to Power." In *Sweden's Development from Poverty to Affluence, 1750–1970*, edited by Steven Koblik and translated from the Swedish by Joanne Johnson, 258–78. Minneapolis: University of Minnesota Press.
Teichova, Alice. 1989. "East-Central and South-East Europe, 1919–39." In *The Cambridge Economic History of Europe*, vol. 8, *The Industrial Economies: The Development of Economic and Social Policies*, edited by Peter Mathias and Sidney Pollard, 887–983. Cambridge: Cambridge University Press.
Tekeli, İlhan, and Selim İlkin. 1977. *1929 Dünya Buhranında Türkiye'nin İktisadi Politika Arayışları*. Ankara: ODTÜ Yayınları.
Tekeli, İlhan, and Selim İlkin. 1981. *Para ve Kredi Sisteminin Oluşumunda Bir Aşama: Türkiye Cumhuriyet Merkez Bankası*. Ankara: T.C. Merkez Bankası Yayını.
Tekeli, İlhan, and Selim İlkin. 1982. *Uygulamaya Geçerken Türkiye'de Devletçiliğin Oluşumu*. Ankara: ODTÜ Yayınları.
Temin, Peter. 1989. *Lessons from the Great Depression: The Lionel Robbins Lectures for 1989*. Cambridge, MA: MIT Press.
Temin, Peter. 1991. "Soviet and Nazi Economic Planning in the 1930s." *Economic History Review* 44, no. 4: 573–93. https://doi.org/10.1111/j.1468-0289.1991.tb01281.x.
Temin, Peter, and David Vines. 2013. *The Leaderless Economy: Why the World Economic System Fell Apart and How to Fix It*. Princeton: Princeton University Press.
Tezel, Yahya S. [1982] 1986. *Cumhuriyet Döneminin İktisadi Tarihi (1923–1950)*. 2nd ed. Ankara: Yurt Yayınları.
Therborn, Göran. 1977. "The Rule of Capital and the Rise of Democracy." *New Left Review*, first series, no. 103: 3–41.
Thomas, Brinley. 1936. *Monetary Policy and Crises: A Study of Swedish Experience*. London: George Routledge.
Thornburg, Max W., Graham Spry, and George Soule. 1949. *Turkey: An Economic Appraisal*. New York: Twentieth Century Fund.
Toniolo, Gianni, and Francesco Piva. 1988. "Unemployment in the 1930s: The Case of Italy." In *Interwar Unemployment in International Perspective*, edited by Barry J. Eichengreen and Tim J. Hatton, 221–45. Dordrecht: Kluwer.

Topp, Niels-Henrik. 1988. "Fiscal Policy in Denmark 1930–1945." *European Economic Review* 32, nos. 2–3: 512–8.

Topp, Niels-Henrik. 2008. "Unemployment and Economic Policy in Denmark in the 1930s." *Scandinavian Economic History Review* 56, no. 1: 71–90. https://doi.org/10.1080/03585520801948534.

Tracy, Michael. 1972. "Agriculture in the Great Depression: World Market Developments and European Protectionism." In *The Great Depression Revisited: Essays on the Economics of the Thirties*, edited by Herman van der Wee, 91–119. The Hague: Martinus Nijhoff.

USBC (US Bureau of the Census). 1965. *The Statistical History of the United States from Colonial Times to the Present*. Stamford: Fairfield.

van Roon, Ger. 1989. *Small States in Years of Depression: The Oslo Alliance, 1930–1940*. Assen: Van Gorcum.

Værholm, Monica. 2010. "Why Did Norwegian Trade Policy Become More Active in the Interwar Period?" In *Managing Crises and De-globalisation: Nordic Foreign Trade and Exchange, 1919–39*, edited by Sven-Olof Olsson, 34–51. London: Routledge.

Villa, Pierre. 2003. "France in the Depression of the Early 1930s." In *The World Economy and National Economies in the Interwar Slump*, edited by Theo Balderston, 58–87. Basingstoke: Palgrave Macmillan.

Welk, William G. 1938. *Fascist Economic Policy: An Analysis of Italy's Economic Experiment*. Cambridge, MA: Harvard University Press.

Wessels, Jens-Wilhelm. 2007. *Economic Policy and Microeconomic Performance in Inter-War Europe: The Case of Austria, 1918–1938*. Stuttgart: Franz Steiner Verlag.

Wigforss, Ernst. 1938. "The Financial Policy during Depression and Boom." *Annals of the American Academy of Political and Social Science* 197, no. 1: 25–39. https://doi.org/10.1177/000271623819700105.

Williams, H. T., ed. 1960. *Principles for British Agricultural Policy*. London: Oxford University Press.

Winch, Donald. 1969. *Economics and Policy: A Historical Study*. London: Hodder and Stoughton.

Wolf, Nikolaus. 2013. "Europe's Great Depression: Coordination Failure after the First World War." In *The Great Depression of the 1930s: Lessons for Today*, edited by Nicholas Crafts and Peter Fearon, 74–109. Oxford: Oxford University Press.

Yamamura, Kozo. 1972. "Then Came the Great Depression: Japan's Interwar Years." In *The Great Depression Revisited: Essays on the Economics of the Thirties*, edited by Herman van der Wee, 182–211. The Hague: Martinus Nijhoff.

Yasuba, Yazukichi. 1988. "The Japanese Economy and Economic Policy in the 1930s." In *Recovery from the Depression: Australia and the World Economy in the 1930s*, edited by Robert G. Gregory and Noel G. Butlin, 135–47. Cambridge: Cambridge University Press.

Zamagni, Vera. 1993. *The Economic History of Italy, 1860–1990*. Oxford: Clarendon Press.
Ziegler, Dieter. 2013. "'A Regulated Market Economy': New Perspectives on the Nature of the Economic Order of the Third Reich, 1933–1939." In *Business in the Age of Extremes: Essays in Modern German and Austrian Economic History*, edited by Hartmut Berghoff, Jürgen Kocka, and Dieter Ziegler, 139–52. Cambridge: Cambridge University Press.
Øksendal, Lars F. 2010. "Re-examining Norwegian Monetary Policy in the 1930s." In *Managing Crises and De-globalisation: Nordic Foreign Trade and Exchange, 1919–39*, edited by Sven-Olof Olsson, 66–81. London: Routledge.

CHAPTER 3

Protectionism: A Safe Haven or Missed Opportunity?

The United Kingdom, Australia, and Canada were among the most consistent followers of protectionism while France dented it only briefly and New Zealand diverged from its British counterparts by adopting eclectic policies from 1935 on. The first group converged in policy despite many things that separated them in other respects, including international status, crisis experience, sectoral and class profile, state organization, and bureaucratic capacity. The United Kingdom was not just a large state but also the "mother country" for Australia and Canada as self-governing Dominions. The three states differed in crisis experience as well, with the United Kingdom having the mildest economic downturn, Canada the sharpest, and Australia an in-between (Safarian [1959] 2009, 98; Schedvin 1970, 44). While all three economies were open/trade-dependent, they each featured a different sectoral and class profile. In contrast to a small agricultural sector (and a large service sector) in the United Kingdom as the first industrialized nation, the Australian and Canadian economies still had sizable agrarian/pastoral sectors which, nevertheless, diverged in class

---

An earlier version of parts of this chapter was published in "Class, politics, and economic policy at a critical juncture: Canada and the Anglo-American 'family of nations' in the Great Depression of the 1930s," Adnan Türegün, Studies in Political Economy, copyright © 2021 Studies in Political Economy, reprinted by permission of Taylor & Francis Ltd, http://www.tandfonline.com on behalf of Studies in Political Economy.

© The Author(s), under exclusive license to Springer Nature Switzerland AG 2022
A. Türegün, *Policy Responses to the Interwar Economic Crisis*, https://doi.org/10.1007/978-3-030-96953-0_3

composition; capitalist class divisions were sharper in the Australian sector whereas independent family farming was dominant in Canada. Moreover, compared with its UK and Australian counterparts, the Canadian labour movement was extremely weak. The three cases also diverged in state organization and bureaucratic capacity. The federal states of Australia and Canada were much weaker than the UK unitary state in bureaucratic capacity.

The underlying cause of the protectionist convergence between the United Kingdom, Australia, and Canada was their rulers' pro-business idea of the economy. Regardless of their formal titles and claims, the ruling parties in all three cases privileged business interests, accommodated agrarian interests as a secondary concern, and largely excluded organized labour from policy consideration. In the United Kingdom, this ideational disposition was carried over from the Labour government to the Conservative-dominated "National" governments. The Australian Labor government handed over a similar disposition to its "bourgeois" successors. In Canada, where there was no comparable labour movement, government changed hands from the Liberals to the Conservatives and back to the former, but a pro-business hierarchy of interests kept defining economic policy. This is the story in a nutshell. Of course, a more complex picture will emerge as I dig into more detail below.

France and New Zealand, too, stuck with protectionism as long as pro-business and labour-excluding parties ruled. However, the conservative cycle was broken in both cases (briefly in France and on an enduring basis in New Zealand) in the mid-1930s. This is where they come in handy for identifying what was missing in the three other cases. Amounting to a coalition of labour and agrarians, the Popular Front government of the Socialist, Communist, and left Radical parties had a different idea of the economy and the crisis that underlaid its proto-Fordist Blum experiment. That the experiment was ended abruptly attested to the need for political will, skill, and flexibility to keep the coalition together and expand it to employers, which Popular Front parties were not able to. Alternatively, the New Zealand Labour Party built an agrarian–labour coalition in its ranks, was not encumbered by the economic dogmatism of its UK and Australian counterparts, and thus took daring initiatives that were domestically reminiscent of proto-Fordism within the confines of a pastoral economy.

This chapter first takes up the cases of the United Kingdom, Australia, and Canada as the exemplars of protectionism. In addition to, and in connection with, the main plot (ideational disposition and political strategies of ruling parties and leaders), I pay attention to the sectoral and class profile of each economy, the configuration of interests arising from that profile, and formal constitutional arrangements, including electoral rules. I do the same, if in less detail, for the French and New Zealand cases representing attempts to go beyond protectionism. Table 3.1 provides a road map for the chapter.

More Than a British Connection

The Ottawa Agreements of 1932 between the United Kingdom and the Dominions constituted the high tide of British imperial protectionism consisting of a low industrial and agricultural tariff zone, which was the Empire, and a high tariff zone, which was the outside world. Ottawa was the culmination of state-level measures taken since the onset of the world economic crisis. Although the crisis was instrumental in unleashing the imperialist drive, the latter had its ideational antecedents. The Tariff Reform Movement of 1903, launched by Joseph Chamberlain within the Conservative–Unionist camp, championed exactly the type of trade arrangements reached in Ottawa (Koning 1994, 139–41). The movement died down in the same decade and the idea was put on the back burner only to be brought out by the Conservatives from time to time, most decisively in the early 1930s, to solve the United Kingdom's industrial and agricultural problems (Williamson 2003, 4–7). The most enthusiastic supporter of the idea in the Dominions was Richard B. Bennett, Conservative prime minister of Canada, who actively pushed it with help from Canadian manufacturers in the lead-up to and during the Imperial Economic Conference held in Ottawa in the summer of 1932 (Clark 1939, 80–103; Drummond 1972, 91, 1974, 191–194, 201).

A preferential trading zone was the realization of a long-held idea among Conservative circles in the increasingly defensive United Kingdom and in some Dominions. It was not a uniquely British idea as similar ideas undergirded other international trading blocs during the crisis. Nor was imperial protectionism the only idea that found its way into UK or Dominion economic policy. As will be seen below, all three country responses unfolded against an ideational background informing governing party strategies.

Table 3.1 Points of convergence and divergence in the protectionist camp

Country group	Key determinants			Policy outcome
	Ruling party approach to sectoral and class interests	Institutional mediators	Structural limits to proto-Fordism	
Exemplary cases				
United Kingdom	Pro-business; agrarian-accommodationist; labour-exclusionary	Majoritarian electoral system; commercial branch banking	Small agricultural sector	Protectionist
Australia	Pro-business; agrarian-accommodationist; labour-exclusionary	Majoritarian electoral system;[a] constitutional division of federal–state powers; commercial branch banking	Weak independent farming class	Protectionist
Canada	Pro-business; agrarian-accommodationist; labour-exclusionary	Majoritarian electoral system; constitutional division of federal–provincial powers; commercial branch banking	n/a	Protectionist
Mixed cases				
France		Majoritarian electoral system;[b] commercial branch banking	n/a	
Pre- and post-1936–1937	Pro-business; agrarian-accommodationist; labour-exclusionary			Protectionist
1936–1937	Coalitional; all-inclusive (pro-labour; agrarian- and business-inclusive)			Proto-Fordist
New Zealand		Majoritarian electoral system; commercial branch banking	Pastoral economy	

(*continued*)

Table 3.1 (continued)

Country group	Key determinants			Policy outcome
	Ruling party approach to sectoral and class interests	Institutional mediators	Structural limits to proto-Fordism	
Pre-1935	Pro-business; agrarian-accommodationist; labour-exclusionary			Protectionist
Post-1935	Coalitional, all-inclusive (pro-labour; agrarian- and business-inclusive)			Mixed

Notes: [a]Preferential voting; [b]Two-step voting

United Kingdom

The UK response under a Labour government from 1929 to 1931 was anachronistic since it maintained all the key pieces of classical liberalism that was on its way out. One exception to this was the maintenance and even expansion of the country's relatively generous unemployment and other insurance services (McKibbin 1975, 112–4). In fact, a proposed cut to unemployment insurance benefits caused turmoil within the Labour Party and instigated the collapse of the government, forcing Prime Minister Ramsay MacDonald and Chancellor of the Exchequer Philip Snowden to leave the party with their orthodox agenda and join forces with the Conservatives in the summer of 1931 (Tanner 2003, 47–9). "It was ironic that the one party whose ultimate goal was the abolition of capitalism by parliamentary means should be in office during capitalism's greatest economic crisis[,]" quipped economic historian Donald Winch (1969, 117): "It was more ironic that the Labour Government should break up as a result of internal dissension over the appropriate methods of saving capitalism."

Several situational factors can be summoned to justify the Labour government's astonishingly orthodox response to the crisis. First, measured by national product and income, the UK economic downturn was one of the mildest in the industrialized world.[1] Nor did the banking system suffer any failure (Born [1977] 1983, 270; Kitson 2003, 94; Mackenzie [1932]

1935, 258–9). Although industry fared relatively poorly with unemployment shooting up to 22% in 1932 (Feinstein 1972, T128), its pressing problems were largely confined to traditional and regionally concentrated industries such as coal mining, steel, ship building, and cotton textiles (Greaves 2000, 123–5; Smith 1998, 41, 64). Second, the pre-existence of a comprehensive unemployment insurance scheme might have created a "path dependency" for the Labour government, which worked to improve the scheme rather than considering other options such as public works in its brief tenure, just as its predecessors' focus was on insurance rather than work creation in the 1920s (Harris 1988, 152–3; McKibbin 1975, 106). Third, as suggested by some (see, e.g., McKibbin 1975, 98; Winch 1989, 118–24), the Labour Party had the "misfortune" of governing at the outbreak of the crisis. That the Australian Labor and German Social Democratic parties faced the same fate lends credence to this reasoning. Fourth, one might add that the UK party was governing only as a minority.

However plausible they may be, these justifications serve to disguise the ideational disposition and political choices of the Labour Party leadership. With a deterministic notion of socialism which would "naturally" follow the self-destruction of capitalism, Labour leaders such as MacDonald and Snowden chose not to take countercyclical action and, instead, threw their support behind the main planks of classical liberalism, including the gold standard, free trade, and macroeconomic orthodoxy (Kavanagh 1973, 180–2; Skidelsky 1967, 27–50, 76–88). By adopting these policies, the Labour government succumbed to the hegemonic coalition of the City representing a highly internationalized financial sector, the Bank of England which privileged external stability over domestic recovery, and the Treasury with its self-advertised orthodox doctrine insisting on the economic futility of government borrowing.

Although Labour was in minority, it had the option of making a coalition with the Liberals, its traditional "Lib–Lab" partners in the transition to democracy (Tanner 2003, 41–2). That it chose not to do so was further proof of an unimaginative mindset at the helm. What made this choice particularly critical was that the Liberals, who had introduced unemployment insurance and other social protection schemes earlier in the century, became a truly reformist party on the domestic front in the 1920s under Lloyd George (Bentley 2003, 25–7). Influenced by Keynes's still-evolving ideas centred on demand management (Winch 1969, 104–9), the Liberal Party outlined a countercyclical platform in its 1928 "Yellow Book," *Britain's Industrial Future*, which Lloyd George would elaborate on in his

1929 booklet titled *We Can Conquer Unemployment* (Clarke 1988, 75–102; Kavanagh 1973, 178–80; Skidelsky 1967, 51–75).[2] The party contested the critical election of 1929 on this platform.

In the election, in which Labour received plurality of the House of Commons seats (47% versus 42% for the Conservatives) but not the votes (37% versus 38% for the Conservatives), the Liberals garnered nearly a quarter (24%) of the votes. Yet their share of the seats was only 10% (Flora et al. 1983, 151, 188). The majoritarian (first-past-the-post) electoral system based on single member constituencies severely punished them especially since their popular support was not geographically concentrated. They still won enough seats to form a possible majority "Lib–Lab" coalition, but not enough to force either Labour or the Conservatives into a demand stimulus coalition. Under proportional representation, the cards would have been shuffled differently. However, there is no way of knowing if or how much parties' ideational disposition and political strategies would have changed. One thing was certain though: With its systemic discrimination against third parties, majoritarian representation hugely contributed to the virtual demise of the Liberals in the mid-1930s.

While the absence of a coalition between Labour and the Liberals was largely by choice, there was no structural base for an agrarian–labour alliance in any form or shape. The UK economy was the first to industrialize, developed a uniquely large service sector, and, with the repeal of the Corn Laws in 1846, relied increasingly on cheap agricultural imports, thus accelerating the relative contraction of domestic agriculture. By the early twentieth century, agriculture had shrunk to an internationally unique size: It accounted for a mere 4% of the national income in 1924 (Dewey 2003, 271) and employed just over 6% of the labour force in 1931 (Tcherkinsky 1939, 13). Consequently, UK agriculture, in which excessively small holdings and large holdings were the dominant pattern (Tcherkinsky 1939, 11–4), did not carry sufficient weight to attract or force labour into an alliance. The Labour Party was in a quandary in its approach to agriculture (Griffiths 2007; see also Dewey 2003, 277–80). On one hand, with its primary base being urban and industrial, it had to defend cheap foodstuffs and thus free trade. On the other hand, to get over the electoral hump for a majority government, it continuously, if not so successfully, strategized in the interwar period to win over rural constituencies—small farmers and agricultural labourers in particular.

The change which the Conservatives effected against this background was no less than paradigmatic. Creating a semblance of coalition with

Labour and Liberal defectors under the rubric of "National" government (Williamson 2003, 11–9), they left the gold standard for a managed currency, replaced generalized free trade with imperial protection, helped regional industries with various schemes (such as cartelization, reorganization, and relocation) and agriculture with marketing and price support, relaxed monetary policy for credit ease, but resolutely defended fiscal orthodoxy at least until the start of the armaments buildup in 1937. It is intriguing that the one party which was most attached to the status quo would oversee the protectionist shift in the UK response. The Conservative Party's choices during postwar reconstruction and the groups of interest it came to articulate during the crisis provide an insight into this puzzle.

The United Kingdom returned to the gold standard at prewar parity under a Conservative government in 1925 (Solomou 1996, 45). The deflationary effects of this decision were felt most strongly in industry, where unemployment registered well over 10% (the so-called intractable million) for the rest of the decade (Feinstein 1972, T128). Moreover, monetary deflation went hand in hand with fiscal expansion as the cost of postwar settlement, including increasing unemployment and other social insurance expenditures, and interest payments on public debt accumulated in wartime (Booth 1989, 37–8). Consequently, the central government ran budget deficits from 1924 on (Feinstein 1972, T31). Back at the helm on the heels of the European financial crisis in 1931, the Conservative Party found the immediate solution in a sort of reversal of the monetary deflation–fiscal expansion duo by abandoning the gold standard, devaluing the pound sterling, and lowering the interest rate, on one hand, and tightening the budget, on the other.[3] Later in the mid-1930s, when the economy had already rebounded, the government would tighten monetary policy but relax fiscal policy to restore social benefit levels.

The Conservative strategy involving the "real" economy was based on the external and internal protection of industry and agriculture. In addition to tariff (and nontariff) protection, each sector received domestic support in the form of marketing and price-fixing arrangements for agriculture, and cartelization and regional relocation for industry. Combined with cheap money, this Conservative package won over both sectors. Like employers, the Trades Union Congress (TUC) was content with tariff protection and monetary reflation (Kaiser 2000, 187–97). Not until after the economy bottomed out in 1932 did the craft union-dominated TUC take up the idea of demand stimulus and push for deficit-financed public works.[4] (A weakened Labour Party itself shifted its focus to microeconomic strategies, particularly planning [Ritschel 1997, 97–143].) As for the commercial-financial complex of City, it did experience a relative decline as a consequence of the crisis and the protectionist response, but its market linkages and relations with the two key public institutions (Bank of England and Treasury) remained unscathed (Ingham 1984, 189–91). For example, commercial branch banking dominated by the "Big Five," which traditionally eschewed investing in industry (Born [1977] 1983, 160–4, 234–6), endured the crisis without any failure.[5]

When measured against the pre-crisis policy set, the UK response can be considered daring and innovative (Middleton 1985, 1998). Indeed, as a nation whose practices had embodied the main principles of classical liberalism, the United Kingdom dropped them all at once except for fiscal orthodoxy. Even in fiscal policy, it proved flexible when spending was felt needed for social, if not economic, purposes. In this sense, the UK response was more innovative than its Australian and Canadian counterparts which, as will be seen shortly, unfolded against a more interventionist background. Compared to some of its democratic contemporaries such as the US New Deal and the Swedish experiment, however, the UK response turns out conservative mainly because of its industrial relations and fiscal outcomes. Many structural and institutional factors, including a couple that I highlighted, played a role in this conservatism. Yet, according to the analysis above, the ideational orientation and political choices of the ruling Labour and Conservative parties had the deciding role.

Australia

Swept to power just before the New York Stock Market Crash in October 1929, the Australian Labor Party (ALP) seemed to have been better positioned than its UK counterpart for a full tenure in office. Although it, too, faced a conservative and uncooperative upper chamber, it had a solid majority in the lower chamber (House of Representatives). Moreover, unlike the UK party, the ALP took part in state building and experienced governance for long spells since the turn of the century. Everything was pointing to another long spell of Labor governance. Yet, like the minority Labour government in the United Kingdom, the majority ALP government lasted just over two years, leaving behind a badly bruised and divided party. To its credit, the UK party was more consistent in applying the orthodox policy mix while resisting cuts to social spending. Operating in an export-dependent economy which relied heavily on one (UK) market,[6] the Australian party admittedly had no choice but to leave the gold standard and devalue the dollar. However, it did choose to deeply cut spending, including wages, salaries, and pensions. At the same time, it continued the protectionist tradition by raising the industrial tariffs and subsidizing primary producers.

Both parties' "labourist" political ideology, although shaped in different historical-institutional settings, produced a commonly conservative response at crunch time which was the Great Depression. They maintained a vague idea of socialization in the interwar period. The UK party's 1918 constitution included a clause adopting "common ownership of the means of production, distribution and exchange" and the ALP followed suit with a similar goal statement in 1921: "socialization of industry, production and exchange" (James and Markey 2006, 32). They thus distanced socialism to an unknown future and, instead, took it upon themselves to do the practical work of weathering the crisis with the least damage to prevailing interests and institutions. What made this response more disappointing for the ALP were its promising initiatives in the previous two decades.

The histories of the ALP and the Australian federation (Commonwealth) were intricately tied to each other. Taking shape in the colonies before the formation of the federation in 1901, the party helped define the Australian political economy, including early democratization,[7] either in alliance with the Liberal Protectionists or on its own.[8] In the process, it became the "party of initiative," forcing its "bourgeois" counterparts to react and regroup as "parties of resistance" (for the contrasting terminology, see Botterill and Fenna 2020; Rydon 1979, 69; also James and Markey 2006, 28). Thus, Labor support to the Liberal Protectionist government of 1903–1908 was instrumental in establishing the parameters of Australian economic and social policy or what Francis Castles (1988, 91–104) calls "politics of domestic defence." Before the decade came to a close, five durable policy pieces were in place: (a) tariff protection for nascent manufactures; (b) marketing and price support for primary products; (c) judicialized industrial dispute resolution and "living wage" determination via the Court of Conciliation and Arbitration; (d) the "White Australia Policy" that helped keep wages high; and (e) a proto-welfare state for the non-working population (Birch 1955, 205–37; Dyrenfurth and Bongiorno 2011, 41; Overacker 1952, 201; Schwartz 1989, 105–63). During its two significant spells of power before 1929 (1910–1913 and 1914–1917), the ALP remained within these parameters, strengthening particular pieces and introducing institutional innovation. After 1929, however, it presided over the fraying of the industrial arbitration and social protection systems under monetary and fiscal orthodoxy.

Stalled by an unimaginative leadership, the ALP failed to live up to its historical record despite growing pressure for countercyclical action from the broader labour movement. In early 1930, the Australian Council of Trade Unions proposed a national unemployment scheme, a national public works programme, establishment of "community settlements" for the unemployed, and nationalization of banking, in addition to further restriction of immigration and higher tariff levels. Later in 1930, the federal executive of the party urged a back-to-work campaign, cheap credit for industry, and an easing of the interest burden on domestic and external public debt. Moreover, under the charismatic leadership of J. T. Lang, the New South Wales wing of the ALP took state office the same year by campaigning on a radical recovery platform that included suspension of external debt payments, reduction of the interest rate on domestic debt to 3%, and establishment of a "goods standard" instead of the gold standard (for these proposals, see Louis and Turner 1968, 42–44, 64, 130–45; also Millmow 2010, 86–7; Overacker 1952, 145). Yet the party leadership did not or could not act on any of these proposals, including the federal executive's recommendations that had received parliamentary caucus support (Louis and Turner 1968, 59).

Labor Prime Minister James Scullin was a middle-of-the-roader between the right and left wings of the party. He went along with the orthodox prescription written by a Bank of England official, Otto Niemeyer, who was on an official visit in Australia in 1930 to report on the state of the Australian economy and public finances. Also receiving the stamp of the Commonwealth Bank, that prescription was accepted by the federal and state governments in the Melbourne Agreement of August 1930 (Dyrenfurth and Bongiorno 2011, 79; Schedvin 1970, 178–84). Between this agreement and its milder version to be actually implemented, the Premiers' Plan of June 1931 (Fisher 1934, 770; Schedvin 1970, 249), Labor would be weakened on its both wings. Deflationist leaders James Fenton and Joseph Lyons, who had been acting prime minister and acting treasurer, respectively, during Scullin's lengthy stay in the United Kingdom for an imperial conference, quit the party upon the latter's return in January 1931 over the reinstatement of Edward Theodore as deputy leader and treasurer, who had expansionary ideas to fight the crisis (Dyrenfurth and Bongiorno 2011, 79–82).[9] Fenton and Lyons joined forces with the opposition Nationalists to form the United Australia Party, which would win the next federal elections and govern for the rest of the decade under the leadership of Lyons. Theodore's expansionary plan was thwarted by the Commonwealth Bank and the politics of federal–state relations, thus clearing the way for macroeconomic orthodoxy and preparing the electoral defeat of Labor in December 1931.

As in the United Kingdom, an agrarian–labour alliance did not take place in Australia primarily for structural reasons. In the Australian case, however, it was not the size but the class composition of the rural sector that constituted a barrier to such an alignment. Unlike its Western European, North American, and New Zealand counterparts sustaining strong and independent farming classes, the Australian development experience generated a polarized class structure in the agrarian/pastoral sector. From the late nineteenth century on, the sector came to be dominated by capitalist pastoralism in which wool figured prominently (Brady 1939, 304, 1941, 219–24; Castles 1988, 110–12; Overacker 1952, 9, 13). Although independent mixed farming grew with the spread of wheat and other crops in the early twentieth century (Graham 1966, 10–1), capitalist relations of production continued to characterize a large part of the rural scene. This had far-reaching political consequences. From the outset, the ALP laid claim to the representation of both industrial and pastoral workers, thus embodying a cross-sectoral coalition of labour and, in the process, providing a model for the less unified "non-Labor" parties (Brady 1941, 224–5, 1958, 204–25; Castles 1988, 112–4; Ehrensaft and Armstrong 1981, 132; Overacker 1952, 197). Sharp class divisions in the rural sector cemented political divisions.

Emulating the political unity of the labour movement, the urban Liberal Protectionist and rural Free Trade/Anti-Socialist parties worked together before merging, in 1909, into the Commonwealth Liberal Party, which would be renamed as the Nationalist Party in 1917. Meanwhile, at the state level, a more radical, anti-Labor agrarian movement sprang up under Country parties across Australia, counterpoising "country-mindedness" against the domination of cities and demanding "all-round" protection instead of exclusively industrial tariffs (Graham 1966). A federal Country Party emerged out of state parties in 1919 and, giving in to industrial protection in return for primary-product marketing and price support, collaborated with the Nationalist/United Australia Party in formal and informal coalition governments throughout the interwar period (Brady 1958, 230; Ellis 1963, 62, 115; Graham 1966, 143–266; Overacker

1952, 220–39; Rydon 1979, 56; Wyatt 1974, 38–56). Unlike the North American and Western European agrarian parties representing independent farming interests, the Country Party was largely a product of capitalist pastoralism and pursued a fierce anti-labour politics along with such goals as creation of new states, decentralization, and protection of rural way of life.[10]

The post-Labor governments in the 1930s were thus based on a labour-excluding alliance of financial-industrial and land-owning interests, a typical configuration for protectionist responses to the crisis. The financial sector cemented this alliance. As in the United Kingdom, the sector was dominated by a small number of large commercial banks (locally known as trading banks) that operated on branch-banking principle, adopted a conservative credit outlook, and weathered the crisis unscathed (Cochrane 1980, 124–41; Louis and Turner 1968, 61–2, 67–70, 155–60; Plumptre 1940, 72–4; Wilson 1952). With strong backing from the Commonwealth Bank, they defended monetary and fiscal orthodoxy most ardently and, in so doing, proved more successful than their UK counterparts.

Australia's complex electoral rules facilitated alignments between the Nationalist/United Australia and Country parties. Under a modified majoritarian arrangement allowing preferential voting in the House of Representatives elections since 1919, voters could enter their first and second choices (Graham 1966, 129; Markey 2008, 71). This is how supporters of the two non-Labor parties exchanged their preferences and ensured comfortable House majorities in the 1920s and 1930s. It is true that the sheer size of the popular vote, 49%, for the ALP in the 1929 election rewarded it with 61% of the House seats (Mackie and Rose 1974, 13, 15). Yet the non-Labor parties retained their majority in the Senate for which there was no election that year and whose members were elected by proportional representation with equal seats for the states. A conservative Senate thus served as a check on the ALP's reform agenda—if and when it had one (Markey 2008, 71–2).

Constitutional arrangements were not on the side of strong national initiatives, either. The Commonwealth Constitution gave major powers to the states in key domestic policy areas such as commerce, industrial organization and relations, welfare provision, wages, and conditions of employment, leaving the federal government with residual powers (James and Markey 2006, 27; Markey 2008, 71). After Labor formed its first majority government in 1910, it held but lost a referendum for constitutional amendment to increase federal powers in some of these areas (Dyrenfurth and Bongiorno 2011, 52; Graham 1966, 76). Even a federal plan for compulsory wheat pooling proposed by the United Australia–Country coalition later in the 1930s was ruled unconstitutional on the same ground (Botterill 2012, 39). It was no coincidence that the establishment of the Australian Wheat Board required federal–state cooperation in the immediate post-World War II period (1948), just as the introduction of a federal unemployment insurance scheme took a wartime (1944) constitutional amendment making welfare provision a federal responsibility with the consent of the states.[11] The other side of the jurisdictional coin was that when New South Wales Premier Lang tried to act on his radical electoral platform, including suspension of loan payments, the governor of the state removed him from office in 1932 "on the grounds that he had caused state public servants to break federal law" (Dyrenfurth and Bongiorno 2011, 82).

As the Wheat Board and unemployment insurance legislation demonstrate, however, institutional obstacles are not insurmountable. It took political will and federal–state cooperation for the two pieces of legislation—as well as the required constitutional amendment—to be passed. The Great Depression was no less costly than World War II in its economic and social consequences. Yet Australian parties, ruling and opposition alike, did not view the former in terms of national urgency as their principal strategies were framed by orthodox ideas. The lack of imagination and boldness was not unique to Australian parties. Canada's two mainstream parties, too, dusted off policies from their past and used institutional obstacles to justify their inaction. It is to the Canadian scene I turn next.

Canada

Canada was better positioned structurally for a proto-Fordist alignment than the United Kingdom and Australia despite the latter's much stronger labour movements as measured by unionization, electoral support, and experience in governance. With independent family farming being its prevalent pattern, the Canadian rural sector was neither extremely small as in the UK case nor sharply divided along class lines as in the Australian case to prevent an agrarian–labour alliance from taking place. The industrial sector did not pose an obstacle, either: In terms of relative size, organization of production, and employment capacity, it was not behind the corresponding sectors that witnessed such alliances. Moreover, Canadian labour and agrarians reached extraordinary levels of mobilization in the depths of the crisis, which was one of the severest in the industrialized world. They did not align with each other at the national level because they were divided internally on multiple dimensions. This left the Liberals and the Conservatives, who alternated each other in government, as the only national political entities with potential to serve as a forum for agrarian and labour demands. Yet these parties did not break out of their traditional pro-business approaches, thus largely remaining within the protectionist fold in their responses.

Canadian cross-sectoral and cross-class alignments during the crisis unfolded against a regionally discriminatory protectionist policy background. Like the Australian "new protection," Canada's National Policy was a nation-building project minus the former's labour and social provisions. Launched by a Conservative government in 1879, the policy consisted of the protective tariffs, transcontinental railways, and Western settlement. The Tariff Act introduced industrial protection, solidifying the tariffs as the main instrument of industrial policy until World War II. The succeeding Liberals made the Canadian tariff system discriminatory by introducing imperial (preferential) and treaty (intermediate) schedules in 1898 and 1907, respectively. Yet, when they proposed a free trade agreement (Reciprocity Treaty) with the United States in 1911, they faced a stiff opposition from the financial-industrial bloc nurtured under the National Policy and were defeated in the election held later the same year (Clark 1939, 13–25; Cudmore 1930, 649–56; English [1977] 1993, 53–69; Mackintosh [1939] 1964, 25–35, 63–8, 99–101; McDiarmid 1946, 155–79, 203–38, 255–71; Perry 1955, 51–73, 93–107, 222–6). The second plank of the National Policy was the construction of transcontinental railways as a key link between tariff-induced industrialization in Central Canada (Ontario and Quebec) and agricultural expansion in the West. Unlike tariff protection, which was the major revenue source for the government, railway building involved lavish public borrowing and spending, as well as being marred by the duplication of lines (Easterbrook and Aitken 1956, 409–44; Laxer 1989, 182–97; Mackintosh et al. 1935, 33–42; Pomfret 1981, 102–11).[12] Western settlement, the third plank of the National Policy, took off with the transcontinental railways. The future farming class would, however, be severely disadvantaged from the outset as railway companies had received big chunks of land and numerous privileges before most of the settlers to be homesteaded actually arrived (Easterbrook and Aitken 1956, 476–513; Fowke 1946, 160–87; Mackintosh et al. 1935, 1–19; Pomfret 1981, 111–9).

Against this background, the Western-based and export-oriented resource sector bore the brunt of the depression and, with its constituent parts (employers, workers, and farmers), demanded tariff reduction and currency devaluation (Brecher 1957, 112–4). The wheat farmers of the Prairies were particularly vocal in articulating these demands, along with central banking, monetary expansion, and fiscal stimulus, since they paid a high price for agricultural implements and faced a strong competition in the UK market (Britnell 1939, 34–68; Fowke 1957, 70–84). Extractive industries and their workforce, too, championed the "inflation" argument and central banking (Brecher 1957, 135–8; Finkel 1979, 119–20). However, tariff protection drew support primarily from the domestic market-serving industries of Central Canada and ambiguously from its workers and farmers. Ironically, US branch plants that dominated the manufacturing sector were at the forefront of the high tariff cause. The Canadian Manufacturers' Association, for example, played an active role both in the tariff increases of 1930–1931 and in the Conservative government's preferential tariff propositions for the Ottawa Conference of 1932 (Clark 1939, 80–103; Drummond 1972, 91, 1974, 191–4, 201).

In stark contrast to the broader productive sector, the powerful financial sector based in Central Canada was unified and unambiguous in its policy demands, including a strong dollar, monetary contraction, and fiscal retrenchment. Like their UK and Australian counterparts, Canada's commercial banks organized along the branch-banking line (locally known as chartered banks) came out of the crisis unscathed.[13] Numbering only 10 in 1931, they even opposed central banking on the grounds that the self-regulating status quo made it unnecessary as demonstrated by their successful record in the ongoing crisis (McLeod 1933, 162–5). At the hearings of the Royal Commission on Banking and Currency in Canada (RCBCC) in 1933, the chartered banks reiterated their case for the adequacy of the status quo (Brecher 1957, 130–5; Plumptre 1940, 175–9). Tellingly, of the five commissioners, three were Canadians but two opposed the establishment of a central bank. Two were from the United Kingdom who, along with one Canadian, recommended it while citing the "excellence of the Commercial banking institutions" (RCBCC 1933, 66, 84–97).

Thus, a dual alignment of sectoral and class interests took place across the geographic divide in Canada. Manufacturing industries and the financial sector based in Central Canada were interested in tariff protection and macroeconomic conservatism, respectively. The federal government combined these two positions in its response, leaving organized labour torn between beneficial tariffs and contractionary policies. A Western Canadian alignment of extractive industries, their "resource proletariat" (Drache 1984), and, most vociferously, wheat farmers opposed the federal response and put forward ideas for an alternative response, but to no avail. However, neither the success of Central Canadian interests nor the failure of Western Canadian interests was inevitable.

Canadian labour picked up steam in the 1930s. Strike activity significantly increased over the 1920s (Cruikshank and Kealey 1987, 86; Urquhart and Buckley 1965, 107). Numerous political campaigns articulated broader policy demands such as unemployment insurance, eight-hour workday, five-day workweek, and minimum wage legislation (Cuneo 1980, 37–44; Struthers 1983, 44–77). Yet the union movement was beset by multiple divisions along the lines of (national–international) affiliation, (craft–industrial) organization, (Eastern–Western) region/(manufacturing–extractive) sector, (English–French) language, and (conservative–confessional–socialist–communist) ideology.[14] Although the national union federations gained ground against the TLC representing (US-based) international unions by mid-decade (Aitken et al. 1959, 168), the rise of industrial unionism in the United States, coupled with the defection of Communist-controlled unions to the TLC, would bring the decline of national unionism among English Canada's industrial unions.

Agrarian movements were politically more experienced than their labour counterparts. During the economic boom of the 1920s, the United Farmers movement became a significant player in provincial politics (Wood [1924] 1975, 273–344). For example, the United Farmers of Alberta (UFA) held provincial office from 1921 to 1935 with a radical anti-tariff position and a notion of "group government" favouring proportional representation of organized interests (Irvine [1920] 1976; see also Finkel 1989, 14–40; Laycock 1990, 69–135; Macpherson [1953] 1962, 28–92; Whitaker 1992, 80–113). Moreover, the United Farmers of Ontario governed from 1919 to 1923 in coalition with the Independent Labour Party (Badgley 2000, 3–20). At the federal level, the largely Western-based National Progressive Party emerged as a political offshoot of the Canadian Council of Agriculture and adopted the latter's anti-tariff "Farmers' Platform" (Brodie and Jenson 1980, 105–10; Conway 1979, 81–2; Laycock 1990, 23–68, 301–5; Morton 1950, 96–209, 302–5; Wood [1924] 1975, 345–64). It contested the 1921 federal election on that platform, which it called the New National Policy, winning the second largest bloc of seats in the House of Commons. Although it was able to extract tariff reductions from the minority Liberal government, it ran out of steam by the mid-1920s.

In the economic dislocation of the 1930s, agrarians had a renewed push to regain their political clout. The Co-operative Commonwealth Federation (CCF) and the Social Credit Party (Socred) represented the left and right versions of this push, respectively (Conway 1978, 118–24, 1979, 84–91; Finkel 1989, 202–13; Laycock 1990, 136–266; Naylor 1972; Sinclair 1975). Socred replaced the UFA to govern in Alberta from 1935 on, seeing the root cause of the crisis in the commercial banking system and its solution in an alternative financial organization based on the proto-Keynesian concept of social credit. Issuing a social credit share to each producer would solve the problems of high borrowing costs and indebtedness in agriculture (Irving 1959, 349–51; Macpherson [1953] 1962, 93–141). Socred tried to put this idea into practice by legislating low interest rate, moratorium on debt collection, and reorganization of banks as community-controlled credit institutions. Yet the legislation could not pass the constitutional test as it was found beyond provincial jurisdiction (Finkel 1989, 41–72; Macpherson [1953] 1962, 169–250; Mallory 1954, 57–122).

Born in 1932, the CCF had as its constituent elements the United Farmers movement (Lipset [1950] 1968, 99–117), provincial labour parties built on the British model (Naylor 2006, 289–91, 2016, 66–111), and Fabian socialist intellectuals (Horn 1980, 219–20; LSR [1935] 1975, ix–xi). It claimed to represent all Canadian interests except for those of "big business" while drawing the bulk of its mass support from Western farmers and, to some extent, workers (Brodie and Jenson 1980, 164–70; Finkel 1979, 154–66; Teeple 1972, 230–41; Young 1969, 12–36). It could not establish a national presence even among its agrarian constituent; it was regionally Western Canadian, ethnically Anglo-Saxon, and Protestant in religion. The CCF policy platform, formulated in the Regina Manifesto of 1933, reflected the party's catch-all philosophy. Interpreting the crisis as the death knell of capitalism, the manifesto envisioned a millennial "co-operative commonwealth" where all financial institutions would be socialized and where planning would replace competition as the guiding principle of economic life (Young 1969, 304–13). Regarding foreign trade, it proposed the abandonment of "insane" protectionism, on one hand, and the establishment of state control over the sector, on the other. An emergency public works programme to be financed by deficit spending, progressive taxation, and labour and social legislation were among the domestic policy proposals.

By mid-decade, the CCF and Socred managed to capture a significant share of the discontent with existing federal policies. In the 1935 federal election, they, along with other dissenting third parties, won 26% of the popular vote, increasing third party vote more than four times over the 1930 election. Yet Canada's majoritarian electoral system based on single member constituencies reduced this strength to 13% of the seats in the House of Commons (Mackie and Rose 1974, 75, 77). Keenly aware of the limitation of majoritarianism on their fortunes, the third parties, old and new alike, consistently pushed for the introduction of proportional representation, to no avail.[15] They would probably have had more (and the two governing parties less) leverage in federal parliament, but how far they would have swayed economic policy even with their combined strength is impossible to know.

In the absence of a unified agrarian or labour movement, let alone an electorally viable alliance between them, either governing party could plausibly serve as a national tent for agrarian, labour, and business interests. That neither did can be explained by their lack of imagination and consequent choices. After all, facing a similar disunity among the agrarian and labour movements as will be seen in the next chapter, the equally pro-business Democrats in the neighbouring United States did just that. In fact, both the Conservatives and Liberals found themselves in a position to attempt a New Deal-style policy innovation but, instead of taking the necessary ideational and political leap, chose to highlight jurisdictional and other institutional difficulties.

In January 1935, Conservative Prime Minister Bennett launched a campaign for economic and social reform in a series of radio speeches, declaring that the "old order is gone" (1935, 9). Coming in the last year of his mandate, this was an unexpected move from a prime minister who had presided over policies that privileged financial-industrial interests, provided bare minimum support to farmers, and were repressive of labour since 1930. Even his own party was caught off guard and some plausibly suggest that the entire move was a ploy by him, who would have to call an election anyway (see, e.g., Forster and Read 1979; McConnell 1969; Struthers 1983, 127–9). Nevertheless, Bennett got his way and parliament passed the "New Deal" policy package in May and June. The legislation included Employment and Social Insurance, Weekly Day of Rest in Industrial Undertakings, Minimum Wages, Limitation of Hours of Work,

Natural Products Marketing, Farmers' Creditors Arrangement, and Dominion Trades and Industry Commission. In its substantive and institutional pieces, the legislation projected a proto-Fordist innovation at the domestic level.

Bennett forced this legislation on his parliamentary caucus and left its fate to the incoming Liberals, who would conveniently put it to constitutional test. Both the Supreme Court of Canada and the UK-based Judicial Committee of the Privy Council serving as Canada's final court of appeal found the key pieces of the legislation outside of federal jurisdiction (Birch 1955, 159–64; Cairns 1971, 322–7; Pal 1986, 77–91; RCDPR 1940a, 247–52; Scott 1937; Simeon and Robinson 1990, 81–2). Instead of rushing the legislation, Bennett could have first remade the Conservative Party as a reformist project inclusive of agrarians and labour as in the US Democratic case, and then taken on the difficult but not impossible task of constitutional change. This is how the Liberal Party introduced unemployment insurance in 1940: Under the altered conditions of war, it begrudgingly broadened its support base to urban workers and collaborated with the provinces for necessary constitutional change to make unemployment insurance a federal responsibility (Cuneo 1979). Yet, as of the mid-1930s, Bennett and his Conservatives were still very much a party of financial and industrial interests based in Central Canada and nurtured under the National Policy (Underhill 1935).

Nor did the Liberal Party and its extremely cautious leader, Mackenzie King, grab the opportunity they were presented with. King contested the 1930 election on a platform of restoring business confidence and lost. In opposition, he summarily dismissed as "reform adventures" proposals for a rethinking of the party strategy in line with what Franklin D. Roosevelt was doing in the United States (Whitaker 1977, 28–84). Back in power in 1935, the Liberals pinned their recovery hopes largely on continentalist trade initiatives, answering the call of resource industries as their traditional business base (Finkel 1979, 1–26). However, they also began to explore alternative ways of dealing with unemployment by establishing a National Employment Commission (NEC). In its final report (NEC 1938), the commission recommended direct federal responsibility in unemployment insurance and other aid as well as federally administered public works. The report was too radical for the cautious Liberal leadership (Bradford 1998, 36–8), who would respond to it by establishing another commission, Royal Commission on Dominion–Provincial Relations (RCDPR). Reporting in wartime (RCDPR 1940b), the royal commission not only reiterated NEC recommendations but also proposed an explicitly Keynesian demand management strategy. That, however, is a postwar story.

From the details of all three protectionist cases, three common patterns emerge. First, regardless of their political party composition, governments catered to business interests, which usually coalesced in a financial-industrial complex, and accommodated agrarian interests only as a secondary concern. Agrarians aligned neither with labour nor with business in a tripartite arrangement for different reasons: They were small in the United Kingdom, weak in Australia, and divided in Canada. Second, governments' approaches to interests and policy decisions were not out of necessity but political choices informed by the ideational disposition of their leaders. What united UK and Australian labour party leadership with that of governing conservative and liberal parties in the three countries was an orthodox idea of the economy in crisis conditions. Third, electoral and constitutional arrangements mediated political and policy choices. Majoritarian rules generally discriminated against innovative third parties in the United Kingdom and Canada whereas Australia's preferential voting favoured a conservative third party. In the latter two cases, the division of powers between national and subnational governments complicated matters but also served as the justification of lack of political initiative.

Expanding the Ideational-Political Space

The mixed cases of France and New Zealand provide a useful reference to see where the three common patterns emerging from the primary cases of protectionism hold and where they do not. Until the mid-1930s, the five countries did not diverge much in terms of either cross-sectoral and cross-class alignments or governing ideas of and strategies for the economy. What changed then in both France and New Zealand was not just replacement of one government by another. A realignment of sectoral and class interests, along with a radical revision of government approach, also took place. The Popular Front government of 1936–1937 in France was a coalition of workers and farmers as represented by the Socialist/Communist and left Radical parties, respectively, and later brought in employers to the fold as well—if only briefly. Critically, an underconsumptionist reading of the economy underpinned the coalition and the policies it pursued. That the Front government discontinued its policy experiment was due in no small measure to the undoing of the tripartite cross-sectoral and cross-class alignment. In New Zealand, a reformist Labour Party came to power in 1935 on the strength of an agrarian–labour alliance that it had built and had a more successful policy experiment within the confines of a pastoral economy. Institutionally, as in the three primary cases, the French and New Zealand governments saw their substantive choices influenced by policy legacies in particular.

France

The French response, except for the Popular Front interlude, was astonishingly conservative under a speedy succession of right-wing and centrist governments. Defending the franc Poincaré (named after Raymond Poincaré, premier at the time of the country's return to the gold standard in 1926) at any cost and preaching balanced budget trumped all other macroeconomic considerations while foreign trade and microeconomic policies were not distinguishable from other protectionist responses. As late as 1933, the daily *Le Figaro* was boasting about French conservatism: "Amidst [international] monetary instability, France is an island of stability, of confidence, of orthodoxy" (quoted in Weber 1994, 29). Part of the reason for this response was that French downturn set in late and, although to prove prolonged, was not particularly severe (Bernard and Dubief [1975–1976] 1985, 180, Salais 1988, 248–9). Unemployment, which provided the most graphic image of the crisis in the industrialized world, did not spin out of control in France largely because the family farm-dominated rural sector provided a domestic outlet for the unemployed and because immigrants were sent back to their countries of origin and women to the home (Bernard and Dubief [1975–1976] 1985, 190).

The underlying reason for French macroeconomic conservatism, however, was governments' pro-business and pro-petit bourgeois prognosis of the crisis. They defended the international and domestic value of the franc religiously because they thought it was the only way, along with fiscal restraint, to maintain business confidence as well as the purchasing power of both rural and urban middle classes (Bernard and Dubief [1975–1976] 1985, 179–89). In so doing, they were also catering to the sensitivities of their electoral and power base. Dominated by smallholding peasantry (Kemp 1972, 129–45; Tcherkinsky 1939, 14–20), the sizable rural sector had long been a bastion of conservative and radical parties, and, in the interwar period, came to equate deficit financing with national bankruptcy (Weber 1994, 39–47). The urban traditional and new middle classes, too, had a conservative outlook: "The essential France of the small capitalist, entrepreneur and shopkeeper, of the liberal professions and much of the public service, feared above all being converted into a proletariat" (Bernard and Dubief [1975–1976] 1985, 158). As for big business, it was dominated by a financial-industrial compact of "two hundred families," who controlled the administration of the Banque de France as central bank until the Popular Front government reorganized it in 1936 (Bernard and Dubief [1975–1976] 1985, 246, 311).

The strong alignment of interests for macroeconomic orthodoxy did not shape in a vacuum. Unlike the United Kingdom, France returned to the gold standard with a devalued currency—at one-fifth of the prewar parity. Reflecting a general pattern for countries experiencing devaluation and inflation in the 1920s (Eichengreen 1992, 394; Schwarz 1993, 99), French governments resisted both for as long as possible. This was the background for the establishment of a national anti-devaluation sentiment that spread, in Tom Kemp's rhetorical words, "from the Regents of the Bank of France to the Central Committee of the Communist Party" (1972, 103). Interestingly, that sentiment engulfed not just urban small savers, who were hurt the most by the inflation of the mid-1920s, but also exporters who benefitted the most from the devaluation of 1926 (officially, 1928). Conservative governments successfully played on the widespread fear of devaluation and inflation to perpetuate their orthodox agenda. Policy legacy became a powerful tool in their hands.

Yet the Popular Front government set aside that legacy during the Blum experiment (named after Socialist premier Léon Blum). The Popular Front was first and foremost a political project to defend French democracy against fascism.[16] Economically, the three constituents favoured neither devaluation nor deflation but were short on specifics (Jackson 1985, 35–49). The left Radicals, representing agrarian and petit bourgeois interests, advocated for *économie dirigée* while remaining faithful to fiscal retrenchment. Both the Communists and the Socialists subscribed to a general notion of socialization but, at the same time, aimed to increase the purchasing power of workers, farmers, and urban middle classes, using as a rationale the Marxian underconsumptionist view of capitalism that was widespread in France (Rosanvallon 1989, 172–83). They similarly proposed expansion of unemployment insurance,[17] public works, wage increases, and various support programmes towards that goal in addition to their industrial reform platform for improving working conditions via shorter hours and equal pay for work of equal value.

The Popular Front itself represented an uneasy alliance of organized labour and smallholding peasantry, a typical formula for policy innovation in democratic nations at the time. In its economic aspect, the Front programme largely reflected the Socialist and Communist platforms (Jackson 1988, 299–302; Pollard and Holmes 1973, 400–2). While reaching out to the left Radicals, the two major left parties also brokered a reunification of organized labour by helping the Socialist-controlled Confédération générale du travail (CGT) and the Communist-controlled Confédération générale du travail unitaire to merge under the umbrella of the former. The CGT thus came to represent the entire union movement except for a small confessional section (Rimlinger 1989, 585–6). Shortly after winning the election and forming a government in June 1936, the Front was met with a wave of strikes, which it would use to bring together the CGT and the main employers' organization, Confédération générale de la production française, to sign the historic Matignon Accord incorporating many economic articles of the Front programme. For a brief moment, it thus seemed that a tripartite alignment of agrarian, labour, and business interests would hold.

Further, the departure from the gold standard and currency devaluation later in 1936 freed monetary policy from deflationary straitjacket. Yet the government could not put together a concerted macroeconomic stimulus programme. It was pulled in different directions, at one extreme, by the Communists whose main interests lay in international issues and, at the other extreme, by large employers who would eventually renege on the Matignon Accord. The Blum experiment failed mainly because the coalition behind it came undone in the absence of a sustained theme. Formal institutions did not seem to play a definite role in the demise or rise of the Popular Front government. The aristocratic Senate was generally obstructive of democratic initiatives, including female suffrage, but did pass the legislative package launching the Blum experiment (Bernard and Dubief [1975–1976] 1985, 249, 288–9). In the Chamber elected by male suffrage, Popular Front parties had a clear majority in part due to a modified majoritarian system requiring two-stage elections (Flora et al. 1983, 115, 167).

The French case is dually useful for comparative purposes. On one hand, it validates the orthodox ideational disposition and labour-excluding political strategies that underlay the protectionist responses as seen previously in the three primary cases. On the other hand, it shows in the Blum experiment what it took to break with protectionism in a democratic polity. The failure of that experiment also serves as a useful contrast to the successful cases of proto-Fordism that will be seen in the next chapter. The New Zealand case, which will be taken up next, provides a similar contrast to the primary cases of protectionism and proto-Fordism while, at the same time, representing a successful coalition-building strategy in the context of a pastoral economy.

New Zealand

The Labour Party experiment of the mid-1930s, a watershed moment in New Zealand's response, had a Liberal beginning. Labour's policy innovation, including the protection of farmers, workers, and non-market population, was rooted in an ideational and political process that went back to the 1890s. Surely, many things changed in-between. What remained unchanged over the five decades, however, was an equitable, "new world" view of the economy and society shared by the Liberals, on one end of the period, and Labour, on the other. In both cases, an agrarian–labour alliance, which was thought not at the expense of the rest of society, predated or coincided with policy innovation. The Liberals had to transform the rural structure to build that alliance and were thus more revolutionary than their Labour successors.

During the extended Liberal governance from 1891 to 1912, New Zealand struck the first agrarian–labour alliance, achieved universal suffrage (1893), and acquired Dominion status (1907). The alliance supported and built on three pillars of public policy: land redistribution, industrial relations and wage arbitration, and proto-welfare state (Brady 1941, 225–32, 1958, 259–327; Castles 1985, 12–21; Hawke 1985, 103–21; Jesson 1987, 22–5; Schwartz 1989, 164–94; Simpson 1990, 51–72). The land reform legislation of 1892 transformed the countryside by breaking up large estates and creating an independent smallholding class as the dominant feature of the sector. What the land reform was to small producers, the Industrial Conciliation and Arbitration Act of 1894 was to wage earners—who were guaranteed state-sanctioned dispute resolution and wage determination. Complementing the legislation for small producers and workers was that for a proto-welfare state in support of non-working population, such as the Old Age Pension Act of 1898.

What made all this possible was a Liberal determination not to repeat the deep divisions of the old world in "God's own country" (Hamer 1988, 37–75; see also Trampusch and Spies 2014, 930–3). The Liberal Party, which was urban-based, identified four divisive issues and dealt with each of them in a specific way: large landownership (concentration of land), the institution of "workhouse" (poor relief), specific urban ills (crime, destitution, disease, and slums), and class rigidity. Land reform was the centrepiece of the Liberal strategy. Breaking up the large estates was devised not only as solution to the land question but also to alleviate urban problems by curbing migration to cities and reduce class inequality in general. Similarly, old age pension was introduced to replace poor relief and help solve other urban problems. As for the pro-labour industrial relations and wage arbitration legislation, "it was needed to equalize labour and capital, not to raise labour above capital" (Hamer 1988, 41).

The Liberal rule can also be seen as a Lib–Lab coalition given the steady support it received from Trades Councils, which also placed several labour representatives in the initial cabinet, and its consequent pro-labour initiatives (Brown 1962, 1–17; Markey 2008, 73). This labour-inclusive atmosphere dominated by the Liberals naturally delayed the arrival of a national labour party. The New Zealand Labour Party was established only in 1916, when the Liberals had lost their founding mission and become part of a conservative coalition dominated by the Reform Party representing the remnants of the old landed class and urban financial-industrial interests. Approaching the different forms of land tenure was one of the stickiest issues that occupied the Labour Party until the late 1920s. Starting from a position of strict nationalization, in the early postwar period it came to accept usehold as a measure to prevent speculation in land and mortgaging under the freehold system. Then, in 1927, it adopted the "new land policy" dropping nationalization and usehold tenure altogether and recognizing private smallholder ownership (Brown 1962, 63–70, 87–95).

Thus, Labour entered the 1930s by removing a major hurdle to reaching out to independent farmers as well as by putting together an economic and social reform package that it would introduce upon taking power (Brown 1962, 150, 161–2). As a result, it came to establish a sizable support outside of its traditional urban base, increasing its rural and country-town seats nearly tenfold in the 1935 election (Sinclair 1976, 117; see also Brown 1962, 181; Markey 2008, 79). The second edition of the agrarian–labour alliance, as in the first, was built by a single party. In this respect, the New Zealand Labour Party distinguished itself from most other labour, social democratic, or socialist parties, which had no claim to represent agrarian interests. The party also inherited from the Liberal tradition a "populist" view of the economy and society that emphasized common, as opposed to sectional, interests among the population (Simpson 1990, 80–2, 102–9). This permitted it a certain flexibility or eclecticism when trying to find solutions to pressing problems. For example, Labour policies of guaranteed prices for direct producers, public works for the unemployed, and wage increases for workers drew as much inspiration from Major Douglas's proto-Keynesian social credit doctrine as from the Marxian idea of underconsumption (Brown 1962, 156–62).

Formal institutional arrangements either facilitated or could not stand in the way of Labour Party performance. The unelected upper chamber (Legislative Council) did not have the (conservative) influence that its UK, Australian, and French counterparts had. Members of the lower house (House of Representatives) were elected by majoritarian rules. Labour pushed for proportional representation until 1934, when it presciently made peace with majoritarianism (Brown 1962, 172). With 47% of the popular vote in 1935, it captured 70% of the House seats (Mackie and Rose 1974, 297, 299). Economically, however, it had to wage a battle to wrest control of the Reserve Bank from powerful commercial (trading) banks and nationalize it as a full-fledged central bank in the late 1930s (Greasley and Oxley 2002, 702–4; Plumptre 1938, 196, 1940, 102–4, 176–78; Quigley 1992, 1–4).

What truly limited the Labour government and its predecessors was a pastoral economy heavily dependent on exports to a single, UK market. In 1928, 94% of New Zealand exports were of pastoral origin (Belshaw 1933, 750). And the United Kingdom accounted for 75% of them (and 46% of imports) in 1929 (Hancock 1942, 310). In responding to this pastoral trade and partner dependency, pre-Labour governments took protectionist measures by minimally accommodating primary producers and discriminating against wage labour. Labour's intervention was in terms of radically raising the level of social protection while, at the same time, keeping market protection at a level bordering on neomercantilism. This is what gave the New Zealand response its mixed character.

Summing Up

The interaction of ideas, interests, and institutions against a structural background in the five democratic cases examined provides sufficient conditions for both turn to protectionism and departure from it. A conservative leadership viewing the economy primarily from the perspective of business found enough policy precedents to rely on and used existing institutional setting to limit change to a minimum, such as monetary ease, agricultural support, and unemployment relief. This is what happened in all the cases for most of the time and in broad contours. The way it happened was no doubt different in each case, but the common thread was a labour-excluding political alignment: In the United Kingdom, Australia, France, and New Zealand, conservative coalitions held sway and, in the first two cases, also co-opted renegade elements from the Labo(u)r parties which were in disarray after their disastrous performance in government. Canada's two conservative parties, which did not need each other when ruling, were less accommodative of agrarians and equally exclusive of labour.

The Popular Front and Labour governments in France and New Zealand, respectively, broke in their own way with protectionism but could not make a paradigm shift to proto-Fordism for different reasons. Informed by unorthodox ideas of the economy and the crisis, both governments embodied an agrarian–labour alliance and, in the French case, also brought in large employers to it. The Front government could not sustain the alliance and abruptly ended the Blum experiment. While maintaining and solidifying the alliance, the Labour government was disproportionately busied by the trade problems of a single market-dependent pastoral economy. The rural sectors of the UK and Australian economies, too, were structurally limiting. The UK sector was too small and Australian independent family farming too weak for a working agrarian–labour alliance. (Nor was that limitation ever tested by potential parties to such an alliance.)

All in all, this group of democracies represented a relatively conservative response to the world-historical crisis of the interwar period. However, this conservatism was not to the exclusion of innovation. Even in the most conservative nations, innovation occurred out of necessity or their own volition. In the United Kingdom, for example, the Conservatives changed everything about classical liberalism except for fiscal policy. Yet whatever change occurred in the broader protectionist camp paled in comparison to those in the second group of democracies, whose combined response would provide the prototype of the Fordist policy paradigm in Western Europe and North America. The next chapter will apply the argument to the second group of democratic responses.

NOTES

1. International statistics are not consistent or comprehensive but give a rough idea about the relative performance of national economies. According to Safarian ([1959] 2009, 98), the UK national income contracted only by 15% from 1929 to 1932, compared to 24% for Australia, 17% for Austria, 45% for Canada, 12% for Denmark, 16% for France, 41% for Germany, 17% for Sweden, and 52% for the United States. The UK real national product contracted only by 14% in the same period, compared to 10% for Australia in 1927–1932, 29% for Canada in 1929–1932, 26% for France in 1929–1936, 16% for Germany in 1928–1932, and 30% for the United States in 1929–1932 (Schedvin 1970, 44).
2. Keynes himself made his case for deficit-financed public works programmes via the Economic Advisory Council and its successor Committee on Economic Information in the 1930s (Howson and Winch 1977).
3. At least in monetary terms, this was the formula used by countries which experienced deflation in the 1920s. Conversely, those countries which experienced (hyper)inflation in the decade were reluctant to leave the gold standard, devalue the currency, or lower the interest rate (Eichengreen 1992, 394; Solomou 1996, 32, 48–9).
4. UK unions were traditionally organized along craft lines and numbered well over 1000 in the interwar period (Mitchell 1962, 68).
5. As of 1930, the "Big Five" were Midland, Lloyds, Barclays, Westminster, and National Provincial banks (Mackenzie [1932] 1935, 20).
6. Even in 1929, when the intra-imperial trade was at a low, Australia sent 38% of its exports to, and received 40% of its imports from, the United Kingdom (Hancock 1942, 306).
7. Full adult suffrage was achieved in 1902 at the federal level and in 1908 at the state level (James and Markey 2006, 24). For the Aboriginals, however, it had to wait until 1962.
8. Before the ALP formed its first majority government in 1910, it briefly ruled as a minority government in 1904—both nationally first by a labour or socialist party in the world. As early as 1899, Queensland had a labour government for a brief stint—the first subnational government of its kind (Dyrenfurth and Bongiorno 2011, 29, 50).
9. Theodore had resigned from the cabinet earlier in 1930 over an investigation into his handling of a government purchase of mines while he was serving as the premier of Queensland in 1922.
10. In this context, efforts (see, e.g., Graham 1966, 1–30) to establish parallels between the Country Party and the North American agrarian third parties are misplaced.

11. Alternatively, John Murphy (2010) argues that the delay in unemployment insurance legislation was because of the presence of compulsory wage arbitration as a "neighbouring policy institution," which presumably made employers reluctant to contribute further to the wage bill.
12. A Canadian commentator observed in 1917: "Consult the annals of Canada for the past fifty years at random, and whatever party may be in power, what do you find? ... The government is building a railway, buying a railway, selling a railway, or blocking a railway" (quoted in Skelton 1922, 244–5).
13. These banks increased their combined asset from 47% of the gross national product in 1929 to 71% in 1933 (Neufeld 1972, 602–3; see also Drummond 1991).
14. The four federations (Trades and Labour Congress [TLC], Confédération des travailleurs catholiques du Canada, All-Canadian Congress of Labour, and Workers' Unity League) represented these divisions (Abella 1973, 1–53; Drache 1984, 56–61, 65–70; Lipton [1967] 1973, 218–65; Pentland 1979).
15. They also wanted the abolition of the Senate as an unelected body. The prime minister of the day appointed its members.
16. It was part of a worldwide movement spearheaded by the Communist International in 1935 in an about-face of its sectarian approach to socialist, social democratic, labour, and other left parties.
17. During the 1930s, French unemployment insurance and general social security schemes had an extremely limited coverage partly because of the large size of the rural sector and the traditional urban middle class (Kemp 1989, 750–1; Salais 1988, 255–6).

References

Abella, Irving M. 1973. *Nationalism, Communism, and Canadian Labour: The CIO, the Communist Party, and the Canadian Congress of Labour, 1935–1956.* Toronto: University of Toronto Press.

Aitken, Hugh G. J., John J. Deutsch, William A. Mackintosh, Clarence L. Barber, Maurice Lamontagne, Irving Brecher, and Eugene Forsey. 1959. *The American Economic Impact on Canada.* Durham: Duke University Press.

Badgley, Kerry. 2000. *Ringing in the Common Love of Good: The United Farmers of Ontario, 1914–1926.* Montreal and Kingston: McGill-Queen's University Press.

Belshaw, H. 1933. "Crisis and Readjustment in New Zealand." *Journal of Political Economy* 41, no. 6: 750–76.

Bennett, Richard B. 1935. *The Premier Speaks to the People – The First Address.* Ottawa: Dominion Conservative Headquarters.

Bentley, Michael. 2003. "The Liberal Party, 1900–1939: Summit and Descent." In *A Companion to Early Twentieth-Century Britain*, edited by Chris Wrigley, 23–37. Oxford: Blackwell Publishing.

Bernard, Philippe, and Henri Dubief. [1975–1976] 1985. *The Decline of the Third Republic, 1914–1938*. Translated from the French by Anthony Forster. Cambridge: Cambridge University Press.

Birch, Anthony H. 1955. *Federalism, Finance and Social Legislation in Canada, Australia, and the United States*. Oxford: Oxford University Press.

Booth, Alan. 1989. *British Economic Policy, 1931–49: Was There a Keynesian Revolution?* Hertfordshire: Harvester Wheatsheaf.

Born, Karl E. [1977] 1983. *International Banking in the 19th and 20th Centuries*. Translated from the German by Volker R. Berghahn. New York: St. Martin's.

Botterill, Linda C. 2012. *Wheat Marketing in Transition: The Transformation of the Australian Wheat Board*. Dordrecht: Springer.

Botterill, Linda C., and Alan Fenna. 2020. "Initiative-Resistance and the Australian Party System." *Australian Journal of Politics and History* 66, no. 1: 63–77. https://doi.org/10.1111/ajph.12639.

Bradford, Neil. 1998. *Commissioning Ideas: Canadian National Policy Innovation in Comparative Perspective*. Toronto: Oxford University Press Canada.

Brady, Alexander. 1939. "Economic Activity of the State in the British Dominions: Some Comments on Comparative Development." *Canadian Journal of Economics and Political Science* 5, no. 3: 300–9. https://doi.org/10.2307/137034.

Brady, Alexander. 1941. "Democracy in the Overseas Dominions." In *Canada in Peace and War: Eight Studies in National Trends since 1914*, edited by C. Martin, 212–44. London: Oxford University Press.

Brady, Alexander. 1958. *Democracy in the Dominions: A Comparative Study in Institutions*. 3rd ed. Toronto: University of Toronto Press.

Brecher, Irving. 1957. *Monetary and Fiscal Thought and Policy in Canada, 1919–1939*. Toronto: University of Toronto Press.

Britnell, George E. 1939. *The Wheat Economy*. Toronto: University of Toronto Press.

Brodie, M. Janine, and Jane Jenson. 1980. *Crisis, Challenge and Change: Party and Class in Canada*. Toronto: Methuen.

Brown, Bruce. 1962. *The Rise of New Zealand Labour: A History of the New Zealand Labour Party from 1916 to 1940*. Wellington: Price Milburn.

Cairns, Alan C. 1971. "The Judicial Committee and Its Critics." *Canadian Journal of Political Science* 4, no. 3: 301–45. https://doi.org/10.1017/S0008423900026809.

Castles, Francis G. 1985. *The Working Class and Welfare: Reflections on the Political Development of the Welfare State in Australia and New Zealand, 1890–1980*. Wellington: Allen and Unwin.

Castles, Francis G. 1988. *Australian Public Policy and Economic Vulnerability: A Comparative and Historical Perspective.* Sydney: Allen and Unwin.

Cochrane, Peter. 1980. *Industrialization and Dependence: Australia's Road to Economic Development, 1870–1939.* St Lucia: University of Queensland Press.

Clark, Samuel D. 1939. *Canadian Manufacturers' Association: A Study in Collective Bargaining and Political Pressure.* Toronto: University of Toronto Press.

Clarke, Peter. 1988. *The Keynesian Revolution in the Making, 1924–1936.* Oxford: Clarendon Press.

Conway, John F. 1978. "Populism in the United States, Russia, and Canada: Explaining the Roots of Canada's Third Parties." *Canadian Journal of Political Science* 11, no. 1: 99–124. https://doi.org/10.1017/S0008423900038774.

Conway, John F. 1979. "The Prairie Populist Resistance to the National Policy: Some Reconsiderations." *Journal of Canadian Studies* 14, no. 3: 77–91.

Cruikshank, Douglas, and Gregory S. Kealey. 1987. "Strikes in Canada, 1891–1950." *Labour* 20: 85–145.

Cudmore, S. A. 1930. "The Economic Development of Canada, 1867–1921: (II) Commercial Policy and the Development of Commerce." In *The Cambridge History of the British Empire*, vol. 6, *Canada and Newfoundland*, edited by J. H. Rose, A. P. Newton, and E. A. Benians, 642–56. Cambridge: At the University Press.

Cuneo, Carl J. 1979. "State, Class, and Reserve Labour: The Case of the 1941 Canadian Unemployment Insurance Act." *Canadian Review of Sociology and Anthropology* 16, no 2: 147–70. https://doi.org/10.1111/j.1755-618X.1979.tb01018.x.

Cuneo, Carl J. 1980. "State Mediation of Class Contradictions in Canadian Unemployment Insurance, 1930–1935." *Studies in Political Economy*, no. 3: 37–65. https://doi.org/10.1080/19187033.1980.11675723.

Dewey, Peter. 2003. "Agriculture, Agrarian Society and the Countryside." In *A Companion to Early Twentieth-Century Britain*, edited by Chris Wrigley, 270–85. Oxford: Blackwell Publishing.

Drache, Daniel. 1984. "The Formation and Fragmentation of the Canadian Working Class: 1820–1920." *Studies in Political Economy*, no. 15: 43–89. https://doi.org/10.1080/19187033.1984.11675625.

Drummond, Ian M. 1972. *British Economic Policy and the Empire, 1919–1939.* London: George Allen and Unwin.

Drummond, Ian M. 1974. *Imperial Economic Policy, 1917–1939: Studies in Expansion and Protection.* London: George Allen and Unwin.

Drummond, Ian M. 1991. "Why Canadian Banks Did Not Collapse in the 1930s." In *The Role of Banks in the Interwar Economy*, edited by Harold James, Håkan Lindgren, and Alice Teichova, 232–50. Cambridge: Cambridge University Press.

Dyrenfurth, Nick, and Frank Bongiorno. 2011. *A Little History of the Australian Labor Party*. Sydney: University of New South Wales Press.

Easterbrook, William T., and Hugh G. J. Aitken. 1956. *Canadian Economic History*. Toronto: Macmillan.

Ehrensaft, Philip, and Warwick Armstrong. 1981. "The Formation of Dominion Capitalism: Economic Truncation and Class Structure." In *Inequality: Essays on the Political Economy of Social Welfare*, edited by Allan Moscovitch and Glenn Drover, 99–155. Toronto: University of Toronto Press.

Eichengreen, Barry J. 1992. *Golden Fetters: The Gold Standard and the Great Depression, 1919–1939*. New York: Oxford University Press.

Ellis, Ulrich R. 1963. *A History of the Australian Country Party*. Parkville: Melbourne University Press.

English, John. [1977] 1993. *The Decline of Politics: The Conservatives and the Party System 1901–20*. Reprint. Toronto: University of Toronto Press.

Feinstein, Charles H. 1972. *National Income, Expenditure and Output of the United Kingdom, 1855–1965*. Cambridge: At the University Press.

Finkel, Alvin. 1979. *Business and Social Reform in the Thirties*. Toronto: James Lorimer.

Finkel, Alvin. 1989. *The Social Credit Phenomenon in Alberta*. Toronto: University of Toronto Press.

Fisher, Allan G. B. 1934. "Crisis and Readjustment in Australia." *Journal of Political Economy* 42, no. 6: 753–82.

Flora, Peter, Jens Alber, Richard Eichenberg, Jürgen Kohl, Franz Kraus, Winfried Pfenning, and Kurt Seebohm. 1983. *State, Economy, and Society in Western Europe, 1815–1975*, vol. 1, *The Growth of Mass Democracies and Welfare States*. Frankfurt am Main: Campus Verlag.

Forster, Donald, and Colin Read. 1979. "The Politics of Opportunism: The New Deal Broadcasts." *Canadian Historical Review* 60, no. 3: 324–49. https://doi.org/10.3138/CHR-060-03-03.

Fowke, Vernon C. 1946. *Canadian Agricultural Policy: The Historical Pattern*. Toronto: University of Toronto Press.

Fowke, Vernon C. 1957. *The National Policy and the Wheat Economy*. Toronto: University of Toronto Press.

Graham, B. D. 1966. *The Formation of the Australian Country Parties*. Canberra: Australian National University Press.

Greasley, David, and Les Oxley. 2002. "Regime Shift and Fast Recovery on the Periphery: New Zealand in the 1930s." *Economic History Review* 55, no. 4: 697–720. https://doi.org/10.1111/1468-0289.00237.

Greaves, Julian. 2000. "British Steel in the 1930s: Adaptation under Duress?" In *After the Slump: Industry and Politics in 1930s Britain and Germany*, edited by C. Buchheim and W. Redvers Garside, 111–30. Frankfurt am Main: Peter Lang.

Griffiths, Clare V. J. 2007. *Labour and the Countryside: The Politics of Rural Britain, 1918–1939*. Oxford: Oxford University Press.
Hamer, David A. 1988. *The New Zealand Liberals: The Years of Power, 1891–1912*. Auckland: Auckland University Press.
Hancock, W. Keith. 1942. *Survey of British Commonwealth Affairs*, vol. 2, *Problems of Economic Policy, 1918–1939*, part 1. London: Oxford University Press.
Harris, Bernard. 1988. "Unemployment, Insurance and Health in Interwar Britain." In *Interwar Unemployment in International Perspective*, edited by Barry J. Eichengreen and Tim J. Hatton, 149–83. Dordrecht: Kluwer.
Hawke, G. R. 1985. *The Making of New Zealand: An Economic History*. Cambridge: Cambridge University Press.
Horn, Michiel. 1980. *The League for Social Reconstruction: Intellectual Origins of the Democratic Left in Canada, 1930–1942*. Toronto: University of Toronto Press.
Howson, Susan, and Donald Winch. 1977. *The Economic Advisory Council 1930–1939: A Study in Economic Advice during Depression and Recovery*. Cambridge: Cambridge University Press.
Ingham, Geoffrey. 1984. *Capitalism Divided? The City and Industry in British Social Development*. London: Macmillan.
Irvine, William. [1920] 1976. *The Farmers in Politics*. Reprint. Toronto: McClelland and Stewart.
Irving, John A. 1959. *The Social Credit Movement in Alberta*. Toronto: University of Toronto Press.
Jackson, Julian. 1985. *The Politics of Depression in France, 1932–1936*. Cambridge: Cambridge University Press.
Jackson, Julian. 1988. *The Popular Front in France: Defending Democracy, 1934–38*. Cambridge: Cambridge University Press.
James, Leighton, and Raymond Markey. 2006. "Class and Labour: The British Labour Party and the Australian Labor Party Compared." *Labour History*, no. 90: 23–41. https://doi.org/10.2307/27516112.
Jesson, Bruce. 1987. *Behind the Mirror Glass: The Growth of Wealth and Power in New Zealand in the Eighties*. Auckland: Penguin.
Kaiser, Claudia. 2000. "Trade Union Reactions to Economic Crisis." In *After the Slump: Industry and Politics in 1930s Britain and Germany*, edited by C. Buchheim and Redvers Garside, 179–200. Frankfurt am Main: Peter Lang.
Kavanagh, Dennis A. 1973. "Crisis Management and Incremental Adaptation in British Politics: The 1931 Crisis of the British Party System." In *Crisis, Choice, and Change: Historical Studies of Political Development*, edited by Gabriel A. Almond, Scott C. Flanagan, and Robert J. Mundt, 152–223. Boston: Little, Brown.
Kemp, Tom. 1972. *The French Economy, 1913–39: The History of a Decline*. London: Longman.

Kemp, Tom. 1989. "Economic and Social Policy in France." In *The Cambridge Economic History of Europe*, vol. 8, *The Industrial Economies: The Development of Economic and Social Policies*, edited by Peter Mathias and Sidney Pollard, 691–751. Cambridge: Cambridge University Press.

Kitson, Michael. 2003. "Slump and Recovery: The UK Experience." In *The World Economy and National Economies in the Interwar Slump*, edited by Theo Balderston, 88–104. Basingstoke: Palgrave Macmillan.

Koning, Niek. 1994. *The Failure of Agrarian Capitalism: Agrarian Politics in the United Kingdom, Germany, the Netherlands and the USA, 1846–1919*. London and New York: Routledge.

Laxer, Gordon. 1989. *Open for Business: The Roots of Foreign Ownership in Canada*. Toronto: Oxford University Press.

Laycock, David. 1990. *Populism and Democratic Thought in the Canadian Prairies, 1910 to 1945*. Toronto: University of Toronto Press.

Lipset, Seymour M. [1950] 1968. *Agrarian Socialism: The Cooperative Commonwealth Federation in Saskatchewan*. Revised ed. Garden City: Anchor Books.

Lipton, Charles. [1967] 1973. *The Trade Union Movement of Canada, 1827–1959*. 3rd ed. Toronto: NC Press.

Louis, L. J., and Ian Turner, eds. 1968. *The Depression of the 1930s*. Melbourne: Cassell Australia.

LSR (League for Social Reconstruction). [1935] 1975. *Social Planning for Canada*. Reprint. Toronto: University of Toronto Press.

Mackenzie, Kenneth. [1932] 1935. *The Banking Systems of Great Britain, France, Germany, and the United States of America*. 2nd ed. London: Macmillan.

Mackie, Thomas T., and Richard Rose. 1974. *The International Almanac of Electoral History*. London: Macmillan.

Mackintosh, William A. [1939] 1964. *The Economic Background of Dominion–Provincial Relations*. Reprint. Toronto: McClelland and Stewart.

Mackintosh, William A., A. B. Clark, G. A. Elliott, and W. W. Swanson. 1935. *Economic Problems of the Prairie Provinces*. Toronto: Macmillan.

Macpherson, C. B. [1953] 1962. *Democracy in Alberta: Social Credit and the Party System*. 2nd ed. Toronto: University of Toronto Press.

Mallory, J. R. 1954. *Social Credit and the Federal Power in Canada*. Toronto: University of Toronto Press.

Markey, Ray. 2008. "An Antipodean Phenomenon: Comparing the Labo(u)r Party in New Zealand and Australia." *Labour History*, no. 95: 69–95. https://doi.org/10.2307/27516310.

McConnell, W. H. 1969. "The Genesis of the Canadian 'New Deal'." *Journal of Canadian Studies* 4, no. 2: 31–41. https://doi.org/10.3138/jcs.4.2.31.

McDiarmid, Orville J. 1946. *Commercial Policy in the Canadian Economy*. Cambridge, MA: Harvard University Press.

McKibbin, Ross. 1975. "The Economic Policy of the Second Labour Government 1929–1931." *Past & Present* 68, no. 1: 95–123. https://doi.org/10.1093/past/68.1.95.

McLeod, J. A. 1933. "Problems Facing Canada." *Journal of the Canadian Bankers' Association* 40, no. 2: 159–65.

Middleton, Roger. 1985. *Towards the Managed Economy: Keynes, the Treasury and the Fiscal Policy Debate of the 1930s.* London: Methuen.

Middleton, Roger. 1998. *Charlatans or Saviours? Economists and the British Economy from Marshall to Meade.* Cheltenham: Edward Elgar.

Millmow, Alex. 2010. *The Power of Economic Ideas: The Origins of Keynesian Macroeconomic Management in Interwar Australia, 1929–39.* Canberra: ANU E Press.

Mitchell, B. R. 1962. *Abstract of British Historical Statistics.* Cambridge: At the University Press.

Morton, W. L. 1950. *The Progressive Party in Canada.* Toronto: University of Toronto Press.

Murphy, John. 2010. "Path Dependence and the Stagnation of Australian Social Policy Between the Wars." *Journal of Policy History* 22, no. 4: 450–73. https://doi.org/10.1017/S0898030610000229.

Naylor, James. 2006. "Canadian Labour Politics and the British Model, 1920–50." In *Canada and the British World: Culture, Migration, and Identity,* edited by Phillip Buckner and R. Douglas Francis, 288–308. Vancouver: UBC Press.

Naylor, James. 2016. *The Fate of Labour Socialism: The Co-operative Commonwealth Federation and the Dream of a Working-Class Future.* Toronto: University of Toronto Press.

Naylor, R. Tom. 1972. "The Ideological Foundations of Social Democracy and Social Credit." In *Capitalism and the National Question in Canada,* edited by Gary Teeple, 251–6. Toronto: University of Toronto Press.

NEC (National Employment Commission). 1938. *Final Report.* Ottawa: J. O. Patenaude.

Neufeld, E. P. 1972. *The Financial System of Canada: Its Growth and Development.* New York: St. Marin's.

Overacker, Louise. 1952. *The Australian Party System.* New Haven: Yale University Press.

Pal, Leslie A. 1986. "Relative Autonomy Revisited: The Origins of Canadian Unemployment Insurance." *Canadian Journal of Political Science* 19, no. 1: 71–92. https://doi.org/10.1017/S000842390005798X.

Pentland, H. Clare. 1979. "Western Canadian Labour Movement, 1897–1919." *Canadian Journal of Political and Social Theory* 3, no. 2: 53–78.

Perry, Harvey J. 1955. *Taxes, Tariffs, and Subsidies: A History of Canadian Fiscal Development,* vol. 1. Toronto: University of Toronto Press.

Plumptre, A. F. W. 1938. "The Arguments for Central Banking in the British Dominions." In *Essays in Political Economy: In Honour of E. J. Urwick*, edited by Harold A. Innis, 191–203. Toronto: University of Toronto Press.

Plumptre, A. F. W. 1940. *Central Banking in the British Dominions*. Toronto: University of Toronto Press.

Pollard, Sidney, and Colin Holmes, eds. 1973. *Documents of European Economic History*, vol. 3, *The End of the Old Europe, 1914–1939*. London: Edward Arnold.

Pomfret, Richard. 1981. *The Economic Development of Canada*. Toronto: Methuen.

Quigley, Neil C. 1992. "Monetary Policy and the New Zealand System: An Historical Perspective." Reserve Bank of New Zealand Discussion Paper No. G92/1, Wellington. https://silo.tips/download/monetary-policy-and-the-an-historical-perspective (accessed 14 June 2021).

RCBCC (Royal Commission on Banking and Currency in Canada). 1933. *Report*. Ottawa: J. O. Patenaude.

RCDPR (Royal Commission on Dominion–Provincial Relations). 1940a. *Report*, book 1, *Canada: 1867–1939*. Ottawa: Queen's Printer.

RCDPR (Royal Commission on Dominion–Provincial Relations). 1940b. *Report*, book 2, *Recommendations*. Ottawa: Queen's Printer.

Rimlinger, G. V. 1989. "Labour and the State on the Continent, 1800–1939." *The Cambridge Economic History of Europe*, vol. 8, *The Industrial Economies: The Development of Economic and Social Policies*, edited by Peter Mathias and Sidney Pollard, 549–606. Cambridge: Cambridge University Press.

Ritschel, Daniel. 1997. *The Politics of Planning: The Debate on Economic Planning in Britain in the 1930s*. Oxford: Clarendon Press.

Rosanvallon, Pierre. 1989. "The Development of Keynesianism in France." In *The Political Power of Economic Ideas: Keynesianism across Nations*, edited by Peter A. Hall, 171–93. Princeton: Princeton University Press.

Rydon, Joan. 1979. "The Conservative Electoral Ascendancy Between the Wars." In *Australian Conservatism: Essays in Twentieth Century Political History*, edited by Cameron Hazlehurst, 51–70. Canberra: Australian National University Press.

Safarian, A. E. [1959] 2009. *The Canadian Economy in the Great Depression*. 3rd ed. Montreal and Kingston: McGill-Queen's University Press.

Salais, Robert. 1988. "Why Was Unemployment So Low in France during the 1930s?" In *Interwar Unemployment in International Perspective*, edited by Barry J. Eichengreen and Tim J. Hatton, 247–88. Dordrecht: Kluwer.

Schedvin, C. B. 1970. *Australia and the Great Depression: A Study of Economic Development and Policy in the 1920s and 1930s*. Sydney: Sydney University Press.

Schwartz, Herman M. 1989. *In the Dominions of Debt: Historical Perspectives on Dependent Development*. Ithaca: Cornell University Press.

Schwarz, L. D. 1993. "Searching for Recovery: Unbalanced Budgets, Deflation and Rearmament in France during the 1930s." In *Capitalism in Crisis:*

International Responses to the Great Depression, edited by W. Redvers Garside, 96–113. London: Pinter.

Scott, Frank R. 1937. "The Privy Council and Mr. Bennett's 'New Deal' Legislation." *Canadian Journal of Economics and Political Science* 3, no. 2: 234–41. https://doi.org/10.2307/136802.

Simeon, Richard, and Ian Robinson. 1990. *State, Society, and the Development of Canadian Federalism*. Toronto: University of Toronto Press.

Simpson, Tony. 1990. *The Slump; The 1930s Depression: Its Origins and Aftermath*. Auckland: Penguin Books.

Sinclair, Keith. 1976. *Walter Nash*. Auckland: Auckland University Press.

Sinclair, Peter. 1975. "Class Structure and Populist Protest: The Case of Western Canada." *Canadian Journal of Sociology* 1, no. 1: 1–17. https://doi.org/10.2307/3340007.

Skelton, Oscar D. 1922. *Life and Letters of Sir Wilfrid Laurier*, vol. 1. New York: Century Co.

Skidelsky, Robert J. A. 1967. *Politicians and the Slump: The Labour Government of 1929–1931*. London: Macmillan.

Smith, Malcolm. 1998. *Democracy in a Depression: Britain in the 1920s and 1930s*. Cardiff: University of Wales Press.

Solomou, Solomos. 1996. *Themes in Macroeconomic History: The UK Economy, 1919–1939*. Cambridge: Cambridge University Press.

Struthers, James. 1983. *No Fault of Their Own: Unemployment and the Canadian Welfare State, 1914–1941*. Toronto: University of Toronto Press.

Tanner, Duncan. 2003. "The Politics of the Labour Movement, 1900–1939." In *A Companion to Early Twentieth-Century Britain*, edited by Chris Wrigley, 38–55. Oxford: Blackwell Publishing.

Tcherkinsky, M. Morduch. 1939. *The Land Tenure Systems in Europe*. Geneva: League of Nations.

Teeple, Gary. 1972. "'Liberals in a Hurry': Socialism and the CCF-NDP." In *Capitalism and the National Question in Canada*, edited by Gary Teeple, 229–50. Toronto: University of Toronto Press.

Trampusch, Christine, and Dennis C. Spies. 2014. "Agricultural Interests and the Origins of Capitalism: A Parallel Comparative History of Germany, Denmark, New Zealand, and the USA." *New Political Economy* 19, no. 6: 918–42. https://doi.org/10.1080/13563467.2013.861414.

Underhill, Frank H. 1935. "The Development of National Political Parties in Canada." *Canadian Historical Review* 16, no. 4: 367–87. https://doi.org/10.3138/CHR-16-04-01.

Urquhart, M. C., and Kenneth A. H. Buckley. 1965. *Historical Statistics of Canada*. Cambridge: At the University Press.

Weber, Eugen. 1994. *The Hollow Years: France in the 1930s*. New York and London: W. W. Norton.

Whitaker, Reginald. 1977. *The Government Party: Organizing and Financing the Liberal Party of Canada 1930–58.* Toronto: University of Toronto Press.

Whitaker, Reginald. 1992. *A Sovereign Idea: Essays on Canada as a Democratic Community.* Montreal and Kingston: McGill-Queen's University Press.

Williamson, Philip. 2003. "The Conservative Party, 1900–1939: From Crisis to Ascendancy." In *A Companion to Early Twentieth-Century Britain*, edited by Chris Wrigley, 3–22. Oxford: Blackwell Publishing.

Wilson, J. S. G. 1952. "The Australian Trading Banks." In *Banking in the British Commonwealth*, edited by R. S. Sayers, 1–38. Oxford: Clarendon.

Winch, Donald. 1969. *Economics and Policy: A Historical Study.* London: Hodder and Stoughton.

Winch, Donald. 1989. "Keynes, Keynesianism, and State Intervention." In *The Political Power of Economic Ideas: Keynesianism across Nations*, edited by Peter A. Hall, 107–27. Princeton: Princeton University Press.

Wood, Louis A. [1924] 1975. *A History of Farmers' Movement in Canada.* Reprint. Toronto: University of Toronto Press.

Wyatt, Alan. 1974. "The Rôle of a Minor Party: A Comparative Study of the British Liberal Party and the Australian Country Party since 1918." Unpublished MA thesis submitted to the Department of Politics, Brock University, St. Catharines.

Young, Walter. 1969. *The Anatomy of a Party: The National CCF, 1932–61.* Toronto: University of Toronto Press.

CHAPTER 4

Proto-Fordism: Seizing the Moment Under Democracy

In a speech delivered at Swedish parliament in 1928, Social Democratic leader Per Albin Hansson lamented that "Swedish society is still not the good citizens' home. ... socially the class society still endures and economically the dictatorship of the few prevails" (quoted in Tilton 1991, 127). He then elaborated on his idea of a "people's home" and emphasized how far Sweden was from it. After experiencing Social Democratic rule for most of the 1930s, however, Sweden was not any less class society. Nor did the "commanding heights" of the Swedish economy cease to be the "dictatorship of the few." What the Social Democrats did introduce was a new way of managing capitalism that would ensure sustained growth and higher standards of living for a few decades to follow. Freer trade, business-friendly investment environment, demand management, centralized bargaining, and social protection were all part of this innovation. That the United States was the only country, large or small, which matched (and, in some ways, surpassed) Sweden in economic policy innovation under democracy constituted one of the most fascinating aspects of the

---

An earlier version of parts of this chapter was published in "Revisiting Sweden's response to the Great Depression of the 1930s: economic policy in a regional context," Adnan Türegün, Scandinavian Economic History Review, copyright © 2017 The Scandinavian Society of Economic and Social History, reprinted by permission of Taylor & Francis Ltd, http://www.tandfonline.com on behalf of The Scandinavian Society of Economic and Social History.

© The Author(s), under exclusive license to Springer Nature Switzerland AG 2022
A. Türegün, *Policy Responses to the Interwar Economic Crisis*,
https://doi.org/10.1007/978-3-030-96953-0_4

period. The United States and Sweden were worlds apart in crisis experience, foreign economic profile, labour movement strength, state organization, and bureaucratic capacity. This makes their economic policy convergence even more intriguing.

The United States and Sweden provided the exemplary cases of proto-Fordism thanks to the innovative thinking and strategizing of their governing parties, Democrats and Social Democrats, respectively. Before taking office, both parties underwent an ideological renewal process and accordingly developed strategies to deal with the crisis. An unorthodox type of leadership was key to that process: Democratic Party leadership was more pragmatic and personal as represented by Franklin D. Roosevelt whereas Social Democratic leadership took on a more programmatic and collective form involving several theoretician-practitioner figures. In both cases, however, the leadership showed creativity and flexibility when strategizing. Under Roosevelt, the Democratic Party became a broker for coalition building between business, organized labour, and agrarians. What is often referred to as the New Deal coalition was in fact a disparate collection of issue-specific, often unstable coalitions. In Sweden, the Social Democrats did not need to be a common medium for cross-sectoral and cross-class coalitions because major groups of interest had their own political representation. Even there, each policy breakthrough required a different coalition: Deficit spending for public works was made possible by a Social Democratic–Agrarian agreement, unemployment insurance by a Social Democratic–Liberal deal, and a centralized industrial relations system by a historic compromise between the union and employers' federations.

I bring in the more conservative cases of Denmark and Norway to point out that cross-sectoral and cross-class alignments alone were not sufficient to lead to proto-Fordist policy innovation. With similar Social Democratic–Agrarian and union–employer compromises, these countries hardly distinguished themselves in the strict sense of economic policy from the mixed cases of post-1935 New Zealand and some of the small states in northwestern Europe. I highlight two factors in separating Denmark and Norway from Sweden and the United States: one structural, one ideational. First, the first duo were heavily resource- and export-dependent with the Danish economy featuring pastoral agriculture and small scale industry, and the Norwegian economy being led by the extractive sector. This structural limitation tilted economic policy towards trade—and, in the Norwegian case, also industrialization—policy. Second, neither the

Danish Social Democratic Party nor the Norwegian Labour Party went through the programmatic innovation that their Swedish counterpart did, or had the bold leadership that the US Democrats did. The Danish party was held by a liberal tradition and the Norwegian by a radical one.

The first section accounts for the proto-Fordist convergence of the US and Swedish responses as primary cases. While not overlooking their differences, I emphasize their common ideational and political threads. The second section deals with the Danish and Norwegian responses with a similar emphasis but also by paying attention to the structural constraints under which they unfolded. An outline of the argument is provided in Table 4.1.

A Curious Convergence

By any conventional measure, the US and Canadian, not Swedish, responses should have converged. The United States and Canada had nearly identical records in economic performance and features in industrial, labour, and state organization. Yet their responses could not be farther apart. In the same fashion, Sweden and Weimar Germany shared many things in common, including sectoral and class profile, economic and political organization, and social democratic governance. Again, they were polar opposites in economic policy. What set apart the United States and Sweden from other democracies was, first and foremost, their innovative and bold leadership. The ideational renewal and political creativity of the Democratic Party in the United States and the Social Democratic Workers' Party (Socialdemokratiska Arbetarepartiet, SAP) in Sweden made the difference.

United States

The United States experienced arguably the severest economic crisis in the industrialized world. At its low point in 1933, the economy was roughly half the size of its former (1929) self. Unemployment climbed to 25% among the active population (USBC 1965, 73) and 38% in industry (Eichengreen and Hatton 1988, 6–7) to remain stubbornly high for the rest of the decade. Moreover, unlike British-style commercial banks which withstood the crisis, over 9000 (39% of) US unit banks failed between 1929 and 1933 (Calomiris 2013, 166; see also Born [1977] 1983, 274–5). That some of this information was *post facto* may lighten the Republican

Table 4.1 Points of convergence and divergence in the proto-Fordist camp

Country group	Key determinants			Policy outcome
	Ruling party approach to sectoral and class interests	Institutional mediators	Structural limits to proto-Fordism	
Exemplary cases				
United States	Coalitional at political and policy levels (pro-business and pro-agrarian; labour-inclusive)	Majoritarian electoral rules; legislative and judicial counterpoints; mixed/universal unit banking	n/a	Proto-Fordist
Sweden	Coalitional at political and policy levels (pro-labour; agrarian- and business-inclusive)	Proportional representation; mixed/universal branch banking	n/a	Proto-Fordist
Mixed cases				
Denmark	Coalitional at political level (pro-labour; agrarian- and business-inclusive)	Proportional representation; mixed/universal branch banking	Pastoral agriculture; small scale industry	Mixed
Norway		Proportional representation; mixed/universal branch banking	Economy driven by the extractive sector	
Pre-1935	Pro-business and pro-agrarian; labour-exclusionary			Protectionist
Post-1935	Coalitional at political level (pro-labour; agrarian- and business-inclusive)			Mixed

administration's burden of responsibility for its unimpressive response. For the most part, however, it was a deliberate business-as-usual response relying on tariff protection to solve the problems of the productive sectors. The incoming Democratic administration did have alternative solutions, but its challenge was how to win over and mobilize these sectors since none of them was speaking with one voice and convincingly.

US labour had the lowest unionization rate among the democratic cases in this study. In 1930, only 7% of the labour force (or 11% of the non-agricultural wage and salary workers) were unionized (Stephens 1979, 115–6).[1] Moreover, 80% of this membership belonged to the Gomperist American Federation of Labor (AFL), which was an umbrella organization of over 100 craft unions (USBC 1965, 97–8). The conservative AFL not only refused to collaborate with the Democratic administration but also actively opposed many of its policies. However, the US union movement would be transformed with the establishment, in 1935, of the Committee for Industrial Organization (CIO, to be renamed as the Congress of Industrial Organizations in 1938) as a federation of industrial unions. Giving a new impetus to labour mobilization, the CIO reached a level of membership comparable to that of the AFL and was thus instrumental in the tripling of the unionization rate by 1940 (Laslett 1989, 539–42). Yet the growing strength and militancy of organized labour were more a consequence of the pro-labour provisions of the National Industrial Recovery and National Labor Relations (Wagner) acts than the other way around (cf. Goldfield 1989). The rise of industrial unionism as represented by the CIO was a class-organizing and class-incorporating effect of the New Deal (Levine 1988; Stryker 1990).

Agrarians were more articulate in their policy demands but were equally multifarious. Three major organizations representing mainly Midwestern corn and wheat farmers, as well as Southern cotton and tobacco planters, proposed policies to dispense domestic surplus in the face of price collapse (Johnson 1963; Kirkendall 1975; Slichter 1956; Trampusch and Spies 2014, 933–5). The American Farm Bureau Federation, the largest and most conservative of the three, promoted an equalization fee scheme under which government would buy the surplus and dump it on the world market and producers who sold on the domestic market at a higher price would cover the difference between domestic and world market prices. For the National Grange (or Patrons of Industry), government would pay for the cost of dumping the surplus on the world market under an export debenture plan. The third and most radical group, National Farmers Union, proposed a price-fixing scheme based on the cost of production.

The way Roosevelt responded to these proposals during his presidential campaign in 1932 was indicative of his coalition-building strategy. Trying not to alienate any one group, he incorporated elements from each proposal into his agricultural policy statements. The Voluntary Domestic Allotment Plan that formed the backbone of the new administration's agricultural adjustment programme met the price maintenance goal of all three groups by paying farmers to reduce production (Johnson 1963, 40; Kirkendall 1975, 88; Slichter 1956, 247). The plan was hugely beneficial to Southern planters and Midwestern farmers, silencing the protest movement that had risen among the latter. In contrast, it discriminated against Southern tenants, especially landless sharecroppers, as well as farm workers who would also be excluded from the pro-labour and social security initiatives of the New Deal (Depew et al. 2013; Eidlin 2018, 177–9; Kirkendall 1975, 90–6; Skocpol and Finegold 1982, 258–60; Trampusch and Spies 2014, 935; Winders 2005, 393–5).

Unlike industrial labour and commercial farmers, no section of business provided a wholesale or sustained support to any policy cluster in either phase of the New Deal.[2] Business approach to fiscal expansion, for example, ranged from outright hostility to active support and defied sectional distinctions (Collins 1978, 371–84). Even traditionally protectionist employers organized in the Republican-dominated National Association of Manufacturers (NAM) could not agree on a point of policy in the New Deal with the notable exception of its pro-labour legislative and regulatory initiatives, which they consistently and publicly opposed (Delton 2020, 107–31; Tedlow 1976). NAM's ambivalence towards the New Deal was displayed most openly in the cases of the National Industrial Recovery and Reciprocal Trade Agreements acts. Concerning the former, it saw a boon to its members in the suspension of antitrust laws while, at the same time, complaining about the lack of import controls and, of course, the entitlement of workers to organize independently and bargain collectively. NAM supported the trade legislation for its promise of expanding trade but had concerns about its unconditional "most favoured nation" clause (Delton 2020, 117–29).

Given this ambivalent business position, the Democratic Party's and Roosevelt's political manoeuvring became all the more important for coalition building. In the absence of organized or institutional business support, the new administration co-opted many of those businessmen from large corporations who had spearheaded the Progressive era's corporate liberalism to serve on various advisory and regulatory boards (McQuaid 1978, 354–62). It had a similar, co-optative approach to the more sympathetic labour and farm groups and their spokespersons. What became known as the New Deal coalition thus lacked an institutional dimension and was in fact a collection of piecemeal, ad hoc arrangements brokered by intermediaries on specific policies. Even policy-specific alignments were not always sustainable over time. While support for the agricultural adjustment legislation strengthened for the rest of the decade and beyond, it held its own for social security but significantly weakened for the pro-labour industrial relations legislation (Winders 2005).

That the Democratic Party mediated and brokered diverse policy alignments was a testimony to the political creativity, skilfulness, and resolve of its leadership. Yet this begs the question of why and how it became willing and able to do so. The answer must be sought in the ideological and political reorientation of the party. With a conservative rural base in the South, the Democrats took a decisive step for self-renewal in the mid-1920s by expanding into the urban and industrial Northeast (Burnham 1967, 301). This was the context which gave rise to a new type of leadership as represented by such figures as Senator Robert Wagner (after whom the New Deal's signature labour relations legislation would be named), Cordell Hull (future secretary of state), and, of course, Roosevelt himself. With the renewal, the Democratic Party became an enlightened liberal party reminiscent of the Lloyd George Liberals in the United Kingdom. Just as the Liberals relied on proto-Keynesian ideas to propose public works programmes, the Democrats had a storehouse of Progressive-era ideas to dip into, particularly the idea of a new, corporate liberalism advocating tripartite economic regulation and protective social legislation (McDonough 1990, 147–8; Weinstein 1968).[3] Although the "roaring" 1920s abated the tide of corporate liberalism, the depression would give it a renewed strength (McQuaid 1978, 346–52).

From a policy perspective, however, the Democrats had three advantages over the Liberals. First, unlike the UK party whose support base was mainly urban, the Democratic Party maintained a strong rural representation, particularly from the conservative South, while building an urban and industrial base. Although the coexistence of the conservative rural and liberal urban wings created tensions within the party (Huthmacher 1968, 134), it would prove to be a blessing in disguise for the type of cross-sectoral and cross-class compromises under the New Deal. Second, while the Liberals were a third party squeezed between the Conservatives and Labour, the Democrats as part of a two-party system had no one to contend with on their left. Except for the Socialist Party, which had sporadic success at presidential elections between 1910 and 1932 (USBC 1965, 682), no socialist, social democratic, or labour party ever established a significant presence at the national level. Third, unlike the Liberals who were facing an uphill battle against the hegemony of neoclassical orthodoxy among the UK financial institutions, policymaking bodies, and leading political parties, the Democrats worked within a relatively open ideational space where neoclassical ideas had less currency. Reflecting late capitalist development in a settler society, institutionalist-historicist economics and unorthodox monetary ideas circulating among the agrarian populist movements of late-nineteenth-century West offset the appeal of the universalizing economic orthodoxy (White 2012, 99–125; Winch 1969, 222–32). In the first three decades of the new century, both microeconomic experimentalist ideas (e.g., scientific management, social engineering, and planning) and underconsumptionist, proto-Keynesian ideas could be heard from urban and industrial United States (Huthmacher 1968, 57–106; Stein [1969] 1990, 131–68; Winch 1969, 237–40).

In hindsight, it is tempting to conclude that formal institutions facilitated the New Deal innovation. This conclusion must be resisted for it simply serves to justify the final policy outcome. At the economic level, the geographically limited but functionally universal (or mixed) unit banking system reflecting a unique pattern of financial organization was particularly vulnerable to economic downturns (Born [1977] 1983, 92–9, 175–81; Mackenzie [1932] 1935, 191–244; Willis 1954). It was thus responsible for massive bank failures in the early 1930s and helped create a situation warranting drastic action. The New Deal's signature banking legislation, Glass–Steagall Act of 1933, separating commercial and investment banking was in response to these failures.

Politically, a presidential executive heavily checked by the bicameral legislature and the judiciary under federalism was not exactly the type of state organization which would anticipate or facilitate the bold departure from US public policy course that was the New Deal. The Supreme Court's repeal of the National Industrial Recovery and Agricultural Adjustment acts in 1935–1936 was a case in point. It may be argued that a "fragmented" state organization, coupled with late and incomplete bureaucratization (Skowronek 1982), was "permeable" to societal interests and thus absorbed progressive initiatives in the 1930s (Skocpol 1980; Steinmo 1993, 69; Weir 1989, 60–73; Weir and Skocpol 1985). Yet this perspective not only assumes the Roosevelt administration's substantive choices and political strategies to build popular support behind them but also overlooks the executive branch's lack of policy capacity to pursue those choices. It is no wonder that the administration would also be occupied with building that capacity throughout the New Deal (Burnham 1967, 302; Skowronek 1982, 288–9).

Electorally, Roosevelt and his Democrats did not need the help of US majoritarianism to win a solid majority of electoral colleges and Congressional seats, respectively, beginning with 1932. Roosevelt received over 57% of the popular vote in the 1932 presidential election and 61% in 1936, compared with 40% and under 37%, respectively, for his Republican opponent (Mackie and Rose 1974, 423). Majoritarian electoral rules may have exaggerated but, certainly, did not manufacture the Democratic majorities in both houses of Congress (USBC 1965, 691). However, one feature of the electoral system that had an impact on political alignments and policy outcomes was the rurally biased apportionment of the House of Representatives seats (Saint-Etienne 1984, 8–16). That the New Deal rewarded commercial farmers most consistently among the major groups of interest was in part due to this bias.

Time was on the Democrats' side in breaking with their predecessors' ways. Like the New Zealand Labour and French Popular Front parties, the Democratic Party had a situational advantage in that, while in opposition, it had the chance to assess what was not working against an unfolding and unprecedented crisis. This observation can be extended to the cases of the Scandinavian social democratic parties, which will be dealt with next, or even the UK Conservatives and the German Nazis. It should not, however, be pushed too far as the assessment of a situation is not a straightforward informational process. Theories, ideologies, programmes, and other ideational designs all come into play. For this reason, the Italian Fascists or the Soviet Communists were able to break with their own old ways just as the Canadian Liberals or the Australian conservative coalitions stayed the course of their predecessors. We will never know if Roosevelt and his Democrats would have still left their mark had they been in office at the beginning of the crisis. What we do know, however, is that they had the political creativity, skilfulness, and resolve to break with the Republican ways.

Sweden

With characteristics similar to those of its UK counterpart, the Swedish downturn would not give any hint of an innovative response. It was mild and short except for unemployment. Falling by only 11% from 1929 to 1932, industrial production already surpassed the level of 1929 by 10% in 1934. By mid-decade, national income would fully recover, too, from a

13% slump during 1929–1932 (Lundberg [1953] 1957, 11, 23). Although general unemployment did not go over 10% at any point, unemployment among the unionized labour force shot up to 23% in 1933 and did not go down below the 1929 mark (10%) until 1939 (Grytten 2008b, 398). The short-lived Conservative and Liberal governments were typically protectionist in their responses. Forming a minority government in 1932, the Social Democrats achieved policy innovation in piecemeal compromises with different political parties and economic actors.

The Social Democratic policy mix represented both success and failure for all major groups of interest. It meant failure in the sense that no single group was able to fully achieve its demands. At the same time, it was a success because it included something from every particular set of demands. Labour wanted free trade in agriculture as well as in industry, the abolition of the pre-existing relief works programmes along with the Unemployment Commission (Arbetslöshetskommissionen, AK) responsible for them, and the establishment of fully market-based and deficit-financed public works programmes under a different institutional arrangement (a new national labour market agency). Unemployment insurance and progressive taxation were among the other things labour wanted. In contrast, employers wanted the continuation of the AK-administered relief works system, lower taxation, and wage restraint. As for farmers, opposing any enlargement of the state's role in fighting unemployment, they demanded higher protection levels, both internationally and domestically (Braatoy 1939, 7–24; Clark 1941, 138–60; Heclo 1974, 100–5; Söderpalm [1973] 1975; Tingsten [1941] 1973, 285–307).

A series of compromises struck after 1932 can be seen as a trade-off between the three groups of interest. In the 1933 Crisis Agreement between the SAP and the Agrarian Party (Bondeförbundet), labour accepted the system of protection and subsidies for agriculture and, with certain pro-labour changes, the continuation of the AK and its relief works programmes. In return, farmers agreed to the introduction of deficit-financed public works programmes as a measure of job creation for the urban population. The introduction of unemployment insurance, which the crisis agreement passed up, required a different deal in 1934, this time, between the SAP and the Liberals. When the SAP government tried to improve the old-age pensions scheme in 1936, however, it met the combined opposition of the Conservative, Liberal, and Agrarian parties and resigned in indignation (Heclo 1974, 211–26). A strong showing by the SAP in the election held the same year convinced the Agrarians to establish a more principled red–green partnership in the form of a coalition government. The industrial peace process to be culminated in the 1938 Saltsjöbaden compromise between the Trade Union Confederation (Landsorganisationen, LO) and the Swedish Employers' Federation (Svenska Arbetsgivareföreningen, SAF) forced labour to give in to key employer demands such as wage restraint and lower corporate taxes. On their part, employers had to go along with an all-inclusive Labour Market Board (Arbetsmarknadsstyrelsen, AMS) to replace the AK.

Central to these cross-sectoral and cross-class compromises was the SAP's ideological and political transformation in the 1920s that favourably positioned it to respond to the crisis in creative ways. Founded in 1889 on Marxist principles like other social democratic parties, it soon adopted a parliamentary road to socialism and aligned with the Liberals in the transition to democracy (Andrae [1973] 1975; Olsen 1992, 93–7; Tingsten [1941] 1973, 345–457; Tomasson 1969). With the achievement of political democracy after World War I, it became the largest party in both popular strength and seats in the second chamber of the Riksdag (national parliament), governing in three short stints between 1920 and 1926. However, the SAP governments of the 1920s were unimpressive in performance not just because of their minority status but also because of their own volition. Still holding on to a broad notion of Marxism and a working-class party model, the SAP established an investigatory commission in 1920 on socialization, whose activities would be limited largely to issuing reports before it was dissolved in the early 1930s (Tilton 1991, 86–102). The party also tried but failed to do away with the AK which was notorious for its anti-union practices during and after World War I. Moreover, making a "left" turn for the 1928 election, the SAP ran on a platform of limited socialization and fielded candidates on a joint ticket with the Communists (Schüllerqvist 2013, 104). The result was a heavy defeat.

At the same time, the 1920s were a decade of Social Democratic ideational and programmatic renewal that the 1928 defeat would only accelerate. The death of the founding leader Hjalmar Branting in 1925 ushered in a new generation of leadership who would piece together a reformist project to expand the party beyond its traditional working-class base and reorient it to manage and tame capitalism (Berman 1998b, 150–75, 2006, 152–76; Eyerman 1985; Higgins 1985; Schüllerqvist 2013, 107–12; Tilton 1991). In 1928, Hansson, new party leader and prime minister after 1932, came up with the concept of people's home (*folkhemmet*) as the organizing principle of the project. To provide a broader roof than that of the working-class ghetto in the old party concept, the people's home would have three pillars: economic democracy, welfare state, and demand management. Nils Karleby, young secretary of the commission on socialization, theorized economic democracy as something that can be achieved by "gradually stripping away the prerogatives of capitalists, like layers of an onion" without socializing the formal ownership of capital (Berman 1998a, 384; see also Tilton 1991, 70–86). The intellectual foundations of welfare state were laid by Gustav Möller (1938), Hansson's minister of social affairs, along with Gunnar Myrdal and Alva Myrdal. As the minister of finance, Ernst Wigforss (1938) built a rationale for demand management by drawing on a variety of proto-Keynesian ideas such as Marxian underconsumptionism, the work of Lloyd George Liberals, and Sweden's own "Stockholm School of Economics" (Gustafsson 1973; Heckscher 1953; Kragh 2012; Lindbeck 1974, 182–93; Tilton 1979; Winch 1966).

After winning the 1932 election, the SAP made good on its promise to introduce a deficit-financed public works programme as well as labour market reforms by sending a legislative package to the Riksdag in early 1933 (Lindvall 2012, 246–9). It was eventually able to pass a watered-down version of the package thanks to a realignment weakening the anti-labour elements within the Agrarian Party. This was the beginning of a durable Social Democratic–Agrarian rapprochement reminiscent of that between the Liberals and the SAP for political democracy earlier in the century. It was by no means the first time Swedish farmers exerted political influence. Just a year previously, a national farmers' group (Sveriges Allmänna Lantbrukssällskap) had exacted a major concession from the Liberal government to gain state sanctioning of production and price controls in dairy farming (Rothstein 1992, 176–84).

Farmers had been an independent force in Swedish politics since the establishment of an estates assembly under absolutism. Occupying half of the cultivated land at the closure of the Middle Ages, freeholder and leaseholder (tax-paying) peasants acquired "fourth estate" status after nobles, clergymen, and burghers. The final consolidation of freeholding, independent peasant farming was completed in the mid-1800s, by which time a state-imposed enclosure campaign had transformed the concentrated village communities owning small, scattered plots into the scattered rural settlements owning concentrated, larger plots (Dahl 1961; Gustavson 1986, 1–17; Heckscher [1941] 1954, 150–73; Scott 1977, 288–92; Østerud 1978, 130–7, 144–8). With the conversion of the Riksdag from an estates assembly into a bicameral parliament in 1866, farmers came to dominate the second chamber and counterbalance crown-appointed, aristocratic-bureaucratic governments (Braatoy 1939, 92; Rustow 1955, 9–42; Tingsten [1941] 1973, 3–6). Organized in the "New" Farmers' Party (Lantmannapartiet), a predecessor of the modern Agrarian Party, they pushed for tariff protection with the decline of agricultural prices in the 1870s and got it in 1888 thanks to an alliance with the aristocratic, large estate owners who dominated the first chamber (Heckscher [1941] 1954, 257–9; Jörberg and Kranz 1989, 1055, 1061–2; Montgomery 1939, 145–50). Not until after the Social Democratic innovation in the early 1930s, however, were they able to exercise political power directly.

Similarly, employers and unions had a history of compromises but not as principled and comprehensive as the one in 1938. In the context of late industrialization, both classes came of age late. Social Democratic unionists founded the LO as a federation of predominantly craft-based unions in 1898. Shortly after taking off the ground, however, the LO underwent profound changes. On one hand, in 1900, it changed its formal and national affiliation with the SAP to an informal and local affiliation between the branches of the member unions and the party (Blake 1960). On the other hand, in 1906, it adopted industrial unionism as an alternative to craft unionism, which had been in decline since the late 1890s (Johnston 1962, 23–9). Its increasing militancy for universal suffrage at the turn of the century had a class-organizing effect on employers, who responded by founding the SAF in 1902 (Gustafsson 1986, 28–31; Johnston 1962, 68–91; Kjellberg 1992, 94–5, 98; Korpi 1978, 55–75; Montgomery 1939, 202–9; Scott 1977, 412–9). In 1906, the LO and the SAF struck the so-called December compromise which, in its recognition of workers' right to organize and strike and of employers' right to organize work and lock out workers, was a prototype of the Saltsjöbaden compromise (Johnston 1962, 139–44). A year earlier, the Metalworkers' Union (Metallindustriarbetareförbundet, Metall) and the Engineering Employers' Association (Verkstadsföreningen, VF) reached an "engineering compromise" amounting to a de facto collective agreement in metalworking industry on a national scale. However, employer–union relations were not always strife-free. In fact, the largest industrial conflict in Swedish history took place shortly after these compromises. Adopting a centralized organizational structure and an aggressive class line from the start, the SAF successfully engaged the LO in the General Strike of 1909 and declared a "general lockout," which ended the strike. After 1909, the two federations "never met until 1938" (Gustafsson 1986, 30).

Big business and "big labour" were at the forefront of industrial relations contention again when the SAP and the Agrarians were negotiating for a crisis agreement in early 1933. Unlike home market industries, export-oriented industries led by large metalworking and engineering companies, including five of the country's largest companies which formed a pressure group called the Directors' Club,[4] opposed the SAP's domestic market-oriented agenda (Gustaffson 1986, 35–41; Korpi 1978, 86, 1982, 133; Olsen 1991, 130–1, 1992, 53–55). For them, wage discipline was essential to competitiveness in international markets. A construction workers' strike launched by Communist-led unions over wage reductions in April 1933 would prove pivotal to the formation of a "wage discipline" coalition involving not just employers and unions in the export sector (e.g., Directors' Club, VF, and Metall) but also the Social Democratic and Agrarian parties as new partners (Johnston 1962, 34–5; Swenson 1989, 43–53, 2002, 100–21). The strike dragged on for over 10 months before the LO forced the unions involved to call it off. Later in the decade, the SAP–Agrarian government bolstered this alignment with public policy, including the corporate tax reform of 1938 which favoured the largest and most profitable companies concentrated in the export sector (Steinmo 1988, 416–22, 1993, 85–91). The road to Saltsjöbaden was thus paved.

As in the US case, economic and political institutions played their mediating role in Swedish innovation. Reflecting a late-follower pattern, Sweden's commercial banks taking on a mixed or universal form to combine commercial and investment functions had been the chief source of industrial financing since the late nineteenth century (Larsson 1991; Melin 1929; Olsen 1991, 125, 1992, 49–53, 61; Olsson 1991, 29–30; Samuelsson 1958). Via their direct and indirect investment activities, these banks came to dominate key industries, including those in the export sector. By 1935, the largest four of the country's 28 commercial banks had their representatives as "captains of industry and finance" on the boards of close to 400 joint-stock companies which accounted for 80% of the capital resources of all joint-stock companies (Braatoy 1939, 118–20; Gaitskell 1938, 100–2; Kjellstrom 1934, 6–12; Montgomery 1939, 129–130).[5] The close bank–industry relations gave rise to a functionally and organizationally unified capitalist class and indirectly helped shape a strong working class. They were also responsible for the vulnerability of the banking system to crises. The country's second largest commercial bank

(Skandinaviska Banken) needed a government bailout in 1932 after the crash of the Kreuger industrial group in which the bank had been heavily involved as creditor (Lindgren 1982). The crash prompted a new banking legislation, in 1933, instructing the commercial banks to sell their shares in industry and not to acquire new shares (Larsson 1991, 94). However, the banks would find loopholes in the legislation to keep their industrial shares in indirect ways.

Proportional representation was a double-edged sword. It was introduced as part of the parliamentary reform of 1907–1909, at the insistence of the Conservatives who saw in it (as well as in maintaining the legislative equality of the two chambers) a mechanism to hold on to their power with the transition to full male suffrage, and much to the consternation of the Liberal and Social Democratic parties favouring a majoritarian system with a weaker first chamber (Braatoy 1939, 51–52; Rustow 1955, 62; Stjernquist 1966, 134, 1987, 288–9; Verney 1957, 138–142, 165). Proportional representation may have solidified the Liberal–Social Democratic coalition in the early twentieth century and helped the Social Democratic–Agrarian rapprochement in the 1930s (Katzenstein 1985, 153–4; Steinmo 1993, 8–9; Tingsten [1941] 1973, 416–57; Verney 1957, 202–14). In the 1932 election, the SAP won 45% of second chamber seats with 42% of the popular vote. Its "cow deal" partner, Agrarians, won 16% of the seats with 14% of the vote (Flora et al. 1983, 143, 185–186). The SAP's share of the vote increased to 46% in 1936, but it came up short of a parliamentary majority, thus needing the Agrarians, whose vote stuck at 14%, to form a majority government—the first since 1917. It is equally true that the same system produced weak minority governments mired in distributional conflicts and instability in Sweden and elsewhere in Europe during the 1920s (Eichengreen 1992, 92–7; Eichengreen and Simmons 1995; Maier 1975). It was not proportional representation per se but its creative use by the Social Democrats in the world-historical context of the 1930s that brought about Swedish compromises. Conversely, majoritarianism did not deter the US Democrats and their Labour counterparts in New Zealand from striking compromises.

In both the US and Swedish cases, governing parties' substantive choices and strategies, rather than some pregiven interests or formal institutions, were the tipping point for economic policy innovation. The two countries could not be more different in interest representation and institutional profile. What drew them closer was their political leaders' drive for experimentation. That brought an economic policy innovation unmatched in the democratic world.

The Limits of Political Alignments

As secondary cases, Denmark and Norway serve a useful comparative purpose on three counts. First, they clearly show that the economy puts structural limits on what government and other actors can do in economic policy. Denmark's export-dependent pastoral economy, like New Zealand's, skewed economic policy towards foreign trade. Similarly, Norwegian economic policy was preoccupied with industrialization in the context of a trade-dependent resource economy. Second, both cases demonstrate that agrarian–labour and employer–union compromises are not a guarantee for economic policy innovation. Denmark was the first country to have a Social Democratic–Agrarian compromise in Scandinavia, and its employers' and union federations had been operating in a general agreement framework since 1899. Yet the Danish response was closer to protectionism than to proto-Fordism, especially in foreign economic relations and macroeconomic policy. Norwegian actors struck agrarian–labour and employer–union compromises in the mid-1930s. Similar to Denmark, however, Norway hardly went beyond protectionism. When it did, it was more in a developmentalist direction than in a proto-Fordist one. Third, both countries' social democratic experience confirms the primacy of ideas and strategies in economic policy outcomes. Neither social democratic party underwent an ideational and strategic renewal that their Swedish counterpart did. The socialization argument died hard in the Norwegian Labour Party and economic liberalism in the Danish Social Democratic Party.

Denmark and Norway diverged from Sweden in their responses despite the fact that all three experienced a mild and short downturn (Hildebrand 1975; Klovland 1998, 328–9). In Denmark, the GNP did, in fact, increase throughout the 1930s except for 1932, when it decreased by only 3% (Johansen 1987, 46). The Norwegian downturn paled in comparison to its predecessor in the 1920s (Øksendal 2010, 68–70). Norway achieved overall recovery by 1935 (Grytten 1998, 100). Its level of industrial production, for example, was 8% higher in 1935 than it had been in 1929 (Hodne 1983, 86). However, as in Sweden, unemployment bucked these trends in both countries, where the rate was 7% in 1929, rose to 11% in 1932, and dropped to 6% in 1939. While these figures were not high internationally, trade union unemployment remained consistently high: It was 16% and 15% in Denmark and Norway, respectively, in 1929, 29% and 33% in 1933, and 18% in 1939 (Grytten 2008b, 398).

Denmark

Unlike Sweden and Norway, Denmark had had a Social Democratic-led government when the international crisis broke out—a coalition formed with the Radical Liberals (Det radikale Venstre) in 1929.[6] To last throughout the 1930s, this was a typical Lib–Lab alliance in the traditional sense of the term although the Radical Liberals had support among small farmers in addition to their main electoral base in urban constituencies. The red–green alliance came with the Kanslergade agreement between the coalition government and the agrarian-based Liberals (Venstre) that was signed on a date (30 January 1933) symbolized by Hitler's coming to power (Lindström 2000, 445; Ruth 1984, 85–6). Reflecting on the agreement, Social Democratic Prime Minister Thorvald Stauning emphasized its defensive, antifascist motive: "We have sacrificed some principles, but we have saved the country" (cited in Larsen 2010, 97). Unlike the Swedish "cow deal," Kanslergade was thus mainly a political, rather than policy, document. It did not change Danish economic policy in any fundamental way. Similarly, while inspiring Saltsjöbaden (Swenson 1991, 518–23), the September agreement (Septemberforliget) of 1899 between Danish employers' and union federations lacked the former's binding power in industrial relations.

The weaker innovative policy thrust of Danish historical compromises was mainly because of the stronger influence of liberalism on the Social Democratic Party in a context of early capitalist development driven by agricultural product processing for export. Taking off in the age of free trade and spurred by the rising UK demand for foodstuffs, Danish industrialization prioritized the processing of locally produced pastoral, particularly dairy, products (Hildebrand 1978; Jörberg 1973). This choice led to a craft pattern of production dominated by small-scale companies producing light consumer goods for both export and the domestic market (Jörberg 1973, 406–15). It also had consequences for the structure of the capitalist class in the form of lower levels of concentration and centralization, and for the organization of unions along craft lines.

Moreover, this pattern of capitalist development created backward linkages in agriculture by transforming it into a leading, high-technology, and export-driven sector (Kristensen 1958, 204; Trampusch and Spies 2014, 928–30).[7] Indeed, in its agricultural export specialization and dependence on the UK market,[8] Denmark was closer to Australia and especially New Zealand than to the other Scandinavian countries. Another feature of Danish agriculture that separated it from its regional counterparts was the relatively large share of middle- and large-holdings (and thus the small share of smallholdings) in the total area of cultivation (Tcherkinsky 1939, 31, 33). This pattern was the consequence of a state-initiated move towards freeholding land use that had begun in the 1790s (Østerud 1978, 125–30).

As in the UK case, Danish capitalist development went hand in hand with political liberalism (Luebbert 1991, 110–58). Democratization began with the Constitution of 1849, which would establish a bicameral parliament and introduce equal but restricted male suffrage. The Conservatives dominated the upper house (Landsting) from the outset and liberal, reformist elements came to control the lower house (Folketing) (Katzenstein 1985, 152–3). This was the liberal political-economic environment to which the United Liberal (Det forenede Venstre) and Social Democratic parties were born in the early 1870s. While also representing urban reformist groups, the United Liberals emerged as the class party of farmers in general and, unlike other agrarian parties elsewhere in Europe, resolutely supported domestic liberalism and international free trade given the competitive position of Danish exports (Andersen and Jensen 2001, 97–104; Esping-Andersen 1985, 73–8; Nevers 2013, 102). The United Liberals could not remain united for long but were able to form Denmark's first parliamentary government in 1901. They soon suffered a final split when the Radical Liberals broke away to form a party of smallholders and urban middle strata, leaving the main group behind as a purely agrarian (middle and large farmers) party which would come to be known simply as the Liberals. In their social and economic outlook, the Radical Liberals were closer to the Social Democrats and began to collaborate with them for political democracy from the 1910s on. With that realignment, the Liberals truly and uniquely became a carrier of the liberal, anti-regulation ideology despite their agrarian base (Nevers 2013, 103–4).

The Danish Social Democrats adopted a parliamentary road to power from the outset, thus setting a moderate example for their counterparts in Scandinavia (Berglund and Lindström 1978, 26–48; Elvander 1979; Lafferty 1971, 176–98; Tingsten [1941] 1973, 6–12). In 1913, they became the first Scandinavian social democratic party in the region to enter a Lib–Lab alliance for political democracy. However, the liberal political-economic environment which they were born to and developed in nurtured conformist tendencies among them, thus constituting a handicap for ideational and programmatic renewal. Although a new programme ("Denmark for the People") espousing a people's party model was launched in 1934 (Krake 2020, 6), it did not propose any specific policy innovation. The party resisted deficit spending (Garside and Topp 2001; Topp 1988) and, at Kanslergade, gave in to the tax cuts and currency devaluation demands of the agrarian Liberals, who had turned protectionist—if only briefly—under pressure from the right-wing Farmers' Union (Krake 2020, 7–9). Unlike the Swedish "cow deal," Kanslergade did not deliver labour market-based public works or deficit spending.

Denmark's (and, as will be seen shortly, Norway's) institutional arrangements were remarkably similar to Sweden's. The former switched to mixed banking in the late nineteenth century, but it came too late to change the craft pattern of consumer goods production with small scale establishments (Glindemann 1929). Proportional representation came as the final piece of a series of guarantees that the Conservatives secured for their continuing domination of the upper chamber. First, a constitutional revision in 1866 strengthened the Landsting in relation to the lower chamber. Second, they secured indirect election for their favourite chamber in return for accepting universal male suffrage in 1915. Third, in the transition to universal suffrage three years later, they exacted a big concession from the left in the form of a switch from the majoritarian to proportional electoral rules (Lafferty 1971, 143–59). Proportional representation checked the power of the Social Democrats but also, in a historical twist, facilitated the Kanslergade agreement. In the 1929 election, they received 42% of the popular vote but needed a partner to take office since their share of Folketing seats was only 41%. Their coalition with the Radical Liberals, who had received 11% of both the votes and seats, secured a majority in the Folketing (Flora et al. 1983, pp. 107, 161–2). Yet the coalition still lacked a majority in the Landsting. After the same picture emerged in 1932, the Social Democratic–Radical Liberal coalition was to negotiate with the agrarian Liberals. The result was political innovation but not necessarily policy innovation.

Norway

If Denmark was at the liberal end of Scandinavian social democracy, Norway was at the radical end. Unlike its Danish and Swedish social democratic counterparts, the Norwegian Labour Party (Det norske Arbeiderparti) took a revolutionary road to socialism, joined the Third International after World War I, and made peace with parliamentary politics only in the late 1920s. The Crisis Agreement that brought the party to power in 1935 was the final end of its oppositional approach to politics since its foundation. Yet, as in the Danish case, the Norwegian red–green agreement lacked innovative thrust in economic policy. Nor did the compromise reached between Norwegian employers' and labour federations later the same year establish a comprehensive or durable framework for industrial relations; it was limited in scope and valid for only two years.

The radicalism of the Labour Party was rooted in Norway's polarized economy coupled with its cultural and regional divisions on a centre–periphery axis (Rokkan 1966, 73–89, 1981, 63–75). In many ways, the Norwegian economy was a prototype of underdevelopment with an enclave urban sector supported by the export-oriented extractive sector and surrounded by a technically backward rural sector that did not produce enough surplus to feed the urban population. The extractive sector was dominated by fisheries until the 1870s and, from then on, by overseas shipping.[9] In this trade-driven economy, while being formally organized along mixed banking, Norwegian commercial banks focused on financing exports rather than industrial investment (Olsson 1991, 29; Swenson 1929). Consequently, foreign capital came to play a large role in Norway's late and incomplete industrialization, making it the only Scandinavian country with high levels of foreign ownership in industry (Jörberg 1973, 434). Import-substituting industrialization became an important policy theme in the 1930s against this background.

In contrast to its Swedish and Danish counterparts, the Labour Party did not contribute to democratization. Norway was the first country in Scandinavia to transition to political democracy. The Constitution of 1814 established a unicameral parliament (Storting) and introduced equal but restricted male suffrage. Parliamentary government was introduced in 1884, universal male suffrage in 1898, and universal suffrage in 1921 (Andrén 1964, 115–35; Lafferty 1971, 116–28). Political democracy came with the impulse of liberal forces while labour stood on the sidelines. There was no Lib–Lab coalition. Although the Labour Party began electoral contestation as early as 1894, it had been an anti-systemic party from its foundation in 1887 to its reformist reorientation in the late 1920s (Lafferty 1971, 82–98). It remained a "section" of the Third International until 1923 and finally reconciled itself with a parliamentary road to socialism later in that decade, when the SAP of Sweden was already proposing a deficit-financed spending programme to fight unemployment. The crisis agreement signed with the Agrarians, Labour's first compromise with a "bourgeois" party, complemented this political turn. Like the Danish Social Democrats, however, it was wary of deficit spending when governing (Grytten 2008a, 272).

Unlike the labour movement, agrarians took part in Norwegian democratization. As in the rest of Scandinavia, the consolidation of freeholding land tenure in the course of the nineteenth century transformed the peasantry into an independent class in Norway (Østerud 1978, 114–25). Although agrarians were not organized as an independent political party until 1920, they formed the rural pillar of the Liberal Party (Venstre) representing both urban and rural constituencies in the struggle for political democracy from the late nineteenth century on. Founded in 1896, the Norwegian Farmers' Union was the first organized expression of the agrarian movement although it was dominated by eastern commercial farmers from the outset (Christensen 2001, 37; Greenhill 1965, 216). The Union became more assertive in the 1910s, demanding equality in tariff protection between industry and agriculture in 1912, and engineering a split from the Liberal Party by founding the Agrarian Party (Bondepartiet) as the political arm of the agrarian movement in 1920 (Allern 2010, 20–3; Christensen 2001, 36; Espeli 2008, 220; Esping-Andersen 1985, 78–9; Greenhill 1965, 214–6; Krake 2020, 12–4). The Agrarian Party remained under the control of the Union and was able to stamp its agricultural protectionism, as well as fiscal conservatism, on the Labour government in the mid-1930s.

In a region-wide trend, Norway transitioned from majoritarianism to proportional representation, which was the concession a privileged, Conservative minority extracted from the Liberal majority in return for accepting universal suffrage with the 1921 election. Proportional representation no doubt helped the Agrarian–Labour agreement. In the 1933 election, the Labour Party won 46% of Storting seats with 40% of the popular vote but was still left out of office. Being in opposition strengthened its reformist resolve and, when opportunity presented itself in 1935, formed Norway's first functioning Labour government with the support of the Agrarians, who had held 15% of the seats with 14% of the vote (Flora et al. 1983, 139, 183–4).[10] However, it was Labour's ideational reorientation, not proportional representation, which made the agreement possible.

For a combination of structural and ideational reasons, the Danish and Norwegian responses diverged from their Swedish counterpart despite the striking similarities between the three countries in terms of both the crisis experience (a mild downturn), institutional arrangements (mixed banking, unitary state organization, parliamentary system, and proportional representation), and political alignments (red–green and employer–union). Shaped in an environment of early capitalist development, Denmark's export-driven pastoral economy resulted in not just a diffuse capitalist and working-class structure but also a pervasive liberal disposition among political actors, including the Social Democrats. The political compromises reached or held in the 1930s thus carried the imprint of this historical development experience. Similarly, Norway's export-dependent, but polarized, economy defined by sharp sectoral and regional divisions fostered a radical, confrontational orientation within the labour movement. Labour's reformist reorientation in the late 1920s and early 1930s made the subsequent political compromises possible but lacked an innovative policy thrust. In contrast, Sweden's mature industrial economy reflecting a pattern of late but rapid capitalist development created closer sectoral linkages as well as leading to higher levels of concentration and centralization within both capital and labour. The Swedish Social Democrats used this structural advantage to the full in organizing while, at the same time, not hesitating to break with orthodox ideas and approaches in strategizing.

Summing Up

The New Deal was the most innovative policy experimentation in the democratic world. And it came from the least expected country by many social and political criteria. The United States had a weak labour movement by any measure, a federal state organization with multiple hurdles for policy legislation, and a low bureaucratic capacity for policy implementation. That the country experienced the severest crisis in the industrialized world may be used to explain its innovative thrust. This situational explanation has some merit as Germany, whose crisis experience was next to that of the United States in severity, fashioned a similar response, albeit in a different direction. Yet Canada's experience was similar to both, but its response was distinctly conservative. Moreover, the United States and Germany, too, remained conservative in the first three full years of the crisis. Conversely, the Swedish response shaped in the context of a mild crisis was nearly as innovative as, and more durable in its consequences than, the New Deal.

As the US case shows, policy innovation in democracies did not require strong labour movements, unitary state organization, proportional representation, or bureaucratic maturity. Nor did it require severe crises or closed economies as shown by the Swedish case. What was necessary though was a rapprochement between agrarians, labour, and employers. In the United States, the Democratic Party engineered this rapprochement on an informal and piecemeal basis. The Swedish rendition was more formal and comprehensive, involving the Social Democratic and Agrarian parties, on one hand, and the union and employers' federations, on the other. Yet similar alignments in Denmark and Norway did not lead to nearly innovative responses. The labour-inclusive alignments were necessary but not sufficient for policy innovation in democracies.

What distinguished the United States and Sweden were the ideational flexibility and political creativity of their governing parties. The US Democrats under Roosevelt developed a progressive liberal outlook before becoming a party of coalitions. Similarly, the Swedish Social Democrats decided to "peel" capitalism by managing it before they had a chance to govern in the 1930s. In both cases, long-term consequences were not as originally intended, but the intention was there. Although the Norwegian Labour Party settled on parliamentary politics in the late 1920s, it did not have a clear idea about what to do with that. In Denmark, the Social Democrats were long accustomed to parliamentary politics, but they had also chosen to conform to, rather than transform, Danish liberalism.

Denmark and Norway also demonstrated the structural limits of economic policy choice. As in the New Zealand case, their economies' dependence on resource exports diverted economic policy away from the macroeconomic and macrosocial areas, where the US and Swedish responses displayed their innovative, proto-Fordist edge. Danish economic policy was pulled towards trade whereas its Norwegian counterpart also emphasized industrialization, a recurring theme of the next two chapters.

Notes

1. According to the same source, corresponding figures were 7% (18%) for France, 8% (14%) for Canada, 12% (21%) for Norway, 17% (36%) for New Zealand, 18% (26%) for Germany, 20% (35%) for Sweden, 21% (42%) for Denmark, 23% (31%) for the United Kingdom, 25% (41%) for Austria, and 38% (57%) for Australia.
2. This goes against two prevalent views on the role of business in the New Deal. Thomas Ferguson (1984, 61–92) and Peter Gourevitch (1984, 112–5, 1986, 147–53) argue that, as the New Deal evolved into the second phase, it moved away from labour-intensive and protectionist industries to rely more and more on a coalition of capital-intensive industries, investment banks, and internationally oriented commercial banks. However, one needs to be cautious about the political importance of this market divergence within the business community since the US economy was extremely closed with exports constituting only 3% of the gross national product (GNP) (USBC 1965, 542). Alternatively, and more contentiously, for Colin Gordon (1994) and Peter Swenson (2002, 192–245), the New Deal was an instrumentation of the capitalist class which, in all its subtlety, coaxed federal policymakers and societal actors such as union leaders into proposing or initiating policies that would be in its interest in the first place.
3. The idea had even taken on an organizational form with the establishment of the National Civic Federation, in 1900, as a tripartite forum with representation from business, labour, and the "public."
4. The "Big Five" were ASEA, Electrolux, LM Ericsson, Separator, and SKF.
5. The "Big Four" were Svenska Handelsbanken, Skandinaviska Banken, Stockholms Enskilda Bank, and Göteborgs Bank.
6. Although the word *venstre* in Scandinavian languages means left, its sociological meaning is closer to liberal. Hence, Det radikale Venstre is known as the Radical (or Social) Liberals in English.
7. During 1910–1914, agricultural, mainly dairy, products accounted for 87% of Danish exports (Jörberg 1973, 412). Their share of the exports was 72% as late as 1936–1939 (Jörberg and Krantz 1976, 406).
8. The UK market accounted for over 56% of Danish exports in both 1929 and 1938 (RIIA 1951, 58).
9. In the 1860s, fisheries accounted for about 45% of Norwegian exports. Overseas shipping would later take over as the chief export activity, accounting for 40% of exports earnings in 1915 (Jörberg 1973, 403, 430).
10. Labour had formed a minority government in 1928, but it lasted less than three weeks.

References

Allern, Elin H. 2010. *Political Parties and Interest Groups in Norway*. Colchester: ECPR Press.
Andersen, Jørgen G., and Jan B. Jensen. 2001. "The Danish Venstre: Liberal, Agrarian or Centrist?" In *From Farmyard to City Square? The Electoral Adaptation of the Nordic Agrarian Parties*, edited by David Arter, 96–131. Aldershot: Ashgate.
Andrae, Carl-Göran. [1973] 1975. "The Swedish Labour Movement and the 1917–1918 Revolution." In *Sweden's Development from Poverty to Affluence, 1750–1970*, edited by Steven Koblik and translated from the Swedish by Joanne Johnson, 232–53. Minneapolis: University of Minnesota Press.
Andrén, Nils. 1964. *Government and Politics in the Nordic Countries: Denmark, Finland, Iceland, Norway, Sweden*. Stockholm: Almqvist and Wiksell.
Berglund, Sten, and Ulf Lindström. 1978. *The Scandinavian Party System(s): A Comparative Study*. Lund: Studentlitteratur.
Berman, Sheri. 1998a. "Path Dependency and Political Action: Reexamining Responses to the Depression." *Comparative Politics* 30, no. 4: 379–400. https://doi.org/10.2307/422330.
Berman, Sheri. 1998b. *The Social Democratic Moment: Ideas and Politics in the Making of Interwar Europe*. Cambridge, MA: Harvard University Press.
Berman, Sheri. 2006. *The Primacy of Politics: Social Democracy and the Making of Europe's Twentieth Century*. New York: Cambridge University Press.
Blake, Donald J. 1960. "Swedish Trade Unions and the Social Democratic Party: The Formative Years." *Scandinavian Economic History Review* 8, no. 1: 19–44. https://doi.org/10.1080/03585522.1960.10411421.
Born, Karl E. [1977] 1983. *International Banking in the 19th and 20th Centuries*. Translated from the German by Volker R. Berghahn. New York: St. Martin's.
Braatoy, Bjarne. 1939. *The New Sweden: A Vindication of Democracy*. London: Thomas Nelson.
Burnham, Walter D. 1967. "Party Systems and the Political Process." In *The American Party Systems: Stages of Political Development*, edited by William N. Chambers and Walter D. Burnham, 277–307. New York: Oxford University Press.
Calomiris, Charles W. 2013. "The Political Lessons of Depression-era Banking Reform." In *The Great Depression of the 1930s: Lessons for Today*, edited by Nicholas Crafts and Peter Fearon, 165–87. Oxford: Oxford University Press.
Clark, Harrison. 1941. *Swedish Unemployment Policy – 1914 to 1940*. Washington, D.C.: American Council on Public Affairs.
Collins, Robert M. 1978. "Positive Business Responses to the New Deal: The Roots of the Committee for Economic Development, 1933–1942." *Business History Review* 52, no. 3: 369–91. https://doi.org/10.2307/3113736.

Christensen, Dag A. 2001. "The Norwegian Agrarian-Centre Party: Class, Rural or Catchall Party?" In *From Farmyard to City Square? The Electoral Adaptation of the Nordic Agrarian Parties*, edited by David Arter, 31–58. Aldershot: Ashgate.

Dahl, Sven. 1961. "Strip Fields and Enclosure in Sweden." *Scandinavian Economic History Review* 9, no. 1: 56–67. https://doi.org/10.1080/03585522.1961.10411433.

Delton, Jennifer A. 2020. *The Industrialists: How the National Association of Manufacturers Shaped American Capitalism*. Princeton: Princeton University Press.

Depew, Briggs, Price V. Fishback, and Paul W. Rhode. 2013. "New Deal or No Deal in the Cotton South: The Effect of the AAA on the Agricultural Labor Structure." *Explorations in Economic History* 50, no. 4: 466–86. https://doi.org/10.1016/j.eeh.2013.06.004.

Eichengreen, Barry J. 1992. *Golden Fetters: The Gold Standard and the Great Depression, 1919–1939*. New York: Oxford University Press.

Eichengreen, Barry J., and Tim J. Hatton. 1988. "Interwar Unemployment in International Perspective: An Overview." In *Interwar Unemployment in International Perspective*, edited by Barry J. Eichengreen and Tim J. Hatton, 1–59. Dordrecht: Kluwer.

Eichengreen, Barry J., and Beth Simmons. 1995. "International Economics and Domestic Politics: Notes on the 1920s." In *Banking, Currency, and Finance in Europe between the Wars*, edited by Charles H. Feinstein, 131–47. Oxford: Clarendon.

Eidlin, Barry. 2018. *Labor and the Class Idea in the United States and Canada*. New York: Cambridge University Press.

Elvander, Nils. 1979. *Scandinavian Social Democracy: Its Strength and Weakness*. Stockholm: Almqvist and Wiksell.

Espeli, Harald. 2008. "Prelude to Extreme Protectionism? Norwegian Agricultural Protectionism in a West-European Context, 1850–1940." *Scandinavian Economic History Review* 56, no. 3: 209–29. https://doi.org/10.1080/03585520802551402.

Esping-Andersen, Gøsta. 1985. *Politics against Markets: The Social Democratic Road to Power*. Princeton: Princeton University Press.

Eyerman, Ron. 1985. "Rationalizing Intellectuals: Sweden in the 1930s and 1940s." *Theory and Society* 14, no. 6: 777–807. https://doi.org/10.1007/BF00174050.

Ferguson, Thomas. 1984. "From Normalcy to New Deal: Industrial Structure, Party Competition, and American Public Policy in the Great Depression." *International Organization* 38, no. 1: 41–94. https://doi.org/10.1017/S0020818300004276.

Flora, Peter, Jens Alber, Richard Eichenberg, Jürgen Kohl, Franz Kraus, Winfried Pfenning, and Kurt Seebohm. 1983. *State, Economy, and Society in Western*

Europe, 1815–1975, vol. 1, *The Growth of Mass Democracies and Welfare States*. Frankfurt am Main: Campus Verlag.

Gaitskell, Hugh. 1938. "The Banking System and Monetary Policy." In *Democratic Sweden*, edited by Margaret Cole and Charles Smith, 96–107. New York: Greystone.

Garside, W. Redvers, and Niels-Henrik Topp. 2001. "Nascent Keynesianism? Denmark in the 1930s." *History of Political Economy* 33, no. 4: 717–41.

Glindemann, Paul. 1929. "The Banking System of Denmark." In *Foreign Banking Systems*, edited by H. Parker Willis and Benjamin H. Beckhart, 489–521. New York: Henry Holt.

Goldfield, Michael. 1989. "Worker Insurgency, Radical Organization, and New Deal Labor Legislation." *American Political Science Review* 83, no. 4: 1257–82. https://doi.org/10.2307/1961668.

Gordon, Colin. 1994. *New Deals: Business, Labor, and Politics in America, 1920–1935*. New York: Cambridge University Press.

Gourevitch, Peter A. 1984. "Breaking with Orthodoxy: The Politics of Economic Policy Responses to the Depression of the 1930s." *International Organization* 38, no. 1: 95–129. https://doi.org/10.1017/S0020818300004288.

Gourevitch, Peter A. 1986. *Politics in Hard Times: Comparative Responses to International Economic Crises*. Ithaca: Cornell University Press.

Greenhill, H. Gaylon. 1965. "The Norwegian Agrarian Party: A Class Party?" *Social Science* 40, no. 4: 214–9.

Grytten, Ola H. 1998. "Monetary Policy and Restructuring of the Norwegian Economy during the Years of Crises, 1920–1939." In *Economic Crises and Restructuring in History: Experiences of Small Countries*, edited by Timo Myllyntaus, 93–124. St. Katharinen: Scripta Mercaturae Verlag.

Grytten, Ola H. 2008a. "A Small Country's Policy Response to Global Economic Disintegration during the Interwar Years of Crisis." In *Pathbreakers: Small European Countries Responding to Globalisation and Deglobalisation*, edited by Margrit Müller and Timo Myllyntaus, 271–96. Bern: Peter Lang.

Grytten, Ola H. 2008b. "Why Was the Great Depression Not So Great in the Nordic Countries? Economic Policy and Unemployment." *Journal of European Economic History* 37, nos. 2–3: 369–403.

Gustafsson, Bo. 1973. "A Perennial of Doctrinal History: Keynes and 'the Stockholm School.'" *Economy and History* 16, no. 1: 114–28. https://doi.org/10.1080/00708852.1973.10418906.

Gustafsson, Bo. 1986. "Conflict, Confrontation and Consensus in Modern Swedish History." In *Economics and Values*, edited by Lennart Arvedson, Ingemund Hagg, Mans Lonnroth, and Bengt Rydén, 16–50. Stockholm: Almqvist and Wiksell International.

Gustavson, Carl C. 1986. *The Small Giant: Sweden Enters the Industrial Era*. Athens: Ohio University Press.

Heckscher, Eli F. 1953. "A Survey of Economic Thought in Sweden, 1875–1950." *Scandinavian Economic History Review* 1, no. 1: 105–25. https://doi.org/10.1080/03585522.1953.10409901.

Heckscher, Eli F. [1941] 1954. *An Economic History of Sweden*. Translated from the Swedish by G. Ohlin. Cambridge, MA: Harvard University Press.

Heclo, Hugh. 1974. *Modern Social Politics in Britain and Sweden: From Relief to Income Maintenance*. New Haven: Yale University Press.

Higgins, Winton. 1985. "Ernst Wigforss: The Renewal of Social Democratic Theory and Practice." *Political Power and Social Theory* 5: 207–50.

Hildebrand, Karl-Gustaf. 1975. "Economic Policy in Scandinavia during the Inter-War Period." *Scandinavian Economic History Review* 23, no. 2: 99–115. https://doi.org/10.1080/03585522.1975.10407818.

Hildebrand, Karl-Gustaf. 1978. "Labour and Capital in the Scandinavian Countries in the Nineteenth and Twentieth Centuries." *The Cambridge Economic History of Europe*, vol. 7, *The Industrial Economies: Capital, Labour, and Enterprise*, part 1, *Britain, France, Germany, and Scandinavia*, edited by Peter Mathias and M. M. Postan, 590–628. Cambridge: Cambridge University Press.

Hodne, Fritz. 1983. *The Norwegian Economy, 1920–1980*. London: Croom Helm.

Huthmacher, J. Joseph. 1968. *Senator Robert F. Wagner and the Rise of Urban Liberalism*. New York: Atheneum.

Johansen, Hans C. 1987. *The Danish Economy in the Twentieth Century*. London: Croom Helm.

Johnson, William R. 1963. "National Farm Organizations and the Reshaping of Agricultural Policy in 1932." *Agricultural History* 37, no. 1: 35–42.

Johnston, Thomas L. 1962. *Collective Bargaining in Sweden: A Study of the Labour Market and Its Institutions*. London: George Allen and Unwin.

Jörberg, Lennart. 1973. "The Industrial Revolution in the Nordic Countries." In *The Fontana Economic History of Europe*, vol. 4, *The Emergence of Industrial Societies*, part 2, edited by Carlo M. Cipolla, 375–485. Glasgow: Fontana.

Jörberg, Lennart, and Olle Krantz. 1976. "Scandinavia, 1914–1970." In *The Fontana Economic History of Europe*, vol. 6, *Contemporary Economies*, part 2, edited by Carlo M. Cipolla, 377–459. Glasgow: Fontana.

Jörberg, Lennart, and Olle Krantz. 1989. "Economic and Social Policy in Sweden, 1850–1939." In *The Cambridge Economic History of Europe*, vol. 8, *The Industrial Economies: The Development of Economic and Social Policies*, edited by Peter Mathias and Sidney Pollard, 1048–105. Cambridge: Cambridge University Press.

Katzenstein, Peter J. 1985. *Small States in World Markets: Industrial Policy in Europe*. Ithaca: Cornell University Press.

Kirkendall, Richard S. 1975. "The New Deal and Agriculture." In *The New Deal: The National Level*, edited by John Braeman, Robert H. Bremner, and David Brody, 83–109. Columbus: Ohio State University Press.

Kjellberg, Anders. 1992. "Sweden: Can the Model Survive?" In *Industrial Relations in the New Europe*, edited by Anthony Ferner and Richard Hyman, 88–142. Oxford: Basil Blackwell.

Kjellstrom, Erik T. H. 1934. *Managed Money: The Experience of Sweden*. New York: Columbia University Press.

Klovland, Jan T. 1998. "Monetary Policy and Business Cycles in the Interwar Years: The Scandinavian Experience." *European Review of Economic History* 2, no. 3: 309–44. https://doi.org/10.1017/S1361491698000148.

Korpi, Walter. 1978. *The Working Class in Welfare Capitalism: Work, Unions, and Politics in Sweden*. London: Routledge and Kegan Paul.

Korpi, Walter. 1982. "The Historical Compromise and Its Dissolution." In *Sweden: Choices for Economic and Social Policy in the 1980s*, edited by Bengt Rydén and Villy Bergström, 124–41. London: George Allen and Unwin.

Kragh, Marrin. 2012. "The Stockholm School, Ernst Wigforss and the Great Depression in Sweden: An Outline." In *The Great Depression in Europe: Economic Thought and Policy in a National Context*, edited by Michalis Psalidopoulos, 75–102. Athens: Alpha Bank Historical Archives.

Krake, Kristina. 2020. "Reconsidering the Crisis Agreements of the 1930s: The Defence of Democracy in a Comparative Scandinavian Perspective." *Contemporary European History* 29, no. 1: 1–15. https://doi.org/10.1017/S0960777318000607.

Kristensen, Thorkil. 1958. "State Intervention and Economic Freedom." In *Scandinavian Democracy: Development of Democratic Thought and Institutions in Denmark, Norway and Sweden*, edited by Joseph A. Lauwerys, 192–219. Copenhagen: Danish Institute.

Lafferty, William M. 1971. *Economic Development and the Response of Labour in Scandinavia: A Multi-Level Analysis*. Oslo: Universitetsforlaget.

Larsen, Hans K. 2010. "Danish Exchange Rate Policy and the Trades: The Interwar Experience." In *Managing Crises and De-globalisation: Nordic Foreign Trade and Exchange, 1919–39*, edited by Sven-Olof Olsson, 82–100. London: Routledge.

Larsson, Mats. 1991. "State, Banks and Industry in Sweden, with Some Reference to the Scandinavian Countries." In *The Role of Banks in the Interwar Economy*, edited by Harold James, Håkan Lindgren, and Alice Teichova, 80–103. Cambridge: Cambridge University Press.

Laslett, H. M. 1989. "State Policy towards Labour and Labour Organizations, 1830–1939: Anglo-American Union Movements." In *The Cambridge Economic History of Europe*, vol. 8, *The Industrial Economies: The Development of Economic and Social Policies*, edited by Peter Mathias and Sidney Pollard, 495–548. Cambridge: Cambridge University Press.

Levine, Rhonda F. 1988. *Class Struggle and the New Deal: Industrial Labor, Industrial Capital, and the State*. Lawrence: University Press of Kansas.

Lindbeck, Assar. 1974. *Swedish Economic Policy*. Berkeley: University of California Press.
Lindgren, Håkan. 1982. "The Kreuger Crash of 1932: In Memory of a Financial Genius, or Was He a Simple Swindler?" *Scandinavian Economic History Review and Economy and History* 30, no. 3: 189–206. https://doi.org/10.1080/03585522.1982.10407986.
Lindström, Ulf. 2000. "Sweden: The Durable Compromise." In *Conditions of Democracy in Europe, 1919–1939: Systematic Case Studies*, edited by Dirk Berg-Schlosser and Jeremy Mitchell, 426–48. London: Macmillan.
Lindvall, Johannes. 2012. "Politics and Policies in Two Economic Crises: The Nordic Countries." In *Coping with Crisis: Government Reactions to the Great Recession*, edited by Nancy Bermeo and Jonas Pontusson, 233–60. New York: Russell Sage Foundation.
Luebbert, Gregory M. 1991. *Liberalism, Fascism, or Social Democracy: Social Classes and the Political Origins of Regimes in Interwar Europe*. New York: Oxford University Press.
Lundberg, Erik. [1953] 1957. *Business Cycles and Economic Policy*. Translated from the Swedish by J. Potter. London: George Allen and Unwin.
Mackenzie, Kenneth. [1932] 1935. *The Banking Systems of Great Britain, France, Germany, and the United States of America*. 2nd ed. London: Macmillan.
Mackie, Thomas T., and Richard Rose. 1974. *The International Almanac of Electoral History*. London: Macmillan.
Maier, Charles S. 1975. *Recasting Bourgeois Europe: Stabilization in France, Germany, and Italy in the Decade after World War I*. Princeton: Princeton University Press.
McDonough, Terrence. 1990. "The Resolution of Crisis in American Economic History: Social Structures of Accumulation and Stages of Capitalism." *Research in Political Economy* 12: 129–83.
McQuaid, Kim. 1978. "Corporate Liberalism in the American Business Community, 1920–1940." *Business History Review* 52, no. 3: 342–68. https://doi.org/10.2307/3113735.
Melin, Hilding. 1929. "The Banking System of Sweden." In *Foreign Banking Systems*, edited by H. Parker Willis and Benjamin H. Beckhart, 1011–74. New York: Henry Holt.
Montgomery, G. Arthur. 1939. *The Rise of Modern Industry in Sweden*. London: P. S. King.
Möller, Gustav. 1938. "The Unemployment Policy." *Annals of the American Academy of Political and Social Science* 197, no. 1: 47–71. https://doi.org/10.1177/000271623819700107.
Nevers, Jeppe. 2013. "The Rise of Danish Agrarian Liberalism." *Contributions to the History of Concepts* 8, no. 2: 96–105. https://doi.org/10.3167/choc.2013.080206.

Olsen, Gregg M. 1991. "Labour Mobilization and the Strength of Capital: The Rise and Stall of Economic Democracy in Sweden." *Studies in Political Economy*, no. 34: 109–45. https://doi.org/10.1080/19187033.1991.11675462.

Olsen, Gregg M. 1992. *The Struggle for Economic Democracy in Sweden*. Aldershot: Avebury.

Olsson, Ulf. 1991. "Comparing the Interwar Banking History of Five Small Countries in North-West Europe." In *The Role of Banks in the Interwar Economy*, edited by Harold James, Håkan Lindgren, and Alice Teichova, 26–34. Cambridge: Cambridge University Press.

RIIA (Royal Institute of International Affairs). 1951. *The Scandinavian States and Finland: A Political and Economic Survey*. London: RIIA.

Rokkan, Stein. 1966. "Norway: Numerical Democracy and Corporate Pluralism." In *Political Oppositions in Western Democracies*, edited by Robert A. Dahl, 70–115. New Haven: Yale University Press.

Rokkan, Stein. 1981. "The Growth and Structuring of Mass Politics." In *Nordic Democracy: Ideas, Issues, and Institutions in Politics, Economy, Education, Social and Cultural Affairs of Denmark, Finland, Iceland, Norway, and Sweden*, edited by Erik Allardt, N. Andrén, E. J. Friis, G. P. Gíslason, S. S. Nilson, H. Valen, F. Wendt, and F. Wisti, 53–79. Copenhagen: Det Danske Selskab.

Rothstein, Bo. 1992. "Explaining Swedish Corporatism: The Formative Moment." *Scandinavian Political Studies* 15, no. 3: 173–91. https://doi.org/10.1111/j.1467-9477.1992.tb00139.x.

Rustow, Dankwart A. 1955. *The Politics of Compromise: A Study of Parties and Cabinet Government in Sweden*. Princeton: Princeton University Press.

Ruth, Arne. 1984. "The Second New Nation: The Mythology of Modern Sweden." *Daedalus* 113, no. 2: 53–96.

Saint-Etienne, Christian. 1984. *The Great Depression, 1929–1938: Lessons for the 1980s*. Stanford: Hoover Institution.

Samuelsson, Kurt. 1958. "The Banks and the Financing of Industry in Sweden, c. 1900–1927." *Scandinavian Economic History Review* 6, no. 2: 176–90. https://doi.org/10.1080/03585522.1958.10411403.

Schüllerqvist, Bengt. 2013. "The Crisis in the 1930s and the Rise to Power of the Swedish Social Democrats." In *Routes into the Abyss: Coping with Crises in the 1930s*, edited by Helmut Konrad and Wolfgang Maderthaner, 102–14. New York and Oxford: Berghahn Books.

Scott, Franklin D. 1977. *Sweden: The Nation's History*. Minneapolis: University of Minnesota Press.

Skocpol, Theda. 1980. "Political Response to Capitalist Crisis: Neo-Marxist Theories of the State and the Case of the New Deal." *Politics and Society* 10, no. 2: 155–201. https://doi.org/10.1177/003232928001000202.

Skocpol, Theda, and Kenneth Finegold. 1982. "State Capacity and Economic Intervention in the Early New Deal." *Political Science Quarterly* 97, no. 2: 255–78. https://doi.org/10.2307/2149478.

Skowronek, Stephen. 1982. *Building a New American State: The Expansion of National Administrative Capacities, 1877–1920.* Cambridge: Cambridge University Press.

Slichter, Gertrude A. 1956. "Franklin D. Roosevelt and the Farm Problem, 1929–1932." *Mississippi Valley Historical Review* 43, no. 2: 238–58. https://doi.org/10.2307/1902685.

Stein, Herbert. [1969] 1990. *The Fiscal Revolution in America.* 2nd ed. Washington, D.C.: American Enterprise Institute.

Steinmo, Sven. 1988. "Social Democracy vs. Socialism: Goal Adaptation in Social Democratic Sweden." *Politics and Society* 16, no. 4: 403–46. https://doi.org/10.1177/003232928801600401.

Steinmo, Sven. 1993. *Taxation and Democracy: Swedish, British and American Approaches to Financing the Modern State.* New Haven: Yale University Press.

Stephens, John D. 1979. *The Transition from Capitalism to Socialism.* London: Macmillan.

Stjernquist, Nils. 1966. "Sweden: Stability or Deadlock?" In *Political Oppositions in Western Democracies*, edited by Robert A. Dahl, 116–46. New Haven: Yale University Press.

Stjernquist, Nils. 1987. "From Bicameralism to Unicameralism: The Democratic Riksdag, 1921–1986." In *The Riksdag: A History of the Swedish Parliament*, edited by Michael F. Metcalf, 223–303. New York: St. Martin's.

Stryker, Robin. 1990. "A Tale of Two Agencies: Class, Political-Institutional, and Organizational Factors Affecting State Reliance on Social Science." *Politics and Society* 18, no. 1: 101–41. https://doi.org/10.1177/003232929001800105.

Swenson, Harold. 1929. "The Banking System of Norway." In *Foreign Banking Systems*, edited by H. Parker Willis and Benjamin H. Beckhart, 869–92. New York: Henry Holt.

Swenson, Peter A. 1989. *Fair Shares: Unions, Pay, and Politics in Sweden and West Germany.* Ithaca: Cornell University Press.

Swenson, Peter A. 1991. "Bringing Capital Back In, or Social Democracy Reconsidered: Employer Power, Cross-Class Alliances, and Centralization of Industrial Relations in Denmark and Sweden." *World Politics* 43, no. 4: 513–44. https://doi.org/10.2307/2010535.

Swenson, Peter A. 2002. *Capitalists against Markets: The Making of Labor Markets and Welfare States in the United States and Sweden.* New York: Oxford University Press.

Söderpalm, Sven A. [1973] 1975. "The Crisis Agreement and the Social Democratic Road to Power." In *Sweden's Development from Poverty to Affluence,*

1750–1970, edited by Steven Koblik and translated from the Swedish by Joanne Johnson, 258–78. Minneapolis: University of Minnesota Press.
Tcherkinsky, M. Morduch. 1939. *The Land Tenure Systems in Europe*. Geneva: League of Nations.
Tedlow, Richard S. 1976. "The National Association of Manufacturers and Public Relations during the New Deal." *Business History Review* 50, no. 1: 25–45. https://doi.org/10.2307/3113573.
Tilton, Timothy A. 1979. "A Swedish Road to Socialism: Ernst Wigforss and the Ideological Foundations of Swedish Social Democracy." *American Political Science Review* 73, no. 2: 505–20. https://doi.org/10.2307/1954894.
Tilton, Timothy A. 1991. *The Political Theory of Swedish Social Democracy: Through the Welfare State to Socialism*. Oxford: Clarendon.
Tingsten, Herbert L. G. [1941] 1973. *The Swedish Social Democrats: Their Ideological Development*, translated from the Swedish by Greta Frankel and Patricia Howard-Rosen. Totowa: Bedminster.
Tomasson, Richard F. 1969. "The Extraordinary Success of the Swedish Social Democrats." *Journal of Politics* 31, no. 3: 772–98. https://doi.org/10.2307/2128497.
Topp, Niels-Henrik. 1988. "Fiscal Policy in Denmark 1930–1945." *European Economic Review* 32, nos. 2–3: 512–8.
Trampusch, Christine, and Dennis C. Spies. 2014. "Agricultural Interests and the Origins of Capitalism: A Parallel Comparative History of Germany, Denmark, New Zealand, and the USA." *New Political Economy* 19, no. 6: 918–42. https://doi.org/10.1080/13563467.2013.861414.
USBC (US Bureau of the Census). 1965. *The Statistical History of the United States from Colonial Times to the Present*. Stamford: Fairfield.
Verney, Douglas V. 1957. *Parliamentary Reform in Sweden, 1866–1921*. Oxford: Clarendon.
Weinstein, James. 1968. *The Corporate Ideal in the Liberal State: 1900–1918*. Boston: Beacon.
Weir, Margaret. 1989. "Ideas and Politics: The Acceptance of Keynesianism in Britain and the United States." In *The Political Power of Economic Ideas: Keynesianism across Nations*, edited by Peter A. Hall, 53–86. Princeton: Princeton University Press.
Weir, Margaret, and Theda Skocpol. 1985. "State Structures and the Possibilities for 'Keynesian' Responses to the Great Depression in Sweden, Britain, and the United States." In *Bringing the State Back In*, edited by Peter B. Evans, Dietrich Rueschemeyer, and Theda Skocpol, 107–63. Cambridge: Cambridge University Press.
White, Lawrence H. 2012. *The Clash of Economic Ideas: The Great Policy Debates and Experiments of the Last Hundred Years*. New York: Cambridge University Press.

Wigforss, Ernst. 1938. "The Financial Policy during Depression and Boom." *Annals of the American Academy of Political and Social Science* 197, no. 1: 25–39. https://doi.org/10.1177/000271623819700105.

Willis, J. Brook. 1954. "United States." In *Banking Systems*, edited by Benjamin H. Beckhart, 839–916. New York: Columbia University Press.

Winch, Donald. 1966. "The Keynesian Revolution in Sweden." *Journal of Political Economy* 74, no. 2: 168–76. https://doi.org/10.1086/259133.

Winch, Donald. 1969. *Economics and Policy: A Historical Study*. London: Hodder and Stoughton.

Winders, Bill. 2005. "Maintaining the Coalition: Class Coalitions and Policy Trajectories." *Politics and Society* 33, no. 3: 387–423. https://doi.org/10.1177/0032329205278461.

Øksendal, Lars F. 2010. "Re-examining Norwegian Monetary Policy in the 1930s." In *Managing Crises and De-globalisation: Nordic Foreign Trade and Exchange, 1919–39*, edited by Sven-Olof Olsson, 66–81. London: Routledge.

Østerud, Øyvind. 1978. *Agrarian Structure and Peasant Politics in Scandinavia: A Comparative Study of Rural Response to Economic Change*. Oslo: Universitetsforlaget.

CHAPTER 5

Neomercantilism, Mark I, Under Dictatorship with an Agro-Industrial Base

In transitioning from democracies to dictatorships, this chapter must first ask and resolve where, not if, the two groups differ in approaching the economy. They do not differ in the primacy they attach to politics or "economics." If the latter is meant to refer to the market institution under democracy as is often the case, even the barest market is a politically constructed and driven priority as Karl Polanyi (1944, 250) convincingly points out in relation to the nineteenth-century "self-regulating" market. Just as the primacy of economics under democracy is a naive proposition, the primacy of politics under fascism (see, e.g., Baker 2006) and other forms of dictatorship is a misleading one. Prioritizing economics over politics or vice versa is not a meaningful divider of democracies and dictatorships in their approaches to the economy. Nor is the quantity of intervention in the economy a useful marker of political regime distinction. It is rather in the quality or type of intervention that political regimes distinguish themselves. As seen in the second chapter, democracies put more weight on macroeconomic and macrosocial measures than did dictatorships, whose relative emphasis was on microeconomic or physical measures, in responding to the interwar crisis.

On a more substantive plane, dictatorships distinguish themselves in their approach to the economy by suppressing organized labour. This is the least common denominator among them. In all three cases of democratic breakdown included in this chapter—Germany, Austria, and Italy—fascist rulers built their dictatorship by crushing the autonomous

© The Author(s), under exclusive license to Springer Nature Switzerland AG 2022
A. Türegün, *Policy Responses to the Interwar Economic Crisis*, https://doi.org/10.1007/978-3-030-96953-0_5

organization of labour. This was fundamentally different from the labour-excluding alignments in protectionist policy regimes such as those of the United Kingdom and France, where labour maintained its economic and political organization. In the Soviet case, to be examined in the next chapter, the self-declared dictatorship of the proletariat was in fact a dictatorship of the bureaucracy which, in addition to eliminating bourgeoisie, large landownership, and independent peasantry as a class, usurped the organization and representation of labour.

In its both Weimar and Nazi phases, the German response was a costly event for domestic and international society. The Weimar period saw a transition from orthodox liberal policies under a Social Democratic-led parliamentary government to protectionist ones under conservative governments appointed by the president. Among the large states, Weimar Germany was in the most advantageous position—situationally, structurally, and institutionally—to make a proto-Fordist breakthrough. It did not do so because, I will argue, its rulers were locked in an orthodox, anti-inflation mindset. Memories of hyperinflation, international obligations and indebtedness, and possibly other factors contributed to this failure, but the deciding factor was the ideational disposition of rulers and other political actors. The policy innovation that democratic forces failed to introduce was brought by the Nazis but at the cost of democracy. In their neomercantilist drive, the Nazis generally observed business priorities and privileged agrarians while also helping the unemployed and the *Mittelstand* (middle strata).

Until the democratic breakdown in 1933, the Austrian response was shaped under strikingly similar circumstances to those of Germany except for difference in size. The Christian Social governments were equally committed to, and more successful in defending, macroeconomic orthodoxy and similarly introduced protectionist measures after the financial crisis of 1931. Ironically, with the establishment of dictatorship in both countries, their economic policies began to significantly diverge especially at the domestic level. Austrian economic policy lacked the *dirigiste* thrust that its Nazi counterpart had. Despite a similar pro-business and pro-agrarian disposition, the Austrofascist regime was tempered with its Christian Social origins and limited in its manoeuvring by international financial tutelage over the economy. The Austrian case shows that fascist politics and policy can take on different forms in similar situational, structural, and institutional settings.

The Italian case differed from the German and Austrian cases in three ways. First, the Italian democratic breakdown occurred in 1922, thus giving the Fascist regime a continuity for the rest of the interwar period. Tracing the regime's changing policy course in different domestic and international contexts will allow us to detect its ideational breaking points. Second, unlike the industrialized economies of Germany and Austria, the Italian economy was still semi-industrial, with agriculture being the single largest sector. Developmentalism thus constituted a major theme of Fascist economic policy as in Soviet fixation on catching up with the West. Third, and related to the second, the Fascists proved much more statist in banking and industry than their German and Austrian counterparts. In fact, they forced the limits of state entrepreneurship and ownership under capitalism.

The first section analyses the German response in its Weimar and Nazi phases. Similarly, the second section examines the Austrian response in its pre- and post-democratic breakdown phases. The Italian response is dealt with as a whole in the third section. Table 5.1 may help the reader follow the argument of the chapter.

Germany's Dual Policy Break

Among the large states, Germany was only next to the United States in severity and scope of its economic crisis.[1] Industrial production declined by over 40% from 1929 to 1932 (Safarian [1959] 2009, 98; Silverman 1988, 186). During the same period, unemployment increased from 9% to 30% among wage earners and from 13% to 44% among union members (Kershaw 1990, 211). The industrial crisis was not an isolated incident, however; it unfolded simultaneously with that of the financial sector given the intimate relations between the country's universal banks and industrial companies. One of the largest banks collapsed and three others ran into severe difficulty during and in the wake of the financial crisis of summer 1931 (Born [1977] 1983, 257–69; Eichengreen 2015, 143–7). The bank–industry symbiosis plunged the entire economy into crisis, thus creating a situational urgency (Weber 1991). Yet the public policy response to Europe's severest crisis could not be more conservative—at least under democracy.

Table 5.1 Neomercantilism, mark I: (semi-)industrial varieties

Country (group)	Key determinants			Policy outcome
	Ruling party approach to sectoral and class interests	Institutional mediators	Structural limits to neomercantilism, mark I	
Industrial cases **Exemplary:** Germany, Phase 2				
Phase 1 (Weimar)	Pro-business and pro-agrarian; labour-exclusionary	Proportional representation; mixed/universal branch banking	Democracy; international financial obligations	Protectionist
Phase 2 (Nazi)	Pro-business and pro-agrarian; labour-repressive	Mixed/universal branch banking	n/a	Neomercantilist
Mixed: Austria, Phase 2				
Phase 1 (pre-1933)	Pro-business and pro-agrarian; labour-exclusionary	Proportional representation; mixed/universal branch banking	Democracy; international financial control	Protectionist
Phase 2 (post-1933)	Pro-business and pro-agrarian; labour-repressive	Mixed/universal branch banking	International financial control	Mixed
Semi-industrial case				
Italy	Pro-business and pro-agrarian; labour-repressive	Mixed/universal branch banking	n/a	Neomercantilist (with a developmental streak)

Phase I: Weimar Period

Viewed against this background, the Weimar Republic's extremely conservative response is baffling. Moreover, in addition to the severe and widespread crisis, the Republic had all the structural and institutional ingredients for a proto-Fordist response. By these criteria, its chances of policy innovation were much better than the United States' and at least as good as Sweden's. That the exact opposite came to pass is worthy of explanation. I argue that this outcome was fundamentally the making of the Weimar ruling bloc, particularly, their ideational disposition and political choices.

The new Germany was made possible first by the defeat of German imperialism in World War I and then by the defeat of the revolutionary, Communist wing of the German labour movement in the aftermath of the war. As one of the most democratic constitutions in Europe, the Weimar Constitution of 1919 enshrined universal suffrage and proportional representation within a parliamentary and federal republican system (Kolb [2002] 2005, 160–74; Lee 1998, 16–35).[2] Although an elected president was given emergency powers and authority to issue decrees to counterbalance the national parliament (Reichstag) in view of the Prussian domination of imperial parliament and government, the system relied on parliamentary government principle. Similarly, Weimar parliament was effectively informed by unicameralism as embodied in the Reichstag. Although a federal council (Reichsrat) was constitutionally enshrined to give states (Länder) representation, it functioned as a consultative body rather than a typically strong upper chamber as in the rest of Europe.

Substantively, the Social Democratic labour movement was a founding partner in the Weimar Republic. Emerging as the largest party by far in early 1919, the Social Democratic Party (Sozialdemokratische Partei Deutschlands, SPD) headed the first few coalition governments and managed to get a Social Democrat elected as the first president of the Republic, as well as taking part in the suppression of Communist insurgency (Flora et al. 1983, 120, 172–3; Kershaw 1990, 204–7; Kolb [2002] 2005, 224–6; Lee 1998, 33). Later the same year, the movement's union wing was reorganized under the General Trade Union Federation (Allgemeiner Deutscher Gewerkschaftsbund, ADGB), which would play a pivotal role in Weimar-era industrial relations and become the centre of innovative policy proposals in the early 1930s (Moses 1986). One year later, when the Works Councils legislation was passed, the unions were elevated to a position of partnership, including formal representation and direct influence, in the workplace (Thelen 1991, 66–71). Moreover, the new regime experimented with peak-level collective bargaining between 1918 and 1924 by establishing the Central Labour Community (Zentralarbeitsgemeinschaft) to serve as a shared forum between union and employers' federations (Swenson 1989, 60–8).

In addition to these political developments, the new Germany inherited from its imperial predecessor a universal banking system that was equally promising for the Weimar political economy. Germany's late capitalist development centred on a rapid industrialization programme financed by commercial banks operating across the country that were small in number but large in size and universal or mixed in function (Born [1977] 1983, 168–75, 241–8; Calomiris 2000, 212–79; Mackenzie [1932] 1935, 154–90; Quittner 1929). This pattern of development resulted in close finance–industry linkages whereby banks did not just extend credit to firms but were also involved in the management of the latter. In the long term, German industrial firm size tended to be larger and capital in general became more centralized, giving rise to theories of finance capital as the fusion of financial and industrial capital.[3] As in the Swedish case, the German working class, not to mention the capitalist class, owed much of its cohesion and strength to bank-financed late industrialization.

To round up the set of conditions potentially advantageous to policy innovation in Weimar Germany, the SPD headed a "grand coalition" government with the pro-Republic parties (namely, confessional [Catholic] Centre Party and its Bavarian wing, Bavarian People's Party, "right" liberal German People's Party, and "left" liberal German Democratic Party) from 1928 to 1930 (Kolb [2002] 2005, 79–81). It was an uneasy coalition but a coalition, nevertheless. In fact, it turned out to be not only the last majority but also the last parliamentary government of the Weimar Republic.

Yet, in its response to the crisis, the SPD-led coalition was a dismal failure. As in the United Kingdom, unemployment insurance became the first target of conservative forces. Introduced just a few years previously (in 1927) for a "normal" business cycle, the Weimar contributory insurance scheme was strained by the mounting number of the unemployed (Moses 1986, 152–7). Rather than accepting to reduce insurance benefits under pressure from its partners, the SPD, like the UK Labour Party, chose to withdraw from government on principle. This paved the way for the first presidential and most deflationary government of the Weimar period, that of Centrist Heinrich Brüning from 1930 to 1932. Using

World War I reparations and other international debt payments as an excuse for inaction, Brüning imposed a crippling regime of deflation on the German population with the acquiescence of the SPD and other system parties (Holtfrerich 1990a, 1990b). At the same time, he instituted a clearing trade regime after the financial crisis of 1931 and managed to effectively bring the reparations issue to an end in 1932. The following two short-lived presidential governments made inconclusive attempts to reverse the deflationary course before Hitler took over.

For every situational, institutional, or other factor conducive to policy innovation, one can bring in a matching factor hindering it in Weimar Germany. First, the harsh terms of the Versailles settlement, particularly war reparations, discouraged expansionary financing (Aldcroft 1977, 144; Overy 1982, 25). This was not, however, a debilitating condition since the Republic found a way to have foreign private creditors finance whatever reparations payment it made and then, in 1931, stopped all foreign debt servicing (Schacht 1956, 196–7, 204). Western creditors, not the German government, thus practically footed the bill for reparations to Western governments. The impact of the reparations issue on Weimar economic policy was rather in the justification it provided for monetary and fiscal orthodoxy (Holtfrerich 1990a, 68). Second, still fresh in the collective memory of Weimar politicians and the people, the hyperinflation of the early 1920s served as a break on leaving the gold standard and easing monetary policy. This was part of a Europe-wide policy trend whereby countries experiencing (hyper)inflation in that decade stuck to the gold standard and a deflationary course (Eichengreen 1992, 394; Solomou 1996, 32, 48–9). Third, the Republic had had a legitimacy problem from its inception. On one hand, the old Prussian landed aristocracy never reconciled itself with Weimar and continued to dominate the upper echelons of the military and civilian bureaucracy. On the other hand, the emerging Nazis and resurgent Communists became increasingly influential as anti-systemic forces especially among the urban middle and working classes, including the unemployed. The Communists' extremely sectarian approach to the SPD as the "class enemy" and their view of Nazism as the last station of capitalism proved fateful for democracy and the labour movement (Kolb [2002] 2005, 127–8; Lee 1998, 25).

Monetary and fiscal orthodoxy prevailed in Weimar Germany not for lack of contrary ideas. In the early 1930s, unions, employers, and cabinet members put forward innovative proposals. Most notably, in late 1931, a group within the ADGB proposed a massive public works programme to employ about one million workers at a cost of two billion Reichsmarks that would be financed partly by savings, taxes, and unemployment insurance contributions and partly by public borrowing (Kaiser 2000, 183; James 1986, 239–40; Moses 1986, 158–60; Woytinsky 1961, 458–81). Known as the WTB Plan after the initials of the group members (Woytinsky, Tarnow, and Baade), the proposal was adopted by the ADGB and its white-collar counterparts at a crisis congress in April 1932, but it was diluted with the SPD's planning and socialization arguments as a condition of its submission to the Reichstag later in the year. Similarly, calls for reflationary policies could be heard from the German Employers' Association and Brüning's own cabinet ministers (Holtfrerich 1990b, 66–70).

These and similar calls were summarily dismissed by the "grand coalition" and Brüning governments from 1928 to 1932. For Brüning, staying the deflationary course for as long as the reparations were in force was non-negotiable (Holtfrerich 1990a, 80, 1990b, 73–4). The case of SPD leadership was more tragic. Not unlike its UK and Australian Labo(u)r counterparts, it believed in the futility of trying to save capitalism by countercyclical policies such as cheap money and deficit budget, and let the economy run its downward course with cyclical measures such as raising the interest rate and lowering spending levels. Hilferding, the SPD's chief economic ideologue and finance minister between 1928 and 1929, symbolized the party's neoclassical orientation. An orthodox Marxist who would not accept any intermediate solution between neoclassical economics and socialization of the economy, he resolutely defended the gold standard, sound money, and balanced budget and opposed the WTB Plan with the same conviction (Darity and Horn 1985, 365–7; James 1986, 327; Woytinsky 1961, 464–72).

Phase II: Nazi Period

Notwithstanding its macroeconomic conservatism, Weimar Germany set a precedent for Nazi economic policy in other areas. The end of the reparations and other foreign debt payments strengthened the hand of the Nazis in refashioning domestic policies. Likewise, the Weimar-instituted clearing trade mechanism became the main pillar of the new regime's drive to extend and consolidate Germany's "living space," and thus achieve self-sufficiency. In its wide and long exposure to public debate, the WTB Plan, too, served as a precedent for Nazi policy breakthrough. And, just as the hyperinflation of the early 1920s put a break on reflationary alternatives in the late Weimar period, the crippling deflation of the early 1930s constituted a negative experience not to be repeated by the Nazi regime. All this, however, presumes willingness to learn from the past, creativity to experiment with new things, and ability to carry on with the choices made, of which the Nazis had a plenty. Their preferences and priorities made German economic policy for the rest of the decade.

Although Nazi dictatorship had an agro-industrial base, it did not owe its rise, let alone its economic outlook or policy, to interest-based alignments in the economy. An economically reductionist account of Nazism was a grave mistake of early post-World War II scholarship and lingered longer in policy studies. According to this account, what brought the Nazis to power was a renewed protectionist "marriage of iron and rye" in Alexander Gerschenkron's apt phrase (1943), that is, of heavy industries and East Elbian Prussia's aristocratic large landowners (Junkers), which had initially been formed during the long stagnation of 1873–1896. Discredited by the disastrous war adventure, the argument continues, the protectionist coalition gave way to the Weimar coalition of export-oriented industries and organized labour that strove to combine international free trade and domestic social reform (Kurth 1979, 22–4; see also Gourevitch 1984, 104–12, 1986, 140–7). The depression, however, irreparably damaged the Weimar coalition and thus paved the way back to a protectionist realignment between big business and big farmers.

Contrary to the "Hitler as the tool of big business and Junkers" view, his and thus the Nazi party's *Weltanschauung* was not sector- or class-specific. In their evolution from a movement to a party state, the Nazis shed their radical pro-worker and anti-capitalist proclivities, moulded themselves into a catch-all party of the ethnically defined German nation, and single-mindedly strove for a "totalitarian" societal project (Baker 2006, 231–8). To the extent that components of the project can be isolated, the "defensive economy" (*Wehrwirtschaft*) was charged to sustain militarism and ensure self-sufficiency (Baker 2006, 233). This framework determined their approach to sectional interests. Industries were forced to readjust their priorities according to the political requirements of the Nazi economy (James 1986, 188). Yet they received incentives to meet these requirements and, as long as they met them, they had significant latitude in their operations (Ziegler 2013, 143–9). Thus, for the Nazis, what mattered was the function business served in the overall "defensive economy," not its formal ownership as demonstrated in the re-privatization, in the mid-1930s, of the banks that had been taken under state control during the financial crisis of 1931. In sharp contrast to business, labour received a statist treatment from the Nazis. They instituted an elaborate system of labour control after crushing all autonomous forms of labour organization.

Unlike big business and labour, the nebulous category of *Mittelstand* in its urban and especially rural components was a constant theme in Nazi public discourse. This theme resonated well with the party's catch-all strategy and its imagery of an unadulterated nation. In the case of independent peasantry, public policy strongly backed up discourse. To borrow from Niek Koning (1994, 151–3), the Nazis were "agrarian fundamentalists" in the sense that they idealized agriculture not just as a vital productive sector but also, more critically, as a vital source of native population, culture, and values. One of the first laws they introduced in 1933 was the Law on Hereditary Peasant Holdings (*Erbhöfe*), which banned the division of these holdings on succession to ensure their preservation through impartible inheritance. The *Erbhöfe* covered about half of the total cultivated area (Tcherkinsky 1939, 20–5). With the other half being owned by larger farmers and the Junkers, German agriculture constituted one of the main streams of the Nazi political economy.

An agrarian–labour rapprochement did not take place in the Weimar period because the SPD had an exclusively urban focus as per its orthodox Marxist thinking and because independent peasantry lacked a political representation *à la* its Scandinavian counterparts (Trampusch and Spies 2014, 925–8). Upon taking power, the Nazis filled the void by effectively appealing to agrarians in a sort of "brown–green" rapprochement instead of a red–green one, just as they appealed to large sections of business. They observed capitalist property relations in both finance, industry, and agriculture except for changing the inheritance rules for independent holdings as just mentioned. In contrast, labour was deprived of its only asset—that is, the power to negotiate the terms of its employment and organize freely—and consequently of the fruits of capitalist neomercantilism.

The Austrian Contrast

No two nations arguably followed more similar paths than Weimar Germany and the Austrian Republic in the first 15 years of the interwar period. They emerged as democratic republics after the collapse of their authoritarian monarchical predecessors, undertook war reparations and other obligations, endured a legitimacy crisis among non-republican sections of society, borrowed heavily from abroad to survive, experienced hyperinflation in the early 1920s and relative stabilization later in the decade, responded astoundingly conservatively to a severe financial-industrial crisis in the early 1930s, and succumbed to fascism shortly thereafter. If anything, Austria experienced all of the above more dramatically except for the hyperinflation. In their responses to the depression, the two nations converged under democracy but diverged under dictatorship. The Austrian Corporate State turned out to be as conservative as the pre-1933, Christian Social governments in many ways and was thus a far cry from Nazi Germany's full-fledged neomercantilism. Continuing international financial control over Austrian finances, along with trade dependency of the Austrian economy, played a role in this divergence. However, the single most important factor was Austrofascism's conservative-clerical orientation and its lack of capacity to regiment the economy.

Phase I: Democratic Period

For many domestic actors, notably including the Social Democrats, the Republic of German Austria was an unwanted child created out of the ruins of the Austro-Hungarian Empire in 1918 (Marcus 2018, 4; Thorpe 2011, 28). They wanted unification (*Anschluss*) with Germany but, since it was banned under the terms of the postwar settlement, went along with a separate republic. The Social Democratic–Christian Social coalition, which emerged from the 1919 election held under universal suffrage and proportional representation (Flora et al. 1983, 99, 155–6), prepared a Weimar-style Constitution the following year. Now simply called the Republic of Austria, the country retained these electoral arrangements and acquired a federal, bicameral parliamentary system whereby a largely ceremonial president cohabited with an executive chancellor and a weak upper house of provincial representatives (Bundesrat) with a strong lower house (Nationalrat) under the Constitution (Griffin 2013, 33; Katzenstein 1985, 187; Marcus 2018, 28–32). Yet the founding Social Democratic–Christian Social coalition failed to last after 1920, giving way to an uninterrupted succession of Christian Social-dominated governments until the collapse of democracy in 1933. Unlike Weimar Germany, Austria had an essentially two-party system with small pan-German and/or Austrofascist parties flanking the extreme right and a much smaller Communist party the extreme left (Katzenstein 1985, 186–7).

The fragility of the Austrian political economy was laid bare in the immediate postwar period. The sudden loss of imperial and neighbouring markets for Austrian finished and semi-finished products, coupled with the imposition of war reparations and low tariffs, provided a context for the hyperinflation of 1921–1922, during which state finances were depleted to keep the administrative machinery going and pay pensioners (Marcus 2018, 35–77; Wessels 2007, 19–32). When efforts to secure foreign private or individual state loan failed, the League of Nations stepped in with a rescue plan via its Financial Committee. However, the terms of the League-arranged loan as stipulated in the Geneva Protocols of 1922 were extremely harsh. The Financial Committee established tutelage over Austrian finances under the supervision of a Vienna-based general commissioner and with an advisor to the central bank (Berger 2003; Cottrell 2013; Deak 2010; Wessels 2007, 114–20). To last until 1926, the tutelary regime delivered a textbook example of neoclassical economics in Austrian economic policy, including deep spending cuts and tight monetary measures to control the inflation. As the general commissioner put it in 1923, "Vienna is at the present moment … the League of Nations' International Reconstruction Laboratory" (quoted in Marcus 2018, 143). Indeed, the regime succeeded in price and currency stabilization, and subsequent return to the gold standard, with the schilling replacing the old crown in 1925.

After a period of relative stability in the second half of the 1920s, Austria was hit hard by the international financial crisis of the early 1930s. Credit-Anstalt, the country's flagship commercial bank with domestic and region-wide industrial concerns, collapsed in May 1931 (Eichengreen 2015, 140–1; Wessels 2007, 121–5). Industrial production plummeted and unemployment soared (Rothschild 1947, 65; Senft 2003, 33–4). The central bank bailed out Credit-Anstalt eventually with a loan arranged by the Bank for International Settlements. Yet the banking crisis was only part of the Austrian crisis and the government, having suspended all its international debt payments, applied to the League of Nations for a second loan. Negotiated in the Lausanne Protocol of 1931 and approved by parliament in 1932, the second loan reinstituted the tutelary regime by the League's Financial Committee over Austrian finances and ensured the ongoing observance of macroeconomic orthodoxy in economic policy— even more so under the Corporate State (Wessels 2007, 250–1).

As in the German case, the experience of hyperinflation bred an "inflation-mindedness" (Rothschild 1947, 60) or "inflation phobia"

(Wessels 2007, 30) among Austrian actors. Despite increasing polarization at the political level, the opposition Social Democratic Workers' Party (Sozialdemokratische Arbeiterpartei, SDAP) generally went along with the governing Christian Social Party (Christlichsoziale Partei) in endorsing the League of Nations' orthodox tutelary regime on both occasions (Berger 2003, 74). Interestingly, the SDAP's macroeconomic pacifism went hand in hand with its political militancy. It organized the Republican Defence League (Republikanischer Schutzbund) in 1923 in response to the growing violence of the right-wing Home Guard (Heimwehr) and even put up a brief armed resistance against the dictatorship in February 1934 (Konrad 2013). Like the SPD, it was exclusively urban-based and informed by orthodox Marxism (locally known as Austromarxism) in its economic ideology. In macroeconomic terms, there was hardly any difference between the SDAP's Austromarxism and the neoclassical orthodoxy of another local current, Austrian School of Economics or Astroliberalism (Klausinger 2002, 18; Thorpe 2011, 26–8; Wessels 2007, 248–9).

The governing Christian Socials were the key party to economic policy both under democracy and, in their fascistic reincarnation, under dictatorship. They held a firm grip on the peasantry by favouring it with generous support programmes while, at the same time, discriminating against wage labour within an extremely restrictive macroeconomic framework. They thus left no room for an agrarian–labour rapprochement. Instead, they built an effective agrarian–business alliance led by financial capitalists. Although the Christian Socials' monetary and fiscal orthodoxy per se was not favourable to employers, they helped them with cartelization and labour-excluding policies.

Phase II: *Ständestaat* Period

Unlike German Nazism and Italian Fascism, which emerged as independent mass movements, Austrofascism emerged out of an established—Christian Social—party and remained largely a top-down project. The latter also distinguished itself by the blatantly open international support it received in the form of the Financial Committee of the League of Nations. Austroliberals, too, saw in dictatorship a guarantee for the continuation of macroeconomic orthodoxy. Moreover, given its conservative-clerical background, Austrofascism did not penetrate society in the totalitarian manner that its German and Italian counterparts did. Thus, on account of its support base and ideological predisposition, the Corporate

State did not deviate much in economic policy from the preceding Christian Social governments under democracy.

Until Hitler's forceful *Anschluss* of Austria with Germany in 1938, Austrofascism tried to steer an independent course from Nazism by relying increasingly on Italian Fascism for both inspiration and support. From the early 1920s on, two streams of the Austrian political right contested for ideological supremacy (Kirk 2003, 15–9). The conservative-clerical main stream, represented by the governing Christian Socials and the rurally based paramilitary Home Guard, projected an independent Austria built on the Catholic notion of corporatism and drew inspiration from Italy. Austrofascism evolved from this stream. While never matching the appeal of home-grown fascism, the fringe pro-German and urban stream was represented by the Greater German People's Party, and direct and indirect agents of Nazism.

The Christian Socials' dictatorial turn took place under the leadership of Engelbert Dollfuss beginning with 1932. With an agricultural background as regional administrator and national minister, 39-year-old Dollfuss began to rule in coalition with the Home Guard and increasingly resorted to rule by decree to implement the terms of the second League of Nations-administered loan, including the reinstallation of the general commissioner representing the Financial Committee (Kirk 2003, 19–22; Konrad 2013, 25). In meeting the requirements of the tutelary regime and answering the calls from neoclassical economists for the undiluted implementation of the orthodox financial programme, he paved the road for dictatorship, which became official with the dissolution of parliament in March 1933 (Berger 2003, 87; Klausinger 2002, 6, 12–5; Wessels 2007, 251). After crushing an SDAP-organized insurrection in February 1934, the new regime faced its most serious challenge interestingly from the local agents of Nazism, who assassinated Dollfuss in a putsch later that year (Griffin 2013, 43–6). Yet his regime would survive for another four years.

In its economic orientation, the Dollfuss regime combined an uncompromising macroeconomic orthodoxy with microeconomic policies favouring businesses and agrarians (Senft 2003). This was the Corporate State version of a similar policy mixture that had encountered the resistance of organized labour under democracy. Reflecting on the professional career of Dollfuss himself, the regime not just materially rewarded farmers but also, in a manner typical of fascism, exalted agriculture and agrarian life as the source of racial purity and the guarantee of cultural survival

(Miller 2003; Thorpe 2011, 30–1). It also succumbed to organizational fetishism, creating layers of hierarchical corporate structures which were devoid of substance. As enshrined in the 1934 Constitution, a rubber-stamp parliament was complemented with four advisory councils and seven estates were created to represent different sectors of the economy (Kirk 2003, 22–7; Wohnout 2003). In addition, a state party called the Fatherland Front replaced the Christian Social Party and the Home Guard. The regime was, however, genuine in its pro-Fascist orientation and established closer linkages with Italy and distanced itself from Germany, for example, in trade (Konrad 2013, 50; Rothschild 1947, 73–5).

Austria was a doubly unique case. It was the only small country with an industrialized economy which came under international financial control and which succumbed to dictatorship in the 1930s. Although Austrian fascism fashioned similar cross-sectoral and cross-class alignments to those of Nazi Germany as another dictatorship with an industrialized economy, its economic policy response fell well short of Nazi *dirigisme* and autarkism. It was not the small open economy per se but the international financial control over Austrian finances which played a limiting role in this divergence. Preference and choice, too, mattered in the form of Austrofascism's embeddedness in a conservative-clerical tradition and its strict adherence to financial orthodoxy.

Italy

Germany, Austria, and Italy all had problems with the post-World War I order. Created out of the ruins of the Austro-Hungarian Empire, Austria was a reluctant republic unable to decide to join Germany or go it alone. When the Dollfuss regime tried to create a sense of independent Austrian nationhood under Austrofascism, it was thwarted by the Nazis. For Germany, it was a sense of injustice that constituted the focal point of opposition against the Versailles settlement. The Nazi regime combined that sense with a renewed claim to Germany's "living space" to launch an assault on the postwar order. As formulated by the Fascists, Italy's problems with the international system ran deeper. Although it ended up on the winning side in the war, Italy was a "proletarian" nation in the eyes of Fascism. This sense of being left behind in international race for supremacy informed Fascist economic policy in its both liberal and neomercantilist iterations.

The Italian case also differed from the German and Austrian cases in the timing of the Fascists' assumption of power. Whereas Nazism and Austrofascism rose to power in the midst of the Great Depression, Fascism took the helm in the aftermath of postwar labour upheaval. It thus ruled in both the expanding and contracting cycles of interwar world economy. This longer tenure and variegated experience allow us to observe how the Fascists reacted to changing economic—and political—circumstances in the international arena. Was their economic liberalism in the early to mid-1920s a concession to world-historical trends or out of a genuine conviction? Similarly, did they switch to neomercantilism out of necessity or as part of a prescheduled agenda?

A third comparative value of the Italian case derives from its parallel trajectory to that of the Soviet Union. The two questions asked above are also relevant for Bolshevik economic policy shifts in the interwar period. The Fascists and the Bolsheviks similarly had a fixed idea of their economies' backwardness in relation to the dominant economies of Western Europe and the United States while differing in their conceptions of, and approaches to, economic interests. This sense of retardation spurred an urgency to catch up with the pacesetters in Fascist and Bolshevik economic policies during both the global upswing of the 1920s and the downswing of the 1930s. Thus, what James Gregor (1979) calls developmental dictatorship formed a common thread between Italy and the Soviet Union (and some of the Balkan countries) to be seen in the next chapter.

The Fascist idea of the economy evolved from its revolutionary socialist or syndicalist beginnings. Mussolini, himself a Socialist Party activist until 1914 when he was expelled for his pro-war stance, initially rejected traditional party notion in favour of a new, group (*fascio*) type of organization. In this, he was informed by revolutionary syndicalism which saw workers' direct, economic organization, rather than their association in political parties, as closer to Marx's vision of a socialist industrial system (Gregor 1979, 22–31). Drawn up in 1919, the movement's coming-out manifesto incorporated syndicalism into a larger radical programme. It promised an eight-hour day, wage floor, and participation in industrial management for workers, a "heavy and progressive" tax on capital, confiscation of all Church property, a near-total confiscation of war profits, as well as universal suffrage with proportional representation, reduction of voting age and age of candidacy, and a constituent assembly (Pollard 1998, 25).

Yet the unprecedented surge of urban and rural labour mobilization in the "red biennium" (1919–1920) helped the Fascists reveal and redefine their priorities. To be culminated in the occupation of factories in the summer of 1920, the strike wave involved both Socialist and Catholic labour organizations (unions and peasant leagues) but was largely spontaneous and lacked a clear strategy (Gregor 1979, 172–3; Pollard 1998, 29–30). It became more important and famous for the response it received from the Fascists. In the countryside, local Fascist squads were formed to guard large landowners and terrorize strikers. Similarly, emerging Fascist syndicates proved their worth to Northern industrialists by engaging in strikebreaking (Gregor 1979, 187; Pollard 1998, 30–2).

Building on their pro-business and pro-agrarian response to the "red biennium," the Fascists wasted no time to engage in a programmatic reorientation. In its 1921 founding programme, the Fascist Party emphasized productivism as the organizing principle of its approach to national development and arranged its economic priorities accordingly. Fascism now exalted productive industrial capital as opposed to "parasitic" rentier capital, promised to "discipline the disorderly struggles between classes and occupational interests," and tasked the state to expand the nation's productive base via tax and administrative reforms (including budget discipline), privatization of public utilities, improvements in physical infrastructure, and tariff protection (Baker 2006, 231–2; Gregor 1979, 129–30; Pollard 1998, 32, 43; Priester 2013, 60). The same year, the Fascists also clarified their position on land tenure in a separate agrarian programme. They opposed the breaking-up of estates (land reform); what mattered was the efficient utilization of land, not its redistribution.

In addition to their economic adaptability, the Fascists also displayed political shrewdness in taking power. They contested the 1921 election by aligning with the fading Liberals against the left (e.g., Socialist and Communist) and Catholic parties, and picked up a small number of seats (Pollard 1998, 40–1). The resulting hung parliament failed to produce a stable government, thus paving the way for the Fascist "March on Rome" in October 1922.[4]

Economic policy in the *Liberista* period (1922–1925) was strikingly consistent with the Fascist programme of 1921 and Mussolini's "[e]nough of the railroad state, the postal state, the state as insurance agent" statement in 1922 (Baker 2006, 232). Minister of Finance Alberto De' Stefani, who was in charge of general economic policy, implemented a radical liberal project, including privatization, incentives for foreign investment, tax benefits for businesses, downsizing of civil service and other spending cuts, downward pressure on salaries and wages, and curtailment of labour rights (Clough 1964, 222–30; de Cecco 1989, 202–7; Priester 2013, 58; Welk 1938, 163). This was a successful project from the standpoint of its authors, producing "a balanced state budget by 1925, a rate of savings and capital accumulation unsurpassed until Italy's 'economic miracle' of the 1950s, and a rate of industrial growth that doubled the peninsula's total output by 1929" (Gregor 1979, 142–3).

Yet economic liberalization went hand in hand with political regimentation in the *Liberista* period. Radical liberal measures required a certain authoritarian fiat. Moreover, as the Fascists consolidated their rule by mid-decade, they turned increasingly *dirigiste* in dealing with the economy. They launched their first autarkic experiment with the so-called Battle for Grain in 1925, which skewed agricultural policy towards self-sufficiency in grains. The following year, they launched another battle, "Battle for the Lira," which would lead to domestic deflation by fixing the exchange value of the currency at a high rate, 90 lire to the pound sterling (Pollard 1998, 78–80). Although there was nothing uniquely nationalist about a deflationary course, it spoke to Fascist pride in the value of national currency as well as creating "path dependency" for monetary policy in the rest of the interwar period. The Fascists also acted on their foundational idea of syndicalism or corporatism from the mid-1920s on. In 1925, they engineered an agreement (to be legislated later the same year) between the General Confederation of Industry and the Confederation of Fascist Corporations (syndicates), which stamped the latter as the representative of all Italian workers. This was the first major curtailment of employers' prerogative to negotiate (Gregor 1979, 198–9). The Labour Charter of 1927 further signalled the state's willingness and readiness to intervene in the economy "when private initiative was lacking or was inadequate, or when the political interests of the state were involved" (Clough 1964, 235).

In the late 1920s and 1930s, the Fascists developed an obsession with pigeonholing every conceivable group into a corporation and organizing the country as a pyramid of corporate structures (see Clough 1964, 230–41; Welk 1938, part 2, for a detailed description of formal structures). As in Germany and Austria, however, corporatism did not matter much to Italian economic policy. Its real function was rather in the area of system maintenance. It served as an apparatus of political control, particularly labour repression, and ideological legitimation for Fascist rule (Baker 2006, 233–4; Maier 1987, 81; Pollard 1998, 87; Priester 2013, 63; Welk 1938, 171).

What drove Italian economic *dirigisme* after 1925 was the consolidation of Fascist totalitarianism combined with the impetus of the Great Depression. As the Fascists got rid of their political opponents and installed a self-styled totalitarian regime in the second half of the 1920s,[5] they grew more confident about what they could do with the economy to lift it internationally. They also become more assertive in relation to both business and agrarian interests. Thus, the Fascist economic agenda was not static. Nor would it have a statist policy component in the 1930s without the world-historical crisis.[6] Although statism and autarky were hinted in Fascist programmes, statements, and speeches or even partially tried before the 1930s, they did not become core sectoral policy priorities until after the onset of the crisis.

This said, the Fascists were able to intervene in agriculture earlier than in industry. The Battle for Grain began 1925 and it was incorporated into a broader "ruralist" agenda later in the decade (Morgan 1995, 101–4; Priester 2013, 67–8; Welk 1938, 181–95). Like their German and Austrian counterparts, they saw small and middle peasantry as the source of, and inspiration for, national rejuvenation. A "demographic battle" was launched in 1927 to encourage rurally based population growth and discourage migration to cities. The following year, this was complemented with a comprehensive infrastructure and public works programme (*bonifica integrale*) for land reclamation, improvement, as well as job creation for the unemployed. By the end of 1937, the programme significantly expanded the acreage of cultivable land, thus strengthening the regime's agrarian base via small proprietorship and tenancy (Tcherkinsky 1939, 27–8).

The world economic crisis served Fascist developmental goals more clearly in industry. The Italian Industrial Finance Institute (Istituto Mobiliare Italiano, IMI), established in 1931 to meet the credit needs of industry in crisis conditions, took control of many of the companies which it helped rescue, thus growing into a state holding company. In 1933, the IMI was joined by the Institute for Industrial Reconstruction (Istituto per la Ricostruzione Industriale, IRI), which began by acquiring the financial and industrial assets of the country's three largest mixed banks that had failed.[7] Originally established as a temporary agency, the IRI kept acquiring failed businesses and thus became a giant financial-industrial conglomerate. After the banking legislation of 1936, which eliminated mixed banking by separating short-term commercial credit and long-term industrial financing, the IRI was given a permanent, state holding company status with separate banking and industrial operations (Morgan 1995, 128–30; Priester 2013, 66; Zamagni 1993, 294–300). By 1937, it "controlled over forty-four percent of all Italian capital stock, and almost eighteen percent of the total capital of the nation" (Gregor 1979, 158). Whether by accident or design, the Italian economy under Fascism came to have the largest state sector in the industrialized and semi-industrialized world outside the Soviet Union (Cohen 1988).

The Fascists' original characterization of Italy as a proletarian nation facing an uphill battle against imperialist and plutocratic nations was certainly an exaggeration. Since the beginning of the unification (*Risorgimento*) in 1861, it had established a significant industrial base. An indirect indication of this was that, by 1920, Socialist and Catholic union confederations reached a combined membership of close to 3.5 million in a country of just over 37 million people (Gregor 1979, 173). Nevertheless, as late as 1936, when Fascist developmentalism was in full swing, industry accommodated only about 25% of the labour force, compared to agriculture's share of over 50% (Toniolo and Piva 1988, 223). Italy had a semi-industrial or, in the language of world-system analysis, semi-peripheral economy. Whether the Fascists elevated the Italian economy to a core industrial status is a question for economic historians. However, at least in the case of the automobile industry, we know that post-World War II Italy reaped the "fruits of fascism" (Reich 1990, 277–302).

Summing Up

All three cases reviewed in this chapter experienced democratic breakdown—Germany and Austria in the midst of the Great Depression, and Italy in the aftermath of World War I. That experience clearly shows that political regime is not a constant structural factor. As long as they exist, both democracy and dictatorship put structural limits to what actors can do, particularly what governments can choose in economic policy. Yet none of the three democracies at issue survived the interwar period. Nor did their dictatorial successors survive World War II. While political regimes change, they do not change as easily or uneventfully as individual institutions. It usually takes a world-historical crisis and/or domestic upheaval for democracy and dictatorship to give way to each other as institutional complexes. In the case of single institutions, change can occur within a given political regime as in the cases of the transition from majoritarian to proportional representation in many European countries, and the replacement of mixed banking with specialized (commercial and investment) banking in interwar United States and Italy.

In transitioning to a modern, fascist form of dictatorship, Germany, Austria, and Italy shared a number of characteristics, including the idea of corporatism, anti-labourism, pro-capitalism, and exaltation of independent peasantry. Prior to democratic breakdown, all experienced a legitimacy crisis exacerbated by sharp sociocultural conflicts. In Germany, no domestic actor was fully content with their country's postwar status as embodied in the Weimar Republic. And the continuing domination of landed (Junker) aristocracy over state apparatus always posed a threat to progressive Weimar coalitions headed by the Social Democrats. Austrians were not even sure about their separate existence in the postimperial period and never embraced the Austrian Republic wholeheartedly. Moreover, the Republic had been built on a fault line between the Catholic Christian Socials and the Marxist Social Democrats. In the Italian case, the founding Liberals were a spent force after World War I and gave way to labour insurgency and two mass parties, the Socialists and the Catholics, who were never willing or able to cooperate. Fascism in a generic sense responded to the legitimacy crisis and sociocultural conflicts with a corporatist solution whereby a Durkheimian integration of functional parts (sectoral, occupational, and all other categories) in a purpose-driven whole would replace the anomic situation and the attending conflicts. All three fascisms were caught up with "corporate mania," building an intricate web of structures. Corporatism may have served the legitimation and coercion functions well, but it was largely an empty shell in terms of the functional representation of economic interests.

Fascist corporatism was closely related to the growing fear of labour's economic and political mobilization. Although they were shaken up by Communist separatism in the immediate postwar period, the three labour movements remained among the strongest in Europe at both union and party levels. In fact, organized labour formed a credible alternative to bourgeois rule. It is no wonder that Hitler, Dollfuss, and Mussolini began by dismantling organized labour and replacing it with party- or state-controlled fronts or corporations. The economic order they established was pro-capitalist but not necessarily submissive to capitalists. Nazism and Fascism steered business according to their political priorities while Austrofascism willingly broadened the space for domestic and international business interests. However, all three were unanimously protective of agrarian interests, not only maintaining existing property relations but also strengthening independent peasantry.

Under dictatorship, each national response was distinguished from the other two by at least one characteristic. The Nazis responded to massive unemployment by launching equally massive public works programmes, which their immediate predecessors could only begin to contemplate. Nazi fiscal innovation can be qualified but not denied. The Austrians were the most business-friendly bunch; they never had the will or capacity to politically regiment businesses. In contrast, the Fascists turned distinctly statist in industrial policy. This was a "mixed economy" position informed by the motto "where business fails or lags, the state intervenes." It was not meant to terminate private enterprise but complement and guide it. In this sense, Italian industrial policy sharply diverged from Soviet industrialization policy. The former's closest counterpart in the Balkans was Turkish *étatisme*. The next chapter will examine different iterations of developmental neomercantilism in the Soviet and Balkan agricultural economies.

Notes

1. As I noted earlier (Chap. 3, Note 1), international statistics give only a very rough idea about the relative performance of national economies. The German national income, for example, contracted by 41%, compared to 52% for the United States, from 1929 to 1932 (Safarian [1959] 2009, 98).
2. As in Scandinavia, conservative forces pushed for proportional representation as a guarantee against Social Democratic dominance. In the German case, however, the Social Democrats, too, were demanding it (Kolb [2002] 2005, 164).
3. In his path-breaking book *Das Finanzkapital* (1910), Austro-German Marxist theoretician Rudolf Hilferding laid the foundations of such theories.
4. Here I take the Italian democratic breakdown, like its German and Austrian counterparts, as a given rather than as a problematic. Its causes, which were probably varied and complex, are outside of this account.
5. The coinage of the term "totalitarian" in its modern sense is attributed to Mussolini, who used it publicly for the first time in his address to a Fascist Party congress in June 1925 (Morgan 1995, 79–80).
6. Here, I am taking issue with a static view of Italian economic policies in the interwar period, which sees them directly and fully flowing from the original Fascist programme (see, e.g., Gregor 1979, 143–54).
7. On Italian mixed banking in historical perspective, see Faro 1929, 803–15; Forsyth 1991, 181–5.

References

Aldcroft, Derek H. 1977. *From Versailles to Wall Street, 1919–1929.* Berkeley: University of California Press.
Baker, David. 2006. "The Political Economy of Fascism: Myth or Reality, or Myth and Reality?" *New Political Economy* 11, no. 2: 227–50. https://doi.org/10.1080/13563460600655581.
Berger, Peter. 2003. "The League of Nations and Interwar Austria: Critical Assessment of a Partnership in Economic Reconstruction." In *The Dollfuss/Schuschnigg Era in Austria: A Reassessment*, edited by Günter Bischof, Anton Pelinka, and Alexander Lassner, 73–92. London and New York: Routledge.
Born, Karl E. [1977] 1983. *International Banking in the 19th and 20th Centuries.* Translated from the German by Volker R. Berghahn. New York: St. Martin's.
Calomiris, Charles W. 2000. *U.S. Bank Deregulation in Historical Perspective.* Cambridge: Cambridge University Press.
Clough, Shepard B. 1964. *The Economic History of Modern Italy.* New York: Columbia University Press.
Cohen, Jon S. 1988. "Was Italian Fascism a Developmental Dictatorship? Some Evidence to the Contrary." *Economic History Review*, 2nd series 41, no. 1: 95–113. https://doi.org/10.2307/2597334.
Cottrell, Philip L. 2013. "Austrian Reconstruction, 1920–1921: A Matter for Private Business or the League of Nations?" In *Business in the Age of Extremes: Essays in Modern German and Austrian Economic History*, edited by Hartmut Berghoff, Jürgen Kocka, and Dieter Ziegler, 59–75. Cambridge: Cambridge University Press.
Darity, William A., Jr., and Bobbie L. Horn. 1985. "Rudolf Hilferding: The Dominion of Capitalism and the Dominion of Gold." *American Economic Review* 75, no. 2: 363–8.
Deak, John. 2010. "Dismantling Empire: Ignaz Seipel and Austria's Financial Crisis, 1922–1925." In *From Empire to Republic: Post-World War I Austria*, edited by Günter Bischof, Fritz Plasser, and Peter Berger, 123–41. New Orleans: University of New Orleans Pres.
de Cecco, Marcello. 1989. "Keynes and Italian Economics." In *The Political Power of Economic Ideas: Keynesianism across Nations*, edited by Peter A. Hall, 195–229. Princeton: Princeton University Press.
Eichengreen, Barry J. 1992. *Golden Fetters: The Gold Standard and the Great Depression, 1919–1939.* New York: Oxford University Press.
Eichengreen, Barry J. 2015. *Hall of Mirrors: The Great Depression, the Great Recession, and the Uses – and Misuses – of History.* New York: Oxford University Press.

Faro, Francesco L. 1929. "The Banking System of Italy." In *Foreign Banking Systems*, edited by H. Parker Willis and Benjamin H. Beckhart, 765–815. New York: Henry Holt.

Flora, Peter, Jens Alber, Richard Eichenberg, Jürgen Kohl, Franz Kraus, Winfried Pfenning, and Kurt Seebohm. 1983. *State, Economy, and Society in Western Europe, 1815–1975*, vol. 1, *The Growth of Mass Democracies and Welfare States*. Frankfurt am Main: Campus Verlag.

Forsyth, Douglas J. 1991. "The Rise and Fall of German-Inspired Mixed Banking in Italy, 1894–1936." In *The Role of Banks in the Interwar Economy*, edited by Harold James, Håkan Lindgren, and Alice Teichova, 179–205. Cambridge: Cambridge University Press.

Gerschenkron, Alexander. 1943. *Bread and Democracy in Germany*. Berkeley: University of California Press.

Gourevitch, Peter A. 1984. "Breaking with Orthodoxy: The Politics of Economic Policy Responses to the Depression of the 1930s." *International Organization* 38, no. 1: 95–129. https://doi.org/10.1017/S0020818300004288.

Gourevitch, Peter A. 1986. *Politics in Hard Times: Comparative Responses to International Economic Crises*. Ithaca: Cornell University Press.

Gregor, A. James. 1979. *Italian Fascism and Developmental Dictatorship*. Princeton: Princeton University Press.

Griffin, Roger. 2013. "Avalanches of Spring: The Great War, Modernism, and the Rise of Austro-Fascism." In *Routes into the Abyss: Coping with Crises in the 1930s*, edited by Helmut Konrad and Wolfgang Maderthaner, 33–54. New York and Oxford: Berghahn Books.

Hilferding, Rudolf. 1910. *Das Finanzkapital: Eine Studie über die jüngste Entwicklung des Kapitalismus*. Vienna: Verlag der Wiener Volksbuchhandlung.

Holtfrerich, Carl-Ludwig. 1990a. "Was the Policy of Deflation in Germany Unavoidable?" In *Economic Crisis and Political Collapse: The Weimar Republic, 1924–1933*, edited by Jürgen B. von Kruedener, 63–80. Oxford: Berg.

Holtfrerich, Carl-Ludwig. 1990b. "Economic Policy Options and the End of the Weimar Republic." In *Weimar: Why Did German Democracy Fail?*, edited by Ian Kershaw, 58–91. London: Weidenfeld and Nicholson.

James, Harold. 1986. *The German Slump: Politics and Economics, 1924–1936*. Oxford: Clarendon Press.

Kaiser, Claudia. 2000. "Trade Union Reactions to Economic Crisis." In *After the Slump: Industry and Politics in 1930s Britain and Germany*, edited by C. Buchheim and Redvers Garside, 179–200. Frankfurt am Main: Peter Lang.

Katzenstein, Peter J. 1985. *Small States in World Markets: Industrial Policy in Europe*. Ithaca: Cornell University Press.

Kershaw, Ian, ed. 1990. *Weimar: Why Did German Democracy Fail?* London: Weidenfeld and Nicolson.

Kirk, Tim. 2003. "Fascism and Austrofascism." In *The Dollfuss/Schuschnigg Era in Austria: A Reassessment*, edited by Günter Bischof, Anton Pelinka, and Alexander Lassner, 10–31. London and New York: Routledge.

Klausinger, Hansjörg. 2002. "The Austrian School of Economics and the Gold Standard Mentality in Austrian Economic Policy in the 1930s." Center for Austrian Studies Working Paper 02-2, University of Minnesota, Minneapolis. https://econwpa.ub.uni-muenchen.de/econ-wp/mhet/papers/0501/0501001.pdf (accessed 8 May 2021).

Kolb, Eberhard. [2002] 2005. *The Weimar Republic*. 2nd ed. Translated from the German by P. S. Falla and R. J. Park. London: Routledge.

Koning, Niek. 1994. *The Failure of Agrarian Capitalism: Agrarian Politics in the United Kingdom, Germany, the Netherlands and the USA, 1846–1919*. London and New York: Routledge.

Konrad, Helmut. 2013. "The Significance of February 1934 in Austria, in Both National and International Context." In *Routes into the Abyss: Coping with Crises in the 1930s*, edited by Helmut Konrad and Wolfgang Maderthaner, 20–32. New York and Oxford: Berghahn Books.

Kurth, James R. 1979. "The Political Consequences of the Product Cycle: Industrial History and Political Outcomes." *International Organization* 33, no. 1: 1–34. https://doi.org/10.1017/S0020818300000643.

Lee, Stephen J. 1998. *The Weimar Republic*. London: Routledge.

Mackenzie, Kenneth. [1932] 1935. *The Banking Systems of Great Britain, France, Germany, and the United States of America*. 2nd ed. London: Macmillan.

Maier, Charles S. 1987. *In Search of Stability: Explorations in Historical Political Economy*. Cambridge: Cambridge University Press.

Marcus, Nathan. 2018. *Austrian Reconstruction and the Collapse of Global Finance, 1921–1931*. Cambridge, MA: Harvard University Press.

Miller, James W. 2003. "Engelbert Dollfuss and Austrian Agriculture." In *The Dollfuss/Schuschnigg Era in Austria: A Reassessment*, edited by Günter Bischof, Anton Pelinka, and Alexander Lassner, 122–42. London and New York: Routledge.

Morgan, Philip. 1995. *Italian Fascism, 1915–1945*. Basingstoke: Macmillan.

Moses, John A. 1986. "The German Free Trade Unions and the Problem of Mass Unemployment in the Weimar Republic." In *Unemployment and the Great Depression in Weimar Germany*, edited by Peter D. Stachura, 148–62. Basingstoke: Macmillan.

Overy, R. J. 1982. *The Nazi Economic Recovery, 1932–1938*. London: Macmillan.

Polanyi, Karl. 1944. *The Great Transformation: The Political and Economic Origins of Our Time*. Boston: Beacon.

Pollard, John. 1998. *The Fascist Experience in Italy*. London and New York: Routledge.

Priester, Karin. 2013. "Fascism in Italy between the Poles of Reactionary Thought and Modernity." In *Routes into the Abyss: Coping with Crises in the 1930s*, edited by Helmut Konrad and Wolfgang Maderthaner, 55–77. New York and Oxford: Berghahn Books.

Quittner, Paul. 1929. "The Banking System of Germany." In *Foreign Banking Systems*, edited by H. Parker Willis and Benjamin H. Beckhart, 627–722. New York: Henry Holt.

Reich, Simon. 1990. *The Fruits of Fascism: Postwar Prosperity in Historical Perspective*. Ithaca: Cornell University Press.

Rothschild, K. W. 1947. *Austria's Economic Development between the Two Wars*. London: Frederick Muller.

Safarian, A. E. [1959] 2009. *The Canadian Economy in the Great Depression*. 3rd ed. Montreal and Kingston: McGill-Queen's University Press.

Schacht, Hjalmar H. G. 1956. *Confessions of "The Old Wizard": The Autobiography of Hjalmar Horace Greeley Schacht*. Translated from the German by Diana Pyke. Boston: Houghton Mifflin.

Senft, Gerhard. 2003. "Economic Development and Economic Policies in the *Ständestaat* Era." In *The Dollfuss/Schuschnigg Era in Austria: A Reassessment*, edited by Günter Bischof, Anton Pelinka, and Alexander Lassner, 32–55. London and New York: Routledge.

Silverman, Dan P. 1988. "National Socialist Economics: The *Wirtschaftswunder* Reconsidered." In *Interwar Unemployment in International Perspective*, edited by Barry J. Eichengreen and Tim J. Hatton, 185–220. Dordrecht: Kluwer.

Solomou, Solomos. 1996. *Themes in Macroeconomic History: The UK Economy, 1919–1939*. Cambridge: Cambridge University Press.

Swenson, Peter A. 1989. *Fair Shares: Unions, Pay, and Politics in Sweden and West Germany*. Ithaca: Cornell University Press.

Tcherkinsky, M. Morduch. 1939. *The Land Tenure Systems in Europe*. Geneva: League of Nations.

Thelen, Kathleen A. 1991. *Union of Parts: Labor Politics in Postwar Germany*. Ithaca: Cornell University Press.

Thorpe, Julie. 2011. *Pan-Germanism and the Austrofascist State, 1933–38*. Manchester and New York: Manchester University Press.

Toniolo, Gianni, and Francesco Piva. 1988. "Unemployment in the 1930s: The Case of Italy." In *Interwar Unemployment in International Perspective*, edited by Barry J. Eichengreen and Tim J. Hatton, 221–45. Dordrecht: Kluwer.

Trampusch, Christine, and Dennis C. Spies. 2014. "Agricultural Interests and the Origins of Capitalism: A Parallel Comparative History of Germany, Denmark, New Zealand, and the USA." *New Political Economy* 19, no. 6: 918–42. https://doi.org/10.1080/13563467.2013.861414.

Weber, Fritz. 1991. "Universal Banking in Interwar Central Europe." In *The Role of Banks in the Interwar Economy*, edited by Harold James, Håkan Lindgren, and Alice Teichova, 19–25. Cambridge: Cambridge University Press.

Welk, William G. 1938. *Fascist Economic Policy: An Analysis of Italy's Economic Experiment*. Cambridge, MA: Harvard University Press.

Wessels, Jens-Wilhelm. 2007. *Economic Policy and Microeconomic Performance in Inter-War Europe: The Case of Austria, 1918–1938*. Stuttgart: Franz Steiner Verlag.

Wohnout, Helmut. 2003. "A Chancellorial Dictatorship with a 'Corporative' Pretext: The Austrian Constitution between 1934 and 1938." In *The Dollfuss/Schuschnigg Era in Austria: A Reassessment*, edited by Günter Bischof, Anton Pelinka, and Alexander Lassner, 143–62. London and New York: Routledge.

Woytinsky, Wladimir S. 1961. *Stormy Passage: A Personal History through Two Russian Revolutions to Democracy and Freedom, 1905–1960*. New York: Vanguard.

Zamagni, Vera. 1993. *The Economic History of Italy, 1860–1990*. Oxford: Clarendon Press.

Ziegler, Dieter. 2013. "'A Regulated Market Economy': New Perspectives on the Nature of the Economic Order of the Third Reich, 1933–1939." In *Business in the Age of Extremes: Essays in Modern German and Austrian Economic History*, edited by Hartmut Berghoff, Jürgen Kocka, and Dieter Ziegler, 139–52. Cambridge: Cambridge University Press.

CHAPTER 6

Neomercantilism, Mark II, Under Dictatorship of the Bureaucracy

If the long stagnation of the late nineteenth century (1873–1896) was instrumental in unleashing a second wave of industrialization in Europe and North America, the Great Depression of the 1930s figured similarly in a third wave involving southern and eastern Europe, Latin America, and Japan. The third wave formed not just in a predominantly agricultural context but also primarily under undemocratic conditions which were much more sweeping than those of the second wave. Politically, countries such as New Zealand and Norway were an exception to the extent that their economic policies revolved around industrialization. The more totalitarian the conditions were, the faster the pace of industrialization became.

Industrialization was the driving force of developmental neomercantilism. As seen in the last chapter, Italian economic policy had a developmental streak. However, Fascist developmentalism was tempered with its semi-industrial context and pro-agrarian disposition. With no such economy or ideology, Soviet and Turkish rulers delivered—in their distinctive ways—the paradigmatic exemplars of developmental neomercantilism

---

An earlier version of parts of this chapter was published in "Policy response to the Great Depression of the 1930s: Turkish neomercantilism in the Balkan context," Adnan Türegün, Turkish Studies, copyright © 2016 Informa UK Limited, trading as Taylor & Francis Group, reprinted by permission, https://www.tandfonline.com/loi/ftur20.

© The Author(s), under exclusive license to Springer Nature Switzerland AG 2022
A. Türegün, *Policy Responses to the Interwar Economic Crisis*,
https://doi.org/10.1007/978-3-030-96953-0_6

among large and small states, respectively. In the Soviet Union, the Stalinists were engaged in a boundless experimentation for socialist industrialization, including central-comprehensive planning and the all-out collectivization of agriculture. In Turkey, the Kemalists did not have such free hand in the economy. Nor did they have the totalizing ideological reach to society. Yet their statist industrialization drive, including planning, investment banking, and anti-agrarianism, was unmatched among small countries. The neighbouring Balkan rulers, too, had a developmentalist outlook but, sticking to their pro-agrarianism, adopted a gradual and private sector-based approach to industrialization.

Rulers' ideas of the economy and their consequent approach to major groups of interest figured prominently in developmental neomercantilism as well. One important difference in this case was that the rulers themselves were part of a larger bureaucratic class independent of traditional classes. Modern, totalitarian dictatorship was the *sine qua non* of this class. It emerged most emphatically in the Soviet Union after the eradication of capitalists and large landowners as a class, and the incorporation of organized labour into party-state apparatus. What happened within, rather than without, the party-state bureaucracy was thus key to the reorientation of Soviet economic policy in the late 1920s. "Socialism in one country" rose on the victory of Stalinism over its "left" and "right" alternatives. Turkish bureaucracy did not have the reach of its Soviet counterpart but, with a submissive commercial bourgeoisie and no industrial labour to deal with, came close to it in acquiring an independent class status. In Turkey, too, an intra-bureaucratic struggle took place that gave way to a new economic policy. However, the Turkish infighting, which resulted in the victory of the mainstream Kemalist faction over its moderate and radical alternatives, was more subdued and unfolded against the background of the world economic crisis in the early 1930s. The other Balkan bureaucracies were weaker in relation to commercial-industrial and agrarian interests, and thus lacked the economic *dirigisme* of their Turkish counterpart.

This is the last substantive chapter dealing with a particular group of national responses. Soviet developmental neomercantilism was unique in many ways but carried a generic affinity with the agro-industrial neomercantilism of Nazi Germany and especially Fascist Italy as well as with the other developmentalist responses. It is thus an indispensable part of our comparative set. The Turkish response, which was exemplary of developmentalism among small countries, constitutes another primary case. With their weaker *dirigiste* thrust, the rest of the Balkan countries were to

Turkey what Austria was to Germany. They are thus included in this analysis as secondary cases for comparison with Turkey. The reader may find Table 6.1 useful for navigating the chapter.

THE TORTUOUS ROUTE TO SOCIALISM IN ONE COUNTRY

The Bolsheviks took power five years before the Fascists' "March on Rome" in October 1922. After the former's War Communism of 1918–1921 necessitated by civil war, the two ruling parties followed near-parallel trajectories in politics and policy in the interwar period. They

Table 6.1 Neomercantilism, mark II: developmental varieties

Country (group)	Key determinants			Policy outcome
	Ruling party approach to sectoral and class interests	Institutional mediators	Structural limits to neomercantilism, mark II	
State socialist case				
Soviet Union	Bureaucratic self-aggrandizing; labour-tutelary; business- and agrarian-liquidationist	War Communism	n/a	Neomercantilist
State capitalist cases				
Exemplary: Turkey	Bureaucratic self-aggrandizing; business- and agrarian-accommodationist; labour-repressive	Young Turk *dirigiste* experience	n/a	Neomercantilist
Mixed: Rest of the Balkans	Limited bureaucratic self-aggrandizing; pro-business and pro-agrarian; labour-repressive	Nineteenth-century liberal tradition	Traditional dictatorship; stronger mercantile-industrial base; independent peasantry	Mixed (protectionist–neomercantilist)

began with a dalliance with economic liberalism, then signalled autarkic tendencies, and finally settled in their trademark *dirigisme*. Politically, they tolerated a measure of contestation while they were busy consolidating their rule but then closed the state and society for any sort of dissent. These parallels, however, hid significant differences between the Bolsheviks and the Fascists in their approaches to the economy and about their place in it. Unlike the latter, who remained pro-agrarian throughout and defended the primacy of private enterprise even at the height of their interventionism, the former would come to eliminate private enterprise and independent peasantry as a class. Moreover, Soviet bureaucracy acquired class-like status with the elimination of capitalists and independent peasants as a class. Despite pompous Fascist rhetoric, Italian bureaucracy never reached that status against the continuing counterweight of business and agrarian interests. These differences were translated into economic policy, whereby Italian mixed-economy route and Soviet all-out socialization formed the main dividing line. How "socialism in one country" came about makes a fascinating story.

As one of the momentous consequences of World War I, the Bolshevik Revolution of 1917 dispossessed the bourgeoisie and landed aristocracy. The Bolsheviks emerged from the ensuing civil war victorious in 1920 but with a regimented economy which could not even feed the population under the so-called War Communism (Nove [1969] 1992, 39–77). The solution they found the following year was the New Economic Policy (*Novaya Ekonomicheskaya Politika*, NEP) which, in the context of the liberal international climate of the time, relaxed restrictions on domestic and foreign trade, allowed intermediaries (who would come to be known as Nepmen) in the sphere of circulation, encouraged independent peasant farming, and carried out tax reforms to ease economic squeeze of the population (Cohen [1973] 1980, 124; Davies 1989, 1008–15; Kuruç 2011, 67–70; Nove [1969] 1992, 78–114). They even initiated currency stabilization in 1923–1924 to replace commodity-based exchange with a gold-backed rouble (Nenovsky 2015, 13–26).

Lenin justified NEP as a strategic retreat to pause and gain breathing space before forging ahead with socialist construction again. He did not mince his words about the nature of NEP: "The New Economic Policy means substituting a tax for the requisitioning of food; it means reverting to capitalism to a considerable extent—to what extent we do not know. Concessions to foreign capitalists … leasing enterprises to private capitalists definitely mean restoring capitalism … the abolition of the surplus-food appropriation system means allowing the peasants to trade freely in their surplus agricultural produce" (Lenin [1921] 1980, 64). That this was an economic retreat and not a political one was confirmed by the concurrent decisions to outlaw all political parties other than the Bolshevik Party and ban organization of factions within that party (Cohen [1973] 1980, 125; Nove [1969] 1992, 77). Nevertheless, the closure of political space for opposition left the party as the only meaningful, de facto arena for expression of different ideas on economic policy in particular.

This became a reality as soon as 1923, when the so-called scissors crisis threatened food supply to cities. Peasants became reluctant to market their goods because the internal terms of trade had turned against agriculture (meaning lower agricultural prices in the face of higher industrial prices) in a high inflation environment (Johnson and Temin 1993, 751–3). The crisis triggered an intense and drawn-out debate among the Bolshevik leadership minus an incapacitated Lenin. Parties to the debate shifted in the course of the decade, but it hinged on two alternative visions of building a socialist economy: a rapid "superindustrialization" on the back of agriculture versus a gradual, market-based industrialization maintaining rural–urban balance (Davies 1989, 1015–24; Erlich 1960, 24–59; Gregory and Sailors 2003, 198–200; Nove [1969] 1992, 115–32).

The "Left" minority headed by Leon Trotsky, who coined the term "scissors crisis," opposed NEP as a petty bourgeois, pro-peasant degeneration of Bolshevism's heroic tradition. What they proposed was a statist, planned, and rapid industrialization prioritizing the production of capital and intermediate goods. The question of how this programme would be financed was answered most cogently by a young economist named Yevgeny Preobrazhensky, who employed the concept of primitive socialist accumulation in analogy to that of primitive capitalist accumulation (Cohen [1973] 1980, 163–5; Davies 1980, 33–4; Lewin [1966] 1968, 142–59). He thought that the rise of capitalism in Europe based on the plundering of colonial possessions gave the Bolsheviks a clue as to the methodology of building socialism. With Soviet Russia currently being an isolated country with no colonial possessions, however, he concluded that the only financing option available for its socialist industrialization was the extraction of surplus value from the peasant economy via taxation and price policy. He thus welcomed the scissors crisis as an unintended consequence of NEP.

The pro-NEP "Right" majority, including Stalin, wanted to continue with the strategic retreat as long as necessary and not to disturb the worker–peasant alliance. However, they still kept socialist industrialization as a long-term goal to be achieved by expanding the peasant-driven domestic market. Nikolay Bukharin was the foremost theoretician of this camp (Cohen [1973] 1980, 165–84 in particular; Davies 1980, 31–3; Erlich 1960, 78–89; Lewin [1966] 1968, 135–42). He agreed with Preobrazhensky that an isolated Soviet Russia would have to create resources for its industrialization internally. Yet, for the former, a prosperous peasantry capable of consuming manufactured goods was necessary for socialist industrialization, which should build up from light industries to heavy ones in a gradual manner, not according to a "Genghis Khan plan." Stalin was, by and large, an economic Bukharinist at this juncture.

While this debate was raging in the mid-1920s, actual policy did not deviate from the NEP course. The "Right" majority in charge of government responded to the scissors crisis by putting in place measures to raise agricultural prices and lower industrial prices (Cohen [1973] 1980, 157; Johnson and Temin 1993, 759). However, the policy context changed both domestically and internationally. First, Stalin, who held the post of general secretary in the Bolshevik Party, steadily increased his control of the party and thus the state with an unmatched organizational and tactical skill. This further marginalized the "Left" opposition. Second, the expected proletarian revolution in Europe, particularly Germany, that would have helped the Bolshevik Revolution internationally did not materialize. A growing consciousness of the failure of European Communist movements gave the mid-decade policy debate special urgency. Third, and as a result of the second, Bukharin implicitly and Stalin explicitly began to speak about building socialism in one country (Lewin [1966] 1968, 159–66). The latter made the point as early as December 1924 while still couching it in an internationalist terminology: "The victory of socialism in one country is not a self-sufficient task. ... For the victory of the revolution in one country, in the present case Russia, is not only the product of the uneven development and progressive decay of imperialism; it is at the same time the beginning of and the pre-condition for the world revolution" (Stalin [1924] 1953, 415).

Until the late 1920s, however, socialism in one country remained as an abstract notion. It was another grain crisis that reshuffled the political deck. When, in 1927, industrial planning initiatives gathered momentum in the party-state hierarchy to threaten NEP and the price equilibrium between industry and agriculture, peasants hit back by withholding the crop of that year from the organized market (Davies 1980, 36–51). In response, authorities began to use extra-economic coercive measures to extract grain from the peasants, particularly rich peasants called *kulak*s who used wage labour.[1] This was the beginning of the end for the Stalin–Bukharin duumvirate. With the Trotskyist opposition having been purged previously, Bukharin and his associates waged a losing battle in 1928–1929 to draw attention to the Stalinist policy "errors" since 1927 and restore economic policy to the NEP framework (Cohen [1973] 1980, 270–336; Lewin [1966] 1968, 294–343). Stalinism had won the battle of ideas. It not only carried on with forced grain collections with further reprisals from the *kulak*s for the rest of the decade but also launched the first five-year plan, in 1928, whose industrialization target, scope, and speed would far outstrip what the "superindustrializer" opposition had proposed (Davies 1989, 1026–44; Erlich 1960, 164–87; Tucker 1990, 91–118). It topped this off with an unprecedented, all-out collectivization blitz in agriculture to be carried out most forcefully in the early months of 1930 (Davies 1980, 203–68 in particular). In December 1929, Stalin would triumphantly declare that "we have passed from the policy of *restricting* the exploiting tendencies of the kulaks to the policy of *eliminating* the kulaks as a class" ([1929] 1954a, 173).

If social revolution means a fundamental change in the class structure of a society, Stalinism achieved a social revolution in the Soviet Union by eliminating independent peasantry as a class and transforming party-state bureaucracy into a class capable of managing the entire political economy. That this was a "revolution from above" (Tucker 1990) does not diminish its world-historical importance. In a sense, it was more radical than the original Bolshevik Revolution, whose main act was to topple the bourgeois and landed upper classes. How Stalinism took over the Soviet Union before the onset of the world economic crisis is a challenging question for this study.

Stalin and his associates' developmentalist ideational resolution provides insight into Soviet policy shift to neomercantilism as part of socialism in one country. Just as Mussolini saw Italy as a proletarian nation up against plutocratic and imperialist nations in formulating a nationalist economic course for his country, the theme of hostile capitalist encirclement was the driving force of Stalin's economic policy reorientation (Gregor 1979, 64–95; Tucker 1990, 44–65). As a nominal internationalist, Stalin went much further than Mussolini in digging up historical instances to chart a nationalist course for his country: "One feature of the history of old Russia was the continual beatings she suffered because of her backwardness. All beat her—because of her backwardness, because of her military backwardness, cultural backwardness, political backwardness, industrial backwardness, agricultural backwardness. ... We are fifty or a hundred years behind the advanced countries. We must make good this distance in ten years. Either we do it, or we shall go under" (Stalin [1931] 1954b, 40–1).

Yet the translation of an idea (developmental or otherwise) into policy is not a foregone conclusion as confirmed by, for example, the failure of the Trotskyist "superindustrialization" thesis. Stalin both showed flexibility by usurping his nemeses' thesis and developed skill by methodically building up an organizational base for his new course. Although the Stalinist ideational reorientation and political preparation took place in the second half of the 1920s, the whole project, including political repression, might not have succeeded had it not been for the concurrent crisis of the world economy and the interstate system in the following decade. For example, the first five-year plan did not foresee crisis-induced constraints such as loss of export markets, deterioration of Soviet terms of trade, and limited availability of foreign credit (Dohan 1976, 635). Consequently, policy shifted on the fly in the direction of further economic closure.

While the Soviet Union and Italy largely settled on a developmentalist course in the late 1920s, Turkey took that course against the overshadowing background of the Great Depression. A Bolshevik-style, if less strident, clash of ideas within bureaucracy preceded the Turkish transition to neo-mercantilism in a small country context and in full view of the Soviet and Fascist policy experiences. The Turkish response adapting Soviet planning and Italian statism also felt the full weight of German trade offensive in southeastern Europe. Turkish politics indeed made strange bedfellows in the 1930s.

Turkey: The Advantages of Backwardness

Reflecting on European economic history, Alexander Gerschenkron observed a correlation between the degree of backwardness and the thrust of industrialization if and when it came: "The more backward a country's economy, the more likely was its industrialization to start discontinuously as a sudden great spurt proceeding at a higher rate of growth" (1962, 353). With the most primary sector-based economy in the Balkans, Turkey indeed had a comparatively remarkable industrial and general economic performance during the Great Depression. Between 1929 and 1939, both manufacturing output and gross national product increased at an annual average rate of over 5% by the most conservative estimates (Owen and Pamuk 1999, 21; Pamuk 2000, 326). Although this performance was not nearly as spectacular as that of the Soviet Union or Japan, it must be viewed against the background of a primary-producing economy whose international linkages had severely been disrupted by the crisis.

The qualification "if and when" in Gerschenkron's observation is critical. Backwardness in and of itself neither triggers nor accelerates industrialization. Its "advantage" for economic spurt lies probably in the room for manoeuvre that it gives to a political force willing and able to act. In the Turkish case, as in the Soviet case, ruling party-state bureaucracy was that force. Unlike its Soviet counterpart, however, the Turkish bureaucracy maintained private property relations in both urban and rural sectors while turning increasingly *dirigiste* towards nascent industries and manipulating the internal terms of trade against agriculture in the course of the crisis. In this respect, Turkish interwar developmentalism was closer to Italian developmentalism in its both liberal and statist iterations. By observing capitalist property relations while, at the same time, privileging its own collective interests, the Kemalist bureaucracy straddled the Fascist–Stalinist divide.

Like all European interwar stories, the story of Republican Turkey began with the end of World War I. Remnants of the Young Turks, or the Union and Progress Party (İttihad ve Terakki Fırkası, İTF), who had taken the Ottoman Empire to war and defeat on the German side, regrouped under Mustafa Kemal to carve a Muslim-Turkish sovereign territory out of the ruins of the multi-ethnic and multi-religious empire (Zürcher 1984, 118–41, 2007, 102). In their campaign known as the national struggle, the Kemalists received support from local notables (large landowners in particular) domestically and the Bolsheviks internationally. This bureaucratic project culminated in the proclamation of the Republic of Turkey in October 1923.[2] Turkey's trajectory in the 1920s paralleled those of Italy and the Soviet Union, combining economic opening with political closure.

The Kemalists picked up where their Young Turk predecessors left off by signalling their intention to help create a national bourgeoisie even before the Republic was proclaimed. In early 1923, they convened a national economy congress with the participation of four "occupational orders" (namely, farmers, merchants, industrialists, and workers), reflecting a penchant for corporatism among interwar authoritarian regimes. While (large) farmers and merchants were self-represented, workers and industrialists were represented mostly by government officials and parliamentarians, indicating the state of industry and labour in the country (Gökmen 2005, 131–2). By convening the congress, the emerging Kemalist regime aimed to send a liberal message abroad in its search for international recognition at the ongoing peace negotiations in Lausanne (Boratav [1974] 1982, 18; Finefrock 1981; Rozaliyev 1978, 56–77; Tezel [1982] 1986, 130–3). The congress itself was notable for its articulation of agrarian, mercantile, and industrial policy demands. Farmers pushed for the abolition of the tithe, the pillar of the Ottoman tax system. "National" merchants demanded protection via increased state involvement in commercial banking. For the "industrial group," tariff protection and fiscal incentives were top priorities.

On the whole, the Republican government favourably responded to these demands, mixing them in with its own priorities in the rest of the 1920s (Boratav [1974] 1982, 7–32, 75–92, 1988, 28–44; Hale 1984; Hershlag [1958] 1968, 47–58; Tekeli and İlkin 1977, 33–74; Tezel [1982] 1986, 119–37). First, it introduced a series of legal reforms, including full recognition of private ownership in land for the first time in Ottoman-Turkish history, and incorporation of the chambers of commerce and industry as professional public bodies. Second, it established a stock exchange market and encouraged national, private commercial banking (Keyder 1981, 97–126; Ökçün 1975, 439–43; Silier 1975, 491–523; Tekeli and İlkin 1981, 176–224). Third, a generous industrial incentives programme was introduced for the private sector in 1927. Fourth, in addition to abolishing the tithe, the government provided various incentives to export-oriented agriculture, including lower freight rates, exemptions from import duties for agricultural implements, and cheap credit (Keyder 1981, 25–37; Önder 1988, 119; Silier 1981, 9–46).

Although the Kemalist regime also took steps to expand the state sector before the world economic crisis, it did so primarily with a view to promoting export-oriented agricultural production. For example, new railway lines built (and those nationalized) in the 1920s were concentrated in the cash-crop growing regions (Keyder 1981, 28–32). The government did, however, take over the tobacco monopoly, *Régie*, which had been the keystone of Western creditors' control over Ottoman finances under the Public Debt Administration. This measure, too, aimed to provide a better, competitive marketing arrangement for export-oriented Turkish tobacco. State industrial activity in the period was limited to the establishment of the Industrial and Mining Bank charged with managing a few textile mills left over from the Ottoman Empire (Boratav [1974] 1982, 82–3).

Turkish export-oriented, liberal developmentalism was a middle-of-the-road orientation between a deliberate strategic retreat as in the Soviet NEP and a wholehearted embrace as in the Italian *Liberista*. What distinguished Turkey was the commercial clause of the Treaty of Lausanne signed in July 1923, which obliged it to maintain the Ottoman tariff schedule of 1916 for imports from the signatory Allied countries for a period of five years and assume two-thirds of the Ottoman debt (Boratav 1981, 168–70, [1974] 1982, 10–1; Hale 1984, 155; Hershlag [1958] 1968, 16–27; Tekeli and İlkin 1977, 34). Nor did Lausanne allow, with certain exceptions, any quantitative restrictions on imports from these countries for the same period. Yet the Republican government did not have to apply the Ottoman tariff schedule to other countries than the signatories, but it did. Moreover, it could have bypassed parts of the commercial clause by making monopoly arrangements in the importation of certain consumer goods, but it would not have (Boratav 1983, 261, 1988, 29; Gülalp 1983, 22; Tezel [1982] 1986, 140). All in all, economic liberalism was a well-considered policy settlement for the Kemalist regime in its initial decade.

Liberal policy direction, however, had an inverse relationship with political democratization. Turkey breathed an air of political openness from the beginning of the national struggle in 1919 to the Kurdish rebellion of 1925 (Çavdar 1989; Frey 1965, 306–13, 323–35; Keyder 1987, 82–90; Özbudun 1981, 80–7; Tunçay [1981] 1989, 27–126). While lacking a democratic impulse, the Kemalist leadership had to live with a measure of pluralism in winning over local notables, including Muslim clerics, for the national struggle. And the first national parliament, whose nucleus was the last Ottoman parliament, had a diverse membership consisting of landed and mercantile elements, clerics, intelligentsia, as well as civil and military bureaucrats. During the national struggle, that parliament functioned as a genuine mechanism of checks and balances, featuring a conservatively minded liberal group in opposition to the Kemalist core group.

With the international recognition of their rule in Lausanne, the Kemalists' stance against the opposition began to harden. First came the exclusion of the conservative-liberal group from the new parliament and the reorganization of the Kemalist group as the People's Party, later to be called the Republican People's Party (Cumhuriyet Halk Fırkası, CHF).

Even in this parliament, however, there was still a dissenting, though much smaller, group advocating political pluralism. The new opposition group would later form the Progressive Republican Party (Terakkiperver Cumhuriyet Fırkası, TCF) (Tunçay [1981] 1989, 370–81). Second came the outlawing of all autonomous institutions and expressions of Islam to reorganize it as an exclusively state institution. What came next was a draconian piece of legislation (Act for the Restoration of Tranquility) to ban all opposition, including the TCF, on the pretext of crushing the Kurdish rebellion of 1925. The act initiated a period of generalized political repression which would last for about two years (Tunçay [1981] 1989, 127–83; Zürcher 1984, 142–67). An alleged attempt on Mustafa Kemal's life in 1926 was used as a further excuse to settle accounts with the pro-TCF, conservative wing of the bureaucracy led by those who had a high-profile Young Turk background. In show trials similar to those in Moscow in the late 1930s, this group was handed over severe punishments, including many death sentences. Not even the economic institutions inherited from the Young Turk era were spared (İlkin 1971).

This first round of intra-bureaucratic struggle was more political, public, and violent than the second one in the early 1930s, which would be confined to economic policy. The former concerned competing visions of society. The Kemalists, who held only middle- and low-ranking positions in the Young Turk movement and assumed no political responsibility during World War I, got the upper hand over the discredited İTF leadership in organizing the national struggle. Ironically, they were closer than leading İTF veterans associated with the TCF to the radical societal engineering of wartime Young Turk experiment (see, e.g., Ahmad 1988; Keyder 1987, 49–69; Toprak 1982).[3] The latter, having seen the tragic consequences of that experiment, came to appreciate political pluralism, adopted gradualism in governance, and thus developed a cautious approach to societal change.

Turkish intra-bureaucratic power struggle had thus been settled decisively in favour of the ruling Kemalists when the New York Stock Exchange crashed in October 1929. It seems that they paused to explore before changing their development model to neomercantilism in 1932. Tariff increases with the expiration of Lausanne's commercial clause, import restrictions, and subsequent exchange controls were still measures taken within the framework of the private sector-driven, export-oriented development model. A review of government-sponsored reports and conferences from 1929 to 1931 reveals no trace of ideas for a definite policy reorientation. For example, two official reports released in early 1930 advised that government incentives to private industry be continued and expanded (Tekeli and İlkin 1977, 227–559, 561–72). They even recommended the establishment of free trade zones and the encouragement of foreign direct investment. A semi-official industrial congress held later the same year had slightly more timely proposals such as a 10-year incentives programme for national private industries (Tekeli and İlkin 1977, 121–4). Similarly, a semi-official agricultural congress held in early 1931 proposed new industries to process cash crops hitherto destined for export markets (Tekeli and İlkin 1977, 190–7).

Although the institution of central banking in June 1930 did not amount to a turn in policy direction, it did occasion the first open policy split within the bureaucracy (İlkin 1975, 542–62; Tekeli and İlkin 1981, 234–307). Those bureaucrats (so-called moderates) who were associated with the semi-official Business Bank promoted it as a candidate to take over central banking functions from the Ottoman Bank, Turkey's de facto but foreign-owned central bank. In contrast, a more statist faction (so-called radicals) pushed for a government-controlled, exclusively central banking institution. Both factions invited foreign expert advice to strengthen their cases (see Tekeli and İlkin 1981, appendices 2–4, 14, for the reporting). The new central bank was a compromise, holding joint-stock company status with fixed shares by the government, Turkish and foreign commercial banks, and other financial institutions. Tellingly, the bank's capital was obtained from the American–Turkish Investment Corporation controlled by the Swedish Kreuger group in return for a concessionary monopoly in the production and marketing of matches and lighters (Boratav [1974] 1982, 85–6).

At this juncture, the regime broadened its search for a new economic policy to include the larger issue of political direction. In August 1930, President Mustafa Kemal convinced a group of deputies to leave the ruling CHF and found the Free Republican Party (Serbest Cumhuriyet Fırkası, SCF) to act as loyal opposition (Barlas 1998, 99–107; Emrence 2006; Tekeli and İlkin 1977, 154–86; Tunçay [1981] 1989, 245–73, 404–5; Weiker 1973). This move was indicative of a general sense of dissatisfaction with the status quo at the highest level of ruling party leadership. Yet it had an unintended consequence in that the SCF, like the defunct TCF, became an outlet for political discontent among the population while, at the same time, criticizing the government's economic policy from a liberal-conservative perspective. The SCF's strong showing in the municipal elections, which were held in a relatively open environment, brought its end; the party "dissolved itself" in November 1930.

The SCF experience helped the ruling party adopt a statist (*devletçi*) import-substituting industrialization policy and evolve from state party to party state. In response to the SCF's criticism of government railway building projects as wasteful, Prime Minister İsmet defended them on grounds of public interest and referred to government policy as "moderately statist" in August 1930 (Boratav [1974] 1982, 43–59; Tekeli and İlkin 1977, 159–65). This was followed by the appointment of a clearly *dirigiste* minister of economy (Mustafa Şeref) a month later and the incorporation of statism (*devletçilik*) into the CHF programme in May 1931 (Tunçay [1981] 1989, 447–54). A ministry of economy report drafted later in 1931 explicitly promoted planning for import-substituting industrialization, also recommending the institutional separation of industrial credit and management functions towards that goal (Tekeli and İlkin 1982, E47–71). However, it took the prime minister's Soviet and Italian trips in the spring of 1932 before the government decided to go all out with statist industrialization in July (Tekeli and İlkin 1982, 137–43). The Kemalist leadership was finally convinced of changing the development model in light of the Soviet planning experience, know-how, and industrial credit, coupled with the more limited Italian experience with the newly launched Istituto Mobiliare Italiano.

Yet the July offensive did not go unchallenged. The "moderate" bureaucrats closely aligned with the Business Bank, as well as private industry itself, opposed the cancellation of private industry's exemptions from customs duties on investment goods imports and the institutional separation of state industrial credit and management functions (Boratav [1974] 1982, 105–8; Buğra 1994, 102–3; Tekeli and İlkin 1982, 155–8, E301–21, E323–42). In a spar over the Business Bank's plan to establish a paper mill, President Mustafa Kemal sided with the "moderates" and replaced Mustafa Şeref with that bank's director general (Mahmut Celal) as minister of economy in September 1932. The ministerial change resulted in a partial reintroduction of the tariff privileges for private industry and a return to the holding company model in state industrial organization. Yet Mahmut Celal's tenure as minister of economy (1932–1937) also gave actually existing *étatisme* its defining characteristics such as Soviet-inspired and -aided industrial planning, and ever-expanding state economic enterprises (Buğra 1994, 104–5; Tekeli and İlkin 1982, E73–299). Moreover, his tenure marked the end of intra-bureaucratic disputes over development model (until after World War II). As the leading "moderate," he came a long way to make this statement: "[I]f industrialization was left in the hands of the private initiative, the country still had to wait for two centuries for its accomplishment" (quoted in Barlas 1998, 68).

The CHF's economic policy reorientation took place in the context of its deepening, if not fully successful, push for political totalitarianism. Not all efforts to unify state and party structures preceded the July offensive as, for example, the principles of Kemalism, including *devletçilik*, were not constitutionally entrenched until 1937 (Karpat 1959, 72–4; Özbudun 1981, 87–98; Tunçay [1981] 1989, 283–322; Webster 1939, 297–318; Weiker 1973, 184–218; Yetkin 1983, 25–132). Yet economic *dirigisme* was always embedded in, and fed by, political *dirigisme*. Like its Fascist counterpart, the Kemalist totalitarian project had a corporatist ideal as epitomized by a functionally integrated, classless society (Belge 1989, 129–131; Bianchi 1984, 92–107; Parla 1985; Parla and Davison 2004).[4] The latter, however, was far more ambitious in the tasks it put before itself: to modernize, secularize, and homogenize society. In the Republican context, modernization meant Westernization involving not just institutional spheres such as administration, education, and law but also cultural markers such as alphabet, calendar, measurements, family names, and the dress (Berkes 1964, 461–78). Kemalist secularism (*laïcité* as locally preferred) was uniquely totalitarian in that, rather than separating the state and religion, it exclusively organized a specific (Hanafi Sunni) interpretation of Islam as part of state apparatus and imposed it on the entire Muslim population, banning the institutions and expressions of any other interpretation (Berkes 1964, 479–503; Hurd 2008, 66–72; Kuru and Stepan 2012; Yavuz 2009, 144–70). With its ethnic, linguistic, and historiographic dimensions, Turkification defined the limits of Kemalist totalitarianism. The state mobilized the intelligentsia to provide support for a Turco-centric view of language and history while, at the same time, subsuming all ethnicities under the category of Turkishness (Beşikçi [1978] 1991b; Webster 1939, 240–6; Weiker 1973, 227–33).

By switching to developmental neomercantilism, the Kemalists added an economic dimension to their overall project. In so doing, they keenly observed concurrent developments abroad and demonstrated a strong sense of threading between them. For example, while Germany became increasingly dominant in Turkish foreign trade via the clearing mechanism,[5] the Republican government did not hesitate to approach the Soviet

Union for financial and technical assistance, or take account of Italy's statist shift, in its industrialization drive. Nor did it confine itself to dealing with dictatorships in this drive. A US delegation was invited to give advice on industrialization while Soviet experts were actually drafting the first Turkish industrial plan in 1933 (Tekeli and İlkin 1982, 172–5; Tezel [1982] 1986, 252). Moreover, later in the decade, the United Kingdom came to counterbalance Soviet industrial assistance and, to some extent, German trade domination (Kuyucak 1939, 51; Mance 1943; Ránki 1983, 180).

Domestically, too, the Kemalists proved pragmatic both when they relied on private enterprise as the engine of development and when they took the matters into their hands.[6] They were not carried away with fervour in either time. Their reaction to a radical, "third way" interpretation of the new economic policy direction in the early 1930s was a case in point. Excited by the increasing pace of policy search, a group of nationalist intellectuals, including ex-communists, began to publish the journal *Kadro* with tacit endorsement from government circles in 1932. As policy took a definite turn to *étatisme*, the group elevated it to an alternative, "whole of nation" form of economic organization to both capitalism and socialism that were based on class conflict, also proposing substantial land reform (Boratav [1974] 1982, 151–60; Gülalp 1983, 89–94; Karpat 1959, 70–2; Kerwin 1959, 239–40; Türkeş 2001; Weiker 1973, 222–7; Yetkin 1983, 112–27). In promoting the Turkish experiment as a development model for all "oppressed nations," this ambitious interpretation smacked of Mussolini's presentation of Italy as an oppressed nation earlier in the century. The message did not go well with the regime and the journal ceased to publish in 1935 in a manner similar to the "self-dissolution" of the SCF.

The story of Turkish neomercantilism was by and large a reflex of the Kemalist bureaucracy in response to the world economic crisis and concurrent experiments in authoritarian Europe. Landed and commercial-industrial interests had some input into the story but generally to check the more radical ambitions of the bureaucracy. Given the level of industrial development and the state of political organization, labour was simply not a factor in economic policy. As for the massive class of peasantry engaged in subsistence and small commodity production, it was close to Marx's characterization of nineteenth-century French peasantry as a sack of potatoes except for export-oriented cash crop farmers in the coastal regions (Akçetin 2000, 89–98). This was the thick line separating Turkish neomercantilism from responses in the rest of the Balkans, where agrarians emerged as an independent class and became a major political force in the aftermath of World War I.

The "European" Balkans in Contrast

The Balkans felt the reverberations of World War I in central and eastern Europe most powerfully at territorial, demographic, and structural levels. Turkey created a largely Anatolian republic with a minor presence (eastern Thrace) in Europe, lost significant human and entrepreneurial potential in atrocities and population exchange but did not attempt land reform, leaving large landownership as a permanent, if regionally specific, fixture of the rural class structure (Duzgun 2017, 415–7; Keyder 1981, 12–20; Silier 1981, 67–70).[7] The rest of the Balkans (Bulgaria, Greece, Romania, and Yugoslavia), too, underwent profound territorial and demographic changes by addition or subtraction, ending up with a substantial ethnic minority who constituted the majority of a neighbouring country (Jelavich 1983, 134–91; Polonsky 1975, 1–25).

At the same time, however, all four states took three major steps that Turkey did not. First, they undertook radical land reforms (Berend 1985, 152–62; Lampe and Jackson 1982, 351–4; Teichova 1989, 897–904) both as part of the "nationalization" (*nostrification*) campaign directed against ethnic minorities (Spulber 1959, 266–7) and in response to the threatening implications of the Bolshevik Revolution (Mitrany 1951, 87–98). The reforms wiped out large landownership, making agriculture a bastion of small peasant ownership (Lampe and Jackson 1982, 357; Polonsky 1975, 167–8). Second, with a significant liberal tradition formed in the late nineteenth century (Mishkova 2014), the four countries concerned had their share of postwar democratization that had swept across Europe. However incomplete and unstable they were, Balkan democracies gave a big spurt to independent agrarian movements in particular (Daskalov 2014). Even after the installation of the so-called royal dictatorships in the 1930s, there was room for political dissent. Third, northern Balkan states (Bulgaria, Romania, and Yugoslavia) in particular established a considerable industrial (import substitution) base in the 1920s by supporting consumer goods production with tariff protection and other incentives (Lampe and Jackson 1982, 486; Ránki and Tomaszewski 1986, 5–21; Spulber 1959, 270–4; Teichova 1989, 904–11). Tellingly, 1927

Turkish legislation for the encouragement of industry drew inspiration from Bulgarian and Romanian examples (Tekeli and İlkin 1977, 64–7).

These three developments formed the immediate context of rulership in the northern Balkans and Greece. Most notably, none of the four bureaucracies nearly approximated the class-like character of the Kemalist bureaucracy, let alone the Stalinist bureaucratic class. Consequently, whether they were popularly elected or executively appointed, these governments stood relatively weaker in relation to societal interests. They were thus more permeable to organized agrarian and commercial-industrial pressures. This is wherein lay the main reason for the better protection of small producers by means of effective rural credit and price support programmes. Similarly, although state ownership in industry and finance increased during the crisis, private enterprise was still a major player in furthering import substitution (Ránki 1985, 71–2; Ránki and Tomaszewski 1986, 35–40; Spulber 1959, 268–70). In general, the Balkan responses, save Turkish neomercantilism, lacked developmental thrust.

What commonly defined the Turkish and other Balkan responses was autarky in the sense of the eclipse of currency transactions in foreign trade and of the maximization of exports at any cost. And the coincidence of balance of payments difficulties in Germany and the region figured prominently in this outcome. The financial crisis of the early 1930s in central and eastern Europe meant the same thing—cessation of Western capital inflows and closure of export markets—for both Germany and the Balkans. The former needed to export its manufactured goods and import primary products while the latter needed the exact opposite and more urgently, given the sharper decline in primary export prices and thus the worsening terms of trade. The clearing trade mechanism devised by Weimar Germany in 1931 was a match made in heaven. Involving no actual currency exchange,[8] it provided an export outlet and an import channel for both parties, thus considerably easing their balance of payments difficulties.

Paradoxically, however, autarky brought an extreme form of dependency for the Balkans. Under the Nazis' New Plan aiming to secure long-term supply of raw materials and foodstuffs, clearing trade became the main tool to integrate the region into Germany's "living space" (Basch 1944, 165–93; Berend and Ránki 1974, 265–84; Ellis 1941, 257–70; Lampe and Jackson 1982, 456–69; Ránki 1983, 123–60). The Nazis used clearing trade as a medium of unequal exchange whereby clearing accounts were settled against an overvalued mark and depreciated Balkan currencies, and whereby Germany delayed exports and thus accumulated huge import surpluses amounting to a "commodity loan" from the region (Dobb [1947] 1963, 377). Moreover, especially northern Balkan states adapted their primary sectors to the requirements of clearing trade. As a result, Germany came to dominate the foreign trade of all countries in the region.[9]

Bulgaria, which developed the highest level of trade dependence on Nazi Germany in the Balkans, passaged from a promising agrarian democracy to a conservative royal dictatorship in the interwar period. While still under nominal Ottoman rule in 1879, it adopted a liberal Constitution modelled after the Belgian example, which limited the powers of the monarch and established a single-chamber parliament to be elected on the basis of universal male suffrage (Bell 1977, 4; Daskalov 2014, 294; Mishkova 2014, 185–92). By the end of the nineteenth century, small peasant ownership had already become the prevalent pattern of Bulgarian agriculture with the confiscation and break-up of Ottoman era estates (Bell 1977, 12–3). Fighting World War I on the losing side, Bulgaria had a period of democratization and radical agrarian experimentation between 1919 and 1923.

The small peasant democracy that the Bulgarian Agrarian National Union (Bŭlgarski Zemedelski Naroden Sŭyuz, BZNS) under the leadership of Alexander Stamboliski tried to put into practice in the immediate postwar period was based on an "estatist," corporatist idea of the economy and society (Bell 1977, 55–84; Daskalov 2011, 93–8, 2014, 298–9; Karaömerlioğlu 2002, 79–86). In this idea, society was composed of estates (occupational groups with common economic interests such as peasants, workers, and artisans) which were entitled to their "labour property" (land, labour power, and shops and tools). Each estate needed to be functionally represented by an "estatist organization" as in the case of the BZNS representing the vast peasant estate. Founded (in 1899) and led by middle-class intelligentsia (Bell 1975), the BZNS got the chance to govern after winning the 1919 election. It carried out further land redistribution, established an extensive network of credit cooperatives and a monopoly body for grain exports, and introduced progressive taxation and other reforms in areas such as housing, labour service, and education (Bell 1977, 154–83; Daskalov 2014, 293–307; Mitrany 1951, 91). Shortly after scoring a massive victory in the 1923 election, however, Stamboliski and his party were overthrown by a bloody coup.

Although the old order defined by a conservative alliance of the royal, military-bureaucratic, and commercial interests was restored after the coup, the egalitarian rural structure established since independence remained intact for the rest of the interwar period. Political space narrowed, but opposition, including the Socialists and Communists in disguise, continued to operate and contested in tightly controlled elections (Jelavich 1983, 166–71, 209; Lampe 1986, 30, 50). In fact, a broad People's Bloc, including remnants of the BZNS, won the 1931 election and ruled the country until another coup in 1934. It was under this coalition that the Bulgarian economy was integrated into the German clearing trade system within a conservative macroeconomic framework (Asenova 2016, 372–4; Penchev and Özgür 2019, 64). Supported by the authoritarian Zveno (Link) movement, the coup ushered in governance by decree after abolishing the Constitution, and suppressing parties and unions. King Boris III staged yet another coup in 1935. Even under the royal dictatorship, however, the Agrarians, Social Democrats, and Communists were able to participate in elections and win seats.

Against the backdrop of the most commercialized and exposed economy in the region, Greece faced particularly severe balance of payments difficulties during the European financial crisis. And it became the only Balkan country to leave the gold standard and devalue its currency in 1932. It did so in defiance of the International Financial Commission, which had been installed back in 1897 to administer its foreign debt load, and went on to default on debt payments in addition to introducing exchange and trade controls (Mazower 1991, 179–202). While these measures set up the economy for clearing trade with Germany, a *dirigiste* turn in domestic policy had to wait for the installation of the Metaxas dictatorship in 1936, when, coincidentally, the United Kingdom began to show a renewed interest in the region (Mazower 1988, 612–9, 1991, 273–305).

In the Balkans as elsewhere, losing war was more transformative than winning it. Greece emerged from the Great War as a nominal victor but ended up with the "Asia Minor disaster" against the Turks in 1922. The defeat caused both a demographic shake-up and a democratic renewal. As a result of the population exchange with Turkey in 1923, Greece accepted over 1.2 million ethnic Greeks bringing about a 20% increase in its population (Mavrogordatos 1983, 186–7). The mass arrival of "refugees" gave a major impetus to the implementation of a land reform legislation that was passed in 1917. With their settlement in the northern, rural New Lands for the most part, Greece completed the land reform process that had begun with the break-up of former Ottoman estates in 1871 (Seferiades

1999, 281–300). However, the consolidation of small peasant ownership in Greek agriculture, unlike the Bulgarian case, was the achievement of urban liberal and conservative parties, which had an early hold over the peasantry via clientelistic linkages, without contribution from an independent agrarian party (Mouzelis 1976).[10] The population influx from Anatolia also became instrumental in the deepening of the "national schism" (*ethnikos dichasmos*) between liberal-republican Venizelism, whose popular support was among the smallholders of the New Lands, and conservative-royalist anti-Venizelism, which drew on the native smallholders of the southern and richer Old Greece for popular support (Mavrogordatos 1983, 296).

Founded in 1924, the First Republic faced a legitimacy crisis from the outset since it was largely the work of the Venizelist camp and never formally accepted by the anti-Venizelist camp. Under Eleftherios Venizelos, the Liberal Party won fairly contested elections by appealing to its support base in a patron–client rewards system and governed until the financial crisis of 1932, when an anti-Venizelist coalition led by the People's Party took over.[11] The coalition restored the monarchy in 1935 and fought the Venizelists to a virtual tie in the 1936 election, putting the small Communist Party in a position to hold the balance of power (Mavrogordatos 1983, 52). King George II broke the stalemate by appointing a former general, Ioannis Metaxas, as prime minister. The royally sanctioned Metaxas dictatorship ruled Greece amid a fanfare of totalitarian rhetoric for the rest of the decade. Nevertheless, its statist industrialization drive came closest to the Turkish experiment in the region.

Until 1917, the Romanian ruling bloc and agrarian structure paralleled those of Czarist Russia. From the formal end of serfdom in 1864 to the most radical land reform of the Balkans in 1918, Romania was ruled by a coalition of large landowners, merchants, and urban professionals held together by the Liberal Party against a peasantry subjected to the "second serfdom" (Daskalov 2014, 307; Mitrany [1930] 1968, 42–92). While adopting a liberal Constitution on the Belgian model in 1866, the Liberals governed in a top-down manner and with a nationalistic modernizing agenda in their long tenure, much like the post-1908 Young Turk government (Mishkova 2014, 171–7). With Romania more than doubling its territory and population in the course of World War I, they changed their agrarian approach and initiated a massive reform in 1918 to endow the peasantry with land by breaking up large estates. What figured prominently in this decisive turn was the fact that most large landowners in the newly acquired lands belonged to ethnic minorities, in addition to the fear of a Bolshevik-style uprising in the countryside (Daskalov 2014, 308; Jelavich 1983, 162; Mitrany [1930] 1968, xxvii, xxxiii, 95–119; Polonsky 1975, 81).

Romania had its share of postwar democratization but with distinct royal manipulation. After the introduction of universal male suffrage in 1917, the National and Peasant parties won the 1919 election and formed a coalition, thus intermitting decades-long Liberal governance. The king, however, summarily dismissed the National–Peasant government and forced a new election in 1920, which gave the conservative People's Party a majority. Only two years later, the Liberal Party was restored to power with a renewed centralist and protectionist agenda and ruled until 1928 (with an interlude in 1926–1927) by "manufacturing" election wins (Janos 1970, 207; Jelavich 1983, 163–4; Polonsky 1975, 83; Turnock 1986, 53–64). Romania had its first truly parliamentary government in 1928, when the National Peasant Party (born out of the merger of the National and Peasant parties in 1926) won a convincing majority in a relatively free election. However, the government and its liberal economic programme fell victim to the Great Depression in 1930 (Daskalov 2014, 319–21; Mitrany 1951, 125, [1930] 1968, 553–66). Following that, power shifted further to the royal court. While electoral politics continued until 1937, winning party leaders were not necessarily appointed as prime minister and the cabinet became a revolving door at the whim of King Carol II (Jelavich 1983, 204–7; Polonsky 1975, 86–8). He ended this charade in 1938 to install a royal dictatorship by bringing a new Constitution and banning political parties in favour of his Front of National Rebirth. At the same time, however, he reined in the more radical, violent politics of mass-based Iron Guard fascism.

Created in 1918, the Kingdom of the Serbs, Croats, and Slovenes was another successor state to the Austro-Hungarian Empire. Although the new state was constitutionally unitary, it was superimposed on geographically distinct communities organized along ethno-religious lines, including the numerically largest and politically dominant Serbs, Croats, Slovenes, and Muslim Bosnians (Singleton and Carter 1982, 47–57). Consequently, ruling parties and opposition alike consumed much of their political capital on inter-community accommodation or separation in the interwar period. The fragmentation of the new political economy on multiple dimensions would prove limiting the space for economic *dirigisme*. Land redistribution did take place, but, since Serbia was already a land of small peasant ownership, it was confined to Croatia, where large landowners were mostly of Austrian and Hungarian origins, and Bosnia, where Muslims had owned large estates (Mitrany 1951, 91).

Despite a fractured party system, the Kingdom tried parliamentary democracy between 1920 and 1928, holding free elections under universal manhood suffrage. The centralist Serbian Radical Party, which had initiated the land reform process, held office for most of the period with varying support from the Slovenian and Bosnian-Muslim parties or the left-leaning Serbian Democratic Party. While the Serbian Agrarian Union remained electorally weak much like the Agrarian Party of Greece (Avakumovic 1979; Daskalov 2014, 339–47), the Croatian Peasant Party grew into the main opposition and tested the postwar settlement (Jelavich 1983, 143–57; Polonsky 1975, 96–9). It was similar to the BZNS in its agrarianism but, being based exclusively in Croatia, took on a more ethnonational character (Biondich 2000). Parliamentary democracy was in a state of constant crisis in this fragmented polity and King Alexander intervened by establishing a royal dictatorship. He renamed the country as the Kingdom of Yugoslavia in 1929 and adopted a new but still unitary Constitution in 1931, which would reduce the roles of political parties, parliament, and the cabinet. However, a regency established following the assassination of Alexander in 1934 gave way to a gradual loosening of dictatorship and, as a result, opposition parties made increasing electoral gains but not parliamentary seats. A further promising development just before the outbreak of World War II was an agreement reached between the government and the Croatian opposition to recognize the autonomy of Croatia (Jelavich 1983, 200–4; Polonsky 1975, 99–105).

The general picture emerging from these developments is that interwar politics in Bulgaria, Greece, Romania, and Yugoslavia significantly diverged from that in Turkey. This was the case both with democratization and with dictatorial reorientation. The four "European" Balkan countries had a considerable democratic experience in the 1920s. It is true that their democracies, unlike Western European ones, failed to create general consent and that their rulers kept changing the rules at will. Nevertheless, compared to Turkey, they developed a broader sphere of rights and liberties for many reasons, including a stronger liberal tradition. More to the point, the "monarcho-fascist" dictatorships installed in the 1930s failed to suppress dissent as opposition parties proved resilient. They were closer to nineteenth-century, conservative dictatorships than to contemporary totalitarian experiments in Europe (Luebbert 1991, 258–66; also Jelavich

1983, 200). In the case of the Kemalist dictatorship, the affinity was in the reverse direction. These political differences contributed greatly to differences in domestic economic policy between Turkey and the rest of the Balkans.

Summing Up

The combined experience of the Soviet Union, Turkey, and, to a lesser extent, the other Balkan countries suggests that their bureaucracies, unlike those of Western democracies, took on an extra-civil service character, developing group interests in a class-style organization. Especially Soviet Stalinist bureaucracy became the only collective actor to be reckoned with after liquidating independent peasantry, which was preceded by a similar act involving capitalists and landlords. Turkey's Kemalist bureaucracy did not have that reach but was unrivalled among other domestic actors it had to live with, including mercantile-industrial and landed groups. Although all other Balkan countries eliminated large landownership in the immediate postwar period, their bureaucracies were both constrained by independent peasantries and mercantile-industrial interests, and fragmented between royal courts and elected offices to the extent that they existed as separate entities.

Given this domestic group profile, intra-bureaucratic contention took the centre stage in determining the direction and pace of economic policy responses to the Great Depression. In the Soviet Union, ideational and political struggle between the Stalinists and the Bukharinists was largely settled in the late 1920s, but the Stalinist industrialization and collectivization drive was aided greatly by the disruption of liberal financial and trade networks, as well as by the collapse of the Versailles settlement. Turkey's Kemalist bureaucrats began to debate and fight over economic policy only after the onset of the crisis but quickly patched up their differences and settled on a statist developmental course. In the rest of the Balkans, intra-bureaucratic contention over economic policy was even less accentuated because legitimacy issues usually took precedence over economic issues. This partly accounts for the weaker developmental thrust of their bureaucracies.

It seems that, under dictatorship, the economic weight of interwar bureaucracies was in inverse relationship to the level of capitalist development. The Nazi and Fascist bureaucracies were certainly no less totalitarian than their Soviet and Balkan counterparts. And the former were equally economic *dirigistes* at the national level. Yet they, not to mention the Austrofascists, did not transform into a collective interest group distinct from their main support base, namely, a well-developed capitalist class and a well-entrenched landed upper class. If dictatorship was the necessary condition for bureaucratic class formation, economic underdevelopment was the sufficient condition.

Notes

1. The word *kulak* in Russian means "tight fist" (Davies 1980, 23).
2. Coincidentally, the date of the proclamation (29 October) fell on the first anniversary of the Fascist takeover in Italy.
3. However, the Kemalist CHF and the Young Turk İTF had their differences. With its collegial leadership, the İTF was a genuine mass party with high levels of popular articulation and mobilization (Tunçay [1981] 1989, 71–2). In contrast, the CHF was defined by a one-man leadership style and remained as an indoor, "congress" party wary of outdoor, mass rallies (Esen 2014, 609, 611).
4. In its Kemalist iteration, corporatism also featured farcical practices such as the selection of a few regime-friendly writers and journalists as workers' representatives in parliament.
5. Germany grew into Turkey's principal partner in both exports and imports. It increased its share of Turkish exports from 14% in 1930 to a record 52% in 1936, and its share of Turkish imports from 21% in 1930 to a record 51% in 1939 (Tezel [1982] 1986, 145).
6. In this context, mention must be made of a local literature viewing *étatisme* as the realization of an economic idea intrinsic to Kemalism (see, e.g., Avcıoğlu 1968, 445; Hershlag 1984; Kuruç 2011, 502–510). The argument is that the young regime had to endure a sort of reluctant liberalism—similar to Soviet NEP—in the 1920s because of the restrictions imposed by the Treaty of Lausanne. After these restrictions were lifted in 1928, however, it was freed to get to its *étatiste* model even without the world economic crisis. In its teleology, this literature closely resembles the argument developed by Gregor (1979) regarding Fascist developmentalism.
7. The 1934 Settlement Act was the only land redistribution measure taken by the Kemalists, but it was motivated by a desire to dispossess Kurdish landlords in particular. The act authorized the government to take confiscatory measures against large holdings in Kurdish (southeastern) provinces (Beşikçi [1977] 1991a, 111–29). Yet the government did not use its man-

date in the face of opposition from the large landowners in other regions (Tezel [1982] 1986, 322–3).
8. Clearing trade still required an agreed-upon exchange measure such as the gold parity of both parties' currencies. It also required a central banking mechanism (or a central trading authority) at each end of the transaction. Thus, importers paid their central bank for imported goods in their own currency while exporters were paid by their central bank for exported goods in their own currency. A final requirement was the clearing of the two central banks' export and import accounts against one another at year-ends (League of Nations 1938, 16; Ránki 1983, 124).
9. Germany's shares in Bulgarian exports and imports increased from 34% and 30% in 1930 to 68% and 66% in 1939, respectively. This compared with the following increases in German shares in the foreign trade of Greece, Romania, and Yugoslavia between the same years (between 1930 and 1938 for Greece): from 26% and 12% to 40% and 30% in Greek exports and imports, respectively; from 28% and 37% to 32% and 39% in Romanian exports and imports; and from 29% and 34% to 32% and 48% in Yugoslav exports and imports (Lampe and Jackson 1982, 458–60).
10. An Agrarian Party of Greece did emerge in 1923, but it would be marred by multiple splits and never gain much electoral traction (Ploumidis 2012).
11. On the importance of clientelism in Greek politics, see Mouzelis (1986, 73–94).

References

Ahmad, Feroz. 1988. "War and Society under the Young Turks, 1908–18." *Review* 11, no. 2: 265–86.

Akçetin, Elif, 2000. "Anatolian Peasants in the Great Depression 1929–1933." *New Perspectives on Turkey*, no. 23: 79–102. https://doi.org/10.1017/S0896634600003393.

Asenova, Vera. 2016. "German Economic Exploitation of Bulgaria: Short-Term Economic Policies and Long-Term Institutional Effects." In *Paying for Hitler's War: The Consequences of Nazi Hegemony for Europe*, edited by Jonas Scherner and Eugene N. White, 364–88. Cambridge: Cambridge University Press.

Avakumovic, Ivan. 1979. "The Serb Peasant Party, 1919–1945." In *The Peasantry of Eastern Europe*, vol. 1, *Roots of Rural Transformation*, edited by Ivan Volgyes, 57–78. New York: Pergamon Press.

Avcıoğlu, Doğan. 1968. *Türkiye'nin Düzeni (Dün-Bugün-Yarın)*, book 1. Ankara: Bilgi Yayınevi.

Barlas, Dilek. 1998. *Etatism and Diplomacy in Turkey: Economic and Foreign Policy Strategies in an Uncertain World, 1929–1939*. Leiden: Brill.

6 NEOMERCANTILISM, MARK II, UNDER DICTATORSHIP... 227

Basch, Antonín. 1944. *The Danube Basin and the German Economic Sphere*. London: Kegan Paul.
Belge, Murat. 1989. *Sosyalizm, Türkiye ve Gelecek*. İstanbul: Birikim Yayınları.
Bell, John D. 1975. "The Genesis of Agrarianism in Bulgaria." *Balkan Studies* 16, no. 2: 73–92.
Bell, John D. 1977. *Peasants in Power: Alexander Stamboliski and the Bulgarian Agrarian National Union, 1899–1923*. Princeton: Princeton University Press.
Berend, Iván T. 1985. "Agriculture." In *The Economic History of Eastern Europe, 1919–1975*, vol. 1, *Economic Structure and Performance between the Two Wars*, edited by Michael C. Kaser and E. A. Radice, 148–209. Oxford: Clarendon.
Berend, Iván T., and György Ránki. 1974. *Economic Development in East-Central Europe in the 19th and 20th Centuries*. New York: Columbia University Press.
Berkes, Niyazi. 1964. *The Development of Secularism in Turkey*. Montreal: McGill University Press.
Beşikçi, İsmail. [1977] 1991a. *Bilim Yöntemi/Türkiye'deki Uygulama*, vol. 1, *Kürtlerin Mecburi İskânı*. Reprint. Ankara: Yurt Kitap-Yayın.
Beşikçi, İsmail. [1978] 1991b. *Bilim Yöntemi/Türkiye'deki Uygulama*, vol. 2, *Türk Tarih Tezi, Güneş-Dil Teorisi ve Kürt Sorunu*. Reprint. Ankara: Yurt Kitap-Yayın.
Bianchi, Robert. 1984. *Interest Groups and Political Development in Turkey*. Princeton: Princeton University Press.
Biondich, Mark. 2000. *Stjepan Radić, the Croat Peasant Party, and the Politics of Mass Mobilization, 1904–1928*. Toronto, Buffalo and London: University of Toronto Press.
Boratav, Korkut. 1981. "Kemalist Economic Policies and Étatism." In *Atatürk: Founder of a Modern State*, edited by Ali Kazancıgil and Ergun Özbudun, 165–90. London: C. P. Hurst.
Boratav, Korkut. [1974] 1982. *Türkiye'de Devletçilik*. 2nd ed. Ankara: Savaş Yayınları.
Boratav, Korkut. 1983. *İktisat Politikaları ve Bölüşüm Sorunları: Politik İktisat Yazıları, 1969–1981*. İstanbul: Belge Yayınları.
Boratav, Korkut. 1988. *Türkiye İktisat Tarihi, 1908–1985*. İstanbul: Gerçek Yayınları.
Buğra, Ayşe. 1994. *State and Business in Modern Turkey: A Comparative Study*. Albany: State University of New York Press.
Cohen, Stephen F. [1973] 1980. *Bukharin and the Bolshevik Revolution: A Political Biography, 1888–1938*. 2nd ed. Oxford: Oxford University Press.
Çavdar, Tevfik. 1989. "Cumhuriyet'in Başlangıcında Filizlenen Demokrasi ve 'Takrir-i Sükûn' Yasası." *Birikim*, no. 4: 33–40.
Daskalov, Roumen. 2011. *Debating the Past: Modern Bulgarian Historiography – From Stambolov to Zhivkov*. Budapest: Central European University Press.

Daskalov, Roumen. 2014. "Agrarian Ideologies and Peasant Movements in the Balkans." In *Entangled Histories of the Balkans,* vol. 2, *Transfers of Political Ideologies and Institutions,* edited by Roumen Daskalov and Diana Mishkova, 281–353. Leiden and Boston: Brill.

Davies, Robert W. 1980. *The Socialist Offensive: The Collectivisation of Soviet Agriculture, 1929–1930.* London and Basingstoke: Macmillan.

Davies, Robert W. 1989. "Economic and Social Policy in the USSR, 1917–41." In *The Cambridge Economic History of Europe,* vol. 8, *The Industrial Economies: The Development of Economic and Social Policies,* edited by Peter Mathias and Sidney Pollard, 984–1047. Cambridge: Cambridge University Press.

Dobb, Maurice. [1947] 1963. *Studies in the Development of Capitalism.* Revised ed. New York: International.

Dohan, Michael R. 1976. "The Economic Origins of Soviet Autarky 1927/28–1934." *Slavic Review* 35, no. 4: 603–35. https://doi.org/10.2307/2495654.

Duzgun, Eren. 2017. "Agrarian Change, Industrialization and Geopolitics Beyond the Turkish *Sonderweg.*" *European Journal of Sociology* 58, no. 3: 405–39. https://doi.org/10.1017/S0003975617000194.

Ellis, Howard S. 1941. *Exchange Control in Central Europe.* Cambridge, MA: Harvard University Press.

Emrence, Cem. 2006. *99 Günlük Muhalefet: Serbest Cumhuriyet Fırkası.* İstanbul: İletişim Yayınları.

Erlich, Alexander. 1960. *The Soviet Industrialization Debate, 1924–1928.* Cambridge, MA: Harvard University Press.

Esen, Berk. 2014. "Nation-Building, Party-Strength, and Regime Consolidation: Kemalism in Comparative Perspective." *Turkish Studies* 15, no. 4: 600–20. https://doi.org/10.1080/14683849.2014.986318.

Finefrock, Michael M. 1981. "Laissez-Faire, the 1923 Izmir Economic Congress and Early Turkish Developmental Policy in Political Perspective." *Middle Eastern Studies* 17, no. 3: 375–92. https://doi.org/10.1080/00263208108700478.

Frey, Frederick W. 1965. *The Turkish Political Elite.* Cambridge, MA: MIT Press.

Gerschenkron, Alexander. 1962. *Economic Backwardness in Historical Perspective: A Book of Essays.* Cambridge, MA: Harvard University Press.

Gökmen, Özgür. 2005. "The State of Labour in Turkey, 1918–1938." *Mitteilungsblatt des Instituts für soziale Bewegungen* 33: 123–36.

Gregor, A. James. 1979. *Italian Fascism and Developmental Dictatorship.* Princeton: Princeton University Press.

Gregory, Paul R., and Joel Sailors. 2003. "The Soviet Union during the Great Depression: The Autarky Model." In *The World Economy and National Economies in the Interwar Slump,* edited by Theo Balderston, 191–210. Basingstoke: Palgrave Macmillan.

Gülalp, Haldun. 1983. *Gelişme Stratejileri ve Gelişme İdeolojileri*. Ankara: Yurt Yayınları.
Hale, William M. 1984. "The Traditional and the Modern in the Economy of Kemalist Turkey: The Experience of the 1920s." In *Atatürk and the Modernization of Turkey*, edited by Jacob M. Landau, 153–70. Boulder: Westview.
Hershlag, Zvi Y. [1958] 1968. *Turkey: The Challenge of Growth*. 2nd ed. Leiden: E. J. Brill.
Hershlag, Zvi Y. 1984. "Atatürk's Etatism." In *Atatürk and the Modernization of Turkey*, edited by Jacob M. Landau, 171–80. Boulder: Westview.
Hurd, Elizabeth S. 2008. *The Politics of Secularism in International Relations*. Princeton and Oxford: Princeton University Press.
İlkin, Selim. 1971. "Türkiye Milli İthalat ve İhracat Anonim Şirketi." *ODTÜ Gelişme Dergisi*, no 2: 199–232.
İlkin, Selim. 1975. "Türkiye'de Merkez Bankası Fikrinin Gelişimi." In *Türkiye İktisat Tarihi Semineri: Metinler/Tartışmalar (8–10 Haziran 1973)*, edited by Osman Okyar and H. Ünal Nalbantoğlu, 537–82. Ankara: Hacettepe Üniversitesi Yayınları.
Janos, Andrew C. 1970. "The One-Party State and Social Mobilization: East Europe between the Wars." In *Authoritarian Politics in Modern Society: The Dynamics of Established One-Party Systems*, edited by Samuel P. Huntington and Clement H. Moore, 204–36. New York: Basic Books.
Jelavich, Barbara. 1983. *History of the Balkans: Twentieth Century*. New York: Cambridge University Press.
Johnson, Simon, and Peter Temin. 1993. "The Macroeconomics of NEP." *Economic History Review*, new series 46, no. 4: 750–67. https://doi.org/10.1111/j.1468-0289.1993.tb01360.x.
Karaömerlioğlu, M. Asım. 2002. "Agrarian Populism as an Ideological Discourse of Interwar Europe." *New Perspectives on Turkey*, no. 26: 59–93. https://doi.org/10.1017/S089663460000371X.
Karpat, Kemal H. 1959. *Turkey's Politics: The Transition to a Multi-Party System*. Princeton: Princeton University Press.
Kerwin, Robert W. 1959. "Etatism in Turkey, 1933–50." In *The State and Economic Growth*, edited by Hugh G. J. Aitken, 237–54. New York: Social Science Research Council.
Keyder, Çağlar. 1981. *The Definition of a Peripheral Economy: Turkey, 1923–1929*. Cambridge: Cambridge University Press.
Keyder, Çağlar. 1987. *State and Class in Turkey: A Study in Capitalist Development*. London: Verso.
Kuru, Ahmet T., and Alfred Stepan. 2012. "Laïcité as an 'Ideal Type' and a Continuum: Comparing Turkey, France, and Senegal." In *Democracy, Islam, and Secularism in Turkey*, edited by Ahmet T. Kuru and Alfred Stepan, 95–121. New York: Columbia University Press.

Kuruç, Bilsay. 2011. *Mustafa Kemal Döneminde Ekonomi: Büyük Devletler ve Türkiye*. İstanbul: İstanbul Bilgi Üniversitesi Yayınları.
Kuyucak, Hazım A. 1939. "Memorandum on Exchange Control in Turkey." Paper submitted to the 12th Session of the International Studies Conference, Bergen, April.
Lampe, John R. 1986. *The Bulgarian Economy in the Twentieth Century*. New York: St. Martin's.
Lampe, John R., and Marvin R. Jackson. 1982. *Balkan Economic History, 1550–1950: From Imperial Borderlands to Developing Nations*. Bloomington: Indiana University Press.
League of Nations. 1938. *Report on Exchange Control*. Geneva: League of Nations.
Lenin, V. I. [1921] 1980. "The New Economic Policy and the Tasks of the Political Education Departments." In *V. I. Lenin: Collected Works*, vol. 33, *August 1921–March 1923*, translated from the Russian and edited by David Skvirsky and George Hanna, 60–79. Moscow: Progress Publishers.
Lewin, Moshe. [1966] 1968. *Russian Peasants and Soviet Power: A Study of Collectivization*. Translated from the French by Irene Nove. London: George Allen and Unwin.
Luebbert, Gregory M. 1991. *Liberalism, Fascism, or Social Democracy: Social Classes and the Political Origins of Regimes in Interwar Europe*. New York: Oxford University Press.
Mance, Osborne. 1943. "The Future of British Trade with Turkey." *Journal of the Royal Central Asian Society* 30, no. 1: 5–18.
Mavrogordatos, George Th. 1983. *Stillborn Republic: Social Coalitions and Party Strategies in Greece, 1922–1936*. Berkeley: University of California Press.
Mazower, Mark. 1988. "Economic Diplomacy between Great Britain and Greece in the 1930s." *Journal of European Economic History* 17, no. 3: 603–19.
Mazower, Mark. 1991. *Greece and the Inter-War Economic Crisis*. Oxford: Clarendon Press.
Mishkova, Diana. 2014. "Balkan Liberalisms: Historical Routes of a Modern Ideology." In *Entangled Histories of the Balkans*, vol. 2, *Transfers of Political Ideologies and Institutions*, edited by Roumen Daskalov and Diana Mishkova, 99–198. Leiden and Boston: Brill.
Mitrany, David. 1951. *Marx against the Peasant: A Study in Social Dogmatism*. Chapel Hill: University of North Carolina Press.
Mitrany, David. [1930] 1968. *The Land and the Peasant in Rumania: The War and Agrarian Reform (1917–21)*. Reprint. New York: Greenwood Press.
Mouzelis, Nicos. 1976. "Greek and Bulgarian Peasants: Aspects of Their Sociopolitical Situation during the Interwar Period." *Comparative Studies in Society and History* 18, no. 1: 85–105. https://doi.org/10.1017/S0010417500008094.

Mouzelis, Nicos. 1986. *Politics in the Semi-Periphery: Early Parliamentarism and Late Industrialisation in the Balkans and Latin America.* London: Macmillan.
Nenovsky, Nikolay. 2015. "The Soviets Monetary Experience (1917–1924) through the Perspective of the Discussion on Unity and Diversity of Money." MPRA Paper No. 79864. https://mpra.ub.uni-muenchen.de/79864/3/MPRA_paper_79864.pdf (accessed 30 June 2021).
Nove, Alec. [1969] 1992. *An Economic History of the USSR 1917–1991.* 3rd ed. London: Penguin.
Owen, Roger, and Şevket Pamuk. 1999. *A History of Middle East Economies in the Twentieth Century.* Cambridge, MA: Harvard University Press.
Ökçün, A. Gündüz. 1975. "1909–1930 Yılları Arasında Anonim Şirket Olarak Kurulan Bankalar." In *Türkiye İktisat Tarihi Semineri: Metinler/Tartışmalar (8–10 Haziran 1973)*, edited by Osman Okyar and H. Ünal Nalbantoğlu, 409–75. Ankara: Hacettepe Üniversitesi Yayınları.
Önder, İzzettin. 1988. "Cumhuriyet Döneminde Tarım Kesimine Uygulanan Vergi Politikası." In *Türkiye'de Tarımsal Yapılar (1923–2000)*, edited by Şevket Pamuk and Zafer Toprak, 113–33. Ankara: Yurt Yayınları.
Özbudun, Ergun. 1981. "The Nature of the Kemalist Political Regime." In *Atatürk: Founder of a Modern State*, edited by Ali Kazancıgil and Ergun Özbudun, 79–102. London: C. P. Hurst.
Pamuk, Şevket. 2000. "Intervention during the Great Depression: Another Look at Turkish Experience." In *The Mediterranean Response to Globalization before 1950*, edited by Şevket Pamuk and Jeffrey G. Williamson, 321–39. London: Routledge.
Parla, Taha. 1985. *The Social and Political Thought of Ziya Gökalp, 1876–1924.* Leiden: E. J. Brill.
Parla, Taha, and Andrew Davison. 2004. *Corporatist Ideology in Kemalist Turkey: Progress or Order?* Syracuse: Syracuse University Press.
Penchev, Pencho D., and M. Erdem Özgür. 2019. "The Role of the State in the Economic Policy and Thought of Bulgaria and Turkey during the Interwar Period." *History of Economic Thought and Policy*, no. 1: 51–66. https://doi.org/10.3280/SPE2019-001004.
Ploumidis, Spyridon. 2012. "Agrarian Politics in Interwar Greece: The Stillborn 'Peasant' Parties (1923–1936)." *Studia Universitatis Cibiniensis. Series Historica*, no. 9: 57–87.
Polonsky, Antony. 1975. *The Little Dictators: The History of Eastern Europe since 1918.* London: Routledge and Kegan Paul.
Ránki, György. 1983. *Economy and Foreign Policy: The Struggle of the Great Powers for Hegemony in the Danube Valley, 1919–1939.* New York: Columbia University Press.

Ránki, György. 1985. "Problems of Southern European Economic Development (1918–38)." In *Semiperipheral Development: The Politics of Southern Europe in the Twentieth Century*, edited by Giovanni Arrighi, 55–85. Beverly Hills: Sage.

Ránki, György, and Jerzy Tomaszewski. 1986. "The Role of the State in Industry, Banking and Trade." In *The Economic History of Eastern Europe, 1919–1975*, vol. 2, *Interwar Policy, the War and Reconstruction*, edited by Michael C. Kaser and E. A. Radice, 3–48. Oxford: Clarendon.

Rozaliyev, Y. N. [1962] 1978. *Türkiye'de Kapitalizmin Gelişme Özellikleri (1923–1960)*. Translated from the Russian by Azer Yaran. Ankara: Onur Yayınları.

Seferiades, Seraphim. 1999. "Small Rural Ownership, Subsistence Agriculture, and Peasant Protest in Interwar Greece: The Agrarian Question Recast." *Journal of Modern Greek Studies* 17, no. 2: 277–323. https://doi.org/10.1353/mgs.1999.0034.

Silier, Oya. 1975. "1920'lerde Türkiye'de Milli Bankacılığın Genel Görünümü." In *Türkiye İktisat Tarihi Semineri: Metinler/Tartışmalar (8–10 Haziran 1973)*, edited by Osman Okyar and H. Ünal Nalbantoğlu, 485–533. Ankara: Hacettepe Üniversitesi Yayınları.

Silier, Oya. 1981. *Türkiye'de Tarımsal Yapının Gelişimi (1923–1938)*. İstanbul: Boğaziçi Üniversitesi Yayınları.

Singleton, Fred, and Bernard Carter. 1982. *The Economy of Yugoslavia*. London: Croom Helm.

Spulber, Nicolas. 1959. "The Role of the State in Economic Growth in Eastern Europe since 1860." In *The State and Economic Growth*, edited by Hugh G. J. Aitken, 255–86. New York: Social Science Research Council.

Stalin, J. V. [1924] 1953. "The October Revolution and the Tactics of the Russian Communists?" In *J. V. Stalin: Works*, vol. 6, *1924*, translated from the Russian, 374–420. Moscow: Foreign Languages Publishing House.

Stalin, J. V. [1929] 1954a. "Concerning Questions of Agrarian Policy in the U.S.S.R." In *J. V. Stalin: Works*, vol. 12, *April 1929–June 1930*, translated from the Russian, 147–78. Moscow: Foreign Languages Publishing House.

Stalin, J. V. [1931] 1954b. "The Tasks of Business Executives." In *J. V. Stalin: Works*, vol. 13, *July 1930–January 1934*, translated from the Russian, 31–44. Moscow: Foreign Languages Publishing House.

Teichova, Alice. 1989. "East-Central and South-East Europe, 1919–39." In *The Cambridge Economic History of Europe*, vol. 8, *The Industrial Economies: The Development of Economic and Social Policies*, edited by Peter Mathias and Sidney Pollard, 887–983. Cambridge: Cambridge University Press.

Tekeli, İlhan, and Selim İlkin. 1977. *1929 Dünya Buhranında Türkiye'nin İktisadi Politika Arayışları*. Ankara: ODTÜ Yayınları.

Tekeli, İlhan, and Selim İlkin. 1981. *Para ve Kredi Sisteminin Oluşumunda Bir Aşama: Türkiye Cumhuriyet Merkez Bankası.* Ankara: T.C. Merkez Bankası Yayını.
Tekeli, İlhan, and Selim İlkin. 1982. *Uygulamaya Geçerken Türkiye'de Devletçiliğin Oluşumu.* Ankara: ODTÜ Yayınları.
Tezel, Yahya S. [1982] 1986. *Cumhuriyet Döneminin İktisadi Tarihi (1923–1950).* 2nd ed. Ankara: Yurt Yayınları.
Toprak, Zafer. 1982. *Türkiye'de "Milli İktisat" (1908–1918).* Ankara: Yurt Yayınları.
Tucker, Robert C. 1990. *Stalin in Power: The Revolution from Above, 1928–1941.* New York: W. W. Norton.
Tunçay, Mete. [1981] 1989. *T.C.'nde Tek-Parti Yönetimi'nin Kurulması (1923–1931).* 2nd ed. İstanbul: Cem Yayınevi.
Turnock, David. 1986. *The Romanian Economy in the Twentieth Century.* London: Croom Helm.
Türkeş, Mustafa. 2001. "A Patriotic Leftist Development-Strategy Proposal in Turkey in the 1930s: The Case of the Kadro (Cadre) Movement." *International Journal of Middle East Studies* 33, no. 1: 91–114.
Webster, Donald E. 1939. *The Turkey of Atatürk: Social Process in the Turkish Reformation.* Philadelphia: American Academy of Political and Social Science.
Weiker, Walter F. 1973. *Political Tutelage and Democracy in Turkey: The Free Party and Its Aftermath.* Leiden: E. J. Brill.
Yavuz, M. Hakan. 2009. *Secularism and Muslim Democracy in Turkey.* Cambridge: Cambridge University Press.
Yetkin, Çetin. 1983. *Türkiye'de Tek Parti Yönetimi, 1930–1945.* İstanbul: Altın Kitaplar Yayınevi.
Zürcher, Erik J. 1984. *The Unionist Factor: The Rôle of the Committee of Union and Progress in the Turkish National Movement, 1905–1926.* Leiden: E. J. Brill.
Zürcher, Erik J. 2007. "The Ottoman Legacy of the Kemalist Republic." In *The State and the Subaltern: Modernization, Society and the State in Turkey and Iran,* edited by Touraj Atabaki, 95–110. London and New York: I. B. Tauris Publishers.

CHAPTER 7

Conclusion

"The stock market will sort itself out. I suspect some good buying opportunities are opening up with some of the panic that we are seeing in the last few days." This advice could easily be given by any stockbroker in the middle of the stock market crash in October 1929. That it was heard from a politician was not too much of a surprise since politicians of all stripes were counselling similarly in the early months or even years of what would become a world economic crisis. That it came from a politician more than 80 years after the onset of the Great Depression and in the middle of the global financial crisis in October 2008 was a little bit of shock: Canada's Prime Minister Stephen Harper was advising his electorate in an interview with the country's public broadcaster (https://www.cbc.ca/archives/entry/harper-calm-about-economy-in-2008). More surprisingly, shortly after that interview, Harper would go on to launch a massive public spending programme in a low-interest rate environment—along with the rest of the Western world.

History did not repeat itself. Western governments acted quickly and cooperatively to resuscitate their economies. They appeared to have learned their lessons from the Great Depression. In other ways, however, history did repeat itself. In the global financial crisis, liberalism (albeit in its neoliberal reincarnation) was again the incumbent economic policy paradigm as in the Great Depression. Likewise, having fallen into disrepute for about 30 years, Keynesianism and interventionism made a sort of comeback via aggressive national spending programmes and government bailout of private businesses during the global financial crisis.

Throughout this book, I wrestled with the issue of the cyclical versus secular nature of change at both international and national levels. I brought in the concept of world-historical context to approach the issue in the case of the interwar period against the background of its pre-World War I antecedent, the extended nineteenth century. Attempts in the 1920s to restore the classical liberal order provided ample evidence for a cyclical notion of change. Return to the gold standard, trade liberalization, creation of the League of Nations as an institution of interstate cooperation, renewed emphasis on market forces, and subsequent withdrawal of the state from wartime spheres of intervention were all real indicators of restitutive change. That these attempts were undone by unprecedented forces in the 1930s highlighted the secular aspect of change. Emergence of regional currency and trading blocs, trade bilateralism and restrictionism, interstate anarchy, increasing recognition of the state's economic responsibility, and installation of totalitarian dictatorships subsequent to politicization of society amounted to a world-historical change. While both aspects of change were more pronounced at the international level, individual nations experienced them unevenly.

I looked at that unevenness in some detail in 18 country cases. No nation ever replicated the classical liberal paradigm in the 1920s. Yet all moved towards it at varying speeds and distances. The same thing happened when nations moved away from the classical liberal orthodoxy in the 1930s. Some turned out to be conservative, limiting the change largely to defensive initiatives in the foreign sector and selective microeconomic intervention in the domestic sphere. This was a protectionist route. Another group went further by also experimenting with macroeconomic demand management and introducing reform in industrial relations, labour market, and social security. I call this policy mix proto-Fordism in reference to the hegemonic postwar policy paradigm in Western nations. A third group stood furthest from classical liberalism with their autarkic initiatives in the foreign sector and differing levels of *dirigisme* in the domestic economy. This was the twentieth-century edition of mercantilism in its industrial and developmental variants.

The brunt of my explanatory effort has been on secular changes in economic policy across nations during the 1930s. Experience of the Great Depression itself loomed large in how far national economic policies changed. I discussed this at some length in the foregoing chapters. What is often overlooked in the comparative public policy literature, however, was the effect that nations' experience of World War I had on their policy behaviour during the world economic crisis. Whether they entered the war, what side they were on, or how they emerged from it all had implications for their economic and political outlook in the interwar period. As a world-historical event, the Great Depression thus has to be seen in light of its immediate antecedent, the Great War. Together, they gave the period its distinctive character.

Within this context, nations had a lot of room for manoeuvre to shape their economic policies. They were by no means free to choose at will. I highlighted political regime, level of economic development, and class composition as structural limits to what nations could do. Democracies did not allow for the autarkic closure and bureaucratic regimentation of the economy, which were the defining features of neomercantilism. Conversely, dictatorships had no room for an industrial relations system requiring free organizations of workers and employers, a system that could only exist under democracy. Predominantly agricultural or underdeveloped economies skewed policy towards microeconomic or physical types of intervention in the economy. Conversely, an extremely small agricultural sector or one that was polarized in class terms between capitalist farmers and hired hands made it impossible for an alignment between independent agrarians and urban workers.

In the remaining and core part of my explanatory effort, I have looked at the 18 country cases—in varying detail—from a "3Is" (ideas, institutions, and interests) perspective. These are extremely broad categories and let me reiterate my position on them. No serious scholarship can overlook any one of them, with each being a cluster of variables rather than a singular one. Yet they also need to be problematized. The comparative public policy literature has in fact been doing just that for 40 years or so. The result is mixed. For me, to put it bluntly, ideas are *primus inter pares* (first among equals). In explaining the economic policy variation across the country cases I took up, I gave primacy to rulers' approach to major groups of interest (e.g., business, labour, and agrarians) and their subsequent strategies in specific institutional settings. In what follows, I revisit some of the main themes from that account at a higher level of abstraction.

The transition between interests and ideas was not problematic in classical Marxism or interest group theory. Interests were (pre)given and pursuit of them naturally followed. This was best expressed by the concept of class consciousness in classical Marxism. As a rule, truly conscious agents pursued their class interests, but there was room for error; some agents could and did pursue someone else's class interests if they had false consciousness. New institutionalism, historical institutionalism in particular, emphasized the constraining or liberating effect of institutions on pursuit of interests while continuing to hold the unidirectional view of the transition between interests and ideas (from the former to the latter). The ideational turn in new institutionalism questioned that view and thus played a corrective role. Interests were no longer (pre)given and ideas were constitutive of interests. In performing this revisioning, however, ideational new institutionalism reversed the direction and opened the door for another unidirectional view: Interests do not exist; it is the ideas that give life to, and determine, interests. While acknowledging that ideas are not necessarily a reflection of interests and that the former can actually frame the latter, I am convinced that there is a material, positional affinity between the two especially at the level of collective action. However, at the level of policy decision, rulers' ideas may not overlap with those of collective actors representing particular interests. The book provides comparative support for that.

In the 1930s, major groups of interest (sectors and classes with their subdivisions) had fairly consistent policy positions and demands as long as they could express themselves freely via autonomous associations and other channels. The institutional context mattered to how they expressed themselves, but, generally, their demands did not vary much across the national cases. Business was divided between financial and industrial sectors. The former was in favour of currency stability (via the gold standard), dear money, and fiscal retrenchment. The industrial sector itself was divided between domestically oriented industries and those serving chiefly foreign markets. Either group did not prioritize currency stability or fiscal retrenchment as their financial counterpart did and both favoured cheap money. Domestic industries pushed for tariff and/or nontariff protection and were more prone to cartelization while export industries feared the retaliatory effects of domestic market protection and were less receptive to government physical intervention. Labour sometimes replicated these market divisions in the industrial sector but was generally supportive of cheap money, public works, and fiscal expansion, as well as pushing for or defending unemployment insurance and social security. As for agrarians, they were in favour of credit expansion but also fiscal contraction and asked for government help regardless of their market orientation. Producers for domestic market demanded insulation from foreign competition while export-oriented farmers sought subsidies to better position themselves in foreign markets.

If groups of interest held consistent policy positions across the cases, their performance in translating their demands into government policies was far from being consistent. First of all, no singular group of interest held positions on all aspects of economic policy; each group was limited by their sectional perspective. This not just strengthened governments' "coordinating" role but also enlarged their room for manoeuvre. Second and most of all, in making economic policy, governments had their ideas and strategies which were not necessarily the sum total of those proposed by sectional groups. Nor were governments refereeing these groups impartially and at an equal distance to each of them. They had their institutional, ideational, and political biases. Moreover, where traditional sectional groups did not exist or were too weak, governments in a broad sense developed their own interests. The Soviet and Turkish ruling bureaucracies were two cases in point.

In the group of countries where economic policy turned out to be most conservative, which I call protectionist, ruling parties of varying type had an unwavering belief in the essentially autonomous recovery of the economy with a little bit of external help from government. Although that help became a lot and went far beyond classical liberal limits, these parties did not think that businesses needed government pump priming to bounce back and create jobs. Their faith in business was complemented with a sense of necessary responsibility for agrarians and a limited understanding of labour's contributing role as consumer in stimulating the economy. The Conservative parties in the United Kingdom and Canada, US Republicans and Canadian Liberals, an assortment of similarly conservative-minded parties in France, their non-Labo(u)r counterparts in Australia and New Zealand, and, most surprisingly, UK and Australian Labo(u)r parties acted on this idea when ruling.

In contrast, in a second group of countries, economic policy change involved macroeconomic and macrosocial areas. Their rulers, too, trusted the capitalist dynamics of the economy. Besides, they were less protectionist in foreign trade and less interventionist in the microeconomic area (except for agriculture) than those of the first group. Yet they came to appreciate the economic contribution of political compromise between sectional interests, and of government spending on public works and social security. In so doing, they informed their post-World War II counterparts in the Western world. The Fordist policy paradigm was built on the interwar experiments of the US Democrats, Swedish (and other Scandinavian) Social Democrats, and, to some extent, French Popular Front and New Zealand Labour parties.

Neomercantilism combining autarky and microeconomic *dirigisme* was the economic policy model of a third group of industrial and semi-industrial countries that were governed by modern dictatorships. Their ruling parties, which equated themselves with the state, accepted the capitalist character of the economy but charged it with politically set goals. Subscribing to a functionalist view of sectional interests, they respected the profit motive as a business rationale, supported agrarians against market forces and ideologically exalted them, and organized labour into a corporate arm of the party state. Nazi Germany was the paradigmatic exemplar of this model, but the Austrian Corporate State was not far behind, especially in the support it gave to businesses and agrarians. Operating in a semi-industrial economy, the Italian Fascists tempered neomercantilism with developmentalism and developed a mixed-economy model by organizing bankrupt and unprofitable businesses into state holding companies.

However, it was the Stalinists in Soviet Russia who gave developmental neomercantilism its paradigmatic expression in a predominantly agricultural economy. Unlike ruling parties in the first three groups of countries, the Stalinist party did not have to deal with capitalists and landed upper classes because they had been eliminated previously and, with the liquidation of independent peasantry and the purge of intra-party opposition in 1929–1930, became the only political force in a nominally workers' state. Moreover, the party-state bureaucracy acquired a class position by controlling the production, distribution, and consumption of goods and services across all sectors of the economy. The Kemalist bureaucrats in Turkey (but not so much their counterparts in the rest of the Balkans) grew into a similar position by adopting an Italian style mixed-economy model of development. Their further aspirations were thwarted by commercial-industrial and landed groups.

Economic policymaking is an ideational and political process. The interwar period, more specifically the 1930s, was the first time this process unfolded concurrently across all states and in full view of broader domestic publics. That is why researchers can reconstruct in their attached ways how policymakers acted at the same world-historical juncture but in different national-structural contexts. My attached mode of explanation is that the ideational orientation and political strategizing of policymakers in their specific institutional settings and against the configurations of interests were the deciding duo of factors in economic policy outcomes.

REFERENCES

Abella, Irving M. 1973. *Nationalism, Communism, and Canadian Labour: The CIO, the Communist Party, and the Canadian Congress of Labour, 1935–1956.* Toronto: University of Toronto Press.
Ahmad, Feroz. 1988. "War and Society under the Young Turks, 1908–18." *Review* 11, no. 2: 265–86.
Aitken, Hugh G. J., John J. Deutsch, William A. Mackintosh, Clarence L. Barber, Maurice Lamontagne, Irving Brecher, and Eugene Forsey. 1959. *The American Economic Impact on Canada.* Durham: Duke University Press.
Akçetin, Elif, 2000. "Anatolian Peasants in the Great Depression 1929–1933." *New Perspectives on Turkey*, no. 23: 79–102. https://doi.org/10.1017/S0896634600003393.
Aldcroft, Derek H. 1970. *The Inter-War Economy: Britain, 1919–1939.* New York: Columbia University Press.
———. 1977. *From Versailles to Wall Street, 1919–1929.* Berkeley: University of California Press.
———. 1997. *Studies in the Interwar European Economy.* Aldershot: Ashgate.
Alhadeff, Peter. 1985. "Public Finance and the Economy in Argentina, Australia and Canada during the Depression of the 1930s." In *Argentina, Australia and Canada: Studies in Comparative Development, 1876–1965,* edited by D. C. M. Platt and Guido di Tella, 161–78. London: Macmillan.
Allen, Christopher S. 1989. "The Underdevelopment of Keynesianism in the Federal Republic of Germany." In *The Political Power of Economic Ideas: Keynesianism across Nations,* edited by Peter A. Hall, 263–89. Princeton: Princeton University Press.

Allern, Elin H. 2010. *Political Parties and Interest Groups in Norway.* Colchester: ECPR Press.
Andersen, Jørgen G., and Jan B. Jensen. 2001. "The Danish Venstre: Liberal, Agrarian or Centrist?" In *From Farmyard to City Square? The Electoral Adaptation of the Nordic Agrarian Parties*, edited by David Arter, 96–131. Aldershot: Ashgate.
Andrae, Carl-Göran. [1973] 1975. "The Swedish Labour Movement and the 1917–1918 Revolution." In *Sweden's Development from Poverty to Affluence, 1750–1970*, edited by Steven Koblik and translated from the Swedish by Joanne Johnson, 232–53. Minneapolis: University of Minnesota Press.
Andrén, Nils. 1964. *Government and Politics in the Nordic Countries: Denmark, Finland, Iceland, Norway, Sweden.* Stockholm: Almqvist and Wiksell.
Arndt, Heinz W. 1944. *The Economic Lessons of the Nineteen-Thirties.* London: Oxford University Press.
Asenova, Vera. 2012. "Small States' Responses to the Great Depression: A Case Study of Bulgaria." Paper presented at the general conference of the European Consortium for Political Research, 25–27 August, Reykjavik.
———. 2016. "German Economic Exploitation of Bulgaria: Short-Term Economic Policies and Long-Term Institutional Effects." In *Paying for Hitler's War: The Consequences of Nazi Hegemony for Europe*, edited by Jonas Scherner and Eugene N. White, 364–88. Cambridge: Cambridge University Press.
Avakumovic, Ivan. 1979. "The Serb Peasant Party, 1919–1945." In *The Peasantry of Eastern Europe*, vol. 1, *Roots of Rural Transformation*, edited by Ivan Volgyes, 57–78. New York: Pergamon Press.
Avcıoğlu, Doğan. 1968. *Türkiye'nin Düzeni (Dün-Bugün-Yarın)*, book 1. Ankara: Bilgi Yayınevi.
Badgley, Kerry. 2000. *Ringing in the Common Love of Good: The United Farmers of Ontario, 1914–1926.* Montreal and Kingston: McGill-Queen's University Press.
Baker, David. 2006. "The Political Economy of Fascism: Myth or Reality, or Myth and Reality?" *New Political Economy* 11, no. 2: 227–50. https://doi.org/10.1080/13563460600655581.
Barlas, Dilek. 1998. *Etatism and Diplomacy in Turkey: Economic and Foreign Policy Strategies in an Uncertain World, 1929–1939.* Leiden: Brill.
Basch, Antonín. 1944. *The Danube Basin and the German Economic Sphere.* London: Kegan Paul.
Béland, Daniel. 2005. "Ideas, Interests, and Institutions: Historical Institutionalism Revisited." In *New Institutionalism: Theory and Analysis*, edited by André Lecours, 29–50. Toronto: University of Toronto Press.
———. 2009. "Ideas, Institutions, and Policy Change." *Journal of European Public Policy* 16, no. 5: 701–18. https://doi.org/10.1080/13501760902983382.

Béland, Daniel, and Robert H. Cox, eds. 2011. *Ideas and Politics in Social Science Research*. New York: Oxford University Press.
———, eds. 2013. "Special Issue: The Politics of Policy Paradigms." *Governance* 26, no. 2: 189–328.
Belge, Murat. 1989. *Sosyalizm, Türkiye ve Gelecek*. İstanbul: Birikim Yayınları.
Bell, John D. 1975. "The Genesis of Agrarianism in Bulgaria." *Balkan Studies* 16, no. 2: 73–92.
———. 1977. *Peasants in Power: Alexander Stamboliski and the Bulgarian Agrarian National Union, 1899–1923*. Princeton: Princeton University Press.
Belshaw, H. 1933. "Crisis and Readjustment in New Zealand." *Journal of Political Economy* 41, no. 6: 750–76.
Bennett, Richard B. 1935. *The Premier Speaks to the People – The First Address*. Ottawa: Dominion Conservative Headquarters.
Bentley, Michael. 2003. "The Liberal Party, 1900–1939: Summit and Descent." In *A Companion to Early Twentieth-Century Britain*, edited by Chris Wrigley, 23–37. Oxford: Blackwell Publishing.
Berend, Iván T. 1985. "Agriculture." In *The Economic History of Eastern Europe, 1919–1975*, vol. 1, *Economic Structure and Performance between the Two Wars*, edited by Michael C. Kaser and E. A. Radice, 148–209. Oxford: Clarendon.
Berend, Iván T., and György Ránki. 1974. *Economic Development in East-Central Europe in the 19th and 20th Centuries*. New York: Columbia University Press.
Berg, Claes, and Lars Jonung. 1999. "Pioneering Price Level Targeting: The Swedish Experience 1931–1937." *Journal of Monetary Economics* 43, no. 3: 525–51.
Berger, Peter. 2003. "The League of Nations and Interwar Austria: Critical Assessment of a Partnership in Economic Reconstruction." In *The Dollfuss/Schuschnigg Era in Austria: A Reassessment*, edited by Günter Bischof, Anton Pelinka, and Alexander Lassner, 73–92. London and New York: Routledge.
Berger, Suzanne. 2013. "Puzzles from the First Globalization." In *Politics in the New Hard Times: The Great Recession in Comparative Perspective*, edited by Miles Kahler and David A. Lake, 150–68. Ithaca: Cornell University Press.
Berglund, Sten, and Ulf Lindström. 1978. *The Scandinavian Party System(s): A Comparative Study*. Lund: Studentlitteratur.
Berkes, Niyazi. 1964. *The Development of Secularism in Turkey*. Montreal: McGill University Press.
Berman, Sheri. 1998a. "Path Dependency and Political Action: Reexamining Responses to the Depression." *Comparative Politics* 30, no. 4: 379–400. https://doi.org/10.2307/422330.
———. 1998b. *The Social Democratic Moment: Ideas and Politics in the Making of Interwar Europe*. Cambridge, MA: Harvard University Press.
———. 2006. *The Primacy of Politics: Social Democracy and the Making of Europe's Twentieth Century*. New York: Cambridge University Press.

Bernanke, Ben S. 2000. *Essays on the Great Depression.* Princeton: Princeton University Press.
Bernard, Philippe, and Henri Dubief. [1975–1976] 1985. *The Decline of the Third Republic, 1914–1938.* Translated from the French by Anthony Forster. Cambridge: Cambridge University Press.
Beşikçi, İsmail. [1977] 1991a. *Bilim Yöntemi/Türkiye'deki Uygulama,* vol. 1, *Kürtlerin Mecburi İskânı.* Reprint. Ankara: Yurt Kitap-Yayın.
———. [1978] 1991b. Bilim Yöntemi/Türkiye'deki Uygulama, vol. 2, *Türk Tarih Tezi, Güneş-Dil Teorisi ve Kürt Sorunu.* Reprint. Ankara: Yurt Kitap-Yayın.
Bianchi, Robert. 1984. *Interest Groups and Political Development in Turkey.* Princeton: Princeton University Press.
Biondich, Mark. 2000. *Stjepan Radić, the Croat Peasant Party, and the Politics of Mass Mobilization, 1904–1928.* Toronto, Buffalo and London: University of Toronto Press.
Birch, Anthony H. 1955. *Federalism, Finance and Social Legislation in Canada, Australia, and the United States.* Oxford: Oxford University Press.
Bishop, Matthew L. 2012. "The Political Economy of Small States: Enduring Vulnerability?" *Review of International Political Economy* 19, no. 5: 942–60. https://doi.org/10.1080/09692290.2011.635118.
Blake, Donald J. 1960. "Swedish Trade Unions and the Social Democratic Party: The Formative Years." *Scandinavian Economic History Review* 8, no. 1: 19–44. https://doi.org/10.1080/03585522.1960.10411421.
Block, Fred L. 1977. *The Origins of International Economic Disorder: A Study of United States International Monetary Policy from World War II to the Present.* Berkeley: University of California Press.
Blyth, Mark M. 1997. "'Any More Bright Ideas?' The Ideational Turn of Comparative Political Economy." *Comparative Politics* 29, no. 2: 229–50. https://doi.org/10.2307/422082.
———. 2002. *Great Transformations: Economic Ideas and Institutional Change in the Twentieth Century.* New York: Cambridge University Press.
Booth, Alan. 1989. *British Economic Policy, 1931–49: Was There a Keynesian Revolution?* Hertfordshire: Harvester Wheatsheaf.
———. 1993. "The British Reaction to the Economic Crisis." In *Capitalism in Crisis: International Responses to the Great Depression,* edited by W. Redvers Garside, 30–55. London: Pinter.
Boratav, Korkut. 1981. "Kemalist Economic Policies and Étatism." In *Atatürk: Founder of a Modern State,* edited by Ali Kazancıgil and Ergun Özbudun, 165–90. London: C. P. Hurst.
———. [1974] 1982. *Türkiye'de Devletçilik.* 2nd ed. Ankara: Savaş Yayınları.
———. 1983. *İktisat Politikaları ve Bölüşüm Sorunları: Politik İktisat Yazıları, 1969–1981.* İstanbul: Belge Yayınları.
———. 1988. *Türkiye İktisat Tarihi, 1908–1985.* İstanbul: Gerçek Yayınları.
Born, Karl E. [1977] 1983. *International Banking in the 19th and 20th Centuries.* Translated from the German by Volker R. Berghahn. New York: St. Martin's.

Borchardt, Knut. 1990. "A Decade of Debate About Brüning's Economic Policy." In *Economic Crisis and Political Collapse: The Weimar Republic, 1924–1933*, edited by Jürgen B. von Kruedener, 99–151. Oxford: Berg.

Botterill, Linda C. 2012. *Wheat Marketing in Transition: The Transformation of the Australian Wheat Board*. Dordrecht: Springer.

Botterill, Linda C., and Alan Fenna. 2020. "Initiative-Resistance and the Australian Party System." *Australian Journal of Politics and History* 66, no. 1: 63–77. https://doi.org/10.1111/ajph.12639.

Boyce, Robert. 2009. *The Great Interwar Crisis and the Collapse of Globalization*. Basingstoke: Palgrave Macmillan.

Boyer, Robert. [1986] 1990. *The Regulation School: A Critical Introduction*. Translated from the French by Craig Charney. New York: Columbia University Press.

Braatoy, Bjarne. 1939. *The New Sweden: A Vindication of Democracy*. London: Thomas Nelson.

Bradford, Neil. 1998. *Commissioning Ideas: Canadian National Policy Innovation in Comparative Perspective*. Toronto: Oxford University Press Canada.

———. 1999. "The Policy Influence of Economic Ideas: Interests, Institutions and Innovation in Canada." *Studies in Political Economy*, no. 59: 17–60. https://doi.org/10.1080/19187033.1999.11675266.

Brady, Alexander. 1939. "Economic Activity of the State in the British Dominions: Some Comments on Comparative Development." *Canadian Journal of Economics and Political Science* 5, no. 3: 300–9. https://doi.org/10.2307/137034.

———. 1941. "Democracy in the Overseas Dominions." In *Canada in Peace and War: Eight Studies in National Trends since 1914*, edited by C. Martin, 212–44. London: Oxford University Press.

———. 1958. *Democracy in the Dominions: A Comparative Study in Institutions*. 3rd ed. Toronto: University of Toronto Press.

Brecher, Irving. 1957. *Monetary and Fiscal Thought and Policy in Canada, 1919–1939*. Toronto: University of Toronto Press.

Brégianni, Catherine. 2012. "The Gold-Exchange Standard, the Great Depression and Greece; Lessons (?) from the Interwar Greek Default." Paper presented at the symposium on "The Euro: (Greek) Tragedy or Europe's Destiny? Economic, Historical and Legal Perspectives on the Common Currency," 11–12 January, Bayreuth.

Britnell, George E. 1939. *The Wheat Economy*. Toronto: University of Toronto Press.

Broadbridge, Seymour A. 1989. "Aspects of Economic and Social Policy in Japan, 1868–1945." In *The Cambridge Economic History of Europe*, vol. 8, *The Industrial Economies: The Development of Economic and Social Policies*, edited

by Peter Mathias and Sidney Pollard, 1106–45. Cambridge: Cambridge University Press.
Brodie, M. Janine, and Jane Jenson. 1980. *Crisis, Challenge and Change: Party and Class in Canada*. Toronto: Methuen.
Brown, Bruce. 1962. *The Rise of New Zealand Labour: A History of the New Zealand Labour Party from 1916 to 1940*. Wellington: Price Milburn.
Brown, C. J. F. 1980. "Industrial Policy and Economic Planning in Japan and France." *National Institute Economic Review*, no. 93: 59–75. https://doi.org/10.1177/002795018009300107.
Brown, William A., Jr. 1949. "Gold as a Monetary Standard, 1914–1919." *Journal of Economic History* 9, supplement S1: 39–49. https://doi.org/10.1017/S0022050700064032.
Bryce, Robert B. 1985. "The Canadian Economy in the 1930s: Unemployment Relief under Bennett and Mackenzie King." In *Explorations in Canadian Economic History: Essays in Honour of Irene M. Spry*, edited by Duncan Cameron, 7–26. Ottawa: University of Ottawa Press.
———. 1986. *Maturing in Hard Times: Canada's Department of Finance through the Great Depression*. Kingston and Montreal: McGill-Queen's University Press.
Buğra, Ayşe. 1994. *State and Business in Modern Turkey: A Comparative Study*. Albany: State University of New York Press.
Burnham, Walter D. 1967. "Party Systems and the Political Process." In *The American Party Systems: Stages of Political Development*, edited by William N. Chambers and Walter D. Burnham, 277–307. New York: Oxford University Press.
Cairns, Alan C. 1971. "The Judicial Committee and Its Critics." *Canadian Journal of Political Science* 4, no. 3: 301–45. https://doi.org/10.1017/S0008423900026809.
Calomiris, Charles W. 2000. *U.S. Bank Deregulation in Historical Perspective*. Cambridge: Cambridge University Press.
———. 2013. "The Political Lessons of Depression-era Banking Reform." In *The Great Depression of the 1930s: Lessons for Today*, edited by Nicholas Crafts and Peter Fearon, 165–87. Oxford: Oxford University Press.
Campbell, John L., and Ove K. Pedersen. 2015. "Policy Ideas, Knowledge Regimes and Comparative Political Economy." *Socio-Economic Review* 13, no. 4: 679–701. https://doi.org/10.1093/ser/mwv004.
———, eds. 2001. *The Rise of Neoliberalism and Institutional Analysis*. Princeton: Princeton University Press.
Cameron, David R. 1978. "The Expansion of the Public Economy: A Comparative Analysis." *American Political Science Review* 72, no. 4: 1243–61. https://doi.org/10.2307/1954537.

Capoccia, Giovanni. 2015. "Critical Junctures and Institutional Change." In *Advances in Comparative-Historical Analysis*, edited by James Mahoney and Kathleen Thelen, 147–79. Cambridge: Cambridge University Press.
Capoccia, Giovanni, and R. Daniel Kelemen. 2007. "The Study of Critical Junctures: Theory, Narrative, and Counterfactuals in Historical Institutionalism." *World Politics* 59, no. 3: 341–69. https://doi.org/10.1017/S0043887100020852.
Carr, Edward H. [1939] 1946. *The Twenty Years' Crisis, 1919–1939: An Introduction to the Study of International Relations*. 2nd ed. London: Macmillan.
Castles, Francis G. 1985. *The Working Class and Welfare: Reflections on the Political Development of the Welfare State in Australia and New Zealand, 1890–1980*. Wellington: Allen and Unwin.
———. 1988. *Australian Public Policy and Economic Vulnerability: A Comparative and Historical Perspective*. Sydney: Allen and Unwin.
Chandler, Lester V. 1970. *America's Greatest Depression, 1929–1941*. New York: Harper and Row.
Checkland, S. G. 1989. "British Public Policy, 1776–1939." In *The Cambridge Economic History of Europe*, vol. 8, *The Industrial Economies: The Development of Economic and Social Policies*, edited by Peter Mathias and Sidney Pollard, 607–40. Cambridge: Cambridge University Press.
Cochrane, Peter. 1980. *Industrialization and Dependence: Australia's Road to Economic Development, 1870–1939*. St Lucia: University of Queensland Press.
Christodoulakis, Nicos. 2012. "Currency Crisis and Collapse in Interwar Greece: Predicament or Policy Failure?" GreeSE Paper No. 60, Hellenic Observatory Papers on Greece and Southeast Europe. http://eprints.lse.ac.uk/44881/1/GreeSE%20No60.pdf (accessed 25 June 2021).
Clark, Harrison. 1941. *Swedish Unemployment Policy – 1914 to 1940*. Washington, D.C.: American Council on Public Affairs.
Clark, Samuel D. 1939. *Canadian Manufacturers' Association: A Study in Collective Bargaining and Political Pressure*. Toronto: University of Toronto Press.
Clarke, Peter. 1988. *The Keynesian Revolution in the Making, 1924–1936*. Oxford: Clarendon Press.
Clavin, Patricia. 1996. *The Failure of Economic Diplomacy: Britain, Germany, France and the United States, 1931–36*. Basingstoke: Macmillan.
———. 2000. *The Great Depression in Europe, 1929–1939*. New York: St. Martin's.
Clough, Shepard B. 1964. *The Economic History of Modern Italy*. New York: Columbia University Press.
Clough, Shepard B., Thomas Moodie, and Carol G. Moodie, eds. 1968. *Economic History of Europe: Twentieth Century*. New York: Walker.

Cohen, Jon S. 1988. "Was Italian Fascism a Developmental Dictatorship? Some Evidence to the Contrary." *Economic History Review*, 2nd series 41, no. 1: 95–113. https://doi.org/10.2307/2597334.

Cohen, Stephen F. [1973] 1980. *Bukharin and the Bolshevik Revolution: A Political Biography, 1888–1938*. 2nd ed. Oxford: Oxford University Press.

Cole, G. D. H. 1938. "Sweden in World Trade." In *Democratic Sweden*, edited by Margaret Cole and Charles Smith, 226–43. New York: Greystone.

Collins, Robert M. 1978. "Positive Business Responses to the New Deal: The Roots of the Committee for Economic Development, 1933–1942." *Business History Review* 52, no. 3: 369–91. https://doi.org/10.2307/3113736.

Conway, John F. 1978. "Populism in the United States, Russia, and Canada: Explaining the Roots of Canada's Third Parties." *Canadian Journal of Political Science* 11, no. 1: 99–124. https://doi.org/10.1017/S0008423900038774.

———. 1979. "The Prairie Populist Resistance to the National Policy: Some Reconsiderations." *Journal of Canadian Studies* 14, no. 3: 77–91.

Cooper, Paul, and Graham Upton. 1990. "An Ecosystemic Approach to Emotional and Behavioural Difficulties in Schools." *Educational Psychology* 10, no. 4: 301–21. https://doi.org/10.1080/0144341900100402.

Cottrell, Philip L. 2013. "Austrian Reconstruction, 1920–1921: A Matter for Private Business or the League of Nations?" In *Business in the Age of Extremes: Essays in Modern German and Austrian Economic History*, edited by Hartmut Berghoff, Jürgen Kocka, and Dieter Ziegler, 59–75. Cambridge: Cambridge University Press.

Crafts, Nicholas, and Peter Fearon. 2013. "Depression and Recovery in the 1930s: An Overview." In *The Great Depression of the 1930s: Lessons for Today*, edited by Nicholas Crafts and Peter Fearon, 1–44. Oxford: Oxford University Press.

Christensen, Dag A. 2001. "The Norwegian Agrarian-Centre Party: Class, Rural or Catchall Party?" In *From Farmyard to City Square? The Electoral Adaptation of the Nordic Agrarian Parties*, edited by David Arter, 31–58. Aldershot: Ashgate.

Cruikshank, Douglas, and Gregory S. Kealey. 1987. "Strikes in Canada, 1891–1950." *Labour* 20: 85–145.

Cudmore, S. A. 1930. "The Economic Development of Canada, 1867–1921: (II) Commercial Policy and the Development of Commerce." In *The Cambridge History of the British Empire*, vol. 6, *Canada and Newfoundland*, edited by J. H. Rose, A. P. Newton, and E. A. Benians, 642–56. Cambridge: At the University Press.

Cuneo, Carl J. 1979. "State, Class, and Reserve Labour: The Case of the 1941 Canadian Unemployment Insurance Act." *Canadian Review of Sociology and Anthropology* 16, no 2: 147–70. https://doi.org/10.1111/j.1755-618X.1979.tb01018.x.

———. 1980. "State Mediation of Class Contradictions in Canadian Unemployment Insurance, 1930–1935." *Studies in Political Economy*, no. 3: 37–65. https://doi.org/10.1080/19187033.1980.11675723.

Curtis, C. A. 1931. "Canada and the Gold Standard." *Queen's Quarterly* 38, no. 1: 104–20.

Çavdar, Tevfik. 1989. "Cumhuriyet'in Başlangıcında Filizlenen Demokrasi ve 'Takrir-i Sükûn' Yasası." *Birikim*, no. 4: 33–40.

Dahl, Sven. 1961. "Strip Fields and Enclosure in Sweden." *Scandinavian Economic History Review* 9, no. 1: 56–67. https://doi.org/10.1080/0358552 2.1961.10411433.

Dahmén, Erik. [1950] 1970. *Entrepreneurial Activity and the Development of Swedish Industry, 1919–1939*. Translated from the Swedish by Axel Leijonhufvud. Homewood: Richard D. Irwin.

Darity, William A., Jr., and Bobbie L. Horn. 1985. "Rudolf Hilferding: The Dominion of Capitalism and the Dominion of Gold." *American Economic Review* 75, no. 2: 363–8.

Daskalov, Roumen. 2011. *Debating the Past: Modern Bulgarian Historiography – From Stambolov to Zhivkov*. Budapest: Central European University Press.

———. 2014. "Agrarian Ideologies and Peasant Movements in the Balkans." In *Entangled Histories of the Balkans*, vol. 2, *Transfers of Political Ideologies and Institutions*, edited by Roumen Daskalov and Diana Mishkova, 281–353. Leiden and Boston: Brill.

Davies, Robert W. 1980. *The Socialist Offensive: The Collectivisation of Soviet Agriculture, 1929–1930*. London and Basingstoke: Macmillan.

———. 1989. "Economic and Social Policy in the USSR, 1917–41." In *The Cambridge Economic History of Europe*, vol. 8, *The Industrial Economies: The Development of Economic and Social Policies*, edited by Peter Mathias and Sidney Pollard, 984–1047. Cambridge: Cambridge University Press.

Day, Richard B. 1981. *The "Crisis" and the "Crash": Soviet Studies of the West (1917–1939)*. London: New Left Books.

Deak, John. 2010. "Dismantling Empire: Ignaz Seipel and Austria's Financial Crisis, 1922–1925." In *From Empire to Republic: Post-World War I Austria*, edited by Günter Bischof, Fritz Plasser, and Peter Berger, 123–41. New Orleans: University of New Orleans Pres.

de Cecco, Marcello. 1989. "Keynes and Italian Economics." In *The Political Power of Economic Ideas: Keynesianism across Nations*, edited by Peter A. Hall, 195–229. Princeton: Princeton University Press.

Delton, Jennifer A. 2020. *The Industrialists: How the National Association of Manufacturers Shaped American Capitalism*. Princeton: Princeton University Press.

Depew, Briggs, Price V. Fishback, and Paul W. Rhode. 2013. "New Deal or No Deal in the Cotton South: The Effect of the AAA on the Agricultural Labor

Structure." *Explorations in Economic History* 50, no. 4: 466–86. https://doi.org/10.1016/j.eeh.2013.06.004.

Dewey, Peter. 2003. "Agriculture, Agrarian Society and the Countryside." In *A Companion to Early Twentieth-Century Britain*, edited by Chris Wrigley, 270–85. Oxford: Blackwell Publishing.

Dobb, Maurice. [1947] 1963. *Studies in the Development of Capitalism*. Revised ed. New York: International.

Dobbin, Frank R. 1993. "The Social Construction of the Great Depression: Industrial Policy during the 1930s in the United States, Britain, and France." *Theory and Society* 22, no. 1: 1–56. https://doi.org/10.1007/BF00993447.

Dohan, Michael R. 1976. "The Economic Origins of Soviet Autarky 1927/28–1934." *Slavic Review* 35, no. 4: 603–35. https://doi.org/10.2307/2495654.

Drache, Daniel. 1984. "The Formation and Fragmentation of the Canadian Working Class: 1820–1920." *Studies in Political Economy*, no. 15: 43–89. https://doi.org/10.1080/19187033.1984.11675625.

Drummond, Ian M. 1972. *British Economic Policy and the Empire, 1919–1939*. London: George Allen and Unwin.

———. 1974. *Imperial Economic Policy, 1917–1939: Studies in Expansion and Protection*. London: George Allen and Unwin.

———. 1981. *The Floating Pound and the Sterling Area, 1931–1939*. Cambridge: Cambridge University Press.

———. 1991. "Why Canadian Banks Did Not Collapse in the 1930s." In *The Role of Banks in the Interwar Economy*, edited by Harold James, Håkan Lindgren, and Alice Teichova, 232–50. Cambridge: Cambridge University Press.

Drummond, Ian M., and Norman Hillmer. 1989. *Negotiating Freer Trade: The United Kingdom, the United States, Canada, and the Trade Agreements of 1938*. Waterloo: Wilfrid Laurier University Press.

Duzgun, Eren. 2017. "Agrarian Change, Industrialization and Geopolitics Beyond the Turkish *Sonderweg*." *European Journal of Sociology* 58, no. 3: 405–39. https://doi.org/10.1017/S0003975617000194.

Dyrenfurth, Nick, and Frank Bongiorno. 2011. *A Little History of the Australian Labor Party*. Sydney: University of New South Wales Press.

Easterbrook, William T., and Hugh G. J. Aitken. 1956. *Canadian Economic History*. Toronto: Macmillan.

Ehrensaft, Philip, and Warwick Armstrong. 1981. "The Formation of Dominion Capitalism: Economic Truncation and Class Structure." In *Inequality: Essays on the Political Economy of Social Welfare*, edited by Allan Moscovitch and Glenn Drover, 99–155. Toronto: University of Toronto Press.

Eichengreen, Barry J. 1988. "The Australian Recovery of the 1930s in International Comparative Perspective." In *Recovery from the Depression: Australia and the World Economy in the 1930s*, edited by Robert G. Gregory and Noel G. Butlin, 33–60. Cambridge: Cambridge University Press.

———. 1992. *Golden Fetters: The Gold Standard and the Great Depression, 1919–1939.* New York: Oxford University Press.

———. 2015. *Hall of Mirrors: The Great Depression, the Great Recession, and the Uses – and Misuses – of History.* New York: Oxford University Press.

Eichengreen, Barry J., and Marc Flandreau. [1985] 1997. "Editors' Introduction." In *The Gold Standard in Theory and History*, 2nd ed., edited by Barry J. Eichengreen and Marc Flandreau, 1–21. London and New York: Routledge.

Eichengreen, Barry J., and Tim J. Hatton. 1988. "Interwar Unemployment in International Perspective: An Overview." In *Interwar Unemployment in International Perspective*, edited by Barry J. Eichengreen and Tim J. Hatton, 1–59. Dordrecht: Kluwer.

Eichengreen, Barry J., and Beth Simmons. 1995. "International Economics and Domestic Politics: Notes on the 1920s." In *Banking, Currency, and Finance in Europe between the Wars*, edited by Charles H. Feinstein, 131–47. Oxford: Clarendon.

Eidlin, Barry. 2018. *Labor and the Class Idea in the United States and Canada.* New York: Cambridge University Press.

Ellis, Howard S. 1941. *Exchange Control in Central Europe.* Cambridge, MA: Harvard University Press.

Ellis, Ulrich R. 1963. *A History of the Australian Country Party.* Parkville: Melbourne University Press.

Elvander, Nils. 1979. *Scandinavian Social Democracy: Its Strength and Weakness.* Stockholm: Almqvist and Wiksell.

Emrence, Cem. 2006. *99 Günlük Muhalefet: Serbest Cumhuriyet Fırkası.* İstanbul: İletişim Yayınları.

Endres, A. M., and Kenneth E. Jackson. 1993. "Policy Responses to the Crisis: Australasia in the 1930s." In *Capitalism in Crisis: International Responses to the Great Depression*, edited by W. Redvers Garside, 148–65. London: Pinter.

English, John. [1977] 1993. *The Decline of Politics: The Conservatives and the Party System 1901–20.* Reprint. Toronto: University of Toronto Press.

Erlich, Alexander. 1960. *The Soviet Industrialization Debate, 1924–1928.* Cambridge, MA: Harvard University Press.

Esen, Berk. 2014. "Nation-Building, Party-Strength, and Regime Consolidation: Kemalism in Comparative Perspective." *Turkish Studies* 15, no. 4: 600–20. https://doi.org/10.1080/14683849.2014.986318.

Espeli, Harald. 2008. "Prelude to Extreme Protectionism? Norwegian Agricultural Protectionism in a West-European Context, 1850–1940." *Scandinavian Economic History Review* 56, no. 3: 209–29. https://doi.org/10.1080/03585520802551402.

Esping-Andersen, Gøsta. 1985. *Politics against Markets: The Social Democratic Road to Power.* Princeton: Princeton University Press.

Evans, Peter B., Dietrich Rueschemeyer, and Theda Skocpol, eds. 1985. *Bringing the State Back In.* Cambridge: Cambridge University Press.

Eyerman, Ron. 1985. "Rationalizing Intellectuals: Sweden in the 1930s and 1940s." *Theory and Society* 14, no. 6: 777–807. https://doi.org/10.1007/BF00174050.

Faro, Francesco L. 1929. "The Banking System of Italy." In *Foreign Banking Systems*, edited by H. Parker Willis and Benjamin H. Beckhart, 765–815. New York: Henry Holt.

Feinstein, Charles H. 1972. *National Income, Expenditure and Output of the United Kingdom, 1855–1965*. Cambridge: At the University Press.

Feinstein, Charles H., Peter Temin, and Gianni Toniolo. 2008. *The World Economy between the World Wars*. Oxford: Oxford University Press.

Ferguson, Thomas. 1984. "From Normalcy to New Deal: Industrial Structure, Party Competition, and American Public Policy in the Great Depression." *International Organization* 38, no. 1: 41–94. https://doi.org/10.1017/S0020818300004276.

Finefrock, Michael M. 1981. "Laissez-Faire, the 1923 Izmir Economic Congress and Early Turkish Developmental Policy in Political Perspective." *Middle Eastern Studies* 17, no. 3: 375–92. https://doi.org/10.1080/00263208108700478.

Finkel, Alvin. 1979. *Business and Social Reform in the Thirties*. Toronto: James Lorimer.

———. 1989. *The Social Credit Phenomenon in Alberta*. Toronto: University of Toronto Press.

Fishback, Price. 2010. "US Monetary and Fiscal Policy in the 1930s." *Oxford Review of Economic Policy* 26, no. 3: 385–413. https://doi.org/10.1093/oxrep/grq029.

Fishback, Price, and John J. Wallis. 2013. "What Was New about the New Deal?" In *The Great Depression of the 1930s: Lessons for Today*, edited by Nicholas Crafts and Peter Fearon, 290–327. Oxford: Oxford University Press.

Fisher, Allan G. B. 1934. "Crisis and Readjustment in Australia." *Journal of Political Economy* 42, no. 6: 753–82.

Flora, Peter, Jens Alber, Richard Eichenberg, Jürgen Kohl, Franz Kraus, Winfried Pfenning, and Kurt Seebohm. 1983. *State, Economy, and Society in Western Europe, 1815–1975*, vol. 1, *The Growth of Mass Democracies and Welfare States*. Frankfurt am Main: Campus Verlag.

Forster, Donald, and Colin Read. 1979. "The Politics of Opportunism: The New Deal Broadcasts." *Canadian Historical Review* 60, no. 3: 324–49. https://doi.org/10.3138/CHR-060-03-03.

Forsyth, Douglas J. 1991. "The Rise and Fall of German-Inspired Mixed Banking in Italy, 1894–1936." In *The Role of Banks in the Interwar Economy*, edited by Harold James, Håkan Lindgren, and Alice Teichova, 179–205. Cambridge: Cambridge University Press.

Fowke, Vernon C. 1946. *Canadian Agricultural Policy: The Historical Pattern.* Toronto: University of Toronto Press.

———. 1957. *The National Policy and the Wheat Economy.* Toronto: University of Toronto Press.

Freris, Andrew F. 1986. *The Greek Economy in the Twentieth Century.* New York: St. Martin's.

Frey, Frederick W. 1965. *The Turkish Political Elite.* Cambridge, MA: MIT Press.

Gaitskell, Hugh. 1938. "The Banking System and Monetary Policy." In *Democratic Sweden*, edited by Margaret Cole and Charles Smith, 96–107. New York: Greystone.

Gallarotti, Giulio M. 1995. *The Anatomy of an International Monetary Regime: The Classical Gold Standard, 1880–1914.* New York and Oxford: Oxford University Press.

Garside, W. Redvers. 2000. "The Political Economy of Structural Change: Britain in the 1930s." In *After the Slump: Industry and Politics in 1930s Britain and Germany*, edited by C. Buchheim and W. Redvers Garside, 9–31. Frankfurt am Main: Peter Lang.

Garside, W. Redvers, and Niels-Henrik Topp. 2001. "Nascent Keynesianism? Denmark in the 1930s." *History of Political Economy* 33, no. 4: 717–41.

Garraty, John A. 1973. "The New Deal, National Socialism, and the Great Depression." *American Historical Review* 78, no. 4: 907–44. https://doi.org/10.2307/1858346.

———. 1986. *The Great Depression: An Inquiry into the Causes, Course, and Consequences of the Worldwide Depression of the Nineteen-Thirties, as Seen by Contemporaries and in the Light of History.* San Diego: Harcourt Brace Jovanovich.

Gerschenkron, Alexander. 1943. *Bread and Democracy in Germany.* Berkeley: University of California Press.

———. 1962. *Economic Backwardness in Historical Perspective: A Book of Essays.* Cambridge, MA: Harvard University Press.

Glindemann, Paul. 1929. "The Banking System of Denmark." In *Foreign Banking Systems*, edited by H. Parker Willis and Benjamin H. Beckhart, 489–521. New York: Henry Holt.

Goldfield, Michael. 1989. "Worker Insurgency, Radical Organization, and New Deal Labor Legislation." *American Political Science Review* 83, no. 4: 1257–82. https://doi.org/10.2307/1961668.

Goldfrank, Walter L. 1978. "Fascism and World Economy." In *Social Change in the Capitalist World Economy*, edited by Barbara H. Kaplan, 75–117. Beverly Hills: Sage.

Gordon, Colin. 1994. *New Deals: Business, Labor, and Politics in America, 1920–1935.* New York: Cambridge University Press.

Gourevitch, Peter A. 1984. "Breaking with Orthodoxy: The Politics of Economic Policy Responses to the Depression of the 1930s." *International Organization* 38, no. 1: 95–129. https://doi.org/10.1017/S0020818300004288.
———. 1986. *Politics in Hard Times: Comparative Responses to International Economic Crises*. Ithaca: Cornell University Press.
Gökmen, Özgür. 2005. "The State of Labour in Turkey, 1918–1938." *Mitteilungsblatt des Instituts für soziale Bewegungen* 33: 123–36.
Göymen, Korel. 1976. "Stages of Etatist Development in Turkey: The Interaction of Single-Party Politics and Economic Policy in the 'Etatist Decade,' 1930–1939." *METU Studies in Development*, no. 10: 89–114.
Graham, B. D. 1966. *The Formation of the Australian Country Parties*. Canberra: Australian National University Press.
Greasley, David, and Les Oxley. 2002. "Regime Shift and Fast Recovery on the Periphery: New Zealand in the 1930s." *Economic History Review* 55, no. 4: 697–720. https://doi.org/10.1111/1468-0289.00237.
Greaves, Julian. 2000. "British Steel in the 1930s: Adaptation under Duress?" In *After the Slump: Industry and Politics in 1930s Britain and Germany*, edited by C. Buchheim and W. Redvers Garside, 111–30. Frankfurt am Main: Peter Lang.
Green, Alan G., and Gordon R. Sparks. 1988. "A Macro Interpretation of Recovery: Australia and Canada." In *Recovery from the Depression: Australia and the World Economy in the 1930s*, edited by Robert G. Gregory and Noel G. Butlin, 89–112. Cambridge: Cambridge University Press.
Gregor, A. James. 1979. *Italian Fascism and Developmental Dictatorship*. Princeton: Princeton University Press.
Gregory, Paul R., and Joel Sailors. 2003. "The Soviet Union during the Great Depression: The Autarky Model." In *The World Economy and National Economies in the Interwar Slump*, edited by Theo Balderston, 191–210. Basingstoke: Palgrave Macmillan.
Griffin, Roger. 2013. "Avalanches of Spring: The Great War, Modernism, and the Rise of Austro-Fascism." In *Routes into the Abyss: Coping with Crises in the 1930s*, edited by Helmut Konrad and Wolfgang Maderthaner, 33–54. New York and Oxford: Berghahn Books.
Griffiths, Clare V. J. 2007. *Labour and the Countryside: The Politics of Rural Britain, 1918–1939*. Oxford: Oxford University Press.
Greenhill, H. Gaylon. 1965. "The Norwegian Agrarian Party: A Class Party?" *Social Science* 40, no. 4: 214–9.
Grytten, Ola H. 1998. "Monetary Policy and Restructuring of the Norwegian Economy during the Years of Crises, 1920–1939." In *Economic Crises and Restructuring in History: Experiences of Small Countries*, edited by Timo Myllyntaus, 93–124. St. Katharinen: Scripta Mercaturae Verlag.
———. 2008a. "A Small Country's Policy Response to Global Economic Disintegration during the Interwar Years of Crisis." In *Pathbreakers: Small*

European Countries Responding to Globalisation and Deglobalisation, edited by Margrit Müller and Timo Myllyntaus, 271–96. Bern: Peter Lang.

———. 2008b. "Why Was the Great Depression Not So Great in the Nordic Countries? Economic Policy and Unemployment." *Journal of European Economic History* 37, nos. 2–3: 369–403.

Guillebaud, Claude W. 1939. *The Economic Recovery of Germany: From 1933 to the Incorporation of Austria in March 1938*. London: Macmillan.

———. 1941. *The Social Policy of Nazi Germany*. Cambridge: At the University Press.

Gustafsson, Bo. 1973. "A Perennial of Doctrinal History: Keynes and 'the Stockholm School.'" *Economy and History* 16, no. 1: 114–28. https://doi.org/10.1080/00708852.1973.10418906.

———. 1986. "Conflict, Confrontation and Consensus in Modern Swedish History." In *Economics and Values*, edited by Lennart Arvedson, Ingemund Hagg, Mans Lonnroth, and Bengt Rydén, 16–50. Stockholm: Almqvist and Wiksell International.

Gustavson, Carl C. 1986. *The Small Giant: Sweden Enters the Industrial Era*. Athens: Ohio University Press.

Gülalp, Haldun. 1983. *Gelişme Stratejileri ve Gelişme İdeolojileri*. Ankara: Yurt Yayınları.

Günçe, Ergin. 1967. "Early Planning Experiences in Turkey." In *Planning in Turkey (Selected Papers)*, edited by Selim İlkin and E. İnanç, 1–27. Ankara: METU Publications.

Hadley, Eleanor M. 1989. "The Diffusion of Keynesian Ideas in Japan." In *The Political Power of Economic Ideas: Keynesianism across Nations*, edited by Peter A. Hall, 291–309. Princeton: Princeton University Press.

Haggard, Stephan. 1988 "The Institutional Foundations of Hegemony: Explaining the Reciprocal Trade Agreements Act of 1934." *International Organization* 42, no. 1: 91–119. https://doi.org/10.1017/S0020818300007141.

Hale, William M. 1981. *The Political and Economic Development of Modern Turkey*. London: Croom Helm.

———. 1984. "The Traditional and the Modern in the Economy of Kemalist Turkey: The Experience of the 1920s." In *Atatürk and the Modernization of Turkey*, edited by Jacob M. Landau, 153–70. Boulder: Westview.

Hall, Peter A. 1989. "Conclusion: The Politics of Keynesian Ideas." In *The Political Power of Economic Ideas: Keynesianism across Nations*, edited by Peter A. Hall, 361–91. Princeton: Princeton University Press.

———. 1993. "Policy Paradigms, Social Learning, and the State: The Case of Economic Policymaking in Britain." *Comparative Politics* 25, no. 3: 275–96. https://doi.org/10.2307/422246.

Hall, Peter A., and Rosemary C. R. Taylor. 1996. "Political Science and the Three New Institutionalisms." *Political Studies* 44, no. 5: 936–57. https://doi.org/10.1111/j.1467-9248.1996.tb00343.x.

Hamer, David A. 1988. *The New Zealand Liberals: The Years of Power, 1891–1912*. Auckland: Auckland University Press.

Hancock, W. Keith. 1942. *Survey of British Commonwealth Affairs*, vol. 2, *Problems of Economic Policy, 1918–1939*, part 1. London: Oxford University Press.

Hanisch, Tore. 1978. "The Economic Crisis in Norway in the 1930s: A Tentative Analysis of Its Causes." *Scandinavian Economic History Review* 26, no. 2: 145–55. https://doi.org/10.1080/03585522.1978.10415624.

Hansson, Sigfrid. 1939. "Employers and Workers in Sweden." In *Sweden's Economic Progress*, edited by the Royal Swedish Commission, 1–113 (separately paged). New York: Royal Swedish Commission.

Harris, Bernard. 1988. "Unemployment, Insurance and Health in Interwar Britain." In *Interwar Unemployment in International Perspective*, edited by Barry J. Eichengreen and Tim J. Hatton, 149–83. Dordrecht: Kluwer.

Hart, Michael. 2002. *A Trading Nation: Canadian Trade Policy from Colonialism to Globalization*. Vancouver: University of British Columbia Press.

Harty, Siobhán. 2005. "Theorizing Institutional Change." In *New Institutionalism: Theory and Analysis*, edited by André Lecours, 51–79. Toronto: University of Toronto Press.

Hawke, G. R. 1971. "New Zealand and the Return to Gold in 1925." *Australian Economic History Review* 11, no. 1: 48–58.

———. 1985. *The Making of New Zealand: An Economic History*. Cambridge: Cambridge University Press.

———. 1988. "Depression and Recovery in New Zealand." In *Recovery from the Depression: Australia and the World Economy in the 1930s*, edited by Robert G. Gregory and Noel G. Butlin, 113–34. Cambridge: Cambridge University Press.

Hay, Colin. 2004. "Ideas, Interests and Institutions in the Comparative Political Economy of Great Transformations." *Review of International Political Economy* 11, no. 1: 204–26. https://doi.org/10.1080/0969229042000179811.

———. 2011. "Ideas and the Construction of Interests." In *Ideas and Politics in Social Science Research*, edited by Daniel Béland and Robert H. Cox, 65–82. New York: Oxford University Press.

Heckscher, Eli F. 1953. "A Survey of Economic Thought in Sweden, 1875–1950." *Scandinavian Economic History Review* 1, no. 1: 105–25. https://doi.org/10.1080/03585522.1953.10409901.

———. [1941] 1954. *An Economic History of Sweden*. Translated from the Swedish by G. Ohlin. Cambridge, MA: Harvard University Press.

Heclo, Hugh. 1974. *Modern Social Politics in Britain and Sweden: From Relief to Income Maintenance*. New Haven: Yale University Press.

Hedberg, Peter. 2010. "Bilateral Exchange Clearing with Germany during the 1930s: The Experiences of the Scandinavian Countries." In *Managing Crises and De-globalisation: Nordic Foreign Trade and Exchange, 1919–39*, edited by Sven-Olof Olsson, 101–20. London: Routledge.

Hentschel, Volker. 1989. "German Economic and Social Policy, 1815–1939." In *The Cambridge Economic History of Europe*, vol. 8, *The Industrial Economies: The Development of Economic and Social Policies*, edited by Peter Mathias and Sidney Pollard, 752–813. Cambridge: Cambridge University Press.

Hershlag, Zvi Y. [1958] 1968. *Turkey: The Challenge of Growth*. 2nd ed. Leiden: E. J. Brill.

———. 1984. "Atatürk's Etatism." In *Atatürk and the Modernization of Turkey*, edited by Jacob M. Landau, 171–80. Boulder: Westview.

Higgins, Winton. 1985. "Ernst Wigforss: The Renewal of Social Democratic Theory and Practice." *Political Power and Social Theory* 5: 207–50.

Hildebrand, Karl-Gustaf. 1975. "Economic Policy in Scandinavia during the Inter-War Period." *Scandinavian Economic History Review* 23, no. 2: 99–115. https://doi.org/10.1080/03585522.1975.10407818.

———. 1978. "Labour and Capital in the Scandinavian Countries in the Nineteenth and Twentieth Centuries." *The Cambridge Economic History of Europe*, vol. 7, *The Industrial Economies: Capital, Labour, and Enterprise*, part 1, *Britain, France, Germany, and Scandinavia*, edited by Peter Mathias and M. M. Postan, 590–628. Cambridge: Cambridge University Press.

Hilferding, Rudolf. 1910. *Das Finanzkapital: Eine Studie über die jüngste Entwicklung des Kapitalismus*. Vienna: Verlag der Wiener Volksbuchhandlung.

Hill, Kim Q. 1988. *Democracies in Crisis: Public Policy Responses to the Great Depression*. Boulder: Westview.

Hirschman, Albert O. 1945. *National Power and the Structure of Foreign Trade*. Berkeley: University of California Press.

Hobsbawm, Eric. 1994. *Age of Extremes: The Short Twentieth Century, 1914–1991*. London: Michael Joseph.

Hodne, Fritz. 1983. *The Norwegian Economy, 1920–1980*. London: Croom Helm.

Holtfrerich, Carl-Ludwig. 1990a. "Was the Policy of Deflation in Germany Unavoidable?" In *Economic Crisis and Political Collapse: The Weimar Republic, 1924–1933*, edited by Jürgen B. von Kruedener, 63–80. Oxford: Berg.

———. 1990b. "Economic Policy Options and the End of the Weimar Republic." In *Weimar: Why Did German Democracy Fail?*, edited by Ian Kershaw, 58–91. London: Weidenfeld and Nicholson.

Horn, Michiel. 1980. *The League for Social Reconstruction: Intellectual Origins of the Democratic Left in Canada, 1930–1942*. Toronto: University of Toronto Press.

Howson, Susan, and Donald Winch. 1977. *The Economic Advisory Council 1930–1939: A Study in Economic Advice during Depression and Recovery.* Cambridge: Cambridge University Press.

Hunter, Holland, and Janusz M. Szyrmer. 1992. *Faulty Foundations: Soviet Economic Policies, 1928–1940.* Princeton: Princeton University Press.

Hurd, Elizabeth S. 2008. *The Politics of Secularism in International Relations.* Princeton and Oxford: Princeton University Press.

Huthmacher, J. Joseph. 1968. *Senator Robert F. Wagner and the Rise of Urban Liberalism.* New York: Atheneum.

Immergut, Ellen M. 1998. "The Theoretical Core of the New Institutionalism." *Politics and Society* 26, no. 1: 5–34. https://doi.org/10.1177/0032329298026001002.

———. 2006. "Historical-Institutionalism in Political Science and the Problem of Change." In *Understanding Change: Models, Methodologies and Metaphors*, edited by Andreas Wimmer and Reinhart Kössler, 237–59. London: Palgrave Macmillan.

Ingham, Geoffrey. 1984. *Capitalism Divided? The City and Industry in British Social Development.* London: Macmillan.

Irvine, William. [1920] 1976. *The Farmers in Politics.* Reprint. Toronto: McClelland and Stewart.

Irving, John A. 1959. *The Social Credit Movement in Alberta.* Toronto: University of Toronto Press.

Irwin, Douglas A. 2011. *Peddling Protectionism: Smoot–Hawley and the Great Depression.* Princeton: Princeton University Press.

———. 2012. *Trade Policy Disaster: Lessons from the 1930s.* Cambridge, MA: MIT Press.

İlkin, Selim. 1971. "Türkiye Milli İthalat ve İhracat Anonim Şirketi." *ODTÜ Gelişme Dergisi*, no 2: 199–232.

———. 1975. "Türkiye'de Merkez Bankası Fikrinin Gelişimi." In *Türkiye İktisat Tarihi Semineri: Metinler/Tartışmalar (8–10 Haziran 1973)*, edited by Osman Okyar and H. Ünal Nalbantoğlu, 537–82. Ankara: Hacettepe Ünüverstesi Yayınları.

Jackson, Julian. 1985. *The Politics of Depression in France, 1932–1936.* Cambridge: Cambridge University Press.

———. 1988. *The Popular Front in France: Defending Democracy, 1934–38.* Cambridge: Cambridge University Press.

James, Harold. 1986. *The German Slump: Politics and Economics, 1924–1936.* Oxford: Clarendon Press.

———. 1989. "What Is Keynesian about Deficit Financing? The Case of Interwar Germany." In *The Political Power of Economic Ideas: Keynesianism across Nations*, edited by Peter A. Hall, 231–62. Princeton: Princeton University Press.

———. 1993. "Innovation and Conservatism in Economic Recovery: The Alleged 'Nazi Recovery' of the 1930s." In *Capitalism in Crisis: International Responses to the Great Depression*, edited by W. Redvers Garside, 70–95. London: Pinter.

———. 2001. *The End of Globalization: Lessons from the Great Depression*. Cambridge, MA: Harvard University Press.

———. 2013. "The 1931 Central European Banking Crisis Revisited." In *Business in the Age of Extremes: Essays in Modern German and Austrian Economic History*, edited by Hartmut Berghoff, Jürgen Kocka, and Dieter Ziegler, 119–30. Cambridge: Cambridge University Press.

James, Leighton, and Raymond Markey. 2006. "Class and Labour: The British Labour Party and the Australian Labor Party Compared." *Labour History*, no. 90: 23–41. https://doi.org/10.2307/27516112.

Janos, Andrew C. 1970. "The One-Party State and Social Mobilization: East Europe between the Wars." In *Authoritarian Politics in Modern Society: The Dynamics of Established One-Party Systems*, edited by Samuel P. Huntington and Clement H. Moore, 204–36. New York: Basic Books.

Jelavich, Barbara. 1983. *History of the Balkans: Twentieth Century*. New York: Cambridge University Press.

Jesson, Bruce. 1987. *Behind the Mirror Glass: The Growth of Wealth and Power in New Zealand in the Eighties*. Auckland: Penguin.

Johansen, Hans C. 1987. *The Danish Economy in the Twentieth Century*. London: Croom Helm.

Johnson, Chalmers A. 1982. *MITI and the Japanese Miracle: The Growth of Industrial Policy, 1925–1975*. Stanford: Stanford University Press.

Johnson, Simon, and Peter Temin. 1993. "The Macroeconomics of NEP." *Economic History Review*, new series 46, no. 4: 750–67. https://doi.org/10.1111/j.1468-0289.1993.tb01360.x.

Johnson, William R. 1963. "National Farm Organizations and the Reshaping of Agricultural Policy in 1932." *Agricultural History* 37, no. 1: 35–42.

Johnston, Thomas L. 1962. *Collective Bargaining in Sweden: A Study of the Labour Market and Its Institutions*. London: George Allen and Unwin.

Jonung, Lars. 1979. "Knut Wicksell's Norm of Price Stabilization and Swedish Monetary Policy in the 1930's." *Journal of Monetary Economics* 5, no. 4: 459–96.

———. 1981. "The Depression in Sweden and the United States: A Comparison of Causes and Policies." In *The Great Depression Revisited*, edited by Karl Brunner, 286–315. Boston: Martinus Nijhoff.

Jörberg, Lennart. 1973. "The Industrial Revolution in the Nordic Countries." In *The Fontana Economic History of Europe*, vol. 4, *The Emergence of Industrial Societies*, part 2, edited by Carlo M. Cipolla, 375–485. Glasgow: Fontana.

Jörberg, Lennart, and Olle Krantz. 1976. "Scandinavia, 1914–1970." In *The Fontana Economic History of Europe*, vol. 6, *Contemporary Economies*, part 2, edited by Carlo M. Cipolla, 377–459. Glasgow: Fontana.
———. 1989. "Economic and Social Policy in Sweden, 1850–1939." In *The Cambridge Economic History of Europe*, vol. 8, *The Industrial Economies: The Development of Economic and Social Policies*, edited by Peter Mathias and Sidney Pollard, 1048–105. Cambridge: Cambridge University Press.
Kaiser, Claudia. 2000. "Trade Union Reactions to Economic Crisis." In *After the Slump: Industry and Politics in 1930s Britain and Germany*, edited by C. Buchheim and Redvers Garside, 179–200. Frankfurt am Main: Peter Lang.
Kalecki, M. 1938. "The Lesson of the Blum Experiment." *Economic Journal* 48, no. 189: 26–41. https://doi.org/10.2307/2225475.
Karaömerlioğlu, M. Asım. 2002. "Agrarian Populism as an Ideological Discourse of Interwar Europe." *New Perspectives on Turkey*, no. 26: 59–93. https://doi.org/10.1017/S089663460000371X.
Karpat, Kemal H. 1959. *Turkey's Politics: The Transition to a Multi-Party System*. Princeton: Princeton University Press.
Katzenstein, Peter J. 1985. *Small States in World Markets: Industrial Policy in Europe*. Ithaca: Cornell University Press.
———. 2003. "*Small States* and Small States Revisited." *New Political Economy* 8, no. 1: 9–30. https://doi.org/10.1080/1356346032000078705.
Kavanagh, Dennis A. 1973. "Crisis Management and Incremental Adaptation in British Politics: The 1931 Crisis of the British Party System." In *Crisis, Choice, and Change: Historical Studies of Political Development*, edited by Gabriel A. Almond, Scott C. Flanagan, and Robert J. Mundt, 152–223. Boston: Little, Brown.
Kemp, Tom. 1972. *The French Economy, 1913–39: The History of a Decline*. London: Longman.
———. 1989. "Economic and Social Policy in France." In *The Cambridge Economic History of Europe*, vol. 8, *The Industrial Economies: The Development of Economic and Social Policies*, edited by Peter Mathias and Sidney Pollard, 691–751. Cambridge: Cambridge University Press.
Kershaw, Ian, ed. 1990. *Weimar: Why Did German Democracy Fail?* London: Weidenfeld and Nicolson.
Kerwin, Robert W. 1959. "Etatism in Turkey, 1933–50." In *The State and Economic Growth*, edited by Hugh G. J. Aitken, 237–54. New York: Social Science Research Council.
Keyder, Çağlar. 1981. *The Definition of a Peripheral Economy: Turkey, 1923–1929*. Cambridge: Cambridge University Press.
———. 1987. *State and Class in Turkey: A Study in Capitalist Development*. London: Verso.

Kindleberger, Charles P. [1973] 2013. *The World in Depression, 1929–1939*. 40th anniversary ed. Berkeley: University of California Press.

———. 1989. "Commercial Policy between the Wars." In *The Cambridge Economic History of Europe*, vol. 8, *The Industrial Economies: The Development of Economic and Social Policies*, edited by Peter Mathias and Sidney Pollard, 161–96. Cambridge: Cambridge University Press.

Kirk, Tim. 2003. "Fascism and Austrofascism." In *The Dollfuss/Schuschnigg Era in Austria: A Reassessment*, edited by Günter Bischof, Anton Pelinka, and Alexander Lassner, 10–31. London and New York: Routledge.

Kirkendall, Richard S. 1975. "The New Deal and Agriculture." In *The New Deal: The National Level*, edited by John Braeman, Robert H. Bremner, and David Brody, 83–109. Columbus: Ohio State University Press.

Kitson, Michael. 2003. "Slump and Recovery: The UK Experience." In *The World Economy and National Economies in the Interwar Slump*, edited by Theo Balderston, 88–104. Basingstoke: Palgrave Macmillan.

Kjellberg, Anders. 1992. "Sweden: Can the Model Survive?" In *Industrial Relations in the New Europe*, edited by Anthony Ferner and Richard Hyman, 88–142. Oxford: Basil Blackwell.

Kjellstrom, Erik T. H. 1934. *Managed Money: The Experience of Sweden*. New York: Columbia University Press.

Klausinger, Hansjörg. 2002. "The Austrian School of Economics and the Gold Standard Mentality in Austrian Economic Policy in the 1930s." Center for Austrian Studies Working Paper 02-2, University of Minnesota, Minneapolis. https://econwpa.ub.uni-muenchen.de/econ-wp/mhet/papers/0501/0501001.pdf (accessed 8 May 2021).

———. 2003. "How Far Was Vienna from Chicago in the 1930s? The Economists and the Depression." In *The Dollfuss/Schuschnigg Era in Austria: A Reassessment*, edited by Günter Bischof, Anton Pelinka, and Alexander Lassner, 56–72. London and New York: Routledge.

Klovland, Jan T. 1998. "Monetary Policy and Business Cycles in the Interwar Years: The Scandinavian Experience." *European Review of Economic History* 2, no. 3: 309–44. https://doi.org/10.1017/S1361491698000148.

Knox, Frank A. 1939. "Dominion Monetary Policy, 1929–1934: A Study Prepared for the Royal Commission on Dominion–Provincial Relations." Unpublished report, Ottawa.

Kolb, Eberhard. [2002] 2005. *The Weimar Republic*. 2nd ed. Translated from the German by P. S. Falla and R. J. Park. London: Routledge.

Kolev, Stefan. 2009. "The Great Depression in the Eyes of Bulgaria's Inter-War Economists." Discussion Paper No. DP/79/2009, Bulgarian National Bank, Sophia.

Koning, Niek. 1994. *The Failure of Agrarian Capitalism: Agrarian Politics in the United Kingdom, Germany, the Netherlands and the USA, 1846–1919*. London and New York: Routledge.

Konrad, Helmut. 2013. "The Significance of February 1934 in Austria, in Both National and International Context." In *Routes into the Abyss: Coping with Crises in the 1930s*, edited by Helmut Konrad and Wolfgang Maderthaner, 20–32. New York and Oxford: Berghahn Books.

Korpi, Walter. 1978. *The Working Class in Welfare Capitalism: Work, Unions, and Politics in Sweden*. London: Routledge and Kegan Paul.

———. 1982. "The Historical Compromise and Its Dissolution." In *Sweden: Choices for Economic and Social Policy in the 1980s*, edited by Bengt Rydén and Villy Bergström, 124–41. London: George Allen and Unwin.

Kragh, Marrin. 2012. "The Stockholm School, Ernst Wigforss and the Great Depression in Sweden: An Outline." In *The Great Depression in Europe: Economic Thought and Policy in a National Context*, edited by Michalis Psalidopoulos, 75–102. Athens: Alpha Bank Historical Archives.

Krake, Kristina. 2020. "Reconsidering the Crisis Agreements of the 1930s: The Defence of Democracy in a Comparative Scandinavian Perspective." *Contemporary European History* 29, no. 1: 1–15. https://doi.org/10.1017/S0960777318000607.

Kristensen, Thorkil. 1958. "State Intervention and Economic Freedom." In *Scandinavian Democracy: Development of Democratic Thought and Institutions in Denmark, Norway and Sweden*, edited by Joseph A. Lauwerys, 192–219. Copenhagen: Danish Institute.

Kuhn, Thomas S. [1962] 1970. *The Structure of Scientific Revolutions*. 2nd ed. Chicago: University of Chicago Press.

Kuhnle, Stein. 1978. "The Beginnings of the Nordic Welfare States: Similarities and Differences." *Acta Sociologica* 21, supplement: 9–35.

Kurth, James R. 1979. "The Political Consequences of the Product Cycle: Industrial History and Political Outcomes." *International Organization* 33, no. 1: 1–34. https://doi.org/10.1017/S0020818300000643.

Kuru, Ahmet T., and Alfred Stepan. 2012. "Laïcité as an 'Ideal Type' and a Continuum: Comparing Turkey, France, and Senegal." In *Democracy, Islam, and Secularism in Turkey*, edited by Ahmet T. Kuru and Alfred Stepan, 95–121. New York: Columbia University Press.

Kuruç, Bilsay. 2011. *Mustafa Kemal Döneminde Ekonomi: Büyük Devletler ve Türkiye*. İstanbul: İstanbul Bilgi Üniversitesi Yayınları.

Kuyucak, Hazım A. 1939. "Memorandum on Exchange Control in Turkey." Paper submitted to the 12th Session of the International Studies Conference, Bergen, April.

Lafferty, William M. 1971. *Economic Development and the Response of Labour in Scandinavia: A Multi-Level Analysis*. Oslo: Universitetsforlaget.

Lake, David A. 1988. *Power, Protection, and Free Trade: International Sources of U.S. Commercial Strategy, 1887–1939*. Ithaca: Cornell University Press.
———. 1999. *Entangling Relations: American Foreign Policy in Its Century*. Princeton: Princeton University Press.
Lampe, John R. 1986. *The Bulgarian Economy in the Twentieth Century*. New York: St. Martin's.
Lampe, John R., and Marvin R. Jackson. 1982. *Balkan Economic History, 1550–1950: From Imperial Borderlands to Developing Nations*. Bloomington: Indiana University Press.
Landes, David S. 1969. *The Unbound Prometheus: Technological Change and Industrial Development in Western Europe from 1750 to the Present*. Cambridge: At the University Press.
Larsen, Hans K. 2010. "Danish Exchange Rate Policy and the Trades: The Interwar Experience." In *Managing Crises and De-globalisation: Nordic Foreign Trade and Exchange, 1919–39*, edited by Sven-Olof Olsson, 82–100. London: Routledge.
Larsson, Mats. 1991. "State, Banks and Industry in Sweden, with Some Reference to the Scandinavian Countries." In *The Role of Banks in the Interwar Economy*, edited by Harold James, Håkan Lindgren, and Alice Teichova, 80–103. Cambridge: Cambridge University Press.
Laslett, H. M. 1989. "State Policy towards Labour and Labour Organizations, 1830–1939: Anglo-American Union Movements." In *The Cambridge Economic History of Europe*, vol. 8, *The Industrial Economies: The Development of Economic and Social Policies*, edited by Peter Mathias and Sidney Pollard, 495–548. Cambridge: Cambridge University Press.
Laxer, Gordon. 1989. *Open for Business: The Roots of Foreign Ownership in Canada*. Toronto: Oxford University Press.
Laycock, David. 1990. *Populism and Democratic Thought in the Canadian Prairies, 1910 to 1945*. Toronto: University of Toronto Press.
League of Nations. 1938. *Report on Exchange Control*. Geneva: League of Nations.
———. 1942. *Commercial Policy in the Interwar Period*. Geneva: League of Nations.
———. 1945. *Industrialization and Foreign Trade*. Geneva: League of Nations.
Lecours, André. 2005a. "New Institutionalism: Issues and Questions." In *New Institutionalism: Theory and Analysis*, edited by André Lecours, 3–25. Toronto: University of Toronto Press.
———, ed. 2005b. *New Institutionalism: Theory and Analysis*. Toronto: University of Toronto Press.
Lee, Bradford A. 1989. "The Miscarriage of Necessity and Invention: Proto-Keynesianism and Democratic States in the 1930s." In *The Political Power of Economic Ideas: Keynesianism across Nations*, edited by Peter A. Hall, 129–70. Princeton: Princeton University Press.

Lee, Stephen J. 1998. *The Weimar Republic*. London: Routledge.
Lenin, V. I. [1921] 1980. "The New Economic Policy and the Tasks of the Political Education Departments." In *V. I. Lenin: Collected Works*, vol. 33, *August 1921–March 1923*, translated from the Russian and edited by David Skvirsky and George Hanna, 60–79. Moscow: Progress Publishers.
Letwin, William. 1989. "American Economic Policy, 1865–1939." In *The Cambridge Economic History of Europe*, vol. 8, *The Industrial Economies: The Development of Economic and Social Policies*, edited by Peter Mathias and Sidney Pollard, 641–90. Cambridge: Cambridge University Press.
Levine, Rhonda F. 1988. *Class Struggle and the New Deal: Industrial Labor, Industrial Capital, and the State*. Lawrence: University Press of Kansas.
Lewin, Moshe. [1966] 1968. *Russian Peasants and Soviet Power: A Study of Collectivization*. Translated from the French by Irene Nove. London: George Allen and Unwin.
Lewis, W. Arthur. 1949. *Economic Survey, 1919–1939*. London: George Allen and Unwin.
Lindbeck, Assar. 1974. *Swedish Economic Policy*. Berkeley: University of California Press.
Lindgren, Håkan. 1982. "The Kreuger Crash of 1932: In Memory of a Financial Genius, or Was He a Simple Swindler?" *Scandinavian Economic History Review and Economy and History* 30, no. 3: 189–206. https://doi.org/10.1080/03585522.1982.10407986.
Lindström, Ulf. 1985. *Fascism in Scandinavia, 1920–1940*. Stockholm: Almqvist and Wiksell International.
———. 2000. "Sweden: The Durable Compromise." In *Conditions of Democracy in Europe, 1919–1939: Systematic Case Studies*, edited by Dirk Berg-Schlosser and Jeremy Mitchell, 426–48. London: Macmillan.
Lindvall, Johannes. 2012. "Politics and Policies in Two Economic Crises: The Nordic Countries." In *Coping with Crisis: Government Reactions to the Great Recession*, edited by Nancy Bermeo and Jonas Pontusson, 233–60. New York: Russell Sage Foundation.
Lipietz, Alain. [1985] 1987. *Mirages and Miracles: The Crises of Global Fordism*. Translated from the French by David Macey. London: Verso.
Lipset, Seymour M. [1950] 1968. *Agrarian Socialism: The Cooperative Commonwealth Federation in Saskatchewan*. Revised ed. Garden City: Anchor Books.
Lipton, Charles. [1967] 1973. *The Trade Union Movement of Canada, 1827–1959*. 3rd ed. Toronto: NC Press.
Louis, L. J., and Ian Turner, eds. 1968. *The Depression of the 1930s*. Melbourne: Cassell Australia.
LSR (League for Social Reconstruction). [1935] 1975. *Social Planning for Canada*. Reprint. Toronto: University of Toronto Press.

Luebbert, Gregory M. 1987. "Social Foundations of Political Order in Interwar Europe." *World Politics* 39, no. 4: 449–78. https://doi.org/10.2307/2010288.

———. 1991. *Liberalism, Fascism, or Social Democracy: Social Classes and the Political Origins of Regimes in Interwar Europe*. New York: Oxford University Press.

Lundberg, Erik. [1953] 1957. *Business Cycles and Economic Policy*. Translated from the Swedish by J. Potter. London: George Allen and Unwin.

Mackenzie, Kenneth. [1932] 1935. *The Banking Systems of Great Britain, France, Germany, and the United States of America*. 2nd ed. London: Macmillan.

Mackie, Thomas T., and Richard Rose. 1974. *The International Almanac of Electoral History*. London: Macmillan.

MacKinnon, Mary. 1990. "Relief Not Insurance: Canadian Unemployment Relief in the 1930s." *Explorations in Economic History* 27, no. 1: 46–83. https://doi.org/10.1016/0014-4983(90)90004-I.

Mackintosh, William A. [1939] 1964. *The Economic Background of Dominion-Provincial Relations*. Reprint. Toronto: McClelland and Stewart.

Mackintosh, William A., A. B. Clark, G. A. Elliott, and W. W. Swanson. 1935. *Economic Problems of the Prairie Provinces*. Toronto: Macmillan.

Macpherson, C. B. [1953] 1962. *Democracy in Alberta: Social Credit and the Party System*. 2nd ed. Toronto: University of Toronto Press.

Maier, Charles S. 1975. *Recasting Bourgeois Europe: Stabilization in France, Germany, and Italy in the Decade after World War I*. Princeton: Princeton University Press.

———. 1987. *In Search of Stability: Explorations in Historical Political Economy*. Cambridge: Cambridge University Press.

Mallory, J. R. 1954. *Social Credit and the Federal Power in Canada*. Toronto: University of Toronto Press.

Mance, Osborne. 1943. "The Future of British Trade with Turkey." *Journal of the Royal Central Asian Society* 30, no. 1: 5–18.

Marcus, Edward. 1954. *Canada and the International Business Cycle, 1927–1939*. New York: Bookman.

Marcus, Nathan. 2018. *Austrian Reconstruction and the Collapse of Global Finance, 1921–1931*. Cambridge, MA: Harvard University Press.

Marjolin, Robert. 1938. "Reflections on the Blum Experiment." *Economica*, new series 5, no. 18: 177–91. https://doi.org/10.2307/2549020.

Markey, Ray. 2008. "An Antipodean Phenomenon: Comparing the Labo(u)r Party in New Zealand and Australia." *Labour History*, no. 95: 69–95. https://doi.org/10.2307/27516310.

Martin, Andrew. 1973. *The Politics of Economic Policy in the United States: A Tentative View from a Comparative Perspective*. Beverly Hills: Sage.

———. 1975. "Is Democratic Control of Capitalist Economies Possible?" In *Stress and Contradiction in Modern Capitalism: Public Policy and the Theory of the*

State, edited by Leon N. Lindberg, Robert Alford, Colin Crouch, and Claus Offe, 13–56. Lexington: D. C. Heath.

Mavrogordatos, George Th. 1983. *Stillborn Republic: Social Coalitions and Party Strategies in Greece, 1922–1936.* Berkeley: University of California Press.

Mazower, Mark. 1988. "Economic Diplomacy between Great Britain and Greece in the 1930s." *Journal of European Economic History* 17, no. 3: 603–19.

———. 1991. *Greece and the Inter-War Economic Crisis.* Oxford: Clarendon Press.

McConnell, W. H. 1969. "The Genesis of the Canadian 'New Deal'." *Journal of Canadian Studies* 4, no. 2: 31–41. https://doi.org/10.3138/jcs.4.2.31.

McDiarmid, Orville J. 1946. *Commercial Policy in the Canadian Economy.* Cambridge, MA: Harvard University Press.

McDonald, Judith A., Anthony Patrick O'Brien, and Colleen M. Callahan. 1997. "Trade Wars: Canada's Reaction to the Smoot–Hawley Tariff." *Journal of Economic History* 57, no. 4: 802–26. https://doi.org/10.1017/S0022050700019549.

McDonough, Terrence. 1990. "The Resolution of Crisis in American Economic History: Social Structures of Accumulation and Stages of Capitalism." *Research in Political Economy* 12: 129–83.

McKibbin, Ross. 1975. "The Economic Policy of the Second Labour Government 1929–1931." *Past & Present* 68, no. 1: 95–123. https://doi.org/10.1093/past/68.1.95.

McLeod, J. A. 1933. "Problems Facing Canada." *Journal of the Canadian Bankers' Association* 40, no. 2: 159–65.

McQuaid, Kim. 1978. "Corporate Liberalism in the American Business Community, 1920–1940." *Business History Review* 52, no. 3: 342–68. https://doi.org/10.2307/3113735.

Mehta, Jal. 2011. "The Varied Roles of Ideas in Politics: From 'Whether' to 'How'." In *Ideas and Politics in Social Science Research*, edited by Daniel Béland and Robert H. Cox, 23–46. New York: Oxford University Press.

Melin, Hilding. 1929. "The Banking System of Sweden." In *Foreign Banking Systems*, edited by H. Parker Willis and Benjamin H. Beckhart, 1011–74. New York: Henry Holt.

Middleton, Roger. 1985. *Towards the Managed Economy: Keynes, the Treasury and the Fiscal Policy Debate of the 1930s.* London: Methuen.

———. 1998. *Charlatans or Saviours? Economists and the British Economy from Marshall to Meade.* Cheltenham: Edward Elgar.

———. 2013. "Can Contractionary Fiscal Policy Be Expansionary? Consolidation, Sustainability, and Fiscal Policy Impact in Britain in the 1930s." In *The Great Depression of the 1930s: Lessons for Today*, edited by Nicholas Crafts and Peter Fearon, 212–57. Oxford: Oxford University Press.

Miller, James W. 2003. "Engelbert Dollfuss and Austrian Agriculture." In *The Dollfuss/Schuschnigg Era in Austria: A Reassessment*, edited by Günter Bischof,

Anton Pelinka, and Alexander Lassner, 122–42. London and New York: Routledge.
Millmow, Alex. 2010. *The Power of Economic Ideas: The Origins of Keynesian Macroeconomic Management in Interwar Australia, 1929–39*. Canberra: ANU E Press.
Milward, Alan S. 1976. "Fascism and the Economy." In *Fascism, a Reader's Guide: Analyses, Interpretations, Bibliography*, edited by Walter Z. Laqueur, 379–412. Berkeley: University of California Press.
Mishkova, Diana. 2014. "Balkan Liberalisms: Historical Routes of a Modern Ideology." In *Entangled Histories of the Balkans*, vol. 2, *Transfers of Political Ideologies and Institutions*, edited by Roumen Daskalov and Diana Mishkova, 99–198. Leiden and Boston: Brill.
Mitchell, B. R. 1962. *Abstract of British Historical Statistics*. Cambridge: At the University Press.
Mitrany, David. 1951. *Marx against the Peasant: A Study in Social Dogmatism*. Chapel Hill: University of North Carolina Press.
———. [1930] 1968. *The Land and the Peasant in Rumania: The War and Agrarian Reform (1917–21)*. Reprint. New York: Greenwood Press.
Moggridge, Donald E. 1989. "The Gold Standard and National Financial Policies, 1919–39." In *The Cambridge Economic History of Europe*, vol. 8, *The Industrial Economies: The Development of Economic and Social Policies*, edited by Peter Mathias and Sidney Pollard, 250–314. Cambridge: Cambridge University Press.
Montgomery, G. Arthur. 1938. *How Sweden Overcame the Depression, 1930–1933*. Translated from the Swedish by Leonard B. Eyre. Stockholm: Alb. Bonniers Boktryckeri.
———. 1939. *The Rise of Modern Industry in Sweden*. London: P. S. King.
Morell, Mats. 2010. "Trade Crisis and Regulation of the Farm Sector: Sweden in the Interwar Years." In *Managing Crises and De-globalisation: Nordic Foreign Trade and Exchange, 1919–39*, edited by Sven-Olof Olsson, 137–57. London: Routledge.
Morgan, Philip. 1995. *Italian Fascism, 1915–1945*. Basingstoke: Macmillan.
Morton, W. L. 1950. *The Progressive Party in Canada*. Toronto: University of Toronto Press.
Moses, John A. 1986. "The German Free Trade Unions and the Problem of Mass Unemployment in the Weimar Republic." In *Unemployment and the Great Depression in Weimar Germany*, edited by Peter D. Stachura, 148–62. Basingstoke: Macmillan.
Mouzelis, Nicos. 1976. "Greek and Bulgarian Peasants: Aspects of Their Sociopolitical Situation during the Interwar Period." *Comparative Studies in Society and History* 18, no. 1: 85–105. https://doi.org/10.1017/S0010417500008094.

———. 1986. *Politics in the Semi-Periphery: Early Parliamentarism and Late Industrialisation in the Balkans and Latin America.* London: Macmillan.

Murphy, John. 2010. "Path Dependence and the Stagnation of Australian Social Policy Between the Wars." *Journal of Policy History* 22, no. 4: 450–73. https://doi.org/10.1017/S0898030610000229.

Möller, Gustav. 1938. "The Unemployment Policy." *Annals of the American Academy of Political and Social Science* 197, no. 1: 47–71. https://doi.org/10.1177/000271623819700107.

Nanto, Dick K., and Shinji Takagi. 1985. "Korekiyo Takahashi and Japan's Recovery from the Great Depression." *American Economic Review* 75, no. 2: 369–74.

Naylor, James. 2006. "Canadian Labour Politics and the British Model, 1920–50." In *Canada and the British World: Culture, Migration, and Identity*, edited by Phillip Buckner and R. Douglas Francis, 288–308. Vancouver: UBC Press.

———. 2016. *The Fate of Labour Socialism: The Co-operative Commonwealth Federation and the Dream of a Working-Class Future.* Toronto: University of Toronto Press.

Naylor, R. Tom. 1972. "The Ideological Foundations of Social Democracy and Social Credit." In *Capitalism and the National Question in Canada*, edited by Gary Teeple, 251–6. Toronto: University of Toronto Press.

NEC (National Employment Commission). 1938. *Final Report.* Ottawa: J. O. Patenaude.

Nenovsky, Nikolay. 2015. "The Soviets Monetary Experience (1917–1924) through the Perspective of the Discussion on Unity and Diversity of Money." MPRA Paper No. 79864. https://mpra.ub.uni-muenchen.de/79864/3/MPRA_paper_79864.pdf (accessed 30 June 2021).

Neufeld, E. P. 1972. *The Financial System of Canada: Its Growth and Development.* New York: St. Marin's.

Nevers, Jeppe. 2013. "The Rise of Danish Agrarian Liberalism." *Contributions to the History of Concepts* 8, no. 2: 96–105. https://doi.org/10.3167/choc.2013.080206.

Noble, S. R. 1938. "The Monetary Experience of Canada during the Depression." *Canadian Banker* 45, no. 3: 269–77.

Nove, Alec. [1969] 1992. *An Economic History of the USSR 1917–1991.* 3rd ed. London: Penguin.

O'Brien, Anthony P., and Judith A. McDonald. 2009. "Retreat from Protectionism: R. B. Bennett and the Movement to Freer Trade in Canada, 1930–1935." *Journal of Policy History* 21, no. 4: 331–65. https://doi.org/10.1017/S0898030609990121.

Olsen, Gregg M. 1991. "Labour Mobilization and the Strength of Capital: The Rise and Stall of Economic Democracy in Sweden." *Studies in Political Economy*, no. 34: 109–45. https://doi.org/10.1080/19187033.1991.11675462.

---. 1992. *The Struggle for Economic Democracy in Sweden*. Aldershot: Avebury.
Olsson, Carl-Axel. 1968. "Swedish Agriculture during the Interwar Years." *Economy and History* 11, no. 1: 67–107. https://doi.org/10.1080/0070885 2.1968.10418874.
Olsson, Sven-Olof. 2010. "Nordic Trade Cooperation in the 1930s." In *Managing Crises and De-globalisation: Nordic Foreign Trade and Exchange, 1919–39*, edited by Sven-Olof Olsson, 17–33. London: Routledge.
Olsson, Ulf. 1991. "Comparing the Interwar Banking History of Five Small Countries in North-West Europe." In *The Role of Banks in the Interwar Economy*, edited by Harold James, Håkan Lindgren, and Alice Teichova, 26–34. Cambridge: Cambridge University Press.
Overacker, Louise. 1952. *The Australian Party System*. New Haven: Yale University Press.
Overy, R. J. 1975. "Cars, Roads, and Economic Recovery in Germany, 1932–8." *Economic History Review*, 2nd series 28, no. 3: 466–83. https://doi.org/10.2307/2593594.
---. 1982. *The Nazi Economic Recovery, 1932–1938*. London: Macmillan.
Ovesen, Thorkild. 1958. "Swedish Agricultural Policy and Agricultural Production from 1930 to 1940." *Economy and History* 1, no. 1: 43–64. https://doi.org/10.1080/00708852.1958.10418864.
Owen, Roger, and Şevket Pamuk. 1999. *A History of Middle East Economies in the Twentieth Century*. Cambridge, MA: Harvard University Press.
Oye, Kenneth A. 1992. *Economic Discrimination and Political Exchange: World Political Economy in the 1930s and 1980s*. Princeton: Princeton University Press.
Ökçün, A. Gündüz. 1975. "1909–1930 Yılları Arasında Anonim Şirket Olarak Kurulan Bankalar." In *Türkiye İktisat Tarihi Semineri: Metinler/Tartışmalar (8–10 Haziran 1973)*, edited by Osman Okyar and H. Ünal Nalbantoğlu, 409–75. Ankara: Hacettepe Üniversitesi Yayınları.
Önder, İzzettin. 1988. "Cumhuriyet Döneminde Tarım Kesimine Uygulanan Vergi Politikası." In *Türkiye'de Tarımsal Yapılar (1923–2000)*, edited by Şevket Pamuk and Zafer Toprak, 113–33. Ankara: Yurt Yayınları.
Özbudun, Ergun. 1981. "The Nature of the Kemalist Political Regime." In *Atatürk: Founder of a Modern State*, edited by Ali Kazancıgil and Ergun Özbudun, 79–102. London: C. P. Hurst.
Pal, Leslie A. 1986. "Relative Autonomy Revisited: The Origins of Canadian Unemployment Insurance." *Canadian Journal of Political Science* 19, no. 1: 71–92. https://doi.org/10.1017/S000842390005798X.
Pamuk, Şevket. 2000. "Intervention during the Great Depression: Another Look at Turkish Experience." In *The Mediterranean Response to Globalization before 1950*, edited by Şevket Pamuk and Jeffrey G. Williamson, 321–39. London: Routledge.

———. 2014. *Türkiye'nin 200 Yıllık İktisadi Tarihi: Büyüme, Kurumlar ve Bölüşüm*. İstanbul: Türkiye İş Bankası Kültür Yayınları.

Paris Peace Conference. 1919. "Treaty of Peace with Germany (Treaty of Versailles)." June 28, 1919. https://www.census.gov/history/pdf/treaty_of_versailles-112018.pdf (accessed 6 March 2022).

Parla, Taha. 1985. *The Social and Political Thought of Ziya Gökalp, 1876–1924*. Leiden: E. J. Brill.

Parla, Taha, and Andrew Davison. 2004. *Corporatist Ideology in Kemalist Turkey: Progress or Order?* Syracuse: Syracuse University Press.

Penchev, Pencho D., and M. Erdem Özgür. 2019. "The Role of the State in the Economic Policy and Thought of Bulgaria and Turkey during the Interwar Period." *History of Economic Thought and Policy*, no. 1: 51–66. https://doi.org/10.3280/SPE2019-001004.

Pentland, H. Clare. 1979. "Western Canadian Labour Movement, 1897–1919." *Canadian Journal of Political and Social Theory* 3, no. 2: 53–78.

Perry, Harvey J. 1955. *Taxes, Tariffs, and Subsidies: A History of Canadian Fiscal Development*, vol. 1. Toronto: University of Toronto Press.

Pierson, Paul. 2000. "Increasing Returns, Path Dependence, and the Study of Politics." *American Political Science Review* 94, no. 2: 251–67. https://doi.org/10.2307/2586011.

Pierson, Paul, and Theda Skocpol. 2002. "Historical Institutionalism in Contemporary Political Science." In *Political Science: The State of the Discipline*, edited by Ira Katznelson and Helen V. Milner, 693–721. New York: W. W. Norton.

Ploumidis, Spyridon. 2012. "Agrarian Politics in Interwar Greece: The Stillborn 'Peasant' Parties (1923–1936)." *Studia Universitatis Cibiniensis. Series Historica*, no. 9: 57–87.

Plumptre, A. F. W. 1938. "The Arguments for Central Banking in the British Dominions." In *Essays in Political Economy: In Honour of E. J. Urwick*, edited by Harold A. Innis, 191–203. Toronto: University of Toronto Press.

———. 1940. *Central Banking in the British Dominions*. Toronto: University of Toronto Press.

Polanyi, Karl. 1944. *The Great Transformation: The Political and Economic Origins of Our Time*. Boston: Beacon.

Pollard, John. 1998. *The Fascist Experience in Italy*. London and New York: Routledge.

Pollard, Sidney, and Colin Holmes, eds. 1973. *Documents of European Economic History*, vol. 3, *The End of the Old Europe, 1914–1939*. London: Edward Arnold.

Polonsky, Antony. 1975. *The Little Dictators: The History of Eastern Europe since 1918*. London: Routledge and Kegan Paul.

Pomfret, Richard. 1981. *The Economic Development of Canada*. Toronto: Methuen.

Priester, Karin. 2013. "Fascism in Italy between the Poles of Reactionary Thought and Modernity." In *Routes into the Abyss: Coping with Crises in the 1930s*, edited by Helmut Konrad and Wolfgang Maderthaner, 55–77. New York and Oxford: Berghahn Books.

Quigley, Neil C. 1992. "Monetary Policy and the New Zealand System: An Historical Perspective." Reserve Bank of New Zealand Discussion Paper No. G92/1, Wellington. https://silo.tips/download/monetary-policy-and-the-an-historical-perspective (accessed 14 June 2021).

Quittner, Paul. 1929. "The Banking System of Germany." In *Foreign Banking Systems*, edited by H. Parker Willis and Benjamin H. Beckhart, 627–722. New York: Henry Holt.

Ránki, György. 1983. *Economy and Foreign Policy: The Struggle of the Great Powers for Hegemony in the Danube Valley, 1919–1939*. New York: Columbia University Press.

———. 1985. "Problems of Southern European Economic Development (1918–38)." In *Semiperipheral Development: The Politics of Southern Europe in the Twentieth Century*, edited by Giovanni Arrighi, 55–85. Beverly Hills: Sage.

Ránki, György, and Jerzy Tomaszewski. 1986. "The Role of the State in Industry, Banking and Trade." In *The Economic History of Eastern Europe, 1919–1975*, vol. 2, *Interwar Policy, the War and Reconstruction*, edited by Michael C. Kaser and E. A. Radice, 3–48. Oxford: Clarendon.

RBNZ (Reserve Bank of New Zealand). 2007. *The Reserve Bank and New Zealand's Economic History*. https://www.rbnz.govt.nz/research-and-publications/fact-sheets-and-guides/factsheet-the-reserve-bank-and-nzs-economic-history (accessed 14 June 2021).

RCBCC (Royal Commission on Banking and Currency in Canada). 1933. *Report*. Ottawa: J. O. Patenaude.

RCDPR (Royal Commission on Dominion–Provincial Relations). 1940a. *Report*, book 1, *Canada: 1867–1939*. Ottawa: Queen's Printer.

———. 1940b. *Report*, book 2, *Recommendations*. Ottawa: Queen's Printer.

Reich, Simon. 1990. *The Fruits of Fascism: Postwar Prosperity in Historical Perspective*. Ithaca: Cornell University Press.

Ricossa, Sergio. 1976. "Italy, 1920–1970." In *The Fontana Economic History of Europe*, vol. 6, *Contemporary Economies*, part 2, edited by Carlo M. Cipolla, 266–322. Glasgow: Fontana.

RIIA (Royal Institute of International Affairs). 1951. *The Scandinavian States and Finland: A Political and Economic Survey*. London: RIIA.

Rimlinger, G. V. 1989. "Labour and the State on the Continent, 1800–1939." *The Cambridge Economic History of Europe*, vol. 8, *The Industrial Economies: The Development of Economic and Social Policies*, edited by Peter Mathias and Sidney Pollard, 549–606. Cambridge: Cambridge University Press.

Ritschel, Daniel. 1997. *The Politics of Planning: The Debate on Economic Planning in Britain in the 1930s*. Oxford: Clarendon Press.

Ritschl, Albrecht O. 2013. "Reparations, Deficits, and Debt Default: The Great Depression in Germany." In *The Great Depression of the 1930s: Lessons for Today*, edited by Nicholas Crafts and Peter Fearon, 110–39. Oxford: Oxford University Press.

Robbins, Lionel. 1934. *The Great Depression*. London: Macmillan.

———. 1971. *Autobiography of an Economist*. London: Macmillan.

Robertson, David. B. 1993. "The Return to History and the New Institutionalism in American Political Science." *Social Science History* 17, no. 1: 1–36. https://doi.org/10.1017/S0145553200016734.

Rokkan, Stein. 1966. "Norway: Numerical Democracy and Corporate Pluralism." In *Political Oppositions in Western Democracies*, edited by Robert A. Dahl, 70–115. New Haven: Yale University Press.

———. 1981. "The Growth and Structuring of Mass Politics." In *Nordic Democracy: Ideas, Issues, and Institutions in Politics, Economy, Education, Social and Cultural Affairs of Denmark, Finland, Iceland, Norway, and Sweden*, edited by Erik Allardt, N. Andrén, E. J. Friis, G. P. Gíslason, S. S. Nilson, H. Valen, F. Wendt, and F. Wisti, 53–79. Copenhagen: Det Danske Selskab.

Rooth, T. J. T. 1986. "Tariffs and Trade Bargaining: Anglo–Scandinavian Economic Relations in the 1930s." *Scandinavian Economic History Review and Economy and History* 34, no. 1: 54–71. https://doi.org/10.1080/03585522.1986.10408059.

Rosanvallon, Pierre. 1989. "The Development of Keynesianism in France." In *The Political Power of Economic Ideas: Keynesianism across Nations*, edited by Peter A. Hall, 171–93. Princeton: Princeton University Press.

Ross, Duncan M., and Dieter Ziegler. 2000. "Problems of Industrial Finance between the Wars." In *After the Slump: Industry and Politics in 1930s Britain and Germany*, edited by C. Buchheim and W. Redvers Garside, 161–77. Frankfurt am Main: Peter Lang.

Rothschild, K. W. 1947. *Austria's Economic Development between the Two Wars*. London: Frederick Muller.

Rothstein, Bo. 1990. "Marxism, Institutional Analysis, and Working-Class Power: The Swedish Case." *Politics and Society* 18, no. 3: 317–45. https://doi.org/10.1177/003232929001800302.

———. 1992. "Explaining Swedish Corporatism: The Formative Moment." *Scandinavian Political Studies* 15, no. 3: 173–91. https://doi.org/10.1111/j.1467-9477.1992.tb00139.x.

Rozaliyev, Y. N. [1962] 1978. *Türkiye'de Kapitalizmin Gelişme Özellikleri (1923–1960)*. Translated from the Russian by Azer Yaran. Ankara: Onur Yayınları.

Rueschemeyer, Dietrich, Evelyne H. Stephens, and John D. Stephens, 1992. *Capitalist Development and Democracy*. Chicago: University of Chicago Press.

Rustow, Dankwart A. 1955. *The Politics of Compromise: A Study of Parties and Cabinet Government in Sweden*. Princeton: Princeton University Press.

Ruth, Arne. 1984. "The Second New Nation: The Mythology of Modern Sweden." *Daedalus* 113, no. 2: 53–96.

Rydon, Joan. 1979. "The Conservative Electoral Ascendancy Between the Wars." In *Australian Conservatism: Essays in Twentieth Century Political History*, edited by Cameron Hazlehurst, 51–70. Canberra: Australian National University Press.

Safarian, A. E. [1959] 2009. *The Canadian Economy in the Great Depression*. 3rd ed. Montreal and Kingston: McGill-Queen's University Press.

Saint-Etienne, Christian. 1984. *The Great Depression, 1929–1938: Lessons for the 1980s*. Stanford: Hoover Institution.

Salais, Robert. 1988. "Why Was Unemployment So Low in France during the 1930s?" In *Interwar Unemployment in International Perspective*, edited by Barry J. Eichengreen and Tim J. Hatton, 247–88. Dordrecht: Kluwer.

Sallius, Per-Ove. 1961. "Swedish–American Treaty Policy, 1920–1935." *Economy and History* 4, no. 1: 65–89. https://doi.org/10.1080/00708852.1961.10418983.

Salmon, Patrick. 2003. "Paternalism or Partnership? Finance and Trade in Anglo-Danish Relations in the 1930s." In *Britain and Denmark: Political, Economic and Cultural Relations in the 19th and 20th Centuries*, edited by Jørgen Sevaldsen, Bo Bjørke, and Claus Bjørn, 231–49. Copenhagen: Museum Tusculanum Press.

Samuelsson, Kurt. 1958. "The Banks and the Financing of Industry in Sweden, c. 1900–1927." *Scandinavian Economic History Review* 6, no. 2: 176–90. https://doi.org/10.1080/03585522.1958.10411403.

Schacht, Hjalmar H. G. 1956. *Confessions of "The Old Wizard": The Autobiography of Hjalmar Horace Greeley Schacht*. Translated from the German by Diana Pyke. Boston: Houghton Mifflin.

Schedvin, C. B. 1970. *Australia and the Great Depression: A Study of Economic Development and Policy in the 1920s and 1930s*. Sydney: Sydney University Press.

Schmidt, Vivien A. 2008. "Discursive Institutionalism: The Explanatory Power of Ideas and Discourse." *Annual Review of Political Science* 11: 303–26. https://doi.org/10.1146/annurev.polisci.11.060606.135342.

———. 2010. "Taking Ideas and Discourse Seriously: Explaining Change through Discursive Institutionalism as the Fourth 'New Institutionalism'." *European Political Science Review* 2, no. 1: 1–25. https://doi.org/10.1017/S175577390999021X.

———. 2011. "Reconciling Ideas and Institutions through Discursive Institutionalism." In *Ideas and Politics in Social Science Research*, edited by Daniel Béland and Robert H. Cox, 47–64. New York: Oxford University Press.

Schüllerqvist, Bengt. 2013. "The Crisis in the 1930s and the Rise to Power of the Swedish Social Democrats." In *Routes into the Abyss: Coping with Crises in the 1930s*, edited by Helmut Konrad and Wolfgang Maderthaner, 102–14. New York and Oxford: Berghahn Books.

Schwartz, Herman M. 1989. *In the Dominions of Debt: Historical Perspectives on Dependent Development*. Ithaca: Cornell University Press.

Schwarz, L. D. 1993. "Searching for Recovery: Unbalanced Budgets, Deflation and Rearmament in France during the 1930s." In *Capitalism in Crisis: International Responses to the Great Depression*, edited by W. Redvers Garside, 96–113. London: Pinter.

Scott, Frank R. 1937. "The Privy Council and Mr. Bennett's 'New Deal' Legislation." *Canadian Journal of Economics and Political Science* 3, no. 2: 234–41. https://doi.org/10.2307/136802.

Scott, Franklin D. 1977. *Sweden: The Nation's History*. Minneapolis: University of Minnesota Press.

Seferiades, Seraphim. 1999. "Small Rural Ownership, Subsistence Agriculture, and Peasant Protest in Interwar Greece: The Agrarian Question Recast." *Journal of Modern Greek Studies* 17, no. 2: 277–323. https://doi.org/10.1353/mgs.1999.0034.

Senft, Gerhard. 2003. "Economic Development and Economic Policies in the *Ständestaat* Era." In *The Dollfuss/Schuschnigg Era in Austria: A Reassessment*, edited by Günter Bischof, Anton Pelinka, and Alexander Lassner, 32–55. London and New York: Routledge.

Shonfield, Andrew. [1965] 1969. *Modern Capitalism: The Changing Balance of Public and Private Power*. 2nd ed. London: Oxford University Press.

Silier, Oya. 1975. "1920'lerde Türkiye'de Milli Bankacılığın Genel Görünümü." In *Türkiye İktisat Tarihi Semineri: Metinler/Tartışmalar (8–10 Haziran 1973)*, edited by Osman Okyar and H. Ünal Nalbantoğlu, 485–533. Ankara: Hacettepe Üniversitesi Yayınları.

———. 1981. *Türkiye'de Tarımsal Yapının Gelişimi (1923–1938)*. İstanbul: Boğaziçi Üniversitesi Yayınları.

Silverman, Dan P. 1988. "National Socialist Economics: The *Wirtschaftswunder* Reconsidered." In *Interwar Unemployment in International Perspective*, edited by Barry J. Eichengreen and Tim J. Hatton, 185–220. Dordrecht: Kluwer.

Simeon, Richard, and Ian Robinson. 1990. *State, Society, and the Development of Canadian Federalism*. Toronto: University of Toronto Press.

Simpson, Tony. 1990. *The Slump; The 1930s Depression: Its Origins and Aftermath*. Auckland: Penguin Books.

Sinclair, Keith. 1976. *Walter Nash*. Auckland: Auckland University Press.

Sinclair, Peter. 1975. "Class Structure and Populist Protest: The Case of Western Canada." *Canadian Journal of Sociology* 1, no. 1: 1–17. https://doi.org/10.2307/3340007.

Singleton, Fred, and Bernard Carter. 1982. *The Economy of Yugoslavia*. London: Croom Helm.

Singleton, John. 2003. "New Zealand in the Depression: Devaluation without a Balance of Payments Crisis." In *The World Economy and National Economies in*

the Interwar Slump, edited by Theo Balderston, 172–90. Basingstoke: Palgrave Macmillan.
Skelton, Oscar D. 1922. *Life and Letters of Sir Wilfrid Laurier*, vol. 1. New York: Century Co.
Skidelsky, Robert J. A. 1967. *Politicians and the Slump: The Labour Government of 1929–1931*. London: Macmillan.
Skocpol, Theda. 1980. "Political Response to Capitalist Crisis: Neo-Marxist Theories of the State and the Case of the New Deal." *Politics and Society* 10, no. 2: 155–201. https://doi.org/10.1177/003232928001000202.
Skocpol, Theda, and Kenneth Finegold. 1982. "State Capacity and Economic Intervention in the Early New Deal." *Political Science Quarterly* 97, no. 2: 255–78. https://doi.org/10.2307/2149478.
Skogstad, Grace, ed. 2011. *Policy Paradigms, Transnationalism, and Domestic Politics*. Toronto: University of Toronto Press.
Skowronek, Stephen. 1982. *Building a New American State: The Expansion of National Administrative Capacities, 1877–1920*. Cambridge: Cambridge University Press.
Slichter, Gertrude A. 1956. "Franklin D. Roosevelt and the Farm Problem, 1929–1932." *Mississippi Valley Historical Review* 43, no. 2: 238–58. https://doi.org/10.2307/1902685.
Smith, Malcolm. 1998. *Democracy in a Depression: Britain in the 1920s and 1930s*. Cardiff: University of Wales Press.
Sobel, Andrew C. 1994. *Domestic Choices, International Markets: Dismantling National Barriers and Liberalizing Securities Markets*. Ann Arbour: University of Michigan Press.
Soifer, Hillel D. 2012. "The Causal Logic of Critical Junctures." *Comparative Political Studies* 45, no. 12: 1572–97. https://doi.org/10.1177/0010414012463902.
Solomou, Solomos. 1996. *Themes in Macroeconomic History: The UK Economy, 1919–1939*. Cambridge: Cambridge University Press.
Spulber, Nicolas. 1959. "The Role of the State in Economic Growth in Eastern Europe since 1860." In *The State and Economic Growth*, edited by Hugh G. J. Aitken, 255–86. New York: Social Science Research Council.
Stacey, C. P., ed. 1972. *Historical Documents of Canada*, vol. 5, *The Arts of War and Peace, 1914–1945*. Toronto: Macmillan.
Stalin, J. V. [1924] 1953. "The October Revolution and the Tactics of the Russian Communists?" In *J. V. Stalin: Works*, vol. 6, *1924*, translated from the Russian, 374–420. Moscow: Foreign Languages Publishing House.
——. [1929] 1954a. "Concerning Questions of Agrarian Policy in the U.S.S.R." In *J. V. Stalin: Works*, vol. 12, *April 1929–June 1930*, translated from the Russian, 147–78. Moscow: Foreign Languages Publishing House.

———. [1931] 1954b. "The Tasks of Business Executives." In *J. V. Stalin: Works*, vol. 13, *July 1930–January 1934*, translated from the Russian, 31–44. Moscow: Foreign Languages Publishing House.

Stein, Herbert. [1969] 1990. *The Fiscal Revolution in America*. 2nd ed. Washington, D.C.: American Enterprise Institute.

Steinmo, Sven. 1988. "Social Democracy vs. Socialism: Goal Adaptation in Social Democratic Sweden." *Politics and Society* 16, no. 4: 403–46. https://doi.org/10.1177/003232928801600401.

———. 1993. *Taxation and Democracy: Swedish, British and American Approaches to Financing the Modern State*. New Haven: Yale University Press.

———. 2008. "Historical Institutionalism." In *Approaches and Methodologies in the Social Sciences: A Pluralist Perspective*, edited by Donatella della Porta and Michael Keating, 118–38. New York: Cambridge University Press.

Steinmo, Sven, Kathleen Thelen, and Frank Longstreth, eds. 1992. *Structuring Politics: Historical Institutionalism in Comparative Perspective*. Cambridge: Cambridge University Press.

Stephens, John D. 1979. *The Transition from Capitalism to Socialism*. London: Macmillan.

———. 1989. "Democratic Transition and Breakdown in Western Europe, 1870–1939: A Test of the Moore Thesis." *American Journal of Sociology* 94, no. 5: 1019–77. https://doi.org/10.1086/229111.

Stjernquist, Nils. 1966. "Sweden: Stability or Deadlock?" In *Political Oppositions in Western Democracies*, edited by Robert A. Dahl, 116–46. New Haven: Yale University Press.

———. 1987. "From Bicameralism to Unicameralism: The Democratic Riksdag, 1921–1986." In *The Riksdag: A History of the Swedish Parliament*, edited by Michael F. Metcalf, 223–303. New York: St. Martin's.

Straumann, Tobias. 2010. *Fixed Ideas of Money: Small States and Exchange Rate Regimes in Twentieth-Century Europe*. New York: Cambridge University Press.

Streeten, Paul. 1993. "The Special Problems of Small Countries." *World Development* 21, no. 2: 197–202.

Struthers, James. 1983. *No Fault of Their Own: Unemployment and the Canadian Welfare State, 1914–1941*. Toronto: University of Toronto Press.

Stryker, Robin. 1990. "A Tale of Two Agencies: Class, Political-Institutional, and Organizational Factors Affecting State Reliance on Social Science." *Politics and Society* 18, no. 1: 101–41. https://doi.org/10.1177/003232929001800105.

Swenson, Harold. 1929. "The Banking System of Norway." In *Foreign Banking Systems*, edited by H. Parker Willis and Benjamin H. Beckhart, 869–92. New York: Henry Holt.

Swenson, Peter A. 1989. *Fair Shares: Unions, Pay, and Politics in Sweden and West Germany*. Ithaca: Cornell University Press.

———. 1991. "Bringing Capital Back In, or Social Democracy Reconsidered: Employer Power, Cross-Class Alliances, and Centralization of Industrial Relations in Denmark and Sweden." *World Politics* 43, no. 4: 513–44. https://doi.org/10.2307/2010535.

———. 2002. *Capitalists against Markets: The Making of Labor Markets and Welfare States in the United States and Sweden.* New York: Oxford University Press.

Söderpalm, Sven A. [1973] 1975. "The Crisis Agreement and the Social Democratic Road to Power." In *Sweden's Development from Poverty to Affluence, 1750–1970*, edited by Steven Koblik and translated from the Swedish by Joanne Johnson, 258–78. Minneapolis: University of Minnesota Press.

Tanner, Duncan. 2003. "The Politics of the Labour Movement, 1900–1939." In *A Companion to Early Twentieth-Century Britain*, edited by Chris Wrigley, 38–55. Oxford: Blackwell Publishing.

Tcherkinsky, M. Morduch. 1939. *The Land Tenure Systems in Europe.* Geneva: League of Nations.

Tedlow, Richard S. 1976. "The National Association of Manufacturers and Public Relations during the New Deal." *Business History Review* 50, no. 1: 25–45. https://doi.org/10.2307/3113573.

Teeple, Gary. 1972. "'Liberals in a Hurry': Socialism and the CCF-NDP." In *Capitalism and the National Question in Canada*, edited by Gary Teeple, 229–50. Toronto: University of Toronto Press.

Teichova, Alice. 1989. "East-Central and South-East Europe, 1919–39." In *The Cambridge Economic History of Europe*, vol. 8, *The Industrial Economies: The Development of Economic and Social Policies*, edited by Peter Mathias and Sidney Pollard, 887–983. Cambridge: Cambridge University Press.

Tekeli, İlhan, and Selim İlkin. 1977. *1929 Dünya Buhranında Türkiye'nin İktisadi Politika Arayışları.* Ankara: ODTÜ Yayınları.

———. 1981. *Para ve Kredi Sisteminin Oluşumunda Bir Aşama: Türkiye Cumhuriyet Merkez Bankası.* Ankara: T.C. Merkez Bankası Yayını.

———. 1982. *Uygulamaya Geçerken Türkiye'de Devletçiliğin Oluşumu.* Ankara: ODTÜ Yayınları.

Temin, Peter. 1989. *Lessons from the Great Depression: The Lionel Robbins Lectures for 1989.* Cambridge, MA: MIT Press.

———. 1991. "Soviet and Nazi Economic Planning in the 1930s." *Economic History Review* 44, no. 4: 573–93. https://doi.org/10.1111/j.1468-0289.1991.tb01281.x.

Temin, Peter, and David Vines. 2013. *The Leaderless Economy: Why the World Economic System Fell Apart and How to Fix It.* Princeton: Princeton University Press.

Tezel, Yahya S. [1982] 1986. *Cumhuriyet Döneminin İktisadi Tarihi (1923–1950).* 2nd ed. Ankara: Yurt Yayınları.

Thelen, Kathleen A. 1991. *Union of Parts: Labor Politics in Postwar Germany.* Ithaca: Cornell University Press.
———. 1999. "Historical Institutionalism in Comparative Politics." *Annual Review of Political Science* 2: 369–404. https://doi.org/10.1146/annurev.polisci.2.1.369.
Therborn, Göran. 1977. "The Rule of Capital and the Rise of Democracy." *New Left Review*, first series, no. 103: 3–41.
Thomas, Brinley. 1936. *Monetary Policy and Crises: A Study of Swedish Experience.* London: George Routledge.
Thornburg, Max W., Graham Spry, and George Soule. 1949. *Turkey: An Economic Appraisal.* New York: Twentieth Century Fund.
Thorpe, Julie. 2011. *Pan-Germanism and the Austrofascist State, 1933–38.* Manchester and New York: Manchester University Press.
Tilton, Timothy A. 1979. "A Swedish Road to Socialism: Ernst Wigforss and the Ideological Foundations of Swedish Social Democracy." *American Political Science Review* 73, no. 2: 505–20. https://doi.org/10.2307/1954894.
———. 1991. *The Political Theory of Swedish Social Democracy: Through the Welfare State to Socialism.* Oxford: Clarendon.
Tingsten, Herbert L. G. [1941] 1973. *The Swedish Social Democrats: Their Ideological Development*, translated from the Swedish by Greta Frankel and Patricia Howard-Rosen. Totowa: Bedminster.
Tomasson, Richard F. 1969. "The Extraordinary Success of the Swedish Social Democrats." *Journal of Politics* 31, no. 3: 772–98. https://doi.org/10.2307/2128497.
Toniolo, Gianni, and Francesco Piva. 1988. "Unemployment in the 1930s: The Case of Italy." In *Interwar Unemployment in International Perspective*, edited by Barry J. Eichengreen and Tim J. Hatton, 221–45. Dordrecht: Kluwer.
Topp, Niels-Henrik. 1988. "Fiscal Policy in Denmark 1930–1945." *European Economic Review* 32, nos. 2–3: 512–8.
———. 2008. "Unemployment and Economic Policy in Denmark in the 1930s." *Scandinavian Economic History Review* 56, no. 1: 71–90. https://doi.org/10.1080/03585520801948534.
Toprak, Zafer. 1982. *Türkiye'de "Milli İktisat" (1908–1918).* Ankara: Yurt Yayınları.
Tracy, Michael. 1972. "Agriculture in the Great Depression: World Market Developments and European Protectionism." In *The Great Depression Revisited: Essays on the Economics of the Thirties*, edited by Herman van der Wee, 91–119. The Hague: Martinus Nijhoff.
Trampusch, Christine, and Dennis C. Spies. 2014. "Agricultural Interests and the Origins of Capitalism: A Parallel Comparative History of Germany, Denmark, New Zealand, and the USA." *New Political Economy* 19, no. 6: 918–42. https://doi.org/10.1080/13563467.2013.861414.

Tucker, Robert C. 1990. *Stalin in Power: The Revolution from Above, 1928–1941*. New York: W. W. Norton.
Tunçay, Mete. [1981] 1989. *T.C.'nde Tek-Parti Yönetimi'nin Kurulması (1923–1931)*. 2nd ed. İstanbul: Cem Yayınevi.
Turnock, David. 1986. *The Romanian Economy in the Twentieth Century*. London: Croom Helm.
Türegün, Adnan. 1994. "Small-State Responses to the Great Depression, 1929–39: The White Dominions, Scandinavia, and the Balkans." Unpublished PhD Thesis, Carleton University. https://curve.carleton.ca/389cf024-c165-4063-8b5a-4ff838e97529 (accessed 17 December 2021).
———. 2016. "Policy Response to the Great Depression of the 1930s: Turkish Neomercantilism in the Balkan Context." *Turkish Studies* 17, no. 4: 666–90. https://doi.org/10.1080/14683849.2016.1227684.
———. 2017. "Revisiting Sweden's Response to the Great Depression of the 1930s." *Scandinavian Economic History Review* 65, no. 2: 127–48. https://doi.org/10.1080/03585522.2017.1286258.
Türkeş, Mustafa. 2001. "A Patriotic Leftist Development-Strategy Proposal in Turkey in the 1930s: The Case of the Kadro (Cadre) Movement." *International Journal of Middle East Studies* 33, no. 1: 91–114.
Tyler, Ken. 1996. "Systems Thinking and Ecosystemic Psychology." *Educational Psychology* 16, no. 1: 21–34. https://doi.org/10.1080/0144341960160102.
UK House of Commons. 1929. "Debates, 15 April 1929." *Hansard*, Series 5, Volume 227: cc53–6. http://hansard.millbanksystems.com/commons/1929/apr/15/disposal-of-surplus (accessed 25 April 2021).
Underhill, Frank H. 1935. "The Development of National Political Parties in Canada." *Canadian Historical Review* 16, no. 4: 367–87. https://doi.org/10.3138/CHR-16-04-01.
Urquhart, M. C., and Kenneth A. H. Buckley. 1965. *Historical Statistics of Canada*. Cambridge: At the University Press.
USBC (US Bureau of the Census). 1965. *The Statistical History of the United States from Colonial Times to the Present*. Stamford: Fairfield.
van Roon, Ger. 1989. *Small States in Years of Depression: The Oslo Alliance, 1930–1940*. Assen: Van Gorcum.
Værholm, Monica. 2010. "Why Did Norwegian Trade Policy Become More Active in the Interwar Period?" In *Managing Crises and De-globalisation: Nordic Foreign Trade and Exchange, 1919–39*, edited by Sven-Olof Olsson, 34–51. London: Routledge.
Veenendaal, Wouter P., and Jack Corbett. 2015. "Why Small States Offer Important Answers to Large Questions." *Comparative Political Studies* 48, no. 4: 527–49. https://doi.org/10.1177/0010414014554687.
Verney, Douglas V. 1957. *Parliamentary Reform in Sweden, 1866–1921*. Oxford: Clarendon.

Villa, Pierre. 2003. "France in the Depression of the Early 1930s." In *The World Economy and National Economies in the Interwar Slump*, edited by Theo Balderston, 58–87. Basingstoke: Palgrave Macmillan.
von Bertalanffy, Ludwig. 1950. "The Theory of Open Systems in Physics and Biology." *Science*, new series 111, no. 2872: 23–9. https://doi.org/10.1126/science.111.2872.23.
Wallerstein, Immanuel M. 1974. "The Rise and Future Demise of the World Capitalist System: Concepts for Comparative Analysis." *Comparative Studies in Society and History* 16, no. 4: 387–415. https://doi.org/10.1017/S0010417500007520.
———. 2011. *The Modern World-System*, vol. 4, *Centrist Liberalism Triumphant, 1789–1914*. Berkeley: University of California Press.
Weber, Eugen. 1994. *The Hollow Years: France in the 1930s*. New York and London: W. W. Norton.
Weber, Fritz. 1991. "Universal Banking in Interwar Central Europe." In *The Role of Banks in the Interwar Economy*, edited by Harold James, Håkan Lindgren, and Alice Teichova, 19–25. Cambridge: Cambridge University Press.
Webster, Donald E. 1939. *The Turkey of Atatürk: Social Process in the Turkish Reformation*. Philadelphia: American Academy of Political and Social Science.
Weiker, Walter F. 1973. *Political Tutelage and Democracy in Turkey: The Free Party and Its Aftermath*. Leiden: E. J. Brill.
Weinstein, James. 1968. *The Corporate Ideal in the Liberal State: 1900–1918*. Boston: Beacon.
Weir, Margaret. 1989. "Ideas and Politics: The Acceptance of Keynesianism in Britain and the United States." In *The Political Power of Economic Ideas: Keynesianism across Nations*, edited by Peter A. Hall, 53–86. Princeton: Princeton University Press.
Weir, Margaret, and Theda Skocpol. 1985. "State Structures and the Possibilities for 'Keynesian' Responses to the Great Depression in Sweden, Britain, and the United States." In *Bringing the State Back In*, edited by Peter B. Evans, Dietrich Rueschemeyer, and Theda Skocpol, 107–63. Cambridge: Cambridge University Press.
Welk, William G. 1938. *Fascist Economic Policy: An Analysis of Italy's Economic Experiment*. Cambridge, MA: Harvard University Press.
Wessels, Jens-Wilhelm. 2007. *Economic Policy and Microeconomic Performance in Inter-War Europe: The Case of Austria, 1918–1938*. Stuttgart: Franz Steiner Verlag.
Whitaker, Reginald. 1977. *The Government Party: Organizing and Financing the Liberal Party of Canada 1930–58*. Toronto: University of Toronto Press.
———. 1992. *A Sovereign Idea: Essays on Canada as a Democratic Community*. Montreal and Kingston: McGill-Queen's University Press.
Whitchurch, Gail G., and Larry L. Constantine. 1993. "Systems Theory." In *Sourcebook of Family Theories and Methods: A Contextual Approach*, edited by

Pauline G. Boss, William J. Doherty, Ralph LaRossa, Walter R. Schumm, and Suzanne K. Steinmetz, 325–52. New York and London: Plenum Press.
White, Lawrence H. 2012. *The Clash of Economic Ideas: The Great Policy Debates and Experiments of the Last Hundred Years*. New York: Cambridge University Press.
Wigforss, Ernst. 1938. "The Financial Policy during Depression and Boom." *Annals of the American Academy of Political and Social Science* 197, no. 1: 25–39. https://doi.org/10.1177/000271623819700105.
Williams, H. T., ed. 1960. *Principles for British Agricultural Policy*. London: Oxford University Press.
Williamson, Philip. 2003. "The Conservative Party, 1900–1939: From Crisis to Ascendancy." In *A Companion to Early Twentieth-Century Britain*, edited by Chris Wrigley, 3–22. Oxford: Blackwell Publishing.
Willis, J. Brook. 1954. "United States." In *Banking Systems*, edited by Benjamin H. Beckhart, 839–916. New York: Columbia University Press.
Wilson, J. S. G. 1952. "The Australian Trading Banks." In *Banking in the British Commonwealth*, edited by R. S. Sayers, 1–38. Oxford: Clarendon.
Winch, Donald. 1966. "The Keynesian Revolution in Sweden." *Journal of Political Economy* 74, no. 2: 168–76. https://doi.org/10.1086/259133.
———. 1969. *Economics and Policy: A Historical Study*. London: Hodder and Stoughton.
———. 1989. "Keynes, Keynesianism, and State Intervention." In *The Political Power of Economic Ideas: Keynesianism across Nations*, edited by Peter A. Hall, 107–27. Princeton: Princeton University Press.
Winders, Bill. 2005. "Maintaining the Coalition: Class Coalitions and Policy Trajectories." *Politics and Society* 33, no. 3: 387–423. https://doi.org/10.1177/0032329205278461.
Wohnout, Helmut. 2003. "A Chancellorial Dictatorship with a 'Corporative' Pretext: The Austrian Constitution between 1934 and 1938." In *The Dollfuss/Schuschnigg Era in Austria: A Reassessment*, edited by Günter Bischof, Anton Pelinka, and Alexander Lassner, 143–62. London and New York: Routledge.
Wolf, Nikolaus. 2013. "Europe's Great Depression: Coordination Failure after the First World War." In *The Great Depression of the 1930s: Lessons for Today*, edited by Nicholas Crafts and Peter Fearon, 74–109. Oxford: Oxford University Press.
Wolfe, David A. 1981. "Mercantilism, Liberalism and Keynesianism: Changing Forms of State Intervention in Capitalist Economies." *Canadian Journal of Political and Social Theory* 5, nos. 1–2: 69–96.
Wood, Louis A. [1924] 1975. *A History of Farmers' Movement in Canada*. Reprint. Toronto: University of Toronto Press.
Woytinsky, Wladimir S. 1961. *Stormy Passage: A Personal History through Two Russian Revolutions to Democracy and Freedom, 1905–1960*. New York: Vanguard.

Woytinsky, Wladimir S., and E. S. Woytinsky. 1953. *World Population and Production: Trends and Outlook.* New York: Twentieth Century Fund.
Wyatt, Alan. 1974. "The Rôle of a Minor Party: A Comparative Study of the British Liberal Party and the Australian Country Party since 1918." Unpublished MA thesis submitted to the Department of Politics, Brock University, St. Catharines.
Yamamura, Kozo. 1972. "Then Came the Great Depression: Japan's Interwar Years." In *The Great Depression Revisited: Essays on the Economics of the Thirties,* edited by Herman van der Wee, 182–211. The Hague: Martinus Nijhoff.
Yasuba, Yazukichi. 1988. "The Japanese Economy and Economic Policy in the 1930s." In *Recovery from the Depression: Australia and the World Economy in the 1930s,* edited by Robert G. Gregory and Noel G. Butlin, 135–47. Cambridge: Cambridge University Press.
Yavuz, M. Hakan. 2009. *Secularism and Muslim Democracy in Turkey.* Cambridge: Cambridge University Press.
Yetkin, Çetin. 1983. *Türkiye'de Tek Parti Yönetimi, 1930–1945.* İstanbul: Altın Kitaplar Yayınevi.
Young, Walter. 1969. *The Anatomy of a Party: The National CCF, 1932–61.* Toronto: University of Toronto Press.
Zamagni, Vera. 1993. *The Economic History of Italy, 1860–1990.* Oxford: Clarendon Press.
Ziegler, Dieter. 2013. "'A Regulated Market Economy': New Perspectives on the Nature of the Economic Order of the Third Reich, 1933–1939." In *Business in the Age of Extremes: Essays in Modern German and Austrian Economic History,* edited by Hartmut Berghoff, Jürgen Kocka, and Dieter Ziegler, 139–52. Cambridge: Cambridge University Press.
Zimmerman, Ekkart, and Thomas Saalfeld. 1988. "Economic and Political Reactions to the World Economic Crisis of the 1930s in Six European Countries." *International Studies Quarterly* 32, no. 3: 305–34. https://doi.org/10.2307/2600445.
Zürcher, Erik J. 1984. *The Unionist Factor: The Rôle of the Committee of Union and Progress in the Turkish National Movement, 1905–1926.* Leiden: E. J. Brill.
———. 2007. "The Ottoman Legacy of the Kemalist Republic." In *The State and the Subaltern: Modernization, Society and the State in Turkey and Iran,* edited by Touraj Atabaki, 95–110. London and New York: I. B. Tauris Publishers.
Øksendal, Lars F. 2010. "Re-examining Norwegian Monetary Policy in the 1930s." In *Managing Crises and De-globalisation: Nordic Foreign Trade and Exchange, 1919–39,* edited by Sven-Olof Olsson, 66–81. London: Routledge.
Østerud, Øyvind. 1978. *Agrarian Structure and Peasant Politics in Scandinavia: A Comparative Study of Rural Response to Economic Change.* Oslo: Universitetsforlaget.

Index[1]

A

Agrarian–labour alliance(s), 12, 23, 25, 27, 28, 105, 110, 112, 120, 123, 124, 126, 140, 150, 153–155
Alexander, king of Yugoslavia, 223
Antipodes, 34
Argentina, 34
Australia, 3, 25, 33, 55–58, 99, 100, 107–112, 119, 126, 127n1, 127n6, 156, 162n1, 239
    Australian Council of Trade Unions, 109
    Australian Labor Party (ALP), 26, 57, 107–111, 127n8
    Australian Wheat Board, 112
    Commonwealth Bank, 58, 109–111
    Commonwealth Constitution, 111
    Commonwealth Liberal Party, 110
    Country Party, 110, 111
    Court of Conciliation and Arbitration, 58, 108
    House of Representatives, 107, 111, 125
    Labor government, 57, 100
    Liberal Protectionist government of 1903–1908, 108, 110
    Melbourne Agreement, 109
    Nationalist Party, 110
    new protection, 113
    New South Wales, 109
    Premiers' Plan, 58, 109
    Queensland, 127n8, 127n9
    Scullin tariff, 57
    Senate, 111
    United Australia–Country coalition, 112
    United Australia Party, 110
    White Australia Policy, 108

---

[1] Note: Page numbers followed by 'n' refer to notes.

Austria, 3, 30, 32, 51, 55, 70–73, 127n1, 162n1, 173, 175, 183, 184, 186, 187, 190, 192, 193, 203
  Anschluss, 183, 186
  Austrian School of Economics, 185
  Bundesrat, 183
  Christian Social government, 71, 174, 183, 186
  Christian Socials, 30, 174, 185, 186
  Communist Party, 183
  Corporate State; Austrofascists, viii, 29, 174, 183, 225; Dollfuss/Schuschnigg regime, 30, 186, 187, 193; Fatherland Front, 187; 1934 Constitution, 187
  Credit-Anstalt, collapse and bailout of, 71, 184
  Geneva Protocols of 1922, 184
  Greater German People's Party, 186
  Home Guard, 186, 187
  hyperinflation of 1921–1922, 184
  Lausanne Protocol of 1931, 184
  Nationalrat, 183
  Republican Defence League, 185
  Social Democratic–Christian Social coalition, 183
  Sozialdemokratische Arbeiterpartei (SDAP, Social Democratic Workers' Party), 141, 185
Austrofascism, 30, 72, 183, 185–188, 193
  See also Fascism; Nazism
Austro-Hungarian Empire, 51, 71, 183, 187, 222
Austromarxism, 185
  See also Marxism
Autarky, 2, 17, 19, 22, 46, 56, 69, 71, 73, 74, 191, 218, 240

B

Balkans, vi, vii, ix, 3, 31, 32, 34, 76, 77, 188, 194, 202, 208, 217–224, 240
Bank for International Settlements, 49, 184
Banking system(s), 103, 116, 146, 152, 178
  commercial banking, 75, 114, 116, 210
  industrial banking, 63, 146, 193, 202
  investment banking (*see* Banking system(s), industrial banking)
  mixed banking, 157, 158, 160, 178, 191, 193, 194n7
  universal banking (*see* Banking system(s), mixed banking)
Belgium, 34, 48, 52
Bennett, Richard B., 59, 60, 101, 117, 118
Berman, Sheri, 7
Blum, Léon, 60, 121
Blyth, Mark M., 6, 35n1
Bolshevism, 205
  See also Communism; Stalinism
Boris III, king of Bulgaria, 220
Bradford, Neil, 35n6
Branting, Hjalmar, 149
Brazil, 35
Britain, *see* United Kingdom
British preferential trading system, 53, 54, 80n7
Brüning, Heinrich, 69, 178–180
Bukharin, Nikolay, 206, 207
Bulgaria, 3, 31, 55, 76, 217, 219, 223
  Bŭlgarski Zemedelski Naroden Sŭyuz (BZNS, Bulgarian Agrarian National Union), 219, 220, 223
  Communists, 220
  People's Bloc, 220
  royal dictatorship, 219, 220, 223

Social Democrats, 220
Socialists, 220
Zveno (Link) movement, 220

C

Canada, 3, 10, 25, 33, 34, 35n3, 53, 55, 56, 58, 59, 99–101, 112–114, 118, 119, 127n1, 128n12, 128n14, 141, 162n1, 235, 239
  All-Canadian Congress of Labour, 128n14
  Bank of Canada, 59
  Bennett New Deal, 59, 60
  Canadian Council of Agriculture, 115
  Canadian Manufacturers' Association, 114
  Central Canada, 113, 114, 118
  Confédération des travailleurs catholiques du Canada, 128n14
  Conservative government, 113, 114
  Conservative Party, 118
  Co-operative Commonwealth Federation (CCF), 35n3, 116, 117
  Dunning tariff, 58
  Farmers' Platform, 115
  House of Commons, 115, 117
  Judicial Committee of the Privy Council, 118
  League for Social Reconstruction (LSR), 116
  Liberal government, 116
  Liberal Party, 118
  National Employment Commission (NEC), 118, 119
  National Policy, 113, 118
  National Progressive Party, 115
  Prairies, 114
  Reciprocity Treaty, proposed, 113
  Regina Manifesto, 116
  Royal Commission on Banking and Currency in Canada (RCBCC), 114
  Royal Commission on Dominion–Provincial Relations (RCDPR), 59, 118
  Senate, 128n15
  Social Credit Party (Socred), 116, 117
  Supreme Court of Canada, 118
  Trades and Labour Congress (TLC), 115, 128n14
  United Farmers movement, 115, 116
  United Farmers of Alberta (UFA), 115, 116
  United Farmers of Ontario, 115
  Wheat Board, 59
  Workers' Unity League, 128n14
Carol II, king of Romania, 222
Cartelization, 5, 16, 17, 25, 27, 30, 54, 57, 59, 60, 63, 65, 67, 71, 76, 77, 106, 185, 238
Castles, Francis G., 58, 108
Chamberlain, Joseph, 101
China, 32, 33
Churchill, Winston, 14
Clearing trade, 17, 29, 51–53, 57, 69, 71, 74, 81n19, 179, 180, 218, 220, 226n8
Communism, 22, 47, 68
  See also Bolshevism; Stalinism
Corporatism, 9, 64, 186, 190, 193, 209, 225n4
Currency blocs, 79n7
  blocked currency bloc, 52
  gold bloc, 30, 52, 60, 72
  sterling bloc (*see* Currency blocs, sterling exchange standard)
  sterling exchange standard, 56, 57, 61, 64, 66, 67
  yen bloc, 52
Customs union between Germany and Austria, proposed, 51

D

Dawes Plan, 48
Deflation, 27, 61, 69, 71, 73, 106, 121, 127n3, 179, 181, 190
Demand stimulus, 6, 9, 12, 13, 17, 28, 66, 105, 106, 239
  See also Proto-Keynesianism
Democratic breakdown, 21, 32, 36n9, 173–175, 192, 193, 194n4
Democratization, 22, 50, 108, 156, 158, 159, 211, 217, 219, 222, 223
  male suffrage, 122, 153, 156–158, 219, 222
  universal suffrage, 22, 50, 55, 123, 157–159, 177, 183, 188
Denmark, vi, 3, 28, 55, 56, 66–68, 127n1, 140, 154–158, 160, 161, 162n1
  constitutional revision in 1866, 157
  Constitution of 1849, 156
  Crisis Agreement, 28, 66
  Denmark for the People, 157
  Exchange Control Office, 66
  Farmers' Union, 157
  Folketing, 156, 157
  Landsting, 157
  Liberals, 155–157
  Radical Liberals, 155, 157
  September compromise of 1899, 67
  Social Democratic Party, 141, 154–156
  Social Democratic–Radical Liberal coalition government, 28, 66, 157
  United Liberals, 156
De' Stefani, Alberto, 189
Devaluation, 15, 16, 28, 51, 61, 65, 67, 69, 71, 74, 76, 114, 121, 122, 157
Dirigisme, 17, 19, 22, 31, 32, 63, 69, 72, 73, 76, 78, 187, 191, 202, 204, 215, 222, 236, 240
Dobbin, Frank R., 5
Dollfuss, Engelbert, 186, 187
Dominions, 32, 53, 56, 99, 101
Douglas, Major C. H., 125

E

Eidlin, Barry, 10, 35n3
Electoral system(s)
  first-past-the-post (*see* Electoral system(s), majoritarian)
  majoritarian, 26, 105, 111, 117, 119, 122, 125, 147, 153, 157, 192
  proportional, 105, 111, 115, 117, 125, 153, 157, 159–161, 177, 183, 188, 192, 194n2
Employer–union compromise(s), 68, 154
Esping-Andersen, Gøsta, 8
Étatisme, *see* Statism

F

Fascism, 12, 22, 34, 47, 50, 64, 68, 71, 72, 121, 173, 183, 185, 187–189, 192, 193, 222
  See also Nazism
Fenton, James, 109
Ferguson, Thomas, 162n2
Fiscal orthodoxy, 5, 6, 26, 57, 58, 61, 69, 71, 106, 107, 109, 111, 179, 185
France, vi, 5, 7, 9, 11, 25, 27, 32, 36n8, 45–49, 51–56, 60, 61, 80n10, 99, 100, 119–123, 126, 127n1, 162n1, 174, 239
  Bank de France, 121
  Blum experiment, 3, 27, 54, 56, 60, 80n10, 100, 121, 122, 126
  Chamber, 122
  Communists, 27, 60, 100, 119, 121, 122

Confédération générale de la production française, 122
Confédération générale du travail (CGT), 122
Confédération générale du travail unitaire, 122
Économie dirigée, 121
franc Poincaré, 120
Le Figaro, 120
Left Radicals, 27, 60, 100, 119, 121, 122
Matignon Accord, 54
Popular Front, 9, 11, 54, 60, 120–122
Popular Front government, 27, 100, 119, 121, 122, 126
Senate, 122
Socialists, 27, 60, 100, 119, 121
Third Republic, 60
Free trade, 2, 14, 25, 45, 52, 53, 56, 60, 64, 104–106, 110, 113, 148, 155, 156, 181, 213

G
George II, king of Greece, 221
George, Lloyd, 104, 145, 150
Germany, vii, 3, 5, 6, 11, 12, 29, 30, 32, 34, 45–48, 51, 52, 55, 64, 69–74, 76, 79n3, 127n1, 141, 160, 161, 162n1, 173–183, 186, 187, 190, 192, 193, 202, 203, 206, 215, 218–220, 225n5, 226n9
East Elbian Prussia, 181
Junkers, 181, 182, 193
Lebensraum, 53, 69
Mittelstand, 174, 182
Nazi Germany; brown–green rapprochement, 182; defensive economy, 181; Law on Hereditary Peasant Holdings, 182; Nazi government, 69, 70; Nazis, 29, 53, 68–70, 73, 147, 174, 179–182, 187, 194, 218; New Plan, 54, 69, 218
Reichsbank, 79n3
Reichstag, 177, 180
unification in 1871, 45
Weimar Germany; Allgemeiner Deutscher Gewerkschaftsbund (General Trade Union Federation) (ADGB), 179, 180; banking crisis, 51, 69; Bavarian People's Party, 178; Brüning government, 69, 180; Central Labour Community, 178; Centre Party, 178; Communist insurgency, 177; Communists, 179; Constitution of 1919, 177; German Democratic Party, 178; German Employers' Association, 180; German People's Party, 178, 186; grand coalition, 178, 180; hyperinflation of early 1920s, 6, 179, 181, 183; Reichsrat, 177; Sozialdemokratische Partei Deutschlands (SPD), 177–180; Weimar coalition, 181, 193; Works Councils, 177; WTB Plan, 180
Gerschenkron, Alexander, 181, 208, 209
Global financial crisis of 2008–2009, v, 235, 236
Gold standard, 2, 14, 15, 21, 25–29, 43, 45–48, 50–52, 56–58, 60–62, 64, 66, 67, 69, 71, 72, 76, 77, 79n2, 79n4, 104, 106, 108, 109, 120–122, 127n3, 179, 180, 184, 220, 236, 238
Gordon, Colin, 162n2
Gourevitch, Peter A., 9, 11–13, 35n4, 162n2
Great War, *see* World War I

Greece, 3, 31, 55, 76, 77, 217, 218, 220, 221, 223, 226n9
  Agrarian Party, 223, 226n10
  Asia Minor disaster, 220
  clientelism, 226n11
  Communist Party, 221
  First Republic, 221
  International Financial Commission, 220
  Liberal Party, 221
  Metaxas dictatorship, 220, 221
  national schism, 221
  New Lands, 220, 221
  Old Greece, 221
  People's Party, 221
  Venizelists, 221
Gregor, A. James, 188, 225n6

H
Hall, Peter A., 13, 16, 35n6
Hansson, Per Albin, 139, 149, 150
Harper, Stephen, 235
Hay, Colin, 10
Heclo, Hugh, 5
Hilferding, Rudolf, 180, 194n3
Hitler, Adolf, 155, 179, 181, 186, 193
Hobsbawm, Eric, 21
Hoover, Herbert, 23
Hull, Cordell, 145

I
Ideas, institutions, and interests (3Is), vii, 2, 4–12, 23, 237
Imperial Economic Conference, 101
India, 32, 33
Industrialization, vii, viii, 2, 3, 19, 23, 27, 30, 31, 45, 49, 54, 73–76, 113, 140, 151, 154, 155, 158, 161, 178, 194, 201, 202, 205–209, 215, 216, 224
  import-substituting industrialization, 29, 56, 62, 158, 214
Irwin, Douglas A., 79n6
İsmet, Turkish prime minister, 214
Italy, 30–34, 45, 46, 52–55, 70, 72, 73, 173, 186–188, 192, 193, 202, 207–209, 216, 225n2
  Battle for Grain in 1925, 190, 191
  Battle for the Lira, 190
  bonifica integrale, 191
  Catholic party, 189, 193
  Communist party, 189
  Confederation of Fascist Corporations, 190
  demographic battle in 1927, 191
  Ethiopia, invasion of, 49, 53
  Fascist government, 72
  Fascist program of 1921, 189, 194n6
  Fascists, 29, 30, 46, 68, 72, 73, 147, 175, 187–192, 194, 203, 204, 240
  General Confederation of Industry, 190
  Istituto Mobiliare Italiano (IMI), 72, 191, 214
  Istituto per la Ricostruzione Industriale (IRI), 72, 191
  Labour Charter of 1927, 73, 190
  Liberals, 189, 193
  Liberista period, 30, 46, 47, 189, 190
  March on Rome, 189
  Quota Novanta, 72
  red biennium, 188, 189
  Risorgimento in 1870, 45, 192
  Socialist party, 189, 193
  syndicates, 189, 190

J

Japan, 34, 36n8, 45, 53, 54
  East Asia Co-Prosperity Sphere, 53
  invasion of Manchuria, 49
  Meiji restoration in 1868, 45
Jonung, Lars, 6

K

Karleby, Nils, 150
Katzenstein, Peter J., 9
Kemp, Tom, 121
Keynesianism, *see* Proto-Keynesianism
Keynes, John M., 6, 104, 127n2
Kindleberger, Charles P., 21, 47
King, W. L. Mackenzie, 118
Koning, Niek, 182
Kuhn, Thomas S., 1

L

Laissez-faire, 5, 12, 45
Land redistribution, *see* Land reform
Land reform, 31, 32, 50, 75, 123, 124, 189, 216, 217, 219–223, 225n7
Lang, J. T., 109, 112
Large state(s), v–viii, 3, 11, 27, 32–34, 36n10, 51, 52, 77, 99, 174, 175
Lausanne Conference of 1932, 48
League of Nations, 21, 47–49, 53, 71, 184–186, 226n8, 236
  Financial Committee, 184–186
Lee, Bradford A., 7
Lenin, V. I., 204, 205
Lib–Lab coalition(s), 105, 124, 158
London Monetary and Economic Conference, 51
Long stagnation of 1873–1896, 45, 181, 201
Luxemburg, 52
Lyons, Joseph, 109, 110

M

MacDonald, Ramsay, 103, 104
Mahmut Celal, Turkish minister, 214
Marx, Karl, 8, 188, 216
Marxism, 7, 30, 149, 185, 237
Mehta, Jal, 24, 25
Metaxas, Ioannis, 221
Mexico, 35
Möller, Gustav, 150
Murphy, John, 128n11
Mussolini, Benito, 188, 189, 193, 194n5, 207, 216
Mustafa Kemal, Turkish president, 209, 212–214
Mustafa Şeref, Turkish minister, 214
Myrdal, Alva, 150
Myrdal, Gunnar, 150

N

Nationalization, 17, 70, 75, 76, 80n10, 109, 124, 217
National-structural limitation(s), 2–5
Nazi Germany, *see* Germany
Nazism, 30, 68, 179, 181, 185, 186, 188, 193
  See also Austrofascism; Fascism
Neoclassical economics, 6, 13, 71, 180, 184
Netherlands, 34, 52
New institutionalism, 4, 6, 8, 11, 238
  historical institutionalism, 4–6, 238
  ideational institutionalism, 8, 238
New York Stock market, crash of, 50, 107, 212
New Zealand, 3, 25, 27, 55, 56, 61, 68, 99–101, 110, 119, 120, 123–126, 140, 153, 156, 161, 162n1, 201, 239
  Court of Arbitration, 61, 62
  House of Representatives, 125

New Zealand (*cont.*)
  Industrial Conciliation and Arbitration Act of 1894, 123
  Labour government, 27, 61, 125, 126
  Labour Party, 27, 100, 120, 123–125
  Legislative Council, 125
  Liberal governance from 1891 to 1912, 123
  Liberal Party, 123
  Liberal/United and Reform party coalition, 61
  Old Age Pension Act of 1898, 123
  Reform Party, 124
  Reserve Bank of New Zealand (RBNZ), 61, 80n11
  Social Security Act, 62
  Trades Councils, 124
Niemeyer, Otto, 109
Norway, 3, 28, 55, 56, 66–68, 140, 154, 155, 158, 159, 161, 162n1, 201
  Agrarian Party, 159
  Constitution of 1814, 158
  Crisis Agreement, 67, 158, 159
  Farmers' Union, 157, 159
  Labour government, 67, 68, 159
  Labour Party, 141, 154, 158, 159, 161
  Liberal Party, 159
  Main Agreement, 67
  Storting, 158, 159

O

Oslo Convention, 53, 64
Ottawa Agreements, 53, 56, 59, 101
Ottawa Conference, 114
Ottoman Empire, *see* Turkey
Oye, Kenneth A., 79n5

P

Planning, 5, 17, 29, 31, 46, 54, 57, 70, 72, 73, 75, 77, 107, 116, 146, 180, 202, 206, 208, 214
Poincaré, Raymond, 120
Poland, 52
Polanyi, Karl, 12, 21, 43, 173
Policy paradigm(s), 2, 3, 13, 15, 16, 18, 21, 22, 26, 51, 55, 60, 77, 126, 235, 236, 239
  classical liberalism, 2, 12–18, 21, 22, 25, 30, 43, 44, 49, 58, 77, 78, 103, 104, 107, 126, 236
  developmentalism (*see* Policy paradigm(s), developmental neomercantilism)
  developmental neomercantilism, 3
  Fordism (*see* Policy paradigm(s), proto-Fordism)
  mercantilism (*see* Policy paradigm(s), neomercantilism)
  neomercantilism, 2, 3, 12, 13, 15, 17–19, 22, 27, 29–31, 34, 36n8, 43, 44, 55, 56, 68, 72, 77, 78, 79n6, 125, 182, 183, 188, 236, 237, 240
  neo-orthodoxy (*see* Policy paradigm(s), protectionism)
  protectionism, viii, 2, 3, 9, 12, 13, 15–18, 22, 25–28, 30, 31, 34, 43, 44, 52, 53, 55–64, 68, 76–78, 79n5, 79n6, 99–101, 116, 119, 122, 123, 125, 126, 154, 159
  proto-Fordism, viii, 2, 3, 12, 15–19, 22, 25, 27, 29, 36n7, 43, 55–57, 62, 68, 77, 78, 100, 123, 126, 140, 154, 236
Political regime(s), 12, 19, 32, 35n4, 43, 55, 78, 173, 192, 237
  democracy, vii, 22, 32, 43, 55, 61, 68, 71, 78, 104, 121, 139,

149, 150, 156–159, 173–175, 179, 183, 185, 186, 192, 219, 223, 237
modern dictatorship, 22, 68, 196, 215, 240
totalitarianism (*see* Political regime(s), modern dictatorship)
traditional dictatorship, 68
Portugal, 35
Preobrazhensky, Yevgeny, 205, 206
Proto-Keynesianism, 4, 11, 13, 14, 16, 35–36n6, 80n16, 235
See also Demand stimulus
Public works, 29, 59, 61–67, 70, 73, 80n13, 104, 106, 109, 116, 118, 121, 125, 127n2, 140, 145, 148, 150, 157, 179, 191, 194, 238, 239
See also Relief works
Pump priming, *see* Demand stimulus

R

Reagan, Ronald, 36n7
Reciprocal Trade Agreement of 1938, 54
Red–green alliance(s), *see* Agrarian–labour alliance(s)
Reflation, 28, 54, 106
Relief works, 28, 59, 65, 80n9, 80n13, 148
See also Public works
Reparations, 21, 48, 49, 51, 69, 71, 79n3, 179, 180, 182, 184
Robbins, Lionel, 12, 35n5
Romania, 3, 31, 55, 76, 77, 217, 221–223, 226n9
Front of National Rebirth, 222
Iron Guard, 222
Liberal Party, 221, 222
National–Peasant government, 222
National Peasant Party, 222

People's Party, 222
royal dictatorship, 222
second serfdom, 221
serfdom in 1864, end of, 221
Roosevelt, Franklin D., 10, 51, 62, 63, 118, 140, 143–147, 161
Ruhr region, occupation of, 48
Russia
Bolshevik/Russian Revolution, 50, 204, 206, 207, 217
serfdom in 1861, abolition of, 45

S

Scandinavia, vi, 9, 11, 32, 34, 54, 64, 66, 154, 156, 158, 159, 194n2
Schacht, Hjalmar H. G., 69, 79n3
Schmidt, Vivien A., 24, 25
Scullin, James, 109
Self-regulating market, 2, 14, 21, 43, 173
Skocpol, Theda, 4
Small state(s), v, vi, viii, 3, 7, 11, 28, 31–34, 36n10, 46, 47, 52, 53, 64, 140, 202
Snowden, Philip, 103, 104
Social credit, 116, 125
Social Democratic–Agrarian compromise(s), *see* Agrarian–labour alliances(s)
Socialization, 108, 121, 149, 150, 154, 180, 204
South Africa, 34
Soviet Russia, *see* Soviet Union
Soviet Union, 3, 11, 12, 14, 17, 23, 31, 32, 34, 46, 52, 54, 55, 72, 73, 188, 192, 202, 205–209, 224, 240
Bolsheviks, 31, 73, 74, 188, 203–206, 209
collectivization, 31, 54, 73, 202, 207, 224

Soviet Union (*cont.*)
  first five-year plan, 31, 207, 208
  kulaks, 74, 207
  Nepmen, 204
  New Economic Policy (NEP), 14, 46, 73, 204
  primitive socialist accumulation, 205
  scissors crisis, 205, 206
  socialism in one country, 52, 74, 202, 204, 206, 207
  socialist industrialization, 31, 202, 205, 206
  Stalinists, 202, 224, 240
  War Communism, 46, 203, 204
Stalin, J. V., 12, 205–208
Stalinism, 202, 207
  See also Bolshevism; Communism
Stamboliski, Alexander, 219
Statism, 5, 13, 72, 74–76, 191, 194, 208, 214, 216, 225n6
Stauning, Thorvald, 155
Straumann, Tobias, 7
Stresa Conference, 53
Sweden, 3–7, 9, 11, 28, 29, 32, 54–56, 62, 64, 66–68, 127n1, 139–141, 150, 152–155, 159–161, 161n1, 177
  Agrarian Party, 28, 148, 150–152
  Arbetslöshetskommissionen (AK), 148, 149
  Arbetsmarknadsstyrelsen (AMS), 149
  Big Four, 162n5
  Conservatives, 148, 153
  Crisis Agreement, 64, 65, 148, 152
  December compromise, 151
  Directors' Club, 152
  engineering compromise, 151
  first chamber, 151, 153
  General Strike of 1909, 151
  Kreuger crash, 153
  Landsorganisationen (LO), 149, 151, 152
  Liberal government, 64, 148, 150
  Liberals, 148–150
  Metallindustriarbetareförbundet (Metall), 151, 152
  New Farmers' Party, 151
  people's home, 139, 149, 150
  Riksbank, 65
  Riksdag, 149, 150
  Saltsjöbaden compromise, 65, 149, 151
  second chamber, 149, 151, 153
  Skandinaviska Banken, collapse and bailout of, 153
  Social Democratic government, 28
  Socialdemokratiska Arbetarepartiet (SAP), 141, 148–153, 159
  Stockholm School of Economics, 7, 150
  Svenska Arbetsgivareföreningen (SAF), 149, 151
  Sveriges Allmänna Lantbrukssällskap, 150
  Verkstadsföreningen (VF), 151, 152
Swenson, Peter A., 9, 162n2
Switzerland, 34, 52
Syndicalism, 188, 190
Systems theory, 19, 20

T

Temin, Peter, 12
Thatcher, Margaret, 36n7
Theodore, Edward, 109, 110, 127n9
Third International, 22, 29, 34, 50, 64, 158, 159
Third World, 11
Tripartite Monetary Agreement, 52, 61
Trotsky, Leon, 205
Turkey, 3, 23, 31, 32, 54, 55, 74, 76, 209, 211, 213, 224, 225n5, 240
  Act for the Restoration of Tranquility, 212

Agricultural Bank, 75
Business Bank, 213, 214
Cumhuriyet Halk Fırkası (CHF), 211, 213–215, 225n3
devletçilik, 214, 215
Etibank, 75, 76
first five-year industrial plan, 75
Industrial and Mining Bank, 211
İttihad ve Terakki Fırkası (İTF), 209, 212, 225n3
Kadro, 216
Kemalists, 74, 202, 209–212, 215, 216, 225n7, 240
Kurdish rebellion of 1925, 211, 212
Lausanne, Treaty of, 211, 225n6
1934 Settlement Act, 225n7
Office for Soil Products, 75
Ottoman Bank, 213
Régie, 210
Republican government, 210, 211, 215
secularism, 215
Serbest Cumhuriyet Fırkası (SCF), 213, 214, 216
statist industrialization, 202, 214
Sümerbank, 75, 76
Terakkiperver Cumhuriyet Fırkası (TCF), 212, 213
Turkification, 215
Westernization, 215
Young Turks, 209

U
Underconsumption, 7, 125
Unemployment insurance, 5, 28, 57–59, 61–63, 65–67, 103, 104, 112, 115, 118, 121, 128n11, 128n17, 140, 148, 178, 180, 238
Unionization, 112, 143
 craft unionism, 151
 industrial unionism, 115, 143, 151

United Kingdom, 3–5, 7, 9, 11, 13, 21, 25, 32, 45–49, 52–58, 61, 64, 99–101, 106, 107, 109–112, 114, 119, 121, 125, 126, 127n6, 145, 162n1, 174, 178, 216, 220, 239
Bank of England, 26, 104, 107, 109
Big Five, 107, 127n5
City, 9, 26, 104, 107
Committee on Economic Information, 127n2
Conservative government, 106
Conservative Party, 106
Corn Laws in 1846, repeal of, 53, 56, 105
Economic Advisory Council, 127n2
House of Commons, 105
Import Duties Act, 56
Labour government, 6, 25, 56, 100, 103, 104, 107
Labour Party, 26, 35n2, 103–106, 178
Liberal Party, 104
National government, 56, 57, 100, 106
Tariff Reform Movement of 1903, 101
Trades Union Congress (TUC), 106
Treasury, 4, 25, 26, 104, 107
United States, 3–7, 9–11, 21, 23, 27, 29, 32, 35n3, 45–49, 51–56, 59, 61, 62, 64, 68, 113, 115, 117, 118, 127n1, 139–141, 146, 160, 161, 175, 177, 188, 193, 194n1
Agricultural Adjustment act, 146
Agricultural Adjustment Administration (AAA), 63
American Farm Bureau Federation, 143
American Federation of Labor (AFL), 143
Civil War in 1865, end of, 45

United States (*cont.*)
  Committee for Industrial Organization/Congress of Industrial Organizations (CIO), 143
  Congress, 21, 23, 49, 62, 147
  corporate liberalism, 144, 145
  Democratic administration, 6, 27, 142, 143
  Democratic Party, 10, 28, 35n3, 140, 141, 144, 145, 147, 161
  Federal Reserve System, 49
  Glass–Steagall Act, 63, 146
  House of Representatives, 147
  National Association of Manufacturers (NAM), 144
  National Civic Federation, 162n3
  National Farmers Union, 143
  National Grange, 143
  National Industrial Recovery act, 143, 144, 146
  National Labor Relations Board, 63, 143
  National Recovery Administration (NRA), 54, 63
  New Deal, 9–12, 28, 54, 63, 64, 107, 117, 140, 143–147, 160, 161, 162n2
  Progressive era, 144
  Reciprocal Trade Agreements Act, 53, 62, 79n5, 144
  Republican administration, 27, 62, 141, 142
  Republican Party, 23
  Smoot–Hawley Tariff Act, 21, 50, 52
  Socialist Party, 145
  Supreme Court, 63, 146
  Voluntary Domestic Allotment Plan, 144
  Wagner Act, 10, 63
Uruguay, 34

V
Venizelos, Eleftherios, 221
Versailles, Treaty of, 47, 48

W
Wagner, Robert, 145
War debts, 48, 51
Washington consensus, 44
Weimar Germany, *see* Germany
Weir, Margaret, 4
Wigforss, Ernst, 150
Winch, Donald, 6, 13, 103
Winders, Bill, 9, 10
World-historical context, 19, 35, 36n9, 44–55, 57, 153, 236
World War I, 5, 20, 21, 30, 32, 43, 45, 46, 49, 68, 71, 149, 158, 177, 179, 192, 193, 204, 209, 212, 217, 219–221, 237
World War II, 14, 43, 113, 192, 215, 223

Y
Young Plan, 48, 49
Yugoslavia, 3, 31, 55, 76, 77, 217, 223, 226n9
  Bosnia, 223
  Croatia, 223
  Croatian Peasant Party, 223
  royal dictatorship, 223
  Serbian Agrarian Union, 223
  Serbian Democratic Party, 223
  Serbian Radical Party, 223